THE MAFIA

THE MAFIA

THE LONG REACH
OF THE INTERNATIONAL
SICILIAN MAFIA

CLAIRE STERLING

HAMISH HAMILTON · LONDON

HAMISH HAMILTON LTD
Published by the Penguin Group
27 Wrights Lane, London W8 5TZ, England
Viking Penguin Inc., 40 West 23rd Street, New York, New York 10010, USA
Penguin Books Australia Ltd, Ringwood, Victoria, Australia
Penguin Books Canada Ltd, 2801 John Street, Markham, Ontario, Canada L3R 1B4
Penguin Books (NZ) Ltd, 182–190 Wairau Road, Auckland 10, New Zealand

Penguin Books Ltd, Registered Offices: Harmondsworth, Middlesex, England

First published in the USA by W. W. Norton & Company, Inc.
First published in Great Britain by Hamish Hamilton Ltd 1990
1 3 5 7 9 10 8 6 4 2

Copyright © 1990 by Claire Sterling

Printed in Great Britain by
Richard Clay Ltd, Bungay, Suffolk

A CIP catalogue record for this book is available from the British Library

ISBN 0-241-12181-7

For my beloved Abby and Luke

Contents

Acknowledgments

Among those who helped me understand what I have written here, my thanks go first to the late Commissario Antonino "Ninni" Cassarà of Palermo and his dedicated aide, the late Commissario Giuseppe "Beppe" Montana, both murdered by the Mafia.

I am deeply indebted to two other superb Italian policemen, fortunately still alive: Gianni De Gennaro, head of Italy's national Anti–Organized Crime Nucleus, and Alessandro Pansa, his indispensable number two.

Judges Giovanni Falcone, Giuseppe Ayala, and Giusto Sciacchitano of Palermo gave me invaluable guidance. Assistant U.S. Attorneys Louis Freeh of New York's Southern District, and Richard Martin, representing the U.S. Department of Justice in Rome, were exceptionally generous in sharing their knowledge, as was Frank Panessa, head of the Drug Enforcement Administration bureau in Italy.

Among my own colleagues, my warmest gratitude goes to Maria Antonietta Calabro of the *Corriere della Sera* (Milan), whose close understanding of the Italian courts and meticulous concern for accuracy were a continuing gift to me through the long years I worked on this book.

I am especially grateful also to Judith Harris, who let me borrow freely from her carefully researched manuscript on the international heroin trade.

Introduction

This book is written in the past tense because the facts I've gathered over the last four years are already receding into history. The Mafia does not wait to be overtaken by events; it has always been ahead of the perceived wisdom.

When I started, in 1985, law enforcers throughout the world were just beginning to find out what the Sicilian Mafia in particular had been doing during the previous quarter of a century. Many still cannot take in the magnitude of their discovery.

Starting in 1957, a small band of criminals presumed to be operating within the confines of a small Mediterranean island grew into a multinational heroin cartel operating around the planet. Today, they are the brokers for much of the world's cocaine as well. Indeed, the Sicilian Mafia is the only organized crime syndicate capable of moving both heroin and cocaine across oceans and continents in massive quantities.

No authority anywhere had an inkling of this until the early 1980s. By then, Sicily's Men of Honor held strategic outposts from Bangkok, London, Munich, and Marseilles to Montreal, Caracas, São Paulo, and some twenty-five key cities in the United States. There was scarcely a country in Europe, Asia, Africa, or the Western Hemisphere that they had not penetrated or corrupted in passing.

What made them invisible for so long—as they still are, in many of these countries—was not so much their own guile as the innocence of the societies they victimized. In spite of accumulating evidence of their brotherhood's nature and purpose, they were protected by a solid wall of popular and official disbelief.

The public had no means of understanding the phenomenon; and law enforcement agencies were neither accustomed nor equipped to deal with it. Agents of the law did not know what the Sicilian Mafia was, or feel the need to know. Not only did they lack curiosity, they were singularly lacking in historical memory. Their failure to look for information in their own archives, to communicate and compare notes, to link one criminal act to another and crimes of the present to those of the past, was central to the success of a calamitous international conspiracy.

Not everybody in law enforcement may welcome the publication of these awkward truths, but the Mafia cannot be defeated as long as they still apply. The same is so for other awkward truths, which are unfailingly said to be an attack on the Sicilian people.

This interpretation has been the Mafia's classic defense for over a century, and it is a transparent fiction. Made members of the Mafia in Sicily constitute only a fraction of 1 percent of the island's population. Those who support them knowingly and willingly are a small minority. Millions of honest Sicilians suffer the Mafia only because they have been terrorized into silence. The bravest and most gallant men and women who have ever fought the Mafia have been the Sicilians themselves.

Some may still be offended by the tarnished image of their island emerging from the facts reported here. That is the Mafia's fault, not mine. Please don't shoot the messenger.

o⌒o

The story told in this book is a complicated one, with many characters and events. The reader may wish to consult, on pp. 14–19, a crime map of Sicily and a chart setting forth the Sicilian Mafia's superclans, and on pp. 321–25, a chronology of events depicted here and a chart listing the Mafia's victims.

The octopus is a sea animal with a soft body and eight arms called tentacles. . . . Rows of round cups on the underside of each tentacle act much like a suction cup. These suckers can fasten tightly to any object, and may hold on even if the tentacle is cut off. If an octopus loses a tentacle, a new one grows in its place. . . .

An octopus has two eyes and sees well. It has the most highly developed brain of all invertebrates. . . .

Some kinds of octopuses inject a poison that paralyzes their prey. . . .

The octopus can also squirt a black fluid forming a dark cloud that hides the animal so it can escape from sharks, whales, human beings and other enemies.

Encyclopaedia Britannica

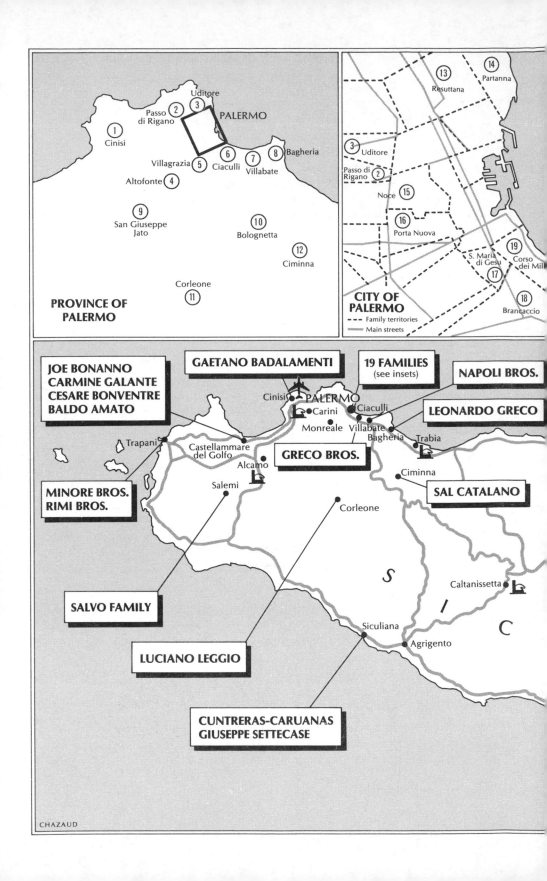

PROVINCE OF PALERMO

Uditore
Passo di Rigano ②③
①Cinisi
PALERMO
Villagrazia ⑤ ⑥ Ciaculli ⑦ ⑧ Bagheria
Villabate
Altofonte ④
⑨ San Giuseppe Jato
⑩ Bolognetta
⑫ Ciminna
Corleone ⑪

CITY OF PALERMO
- - - Family territories
—— Main streets

⑬Resuttana
⑭Partanna
③Uditore
②Passo di Rigano
⑮Noce
⑯Porta Nuova
⑲Corso dei Mil
S. Maria di Gesù
⑰
⑱Brancaccio

JOE BONANNO
CARMINE GALANTE
CESARE BONVENTRE
BALDO AMATO

GAETANO BADALAMENTI

19 FAMILIES
(see insets)

NAPOLI BROS.

LEONARDO GRECO

Cinisi ✈ PALERMO
Carini
Monreale Villabate Ciaculli
Bagheria
Trabia
Trapani
Castellammare del Golfo
GRECO BROS.
Alcamo
Ciminna
SAL CATALANO
MINORE BROS.
RIMI BROS.
Salemi
Corleone
S
SALVO FAMILY
Caltanissetta
/
LUCIANO LEGGIO
Siculiana
Agrigento
C
CUNTRERAS-CARUANAS
GIUSEPPE SETTECASE

CHAZAUD

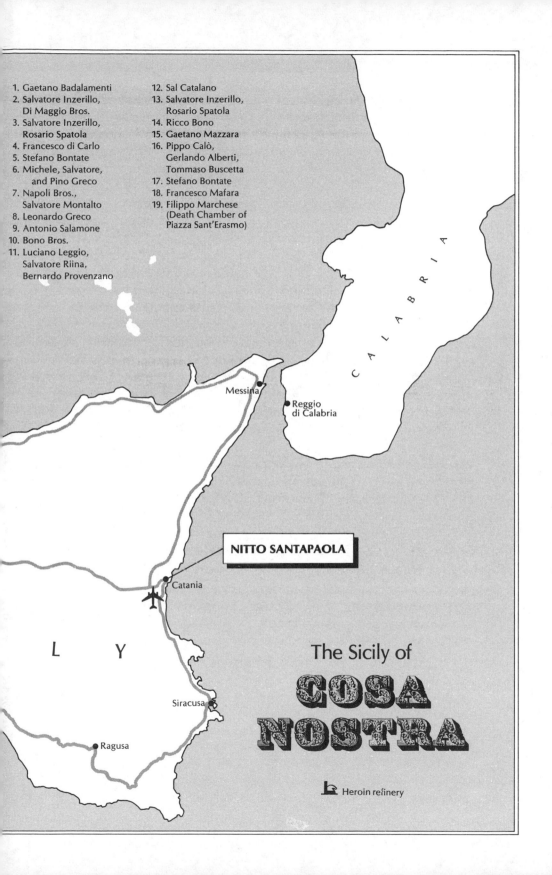

1. Gaetano Badalamenti
2. Salvatore Inzerillo, Di Maggio Bros.
3. Salvatore Inzerillo, Rosario Spatola
4. Francesco di Carlo
5. Stefano Bontate
6. Michele, Salvatore, and Pino Greco
7. Napoli Bros., Salvatore Montalto
8. Leonardo Greco
9. Antonio Salamone
10. Bono Bros.
11. Luciano Leggio, Salvatore Riina, Bernardo Provenzano
12. Sal Catalano
13. Salvatore Inzerillo, Rosario Spatola
14. Ricco Bono
15. Gaetano Mazzara
16. Pippo Calò, Gerlando Alberti, Tommaso Buscetta
17. Stefano Bontate
18. Francesco Mafara
19. Filippo Marchese (Death Chamber of Piazza Sant'Erasmo)

CALABRIA

Messina

Reggio di Calabria

NITTO SANTAPAOLA

Catania

ITALY

Siracusa

Ragusa

The Sicily of

COSA NOSTRA

⚑ Heroin refinery

Sicilian Mafia Superclans

WINNING CLANS IN THE GREAT MAFIA WAR, 1981–83
(UNTIL 1988; A PARTIAL LIST)

Corleone: Luciano Leggio
 Salvatore Riina
 Bernardo Provenzano

Catania: Nitto Santapaolo
 Giuseppe Ferrara and two brothers

Agrigento
 (Siculiana): Cuntrera and Caruana Families

Trapani: Minore brothers

Altofonte: Francesco Di Carlo, replaced by his brother

Bagheria: Leonardo Greco
 Giovanni Scaduto

Ciaculli:	Michele Greco
	Salvatore Greco
	Pino Greco
	Prestifilippo Family
Salemi:	Salvo Family
Partinico:	Nene Geraci
Villabate:	Salvatore Montalto
	Salvatore Buscemi

PALERMO

Corso dei Mille:	Filippo Marchese
San Giuseppe Jato:	Bernardo Brusca
	Antonio Salamone
Noce:	Ino Picone
	Gaetano Mazzara
Porta Nuova:	Giuseppe "Pippo" Calò
	Tommaso Spadaro
	Gerlando Alberti
	Antonino Rotolo
Resuttana:	Francesco Madonia
San Lorenzo:	Vincenzo Puccio
Brancaccio:	Carmelo Zanca and four brothers
Uditore:	Francesco Bonura

(All territory west of Resuttana is the Piana dei Colli, dominion of the Corleonesi's Salvatore Riina.)

LOSING CLANS

Santa Maria di Gesu:	Stefano Bontate
	(now Pullara brothers)
	Salvatore Contorno
	Grado brothers
	(Contorno's cousins)

Brancaccio:	Giuseppe Di Maggio (taken by Giuseppe Savoca)
Uditore:	Salvatore Inzerillo Rosario Spatola
Passo di Rigano:	Salvatore Inzerillo Salvatore Buscemi Di Maggio brothers
Cinisi:	Gaetano Badalamenti
San Lorenzo:	Filippo Giacolone (now Pedone, father and son)
Borgetto:	Frank Rappa Salvatore Lamberti
Catania:	Giuseppe Calderone Alfio Ferlito
Riesi:	Giuseppe Di Cristina

THE MAFIA

Prologue

The two men were dining at the Palace, one of New York's most exquisitely expensive East Side restaurants in those days—the winter of 1977. (Customers spending more than $10,000 a year there were given twenty-four-karat-gold credit cards.) Both were dressed with killing elegance: hand-tailored suits, fairly quiet designer ties, no diamond pinkie rings. Only their language might have betrayed them, could their murmured half-sentences have been overheard.

The one addressed as Enzo had very little English and a thick Italian accent. His companion, Tommy, spoke unbroken Brooklynese. Over a rack of lamb and a bottle of Château Lafite-Rothschild '55, they talked business:

ENZO: It's a painting from a museum.
TOMMY: Excuse me?
ENZO: It's a painting . . .
TOMMY: Oh yeah, inna museum. . . . You got these people that put 'em in their fucking bathrooms and leave 'em there for years, they don't care. . . .

ENZO: Yeah. . . . Look, from the time you was away I done a lotta research. A hundred thousand dollars, right?

The stolen painting they discussed was a "Tiepido," as far as they could make out (Giovanni Battista Tiepolo, an eighteenth-century Italian master). Enzo could arrange to have other museum pieces lifted on order, he said.

TOMMY: Rembrandt.
ENZO: Rembrandt what?
TOMMY: Rembrandt, there's a million of 'em. Da Vinci, van Gogh, ya want me to go down the list? Van Gogh, Da Vinci . . . Y'know what I'm saying?
ENZO: V-A-A, G-O-R-A. Van Go?

They moved on to musical instruments.

ENZO: Violins . . . Stradinoff . . .
TOMMY: Stradius?
ENZO: Stradivar . . . I don't remember the name. Six. They're worth a million dollars.
TOMMY: What do they want for two?
ENZO: They want two hundred ten thousand dollars, all six. Divided by six, which is thirty-five thousand apiece.
TOMMY: Y'know, you're a pain in the ass to fucking bargain. . . . I'll take one Stradivarus or whatever. Who the fuck is gonna buy six Stradivarus?

From there, the two men got into embezzled securities.

TOMMY: Gimme a hundred thousand dollars' worth of Treasury bonds. I'll pick 'em up next weekend. If they're cold. Okay?
ENZO: We wait. It would blow everything out. . . . There's gonna be ten million dollars. . . . Ten percent up front, fifteen percent after they're cashed. Right?
TOMMY: Right. . . . Well, gimme a hundred to a hundred and a quarter, and then maybe next time we'll take a million. . . .

Finally, the talk turned to more sensitive matters.

TOMMY: What about a federal judge?
ENZO: What?

TOMMY: Do y'know any federal judge?
ENZO: New York?
TOMMY: Yeah.
ENZO: If it's junk it's very hard, anything else the bottom figure is fifty thousand dollars.[1]

By the time the men got to the brandy—vintage Napoleon wheeled in on a cart, $1,800 a bottle—they had covered a lot more ground. Enzo had offered fake Cartier watches at $65 apiece, counterfeit $20 bills at twenty points on the dollar, truckloads of copper slugs for cigarette machines, and twenty thousand pounds of scallops at 15 cents a pound below market price.

He had mentioned skilled labor: "Listen, Tommy, if you ever want anybody bumped or beat up, just ask. I got very good people, I can have it done for you." He could arrange a torch job "to get rid of a building or something" for a couple of hundred dollars. He knew a pilot who would smuggle in any package from Italy weighing under ten pounds. He could clear a package the size of a shoe box through customs, mailed from Europe. "It's dangerous. It's only worth it for diamonds or junk," he explained.

Much of the cryptic conversation that evening defeated the agents listening in and even, at times, the two men themselves:

TOMMY: Let me know about the other thing, that other thing y'know that we talked about that time. . . . Y'know what I'm saying?
ENZO: No.

Neither did the agents (who cracked up). They had been taping encounters between these two for some months. "Tommy," who wore a minuscule AID recorder in a special pocket sewn into the crotch of his shorts, was really Detective Douglas Le Vien, attached to the elite Central Investigation Section of the New York City Police Department's Organized Crime Control Bureau.

Both before and since, Detective Le Vien has worked many sensational cases over the years. He was the agent who wore the electronic bug in the famous Goldbug case of 1972. Posing as a cop on the take in a Brooklyn junkyard in that case, he nailed the boss of the Mafia's Lucchese Family, Carmine Tramunti, along with forty other mobsters and twenty-one corrupt policemen. As a result, for the press, he became "The Cop Who Couldn't Be Bought." Later, he worked on the celebrated Abscam case, "the Sting," exposing corruption in high public office. Detective Le Vien has collected meritorious awards from the New York Police Department, the U.S. Department of Justice, the Treasury, the Internal Revenue Service, and the Federal Bureau of Investigation. The FBI's then director, Judge William Webster, commended him personally for his "invaluable services" on Abscam. He did a superlative job for the President's Commission on Organized Crime in the early 1980s. "Doug Le Vien's street smarts and insights formed the basis for the commission's most important recommendations to the president," said the commission's head and chief counsel, James Harmon. Today Le Vien ranks among the best investigators in America.

But he got no thanks for his remarkable investigation of Vincenzo Napoli, "Enzo." He was on to something perfectly concealed from the police of two continents for a quarter of a century, perhaps the biggest story in the contemporary history of organized crime. Left to pursue the story, Le Vien might have uncovered an international criminal conspiracy of monstrous proportions—but he was stopped cold. Whether this was a matter of chance or design, of ignorance, indifference, incompetence, or deft interference, the few who knew what Le Vien was doing could hardly wait to close the Napoli case. They still have no idea of the grievous mistake they made.

"Enzo" was Doug Le Vien's discovery, and his affliction. A curious inertial drag impeded the detective from the day of his fabulous find, in June 1976. His superiors simply could not see what he was so excited about. The more obsessively he argued, the less they seemed to listen. "They would look at me like something was wrong with me. Why was I talking so loud? Was I drunk or something?"

Eventually, they stopped listening altogether. The money for the investigation, never bountiful, dried up. Le Vien's reports never saw the light of day, in or out of a courtroom; the contents are published here for the first time. The secrets he stumbled on were never explored. His findings were buried under bureaucratic bumf, his rare Mafia specimen was allowed to get away, and the case died of neglect. "Un-fucking-believable," says Le Vien.

At the time, to be fair, not even he could have known how right he was. He thought he was infiltrating the American Mafia, as many undercover agents had done. But in fact, he was infiltrating the Sicilian Mafia in America, a feat nobody else had managed.

The operation was all over before he began to wonder just who his target had been. Like his colleagues at headquarters, Le Vien had taken Enzo Napoli for a soldier in the Gambino Family, America's mightiest

Mafia clan. "Then the guy goes to jail, and we get a tip that he put out a contract on me," says Le Vien. "I don't believe it. But the source says, 'You gotta take it serious. This ain't no American guy. This guy is a geep. They [the Gambinos] don't control him.' "

"Geeps" were Sicilians in the New York mob's lexicon. Enzo Napoli, born in Villabate, Sicily, was regularly sworn in as a "made" member of the Sicilian Mafia, to which he was bound by a blood oath for life. The Gambinos in New York did not control him. He worked with them, not for them, only when it was necessary or expedient.[2] From New York his operations extended to Detroit, Milwaukee, Chicago, Anaheim, Houston, Virginia Beach, and Miami, to Montreal, Puerto Rico, the Bahamas, Grenada, and Caracas, to Munich, Zurich, Lugano, Paris, Milan, Rome, Palermo, Bangkok, and Hong Kong.[3] "He was a world-class guy," conceded an assistant U.S. attorney in Brooklyn, a decade after Doug Le Vien had him and lost him.

Le Vien was not looking for heroin when he stumbled on Napoli. He was just intrigued by a crook who was obviously "connected" and utterly engrossed in making enormous sums of money. The fact that Napoli was part of a sprawling underground network directed from a distant island in the Mediterranean would have astounded him.

The first meeting between Le Vien and Napoli, in June 1976, was arranged by an underling of Napoli's, who thought the detective was a wealthy businessman from Connecticut buying for his own shady crowd. (Such a man had been dealing with Napoli through the underling for years, sight unseen.) The information on Napoli was scanty, consisting mostly of a scrap of conversation on a tapped telephone in a Manhattan vice case. The caller, evidently not Sicilian, worked at a sumptuous gambling club that Napoli owned, the Murray Hill Townhouse, which featured girls, food and drink, instant credit, baccarat, and a Sicilian card game called *zigonet*. Excerpts of their dialogue offered a tantalizing glimpse of Enzo Napoli:

I think he possibly has a little respect, you know what I mean. . . . But he's a fucking schemer. I've always held this guy in the highest esteem cause he always had money, he's got shit now so I don't hold him so high anymore. . . . [Napoli customarily talked poormouth to ward off pressing financial demands from his employees.]
He tells me they cut thirteen thousand last week, the whole week. He's full of shit. . . . This game does half a million a week. . . . He tells me the eight thousand left has to be split sixteen shares. He says every fucking Family in

New York got a piece of this here, everybody. . . . There's big Mafia people getting a piece of this game. . . .

Y'know, these other guys wanted to take the joint over. [These were "Fat Andy" Ruggiano's people in the Gambino Family.] They had a sit-down, and Napoli's people said, "Hands off—we're taking it." . . . He says, "Don't ever think you can run us outta there, because we stay. Nobody else comes in. We stay." . . .

Hey, lemme tell ya, as far as I'm concerned, I'd like to walk in there with two machine guns, heist the joint, take their money, and ah, forget everything. . . .

They got too many Sicilians there [says his interlocutor].

You better believe it. They'd tear ya up.

Chop your balls right off [the other agrees].[4]

With little more than this tape to go on, Le Vien met his man at a gentleman's hairdressing salon in lower Manhattan. Le Vien came as "Tommy Russo," the bent millionaire from Connecticut. Enzo Napoli, forty-six years old, six feet tall, and well over two hundred pounds, had the beginnings of a paunch and a middle-aged slouch. His features were fleshy, his eyes closely set and slightly squinty, his hands sweaty. He dressed well and spoke softly, to lethal effect.

Napoli wanted to sell Tommy a .9mm Beretta with a custom-made silencer for $1,000. "I used it myself; it don't make much noise," he said. He had even better weapons for sale, including an automatic rifle with a silencer "made exclusively for the CIA," and much bigger deals to propose. He was an "earner," Le Vien could see that at once: a versatile money-maker, smart, cautious, and decidedly dangerous. "I told him I just wanted him and me to earn together," Le Vien reported afterward. "I says to myself, 'Who's Enzo Napoli?' and I start looking. He's never been caught. He's an unknown, and we don't know a lot about what's going on out there. . . . I says to myself, there's no way I could ever get higher than this guy. I'm gonna key in on this guy."

But he ran into instant resistance. Back at headquarters, where only top priority cases were handled, "they didn't wanna know. . . . I come up with the gun, they say, 'Why buy from this guy? We can buy that anywhere.' I say, 'Are you kidding me? This guy has it. He's got quality. He knows how to operate."

With tentative permission (but no funds) from his captain, Le Vien began his new double life. He had been an undercover cop for six years when he took on Enzo Napoli in 1976, and was moving up fast. At twenty-nine, he was a thorough, dogged, imaginative, and courageous—as well as funny and likable—detective. He made a wonderfully convincing con man. Growing up on the seamier side of Brooklyn, Le Vien had been a wild street kid mingling with the Mafia's young. At fifteen, he was running his own book and leading a street gang, the Hilltoppers. Today, he walks, talks, and, if necessary, can think like one of them. And, though he is French-Canadian, he even looks Italian. Dark and stocky, with the stance of a ballpark tough and the hooded eyes of a George Raft (though a slight stutter tends to mar the effect), he could easily be taken for a Mafia wise guy. "I mighta been, if I hadn't joined the marines," he observes. (He served with the marines in Vietnam.)

Expensively clothed—"vined out," he would say—Le Vien could get by as a self-made millionaire. Certainly, he could pass for a crook. Over the next two years, Napoli would never doubt that he was both.

A formal investigation of Enzo Napoli, code-named Operation Earn, finally began in November 1976. Le Vien had had to circumvent the whole New York Police Department to get that far. Unable to budge his superiors, he turned secretly to a U.S. Customs officer who knew a little about Napoli. Customs leaned on the police department until it gave in. A joint operation was then launched "on a trial basis" by the Eastern District's Strike Force.[5] This was a multi-agency unit headed by the U.S. attorney's office in Brooklyn-Queens, bringing together the New York police, customs, the IRS, the INS (Immigration and Naturalization Service), the ATF (Bureau of Alcohol, Tobacco, and Firearms), the DEA (Drug Enforcement Administration), and the FBI.

The investigation covered not just Vincenzo Napoli, but his brothers Antonino and Gaetano, known respectively as Nino and Tommy. All three were held to be "high-ranking and trusted members of the Gambino Crime Family." Antonino had been Target of the Month for the 123rd Police Precinct some years back, for his countless suspected sins. Enzo himself was described as a "money-maker" or "mover," a "major source of income . . . for the highest echelons of organized crime."[6]

By the end of 1976, a trailer had been fitted out at Manhattan's 23rd Street Pier for Le Vien's confidential base. A chart of New York's five Mafia Families and a map of the United States were tacked to the ceiling. (A map of the world went up later.) An apartment was rented for the detective in Fairfield, Connecticut, and a telephone circuit was patched through, relaying calls from Fairfield to the trailer. Driving license, car sticker, bank account, and funds for a wardrobe were all arranged.

A dazzling "Tommy Russo" emerged. He had studied up on wines and art. He had gotten a $27 haircut and manicured fingernails. He wore a $25,000 Piaget watch (borrowed from customs), a cashmere topcoat, an Oleg Cassini suit (with a label inside saying "Made Specially for Tom"), a Valentino scarf and tie, Saks Fifth Avenue socks, and Gucci shoes. "If Enzo sees me in Thom McAn's, that's it," he noted on his private tape recorder. Le Vien's Gucci wallet was stuffed with cash, ready to be dispensed as lordly $50 tips to maître d's and "the guys with a Ph.D. in wines." "This is a nice wine, this here '55 Château Morton [Mouton]-Rothschild," he would assure Enzo. "The one we had last time, we had the Château La Fête [Lafite] '62. That wasn't bad. . . . You like Havanas?"

He ordered escargots and Dom Perignon champagne at the "21" and eggs Benedict for breakfast at the St. Regis. Fellow agents in snappy business suits would drop by their table to say, "How ya' doin', Tommy? How'd it go in Acapulco [or Paris or Costa Rica]?" Once he swanned in with an undercover playing chauffeur: "Sal, my schlep." To top it off, customs threw in a black Mercedes for his use. "Now Enzo knows I got a thirty-thousand-dollar car; I couldn't be a cop," he told himself.

But underneath his carefree exterior, Le Vien was full of foreboding: "This is like out of a fairy book, and I tell ya', I'm scared. . . . I haven't enjoyed a single minute with this guy. . . . He's got a mind like a brain surgeon. . . . You gotta be extra, extra, extra sharp with this guy. . . . He frightens the shit outta me."

For all his reports on the target—piece after piece of amazing information—Le Vien kept running into the same odd inertia. "The inspectors didn't wanna hear," he would say into his recorder. Or, "My office didn't wanna know a fucking thing." In thirty-five tapes of the diary he kept, his recurrent baffled and frustrated question was: Why?

As Le Vien later discovered, everybody in law enforcement already had something on Vincenzo Napoli. He was in the U.S. Secret Service files for hawking $100,000 Treasury notes; in the ATF files for selling guns; in the INS files for smuggling aliens; in customs files for smuggling currency; in the files of the DEA and Department of Justice for suspected heroin trafficking; in the FBI files for a million-dollar bank swindle; in various police files for fraud, grand larceny, illegal gambling, loan-sharking, drug-running, and consorting with the innermost circles of Cosa Nostra.[7]

Only a fraction of this information was in Le Vien's hands when Operation Earn began. Several law enforcement agencies, starting with the Eastern District's Strike Force, had forgotten about documents in their own archives. Many disliked sharing information, on principle. Few had a compelling interest in crimes beyond their own jurisdiction. Even within their jurisdiction, what mattered was not so much the nature of the crime as the score: numbers of arrests, convictions, citations, commendations, promotions.

Nobody had thought of matching up the files. Enzo Napoli was too *busy.* He would require too much paperwork. He was transgressing too many agency boundaries, his case was too remote from the comfortably familiar, too perplexing, too exotic. "Big cases, big problems," law enforcers are wont to say. The Napoli case was too big.

Conventional wisdom about Cosa Nostra in America could not account for Napoli. His multifarious transactions were largely untraceable to the Mafia's usual operators, and incredible in scale—millions upon millions of dollars' worth of contraband gold, diamonds, emeralds, junk, securities, and weapons, a seemingly bottomless supply of U.S. Treasury bonds, countless American Express credit cards, priceless stolen paintings from Europe, phony currency from Italy, pilfered money orders from London, counterfeit bank checks from Tokyo and Sydney, and embezzled funds passing through his own shell bank in Grenada.

There were times when Le Vien wondered who was conning whom. Not only did Napoli talk incessantly in improbable seven- or eight-digit figures, he also tried to palm off some egregious fakes. The Tiepolo was one. Others included a couple of so-called Ming Dynasty vases and two volumes of "Paccio" (Picasso) sketches. Over breakfast at the St. Regis, Le Vien was suitably outraged. "I'm not your fucking appraiser," he told Enzo. "That Tripoli—Tiepolo—is no good. My people won't tolerate this fegazy stuff, they want quality." (He had no money to buy it with anyway.)

Other artworks Napoli had on offer were no fakes, though. Two stolen bronzes by the American Frederic Remington were worth $100,-000 apiece (at 1976 prices). A pair of seventeenth-century paintings from Europe were valued at $150,000 each: a Rubens and an oil sketch by Gerard Terborch, among the finest of the Dutch Little Masters.[8]

The weapons he had for sale were no fakes either. He specialized in every kind of hit gun: machine guns, handguns, rifles, .45s, .38s, .22s. "The best one for hits is a .22," he had assured Le Vien the first day they met. "It's nice, it's quiet, it don't make problems." Just before Christmas 1976, Napoli presented his friend Tommy Russo with a "Christmas present" (for only $2,500). It was the perfect assassin's weapon: a

.22-caliber AR-7 High Standard automatic rifle with, according to Le Vien, "the most sophisticated silencer and scope you'll ever see. . . . You could hit a guy walking down the street a block away from a tenth-floor window, and nobody in the next room would hear a thing."

Seemingly identical .22s were used that year to execute twenty-odd men on the Mafia's hit list in America from coast to coast. The victims, potential courtroom witnesses or confidential police sources, included Sam Giancana, retired boss of Chicago, and Frank Bompensiero, the FBI's highest-ranking Mafia informant. The FBI was disturbed enough to call an emergency conference of twenty agents in San Diego. "The thing is a mess. No one knows who's doing it or why, but people in Washington are in a near-panic," said one to the *New York Times*. "Some Mob insiders believe the killers are a squad of 'greenies,' brought illegally into this country from Sicily," reported *Time,* closer to the truth than its editors dreamed.[9]

Yet the perfect assassin's weapon stayed on a shelf in its Christmas wrappings for a full year before getting to the FBI. "This is a fucking joke! Why don't they ever want the FBI to just examine the .22? Would that hurt? It's so fucking *par!*" Le Vien shouted into his tape recorder.[10]

He ran into other unbelievable roadblocks. Soon after their first meeting, in the summer of 1976, Napoli had told Le Vien about buying off a federal judge in Miami to get out of trouble. "You mean the judge down there did the right thing?" the detective asked for the benefit of his AID recorder. "Yeah . . . it cost me forty thousand bucks," Napoli replied.

Bribing a federal judge is an exceptionally grave offense in America. Yet the Strike Force failed to react when Le Vien reported Napoli's own admission. Exasperated, he hammered at his superiors to get the facts about Napoli, and went after them himself.

He discovered that Napoli had been arrested in Miami by the FBI, in August 1976. He was waiting on a street corner while two Sicilian *picciotti* (young Mafia apprentices or gofers) in his employ cashed $65,000 worth of phony checks at the Biscayne Bank. A federal judge released him without his even being arraigned; his accomplices were freed soon after, without trial. The judge who let him go was one Jacob Eshkenazi, who became a U.S. attorney the following year. Le Vien reported his name to the Eastern District, but nothing ever happened to him.[11] Nothing happened to Enzo Napoli either, for this or several other scabrous criminal acts known to his undercover detective friend. Le Vien caught him out in half a dozen multidigit scams, but to his eternal mystification—it would mystify anybody—Napoli has never been questioned about them.

Once Napoli told Le Vien how he planned to rip off an Off-Track Betting office in midtown Manhattan; a month later, the office was taken for a quarter of a million dollars in the way Napoli had described. On another occasion, he showed Le Vien a sample stolen money order from USN of Milford, Connecticut, one of the country's largest private money order houses. The company went bankrupt soon afterward, blaming a $5 million "seepage."[12]

Also in 1976, Napoli swindled a Staten Island bank out of $1 million, laundering the money through his own shell bank in St. George, Grenada; Le Vien found the proof in a forgotten customs report in the Eastern District's own files.[13] The next year, Napoli got away scot-free with a million-dollar diamond heist—this when the FBI and a special police task force admitted to making "no progress" on a succession of million-dollar robberies in New York's diamond district.[14] The diamonds were stolen for Napoli on April 18, 1977, by the same two *picciotti* in his employ.[15] He threw the glittering stones on the table before "Tommy" the next night.

To avoid having to buy them, Le Vien persuaded customs agent Steve Rogers to lay on a yacht at the 79th Street Pier, a nautical captain and crew, a sexy girl agent to lounge in the stateroom, and an alternative million-dollar batch of gems. Fitted out in white ducks and a yachting cap from Abercrombie and Fitch, he ushered Napoli aboard and threw his own stash on the table. "What the fuck would I do with your diamonds? I *got* diamonds!" he exclaimed. Then he took Napoli for a leisurely moonlight cruise up the Hudson.

Operation Earn had been under way for barely half a year by then—the spring of 1977—and pressure was already mounting to end it. Le Vien could not make anybody listen. He became a nag and a nuisance, and perhaps an inconvenience. As the next months went by, he was shunted aside, stripped of his aides, denied buy money, and left unnervingly exposed. (He was ordered twice by the New York Police Department to appear publicly in police uniform, which might easily have gotten him spotted and killed.)

He took to reading Agatha Christie in his confidential trailer-base, where the phone never rang. The head of the Eastern District's Strike Force, U.S. Attorney Tom Puccio, hardly ever returned his calls, claiming once to have forgotten the number. Not only were Le Vien's reports ignored, they seem to have gone unread.

Le Vien had pried a lot of information out of various police intelligence units and federal agencies. He had obtained the records of Napoli's long-distance phone calls to most states in the Union, South America, Europe, and Asia; credit card travel charges, crisscrossing the United States and the European continent; old classified correspondence with the Italian police; printouts of the Napoli brothers' close associates going back to the early 1960s. Entombed in this long-buried dossier were secrets that the Sicilian Mafia would have killed to defend—has killed for, many times over, since Le Vien worked the case a dozen years ago.

The associates' names gave the game away, which isn't to say that Le Vien realized how big the game was. Nobody in the 1970s knew what experts know now. Italy and the United States exchanged virtually no information in those days. Americans understood very little about their own Mafia and next to nothing of its mother cell in the Old Country. Members of both Mafias looked alike, spoke the same incomprehensible jargon, had the same deplorable habits, bore the same unpronounceable names. The names alone, a glop of fused vowels and insistent consonants for most investigators, were hopelessly defeating.

Nevertheless, it didn't take much to perceive that Enzo Napoli kept singular company. Although both Mafias were engrossed in making huge sums of money by every imaginable means, the Americans' "earners" had nothing like his scope.

Napoli never told Le Vien who "his people" were, but he often spoke of their activities and whereabouts. His people in Sicily were setting up gambling casinos in Morocco, he said. His people in Canada were ferrying in Sicilian aliens. His people in Brazil were smuggling emeralds. His people in Venezuela owned a ship that he was going to bring up to Atlantic City and turn into a gambling casino. His people in Rome had counterfeited $8 million worth of the $20 bills he provided for Le Vien's inspection.

His people in Sicily were also "getting the best-quality heroin from the Golden Triangle" in Asia, and his people in South America could "do very safe heroin deals." "You people interested in heroin?" he had murmured to "Tommy" over dinner at the "21." "In a way, yes, and in a way, no," answered the detective truthfully.

This was the one report of Le Vien's that registered among his superiors, and the one that finally closed the case. The DEA put Napoli under immediate surveillance, tracked a courier of his to Bangkok, and arrested the pair of them when the courier returned with a kilo of heroin. The entire investigation thereupon wound down, for a single kilo of dope: 2.2 pounds. Small cases, small problems.

Actually, the single kilo was just a trial run. Napoli was going to be the conduit in New York for twenty kilos of heroin a month from Thailand, a quarter of a ton a year, five million fixes.[16] And judging from reports Le Vien had gathered, starting with the DEA's, that wasn't the half of it.

The Napoli brothers were a window on an immense hidden landscape, as we will see. Enzo was part of the biggest heroin circuit in the world. His older brother, Antonino, was on file in the New York Police Department as "the biggest mover of junk into the United States"—and in the Eastern District as "one of the world's major narcotics dealers." The Napolis' close associates, listed in U.S. government printouts, were among the biggest known international traffickers up to the present day. All were made members of the Sicilian Mafia.

They had just completed their conquest of the world's heroin market—the most profitable multinational on earth—when Le Vien strayed on the scene. This conquest was what they had been working toward since reaching a secret agreement with the American Mafia, twenty years before. That very winter—the winter of 1976–77—the Sicilian Mafia opened a massive heroin pipeline into the United States. Its own men were then in place to move the merchandise, up and down the country and at strategic points throughout the Western Hemisphere. Rivers of junk spilled out over America before this secret army was detected, halfway through the next decade.

Le Vien was there watching: the only investigator who has ever gotten close enough to see the Sicilian Mafia at work anywhere abroad. Had his superiors taken notice, they might have learned enough to contain the spreading heroin plague before it got out of control. They didn't, and it did.

The View from Palermo

n the spring of 1988, the primary purveyors of heroin to the world were said to be finished. Their destruction was assured in "the largest arrest ever to take place in the history of mankind," said the FBI's top expert on organized crime. A hundred Sicilian narcotics traffickers had been rounded up in Italy and the United States, and another 150 warrants were out. "The Sicilian Mafia's drug connection has been dismantled," announced an FBI spokesman in Washington.[1]

This was heartening news from the front, in what has come to be called the Third World War—society's seemingly lost war on drugs. Obsessed by the spreading scourge of cocaine, the press and public and even law enforcers were tending to overlook the continuing inexorable advance of heroin. The hardest drug, deadliest of all narcotics killers, heroin had survived every onslaught up to then. By 1988, it was worth ten times its weight in gold.

It was bringing in from $12 to $20 billion a year on American streets, in an overall narcotics trade generating $110 billion a year in the United States, $35 billion more in Italy, and another $300 billion or so around the planet.[2] The yield per heroin dollar invested at the source was around 1,600 percent. Profits were such that those in charge in New York often didn't bother to count the cash on the way to the bank; they simply weighed it.[3]

The cash was mostly in small bills, from customers turning their cities into war zones to pay for their fixes. The number of America's heroin addicts was up tenfold since the boom began, and holding steady at half a million, officially; the unofficial figure was probably closer to a million.[4] Elsewhere in the world, the addict community population was approaching three million and growing exponentially.

Western Europe had not only caught up with but surpassed the United States in addicts. By unofficial State Department estimate, Europeans were consuming ten to fifteen tons of heroin a year in 1988, at least half again as much as per capita figures for the United States.[5] Italy had 300,000 heroin addicts by 1988, three times as many as in the United States per capita; and the number of its overdose deaths reached 800 that year, up fourfold in just five years.[6] West Germany had half a million users, of whom 150,000 were officially addicts—this from a total of 27 heroin addicts a decade earlier; and new heroin users were increasing by nearly a third yearly.[7] In West Berlin there were 9,000 addicts in a population of 2 million, more than double the U.S. rate. Spain had 125,000, higher than the U.S. rate by 50 percent. France and Great Britain were up to around 120,000 apiece, and the British rate was rising 25 percent yearly.[8]

Seizures of heroin were seven times bigger in Western Europe than in the United States: around three and a half tons in 1987. By their own rule of thumb, narcotics agents would estimate that at least ten times as much must have been circulating on the Continent that year: 1.5 billion fixes.[9]

The Sicilian Mafia, largely responsible for creating and feeding this habit in the West, had been a pillar of the trade since the 1950s, and a dominant force since the 1970s. According to FBI Director William Sessions in 1988, the organization had "supplied most of the heroin sold in the United States from 1975 to 1984." Earlier, the DEA had put the figure at 85 percent.[10] For Sicilian magistrates, the Sicilian Mafia, or the Octopus, as Italians call it, was "the central directorate of the world drug trade."[11]

Nearly all of Sicily's Mafia Families were in the business—150 clans with 50 to 100 members apiece, at last count. They had envoys all across the United States and in dozens of way stations from Bangkok to London, Caracas, and Montreal. Thousands of foreign nationals worked for or with them around the globe: Belgians, Dutch, Britons, Thais, Lebanese, Palestinians, Israelis, Turks, Chinese, Nepalese, Brazilians, Canadians, Americans.

A part of this network may have been dismantled in the spring of 1988; not all. Its magnitude has been a continuing surprise. Invisible for a quarter of a century, the Sicilian Mafia's secret army abroad was not even noticed by law enforcement agencies anywhere until 1984. Years passed before they began to grasp the nature of this enormous subterranean enterprise, insofar as they have grasped it yet. Almost every discovery has come as a shock.

The big drug bust of 1988 brought several disquieting new facts to light. American authorities had thought that the Sicilian Mafia was implanted only along the eastern seaboard. Now they found it operating in at least twenty-five major cities coast to coast.[12] They had assumed that exposure and spectacular arrests on both sides of the Atlantic had hampered the Mafia's traffic severely; its share of the U.S. heroin market was supposed to be down to a mere 30 percent, surpassed by the Chinese Triads' with 40 percent. Actually, the Chinese were turning much of their heroin over to the Sicilians in New York for distribution (see chapter 20).[13]

The Mafia's refineries in Sicily were held to be closed down, and its heroin shipments to be dwindling because narcotics agents were finding none on familiar transatlantic routes. In fact, the Mafia had simply switched to carriers the agents were no longer watching: from jumbo jets under heavy surveillance to old-fashioned cargo ships. Some of its heroin came from the Middle and Far East, but much was unmistakably made in Sicily or mainland Italy. American and Italian narcotics agents are still hunting for new refineries there.[14]

Even as the FBI announced the end of the Sicilian Mafia's drug connection, the evidence showed it to be in a phase of frightening expansion. The Sicilian traffickers caught in 1988 were a portent of the calamitous future: in exchange for the heroin they brought to New York, they were taking payment in cocaine to carry back to Europe.

It was a stupendous deal. Heroin sold for $50,000 a kilo in Italy and around $200,000 in New York. Cocaine sold for $11,000 a kilo in New York and $50,000 in Italy. Nobody could handle such a swap the way the Sicilian Mafia could. Therefore, the organization was going into the cocaine business, naturally, ineluctably.

The cocaine explosion of the 1980s had almost put heroin in the shade. Consumption had more than doubled in America halfway through the decade, from thirty-one to seventy-two metric tons, for some six million regular users. By 1988, users were tripling yearly in Europe; the increase there over 1987 was 350 percent.[15] Most of the cocaine traffic was controlled from the city of Medellin in Colombia. By 1988, however, Colombia's cocaine merchants needed Sicily's heroin merchants. The American market was saturated; the price of cocaine had dropped by more than two-thirds in two years.

In Europe, on the other hand, cocaine was selling for four times as much. The rage for it was just beginning to devour the Old Continent. Great Britain, France, West Germany, Denmark, Sweden, Holland, Italy, and Spain were succumbing at terrifying speed. In Spain alone, police seized over three tons of cocaine between January and June of 1988. Presumably, ten times more must have been getting into Europe through this single channel—perhaps as much as sixty tons a year. It would not be long before Europe caught up with or surpassed America in the cocaine market too.

Here, the Sicilian Mafia could do what Colombia's Medellin cartel could not. Europe had been the Mafia's practically exclusive marketplace for upward of twenty-five years. Moreover, the Sicilians were already much closer to Colombia's cocaine traffickers than many realized. The Sicilian Mafia's Venezuelan branch had been sending "huge amounts" of cocaine to Europe since at least 1978, according to the DEA.[16] By 1982, it was brokering 60 percent of all the cocaine in transit—this according to DISIP, the Venezuelan intelligence service; and four-fifths of the cocaine shipped to the United States and Europe was moving by way of Venezuela.[17] By 1984, the Sicilian branch in Venezuela was engaged in "a gigantic exchange of cocaine for heroin."[18]

Now, experts were finding proof of a full partnership. Talks to that effect were known to have been held between the Mafia and the Medellin cartel in the spring of 1988. "We expect the Sicilian Mafia to take over cocaine distribution in Europe. They have the network; the Colombians don't," said Assistant U.S. Attorney Louis Freeh, head of the Organized Crime team for New York's Southern District at the time.[19] By the following year, the Sicilian-Colombian-European partnership was in full swing.

The combination looked hair-raising. Colombia's drug traffickers were probably the most vicious on earth; Sicily's, only a shade less so, were the most sophisticated and best placed. The global turnover for the merchandise they dealt in would run to an estimated $200 billion a year.[20] Together, the two organizations were capable of spreading unimaginable havoc.

There things stood as the decade drew to a close. By rights, the

Sicilian Mafia should have been dead or dying. In the course of the 1980s, it had been hit with sensational defectors, tremendous revelations, massive arrests, trials, and convictions in Italy and America. Its secrets were betrayed, its drug traffic disrupted, a whole generation of its leaders jailed or forced into hiding and stripped of their wealth. Yet it appeared to be as strong as always—stronger. It seemed beyond human reach: a faceless, disembodied, malevolent power impervious to the law, emanating death and destruction. But the Mafia was not a force of nature. It was a very small band of insatiably avaricious men, inflamed by the money in drugs and therefore vulnerable. The fabulous fortune within their reach was an incitement to uncontrollable greed. Sicily's Men of Honor were never so murderous as when they grew prodigiously rich. They might have beaten the law, but they still had to reckon with one another.

At the start of the 1980s, when the heroin trade was peaking, a frenzy of bloodletting decimated Sicily's warring clans. The Mafia was producing a corpse a day in Palermo, the island's capital. A growing number were eminent public figures, gunned down in broad daylight or blown up by car bombs: five judges, a prosecutor-general, a state prosecutor, two police chiefs, a colonel and a captain of the Carabinieri (Italy's elite paramilitary police), a crusading journalist, the Christian Democratic provincial secretary, the Communist party's regional secretary, the president of Sicily's regional government, and Italy's towering antiterrorist hero, General Carlo Alberto Dalla Chiesa. "Distinguished cadavers," the Italians called them.

Lesser cadavers were turning up in bars, dumps, hallways, villas at the beach, cars parked on downtown streets. Many were obscenely mutilated, genitals stuffed into the mouth, dollars shoved into the crotch. Some were headless. Others had died of slow self-strangulation, with slipknots binding their throats to their arms and legs, joined behind their backs. These were the *incaprettati,* or trussed goats.

Nobody in Italian law enforcement understood the war. Palermo's clans appeared to be settling mysterious tribal accounts. The police at that time did not know that the Sicilian Mafia had a corner on the worldwide heroin market by then—as the courts would soon determine—and that whoever won supremacy in Palermo would control that market. They had no idea that the Mafia had a dozen heroin refineries in Sicily and half as many again in the Italian north, an army deployed overseas to handle the traffic, and the franchise for the most voracious of heroin markets: the United States.

Not a word of all this leaked out, at home or abroad, until nearly the end of the Great Mafia War of 1981–83.

o◯o

Silence is a race memory in Sicily. Two thousand years of foreign occupation and despotic rule have taught the five million inhabitants of this Mediterranean island to keep their mouths shut. The state is the enemy, whether in the guise of Norman conquerors or Bourbon kings or modern Italy (which has included Sicily since 1860). To help the police detect a crime, to collaborate with forces of the law or turn to the courts for justice, is to be an *infame*—a rat and a renegade. Justice, honor, and vengeance are for a man to take care of himself. They have a word for this code of conduct: *omertà,* to be a man.

Hardly a soul in Sicily would inform on the Mafia up to the 1980s. Fear held people back—stark terror, often—but so did pride and fierce ethnic loyalty. The same passionate pride has produced the bravest men and women who ever fought the Mafia: Sicilian writers, deputies, policemen, magistrates, trade unionists, housewives. By and large, however, the ancient Sicilian code of *omertà* held a whole populace in bond.

Secret by nature, the Mafia was doubly secret as a result of this great popular wall of silence around it. Even as it robbed, kidnapped, extorted, murdered, bought and sold government officials, rifled the public till, terrorized judges and juries, trafficked in drugs and amassed colossal fortunes, many experts insisted that the Mafia did not exist. There was no damning, unanswerable evidence to the contrary—no smoking gun. The Mafia puts nothing in writing; no outsider can be initiated into its mysteries; made Men of Honor are bound by oath to swear Cosa Nostra is a fiction, on pain of death. Thus, it is probably the only structured criminal organization extant that has operated without leaving a material trace for over a hundred years.

Generations of scholars were duped by this expedient. For all the suffocating sense of a Mafia *presence* in Sicily, they could not get past the absence of tangible proof that the organization was there. They concluded that it really was a fiction.

"There does not exist, nor has there ever existed, an organized, secret, hierarchical criminal society called 'Mafia,' " wrote a leading Italian crime analyst, Pino Arlacchi, as late as 1983, echoing a long line of others. "No such organization has ever existed," agreed the meticulous German academic Henner Hess. The Mafia was only seen in that light "thanks to journalists avid for scandal, confused jurists from northern Italy, and foreign authors," he added.[21]

Actually, foreign authors usually quoted sources like Hess. Blood-curdling tales of a sinister, stiletto-wielding Mafia brotherhood had gone out with the bustle. The Mafia's early appearance in the United States had prompted ferocious assaults on all Sicilians and Italians: "swarthy-looking, jabbering foreigners," who "delight in lopping off another's finger or slashing his cheek." ("What Shall We Do with the Dago?" ran a *Popular Science Monthly* headline in 1890.)[22] The conspiracy theory thus became ugly racism, and intellectuals soon rejected it. The perceived wisdom from then on was that the Mafia was not a secret society, but a peculiarly Sicilian way of life: a "mental affinity," a "point of view," a "frame of mind."

In any event, the Mafia purportedly had nothing to do with America. The idea seemed to offend both Italians and Americans. Italians were inclined to think of America's Cosa Nostra as "gangsterism"; Americans tended to see the Sicilian Mafia as folklore. "The myth persists that Cosa Nostra in the United States is controlled by a mystical and somewhat romantic Sicilian Mafia with secret initiation rites that include bloodletting, holding a burning paper in cupped hands, and oath taking," wrote the former head of Chicago's Crime Commission, Virgil Peterson, a presidential consultant on organized crime. He still considered the Mafia a myth in 1985.[23]

So did many others whose honesty was not in question. Indeed, they refused to believe that the United States was home to any Mafia at all—this even after its governing body was finally hauled before the courts. "Some say the Mafia is an organization; I say that's a lot of baloney," declared New York governor Mario Cuomo in December 1985, just as the American Mafia's entire national Commission was going into the dock.[24] Hardy American skeptics had been saying as much since the reign of J. Edgar Hoover. Director of the FBI from 1924 to 1972, Hoover would not allow the bureau to acknowledge the Mafia's existence until the day he died.

No "friends of the friends" in the Mafia sense could have served it so well as these upright, obstinate disbelievers. Their refusal to see the plain truth was worse than misleading; it effectively blocked any assault on the Mafia *as an organized criminal body* for over a century.

Yet Italians had the benefit of repeated, laborious parliamentary investigations going back to 1867; the latest had lasted ten years, up to 1974. And Americans had been warned of the Mafia's existence in two exhaustive congressional investigations. Senator John McClellan's had actually produced the American Mafia's first defector, Joseph Valachi, who revealed its vows, structure, leadership, pursuits, and even its in-house name—La Cosa Nostra—in 1963. Senator Estes Kefauver had presented voluminous evidence as far back as 1951. "There is a nation-wide crime syndicate known as the Mafia," Kefauver concluded. "It does exist in the United States, despite the protestations of a strangely assorted company of criminals, self-serving politicians, plain blind fools and others who may be honestly misguided." Furthermore, he said, it was linked to a "mysterious international criminal organization going under the name of 'Mafia,' so fantastic that most Americans have dif-ficulty in believing it really exists."[25]

Cosa Nostra's soldiers were aghast at the threat of exposure, as a tapped phone conversation in New York disclosed in the sixties:

"We got to retrench ourselves. We got to go deep, deep, deep, deep . . . in the fucking holes and make new tunnels."

"Underground?"

"Underground. Underground and reorganize and come up. And leave a couple of fucking bodies on every fucking corner. . . ."

"You know where you got to put a rat who talks? Hang him on a lamppost. You understand? You got to cut his prick off. You got to put it in his pocket and you got to give him a nice slash and leave him up there."[26]

They needn't have worried. What with self-serving politicians, plain blind fools, and the honestly misguided, nobody went after the Mafia in spite of Senators Kefauver and McClellan. For Daniel Bell, Harvard professor and leader of intellectual fashion, the Kefauver Committee was "misled by its own hearsay."[27] For presidential consultant Virgil Peterson, the McClellan Committee's star witness—Joe Valachi—had "very likely coined the name La Cosa Nostra himself."[28]

So it went until the 1980s. The Sicilian and American Mafias ad-vanced inexorably in their respective countries, Sicily's Men of Honor settled into place abroad, and the Heroin Age got under way. Then the wall of silence cracked. The Mafia was trapped in America by superb electronic surveillance, and in Italy by an extraordinary phenomenon that came to be known as *pentitismo*.

Sicily's Great Mafia War was too much to stomach for some of the war's losers. Loosely referred to as penitents, the *pentiti* were not neces-sarily repentant but were willing to give away the Mafia's secrets. Just one *pentito* would have been astonishing—and there were thirty or more to start with, soon to grow into hundreds. They exposed an under-

world as hidden as the dark side of the moon. In the space of three or
four years, beginning around 1982, the myths and mysteries of a century fell away. The real Mafia, a startlingly dangerous secret society,
grew visible for the first time.

Its nature emerged in a succession of dramatic trials, in Palermo
and New York. The proceedings differed, but the findings matched.
Witness after witness took the stand, revealing the Mafia's depths of
depravity and ancestral capacity for deceit. The smoking gun turned up
in several million pages of courtroom testimony.

There really is an organized, conspiratorial, and hierarchical brotherhood calling itself Cosa Nostra, Our Affair. It is tightly structured—a
Sicilian court calls it a "paramilitary pyramid"—with rituals and rules,
meetings and vote-taking, and is led by elite boards of directors in Sicily
and the United States. The two boards are separate but not equal. The
Americans yield to the Sicilians; the Sicilians, not the Americans, operate on a global scale; the center of Mafia power is in Palermo, not New
York. Of all the discoveries in recent years, this is the most momentous.

Heroin has made the difference: the American Mafia merely traffics
in it, whereas the Sicilian directs the traffic. To do so, it functions as an
independent entity in the United States and everywhere else. Its men,
fanning out across America since the late 1950s, were thought to belong
to the American Cosa Nostra until just a few years ago. In fact, they
have encroached steadily on its sovereignty and living space. Sicilians
directly responsible to Palermo occupy several of the American Mafia's
exclusive enclaves, and poach all over its criminal preserves. For the
American Mob, they are the "zips," the "geeps," the "fucking siggies":
secretive, predatory, disliked, and resented, but not molested.

The American Mafia invited them in, to divest itself of the risks in
dealing heroin while collecting a share of the profits. Some might say
this was an early sign of decline; it has at any rate proved to be an act of
surrender. The U.S. heroin franchise has propelled the Sicilian Mafia to
the heights of the international underworld, and brutalized it to a degree that frightens even its American offspring.

"Why no Sicilian bodies in New York? How come our guys aren't
fighting back?" asked an FBI agent covering Brooklyn in the mid-
1980s. "The American Mafia will not take them on," responded Robert
Stutman, New York director of the DEA. Compared with the Sicilians,
America's Mafiosi look flabby. Their dons are a hybrid strain two or
three generations removed from pure Mafia stock. Their average age is
between seventy and eighty, whereas Sicilian leadership is constantly
renewed in blood. Americans let anybody in who has an Italian father;

both parents of a made member in Sicily must be Sicilian. They lease out rackets to others: New York's Families have rented twenty-seven of their thirty-six numbers games to Cubans. They kill less, and don't like to kill cops at all. In a word, they lack the Sicilian Mafioso's amoral fiber.

If they defer to the men from Palermo, however, they have yet to submit to anyone else. For all their vicissitudes, they are still regarded by FBI experts as "the most important criminal organization in the United States."[29] Indeed, the Mafia has outlived every crime ring in the country since the 1890s.

The wealth of both Mafias is incalculable. Drugs alone make it the twentieth richest "nation" in the world—richer than 150 sovereign states.[30] More pours in from any enterprise capable of making money, licit and illicit (gambling, extortion, loan-sharking, fraud, etc.). Government sources, on the cautious side, estimate that the Sicilian and American Mafias combined have an annual turnover approaching a quarter of a trillion dollars. The U.S. figure was $168 billion in 1984, according to President Reagan's Commission on Organized Crime. Net of costs, the take on strictly criminal operations came to $30 billion. The Sicilian Mafia's income *solely* from drugs, extortion, kidnapping, and gambling was put at $30 billion in 1989—three times the yearly budget of Sicily's regional government, $6,000 a head for every Sicilian man, woman, and child.[31]

The ultimate beneficiaries are astoundingly few. Limited points on the dollar go to about ten "associates" and "earners" for every made Mafioso, and there are legions of "protectors" to pay off: businessmen, attorneys, politicians, judges, cops. But Cosa Nostra itself has only 1,700 sworn members in the United States, out of nearly 250 million people. Even in Sicily, there are a mere 15,000 made members, a fraction of 1 percent of the island's inhabitants.[32]

The Mafia's size is kept down deliberately. Men have paid for the privilege of joining, much as if they were buying a seat on the stock exchange. Albert Anastasia, heading what became the Gambino Family in New York, sold memberships for $50,000 apiece in the 1950s. A powerful Gambino captain today reportedly paid $100,000 for his entry fee.[33]

The numbers seem to belie the whole story. How could a band so small wield such immense power? Who would believe that a few thousand barely literate criminals could inflict the scourge of heroin upon the world, hold entire nations to ransom, steal more money in a year than the gross domestic product of Norway or Denmark? It is not so improbable. A few thousand political terrorists have been able to bring half the world to its knees in recent years. "Kill one, frighten ten thousand" is their elementary premise. It was the Mafia's long before these terrorists were born.

Sicilian Men of Honor are required to kill before they can be sworn in; they have testified so in court. Those who kill best are called Men of Valor. Those who get sick of killing may be killed in turn. "A Man of Honor's prestige inside a Mafia Family depends above all on the consummation of homicides. The more important the homicide, the greater his prestige," testified a defector in Italy.[34] The entire system of Mafia power rests above all else on being *seen* to be ready to kill—instantly, any time, anywhere.

The force of this system can bend the will of a great many to a very few, if properly applied. "Give me a place to stand and I will move the world [with a lever]," said the master mathematician-inventor of antiquity, Archimedes, around 240 B.C. Archimedes lived in Syracuse, Sicily.

Contrary to legend, the Mafia is not nearly so many centuries old, but it was born old. The key to its singular strength—its ability to spread devastation around the globe and get away with it—lies in its artful use of Sicily's geography, separate culture, misery, and millennial history.

The history of Sicily is awful. Every kind of invader since the mythical Cyclops has been lured to its nine thousand square miles of choice real estate. The island lay in the middle of their Mediterranean sea lanes, and the Mediterranean was the center of their universe. The Phoenicians took it, followed by Greeks, Romans, Vandals, Ostrogoths, Byzantines, Arabs, Normans, Germans, Aragonese, Spaniards, and Bourbons. Some were more enlightened than others, but they were all incorrigible colonialists. Sicilian wheat fed their armies, Sicilian slaves grew their wheat, Sicilian land in vast tracts enriched them. Sicily abounded in secret sects under foreign occupation: avengers or plain bandits or both, reflecting popular hatred and rage. They are often called "Mafia," but they were only its precursors.

The word itself has been traced to nationalists in the thirteenth-century Sicilian Vespers uprising; to Freemasons in a Sicilian fishing village in 1799; to a witch in the Inquisition nicknamed "Catarina la Licatisa nomata ancor Maffia," meaning one with audacity, power madness, and arrogance.

Some say "Mafia" comes from the archaic French *maufer*, god of evil. Others attribute it to the Arabic *mihfal,* assembly of many people (plus *mahyas* for braggadocio). It is more often said to stand for "Mazzini Autorizza Furti, Incendi, Avvelenamenti": Giuseppe Mazzini, nineteenth-century leader of the Risorgimento that freed and unified Italy, is held to have "authorized robberies, arson, and poisoning" in Sicily to fight the Bourbon monarchy. He did have a secret band working for him there, which could be relevant.

Historians generally agree that the authentic Mafia got its start with Mazzini's flamboyant ally Giuseppe Garibaldi.[35] It was Garibaldi who drove out the last of the Bourbon kings and united Sicily to the new Italian state. Sicilians flocked to join him in an explosion of joyous excitement when his Red Shirts landed in Palermo in 1860. About two thousand *picciotti* were among them—bold young peasants, half-brigand, half-rebel, who used to hide in caves of tufa stone called *maha* in Arabic. That is probably where "Mafia" comes from; Garibaldi's *picciotti* were spoken of as *squadri della mafia.*[36]

They were dazzled by Garibaldi's promises of dignity and social justice. Sicily was prostrate after two millennia of foreign rule—humiliated, eaten with corruption, destitute—but the young Italian nation failed to redeem it. The promises were broken, the Sicilians forgotten. In the absence of a state, the *picciotti* banded together and took over.

There is no document stating that this band was the Mafia. Nevertheless, an official dispatch dated 1865 cites it by name for the first time as a virulent, criminal secret society.[37] A now-celebrated play in Sicilian dialect, *I Mafiusi della Vicaria,* had just appeared in 1863. This comedy of prison life in Palermo described a *consorteria mafiusa:* a "society," complete with initiation rites and a hierarchical structure, of Mafiosi who commanded special respect inside the jail, imposed their own rules, exacted payoffs, daunted prison guards, and smuggled in clothing, food, and arms.[38]

The hierarchical structure was lost to sight for the next 120 years, but the *consorteria* flourished. The crime rate in Sicily shot up so wildly that a state of siege was formally declared in 1893.[39] By then, the Mafia had already grown so useful to the rich and mighty that it could never be dislodged. Feudal barons relied on it to keep unruly peasants in line. The Catholic church counted on its protection for enormous land holdings. Candidates for office would kiss the hand of a *Capo-Mafia* in public squares. A future prime minister used the slogan "Vote for X, a friend of the friends"—the classic Mafia label. Not a single Sicilian politician was elected to the Italian Parliament without the Mafia's stamp of approval from 1860 to 1924.[40] Not too many are even now.

The poor turned to the Mafia because they had nobody else. There was no state apart from tax collectors, where they were concerned. The church, omnipotent in a solidly Catholic country, was in league with the barons and the establishment in Rome. The Mafia, though in league with all three, took pride in administering a degree of even-handed justice. This was a necessary ingredient of power; and power was once thought to be more intoxicating than money for a Mafia don. A simple citizen with none but honorary titles, he could command respect bordering on reverence, dispense wisdom and patronage, mediate disputes, choose public servants (including police chiefs and judges), elect lawmakers, and shape governments. Some peasants, therefore, got satisfaction from their *capo-cosca* (head of the clan); others received a blast from the *lupara,* the island's traditional sawed-off shotgun. It was rough, but it was justice of a kind.

From this confused and tormented scene, the Mafioso in Robin Hood's image emerged. He was manly and flagrantly contemptuous of the law, defended himself with bravura, and could even appear to be generous and wise, depending on who was looking. Foreign visitors thought him dashing, and romantic poets praised him. He was the essence of "beauty, grandeur, perfection, excellence," wrote the most celebrated of these last, Giuseppe Pitrè.

Men of Honor love to quote Pitrè. Probably no single man has done more to glorify a fraternity of murderous villains than this turn-of-the-century authority on Sicilian folklore. "The Mafioso is not a thief, not a blackguard. . . . The Mafioso is simply a valorous man with no flies on his nose," he wrote. "Mafia is the force of the individual, intolerance toward the arrogance of others. . . . Mafia unites the idea of beauty with superiority and valor in the best sense of the word, and something more: awareness of being a man, sureness of soul . . . audacity but never arrogance, never haughtiness."[41]

There has never been such a Mafioso. Pitrè was drawing on "distant and scented childhood memories," we are told tactfully by a former curator of the Pitrè Museum in Palermo. "He did not invent facts but lived inside fantasy," explains this knowledgeable source. "He was not a historian, not a professional."[42] No indeed.

o◯o

The two faces of the Mafia could best be seen in a contemporary of Pitrè's named Vito Cascio Ferro: Don Vito to a deferential public, Sicily's first grand *capo di tutti capi.*

Don Vito was born in Palermo in 1862 and grew up illiterate, which was no handicap. Never again would the Mafia produce a man so warmly admired. Describing him in *The Italians,* the late Luigi Barzini, Jr., wrote:

Don Vito brought the organization to its highest perfection without undue recourse to violence. . . . The Mafia leader who scatters corpses all over the island in order to achieve his goal is considered as inept as the statesman who has to wage aggressive wars. Don Vito ruled and inspired fear mainly by the use of his great qualities and natural ascendancy.

In point of fact, Don Vito was accused in his lifetime of twenty homicides, five burglaries, thirty-seven cases of extortion, a sensational kidnapping, and fifty-three other crimes of physical violence. One of his murder charges included cutting up the victim and stuffing the pieces into a barrel. He was formally indicted on such charges sixty-nine times, and acquitted sixty-nine times.[43]

It was Don Vito who fathered the American Mafia. Fleeing to the United States in 1901 to escape arrest, he was the first Mafioso *di rispetto* (Man of Respect) to set foot on American shores. New York's Lower East Side teemed with Sicilian immigrants then, hardworking peasants slaving in sweatshops to survive. Sheltering among them, and preying mercilessly upon them, were scores of Mafia fugitives from the first government crackdown in Sicily in 1893. The press called them the Black Hand.[44]

The United States was their Land of Promise not only for the usual reasons, but because it was so safe. "Here, there is practically no police surveillance," read a New York police report at the time. "Here it is easy to buy arms and dynamite. Here there is no penalty for using a false name. Here it is easy to hide [thanks to] our enormous territory and overcrowded cities."[45] The report's author was Italian-born Joseph Petrosino, the only cop in New York (if not all America) who knew something about the Sicilian Mafia. Head of the Police Department's special Italian Branch, he was New York's answer to the violently criminal Black Hand.

By the turn of the century, the Black Hand was operating in St. Louis, Detroit, Chicago, Kansas City, New Orleans, New Jersey, and New York. The press and public were convinced that it was an extension of the Sicilian Mafia, stealthily overrunning America (in 1901!). Petrosino disagreed. To him, the group was no more than a natural product of the Sicilian émigré environment: a loose association of calloused criminals, cruel and rapacious, but disorganized. Then Don Vito

Cascio Ferro showed up, and he changed his mind.

Petrosino came across Don Vito in 1903, when a dismembered head with genitals stuffed into its mouth was found in a barrel on New York's Eleventh Avenue. The victim was a Sicilian immigrant who had worked for Black Hand higher-ups. Petrosino was persuaded by the evidence that Don Vito was responsible.

Sicily's future overlord, a superlative organizer, had quickly gained ascendancy over the Black Hand. He personally had helped many of its members slip over from Sicily to the United States. Now he taught them discipline and established regular ties with Sicily—the Mafia's first Palermo–New York circuit. In the process, Don Vito perfected the most serviceable and durable of Mafia methods for making money: 'u pizzu. Fari vagnari 'u pizzu means wetting a small bird's beak, a Mafia euphemism for buying protection by means of a monthly payoff.

The pizzu, first devised in New York in 1903, was exceedingly crude at the start. The Black Hand favored bleeding victims white, but Don Vito did not (or not quite). "You've got to skim the cream off the milk without breaking the bottle," he advised. "Don't ruin people with absurd demands for money. Offer your protection instead. Help them prosper in business and they'll not only be happy to pay the pizzu but they'll kiss your hands in gratitude."[46]

Some did kiss Don Vito's hands. Unschooled though he was, he could calculate the limits of their financial tolerance to a nicety. By 1904, the Black Hand had become as coldly methodical as the Internal Revenue Bureau. Its demands for the pizzu arrived punctually, omitting no Sicilian immigrant with an income to tax—shopkeepers, peddlers, bricklayers, longshoremen—the sums fixed by sliding scale.

Don Vito took the system back to Sicily that same year. He might have ended his days in America if not for the Man in the Barrel murder case, a national sensation. Once on his trail, Lieutenant Joe Petrosino would not let go. Don Vito was forced to skip town, hide out in New Orleans for a while, and finally head home. He carried a photograph of Joe Petrosino in his pocket—an assassin's mark—when he sailed for Italy in 1904. There he became the island's reigning prince: a tall, distinguished gentleman with a "Mephistofelian beard" and "Mafiuso bearing" (read a police report), whose hand would be kissed by mayors and local dignitaries when he toured "his" towns. All Sicily was in his pocket when Petrosino showed up in Palermo five years later.

The visit was an insufferable affront. The Black Hand was under Don Vito's personal protection, and Petrosino's mission was to destroy it. He was going to track down its members' Italian criminal records, get them deported from the United States, and break up the whole Sicilian-American Mafia partnership. But Petrosino was shot and killed in Palermo's Piazza Marina before he could even begin.

The folklore tale is that Don Vito Cascio Ferro left a parliamentary deputy's table, drove to the Piazza Marina in his carriage, fired, and returned to finish his dinner. In fact, leaders of the Black Hand had met in New Orleans to discuss the problem, and dispatched two emissaries to meet with Don Vito in Sicily. The three of them shot Petrosino twice in the back of the head and once in the face.[47]

Long afterward, Don Vito claimed personal credit for the murder. "Petrosino was a courageous adversary who did not deserve an ignoble death at the hands of a common *sicario* [killer]," he declared. It was the eve of World War II, and Sicily's peerless *capo di tutti capi* was dying in prison. Mussolini, dictator of fascist Italy, had put him there.

Mussolini had decided, on his first tour of Sicily in 1924, that the Mafia would have to go. The mayor and *Capo-Mafia* of Piana dei Greci, Don Ciccio Coccia, was showing him around, and remarked of his large police escort: "Excellency, you're with me, and you have nothing to worry about. Why do you need so many cops?"[48] Il Duce instantly understood the Mafia in Sicily. This was its kingdom, and he its guest— not at all his style. He was unlikely in any case to put up for long with this alternative power to his own. Within a month, Don Ciccio was in jail, and Mussolini's war on the Mafia had begun.

His Iron Prefect, Cesare Mori, set out to uproot the Mafia "as a surgeon penetrates the flesh with fire and steel, until he cauterizes the pus sacks of the bubonic plague." Thousands were flung into prison and tortured, guilty or innocent, their property seized and their families ruined. Where evidence was lacking, they were framed.

Sicily held fifteen mass trials between 1927 and 1929. An enormous cage, fifty yards long, was erected to hold 154 defendants in the first trial. "Fascist justice must be rapid and decisive. If the trial does not go faster, the liquidation of the Mafia will not be done until the year 2000," telegraphed Mussolini. Fascist justice triumphed; all but 6 were convicted. "The Mafia is dead, a new Sicily is born," affirmed the *New York Times*. "Mussolini has strangled the monster in its native lair," commented the *Times* of London.[49] And the monster did retreat. Officially, the Mafia's kill rate on the island dropped from *ten a day* to three a week. Even unofficially, the rate fell by about three-quarters.[50]

But the monster had not been beaten. The Mafia reappeared as if by magic when Mussolini fell at the end of World War II. Men of Honor, stout antifascists all, went straight from prison to public office. Their new *capo di tutti capi,* Don Calogero Vizzini, was installed as mayor of Villalba, his hometown; "Long live the Mafia! Long live Don Calò!" shouted friends in the crowd attending the ceremony.[51]

Tall, heavy, and sturdy, jacket slung over his shoulder, and traditional Mafia *coppola* (beret) tilted over his eyes, Don Calò would hold daily audience at a café in the piazza as if the Duce's long reign had never happened. Describing his days, Barzini wrote:

> From the shadows along the walls and narrow sidestreets, people would come out and line up to see him—peasants, old women in black, young Mafiosi.
>
> His magnanimous and protective manner, the respectful greetings of passersby, the humbleness of those approaching him, the smiles of gratitude when he addressed them, all recalled an ancient scene: a prince holding court in the open air.[52]

Meanwhile, hundreds of his subjects had regrouped across the ocean. Eluding Mussolini's Iron Prefect during the 1920s, they had fled to America just in time for Prohibition and a fortune in bootleg booze. Several became famous fathers of Mafia Families: Joe Profaci from Villabate, Carlo Gambino from Palermo, Gaetano Lucchese (alias Tommy "Three-Finger" Brown) from Palermo, Joe Bonanno from Castellammare del Golfo. An especially large contingent had set forth from Castellammare, whose native sons would one day inaugurate the Sicilian-American heroin trade. So well did they fare that a replica of the Statue of Liberty stands in the town's main square, in homage to their adopted land.

These immigrants were the stalwarts of the Unione Siciliana, into which the Black Hand merged. A popular ethnic fraternity, the Unione Siciliana was comprised of thirty-eight lodges and forty thousand members across the country. Sheltering within it, the secretly organized Mafia muffled its criminal ventures in philanthropic works, religious sodalities, social clubs, and festive tours to the Old Country.

The Mafia made millions in bootlegged liquor, on top of its customary income from gambling, usury, blackmail, and *'u pizzu;* and it was a formidable political force besides. Al Smith, bucking for the Democratic presidential nomination in 1928, was the first aspirant to the White House to solicit its help, though certainly not the last. "Line up overwhelming support for me from Manhattan, Brooklyn and the Bronx, where you fellows control the delegates [and] I'm prepared to make things good for you," Smith is reported to have said.[53]

The Unione was plagued by tribal warfare, however, until Salvatore Lucania, alias "Charlie Lucky" Luciano, took over in 1931. Luciano had come to America from Lercara Friddi, Sicily, as a child. He was a made Mafioso, but he embodied the very spirit of American enterprise, a captain of industry whose talents might have carried him to the top of the capitalist world.

"All us younger guys hated the old mustaches and what they was doin'. We was tryin' to build a business that'd move with the times and they was still livin' a hundred years ago," he explained.[54]

Accordingly, Luciano murdered the two Sicilian bosses currently killing each other's soldiers off in New York—Joe "The Boss" Masseria and Salvatore Maranzano—and became The Boss himself. "All we have to do is eliminate the two roadblocks and from then on, Charlie sits on top. That's what we want, isn't it?" his money wizard, Meyer Lansky, had observed.[55] The event was celebrated at Chicago's Blackstone Hotel in the autumn of 1932. Al Capone played host, and delegations came from all over the nation. Lucky Luciano was acclaimed as the undisputed leader of a modern, managerial crime corporation, nationally organized and distinctly American in outlook.

One of the first things Luciano did was to close Cosa Nostra's books: a figurative way of saying that no more Sicilian immigrants could be sworn in.[56] He was not interested in rituals, vendettas, or Sicilianesimo (the art, or state, of being Sicilian). He simply wanted to "build a business that'd move with the times."

As the American Cosa Nostra's frontiers expanded, its visible foreign origins receded. The Sicilian connection appeared to be eclipsed in the United States over the next half-century, but actually the reverse was true. A complex succession of events made the Sicilian Mafia necessary—indispensable—to its American counterpart. With the active connivance of Lucky Luciano and the entire American high command, Sicily acquired its exclusive heroin concession, and the drugging of America began.

Don Luciano Leggio,
the Winner

Corleone, a huddle of rooftops surrounding the stony outcrop of an abandoned prison, might be any of a hundred dreary hill towns in Sicily. Fame once singled it out for the inordinate number of Mafia murders taking place there. Nowadays, it is better known as the place Luciano Leggio comes from.[1]

Don Luciano has been serving a life sentence for murder since 1974, and is getting on. He passes his days reading Dickens and the Greek philosophers, writing poetry, and painting nostalgic landscapes of his hometown. Some might think he is finished, but he is still the most feared *capo di tutti capi* of all time.

Leggio did not create the Mafia's global heroin network; he won it in the Great Mafia War of 1981–83, plotting strategy from his prison cell. The assault by his Corleonesi and their allies took three years, spreading from Sicily to the Italian mainland, Western Europe, Canada, South America, and the United States. When it was over, around a thousand ex- or would-be opponents had been shot, strangled, poisoned, bombed, or stabbed to death, and perhaps as many again had disappeared.[2] Few, if any, of importance remained.

The story of Leggio's ascent to power follows the Mafia's progression from bad to worse in the forty-odd years since World War II. In the course of those years, the rustic Mafioso of Leggio's youth became a broker in a double-breasted suit. The old code of honor, such as it was, fell apart. The killing, a constant in brotherhood affairs, grew more methodical, impersonal, and comprehensive. The Mafia ceased to be a mere provincial or even national affliction and became a multinational criminal conspiracy.

Many have blamed these things all on Leggio. His story has been used to perpetuate the seemingly imperishable fiction of a "good" and "bad" Mafia. The good one is supposed to have presided over Sicily for a hundred years, after which it was overrun by Leggio's. Thus, the most important Mafia defector anywhere, ever—Tommaso Buscetta, star witness for the state in Palermo and New York—explained Leggio away as the countermodel of a true Mafioso. Actually, Leggio is a pure specimen, more than a century in the making. His emergence puts finish to the relatively benign godfather of popular legend: a patriarch who appeared to have a gentlemanly code of sorts and even, on occasion, to have a heart.

Luciano Leggio was born in Corleone on a winter's morning in 1925. The tenth child of a penniless and illiterate peasant family, he arrived unnoticed. No hint of his conspicuous talents appeared until his nineteenth year, when he killed an estate guard who had sent him to jail for stealing grain.

The shaping of what was then an ignorant and coarsely brutal peasant boy began that year, when Leggio joined Corleone's *cosca,* or clan. It was 1944. World War II was ending, Mussolini had fallen, and Cosa Nostra had made a stunning comeback.

Men of Honor were everywhere after the Allies invaded Sicily in July 1943. The entire fascist establishment having collapsed, they took its place. Local Mafia bosses were doubling as mayors in scores of Sicilian towns. Their incoming *capo di tutti capi,* Don Calogero Vizzini, ran a thriving black market from the City Hall of Villalba, his hometown. Vizzini, whose onetime criminal dossier had included thirty-nine murders, six attempted murders, thirty-six robberies, thirty-seven thefts, and sixty-three extortions, now owned a gun permit "for protection against fascist attacks." The U.S. Army had made him an honorary colonel.

This turn of events has long been ascribed to a plot, supposedly thought up by the American government and carried out by Lucky Luciano. After being sentenced to thirty years for running a prostitution ring, Luciano was approached in Dannemora prison during the war, the story goes. The Americans wanted him to help smooth the way for an Allied landing in his native Sicily. In exchange, he would be freed. He is supposed to have flown over Villalba in a light U.S. Army plane, and dropped a yellow silk kerchief marked with a black "L" on Don Calogero Vizzini's doorstep. Vizzini then organized a proper welcome for Allied troops, after which the Americans gave him the run of the island. So it is said.

Historians are inclined to dismiss the tale today; and investigators starting with Senator Estes Kefauver's committee have yet to find conclusive proof.[3] Luciano has denied the legend himself. U.S. Naval Intelligence did solicit his help during the war, he asserted, but only to deal with Nazi sabotage on the New York waterfront. He was paroled in 1946 and deported to Italy for his "extensive and valuable aid to the Navy in the war."

Nevertheless, Luciano did have splendid opportunities to further the Mafia's postwar growth in Sicily; and the American military did help in this process, wittingly or otherwise. The Americans were interested in blocking a communist advance at the time, something the Mafia was especially good at. But the Allied forces were also hoodwinked: taken by practiced con men, infiltrated and robbed blind, their officers corrupted or grievously misled.[4]

The Allies were only in Sicily for seven months, facing half a million German and Italian troops; their sole concern was winning the war. Sicily had to be governed in the meanwhile. The Allied Military Government (AMGOT) wanted antifascists in charge, and the Mafiosi were certainly antifascist; they had spent years in Mussolini's jails. Furthermore, they contrived to look like the only antifascists around.

Mafia notables were on every list of "those to be trusted," and were recommended to AMGOT by leading citizens, the clergy, and AMGOT's own local employees. "Many of my officers fell into the trap of . . . following the advice of their interpreters," said the British military governor for Sicily, Lord Rennell. Many interpreters proved to be Mafiosi, he added.[5] The prime example was Vito Genovese, official interpreter at U.S. Army headquarters near Naples, on the Italian mainland. Lucky Luciano's longtime underboss in New York, Genovese was the most assiduous dope dealer of his day. An inveterate racketeer, crook, and killer besides, he was hiding out in Italy to dodge a U.S. murder charge.

Luciano, who loathed Genovese, had nevertheless sent word from prison "to make sure Vito wound up on his feet in Italy. . . . I might need [him] over there." As it happened, Luciano went on, "the Army appointed Charlie Poletti, who was one of our good friends, as the Military Governor in Italy." Genovese thereupon landed on his feet as the military governor's interpreter and confidant. Although Genovese served under Colonel Poletti for less than a year (a sergeant in U.S. Army intelligence shipped him back to America in the summer of 1944), in that time he had greased his way through the armed forces and built a monumental black market. Upon arriving in Italy, Luciano promptly took it over.

A great deal of what the Italians ate, wore, smoked, and got around in after the ravages of war came from the Americans' PX. Such local produce as might be lacking there—flour, oil, sugar, beans, salt—was fed into the pipeline by Sicily's Men of Honor. This was the kind of service to the public that Luciano liked best.

Naturally, everybody in the Sicilian Mafia was making a bundle, from Don Calogero Vizzini down to the lowest *picciotto.* So it was that the young Luciano Leggio earned the first dishonest dollar of his richly rewarding career. "How did I accumulate my fortune? I did the black market during and after the war," he explained in court many years later. "Just think! You could buy a quintal of grain from the Farm Board for 2,000, 2,500 lire and sell it on the black market for 15,000."[6]

Otherwise, the fifty-odd members of Corleone's Mafia clan were engaged in their habitual pursuits. Like most Men of Honor in Sicily then, their felonies were largely rural. They stole cattle, sold water rights for irrigation, ran the shape-up for hired farmhands, collected protection money to ward off rustling, vandalism, arson, and theft, kidnapped for ransom, and resorted to the "pitiless elimination of inconvenient rivals by homicide," as a report to the Italian Parliament put it. Indeed, they would rack up 153 homicides in Corleone during Leggio's first four years of membership; this in a town of 11,000 souls.[7] An equivalent figure per head of population would come to well over 100,000 in Paris, London, or New York.

The clan's latest addition was no prize. Leggio had dropped out of school in the fourth grade, foiling a parental scheme to make a priest out of him. He could not read or write, a shortcoming he remedied later by forcing a schoolteacher to give him lessons at gunpoint.[8] He was also crippled by Pott's disease, a tubercular spinal ailment that obliged him to wear a tormenting wooden (later silver) brace.

He was an odd-looking boy: hunched in his brace and pasty pale, with a big round face and thick, sensuous lips. Only the clever eyes held latent promise—these and his skill with the *lupara,* acquired by shooting the brains out of grazing sheep and goats.

It did not take Leggio long to discover the frailties of the democratic judicial process. He had only to kill his first victim, the estate guard who had gotten him arrested for stealing wheat. Though the guard's wife actually saw him shoot, and an accomplice confessed, the case dragged on for eighteen years. Never apprehended in that time, during which he more or less openly went about his business, Leggio was acquitted twice *in absentia.* A court of assizes, upheld on appeal, found the accomplice's confession to have been extorted and the widow's testimony "incoherent."[9]

This was not at all unusual. Men of Honor wore such acquittals like so many scalps, a mark of their prowess in outwitting the law. The key to their success lay in the prerogatives of an Italian court, which could find a defendant neither innocent nor guilty, and acquit him simply "for insufficient evidence."[10] It is not hard for a Mafioso to render the evidence insufficient, by removing a witness.

Doubtless Leggio committed his first killing out of sheer vengeful fury. But the manner of his shooting, daring and precise, attracted the attention of his superiors. They began to use him regularly as a hit man. He became their favorite killer, and a small but raptly admiring band gathered around him. His upward path from then on was littered with the bodies of his victims. Beyond killing to punish, he killed to impress, to instruct, to amass a fortune, to mock the authorities and make a comedy of the courts, and above all to rule over his peers.

Among his early victims was a fearsome Mafia boss, a certain Barbaccia, who controlled most of the cattle rustling in the region. Leggio began to rustle cattle on his own, and was given the usual ultimatum. He responded as he usually would thereafter. Barbaccia's men were picked off one by one, their bullet-riddled bodies found strewn along outlying mountain paths. Eventually, Barbaccia himself disappeared and was never seen again.[11]

Casting around for a place to slaughter the cattle, Leggio decided to become a *gabellotto.* Overseers of Sicily's vast landed estates—thousands of acres, usually—the *gabellotti* had long been the Mafia's best earners. They were cut down under Mussolini's rule, but were infesting the Sicilian countryside again by 1945 when the Carabinieri observed: "The Mafia has already imposed its own *gabellotti* on landowners, many of whom dare not visit their estates for fear of kidnapping or worse. Certain areas have had tens and tens of homicides, mass executions, people who vanish without a trace."[12]

Though the position was privileged and usually went with rank,

Leggio managed to become the youngest *gabellotto* in Sicily. He did it with characteristic simplicity, by shooting one in the back. "I will take the place of the dear departed," he informed the landlord.[13] His new employer, a good-tempered young man, was forced to fire his farmhands, convert his wheat fields to fodder, sell off his own cattle, and finally stay off his own land. He died of a broken heart, people said.

Within a year or so, Leggio was rich enough to buy an estate of his own. He selected Piano della Scala, a prosperous holding conveniently hidden in the gaunt shadow of a mountainous wilderness called Rocca Busambra. It was not for sale, until he garroted the herds, poisoned the dogs, chopped down the lemon trees, burned the crops, and then dropped in on the owner. "Your farm doesn't pay, and you want to sell," Leggio informed the owner, who promptly complied.[14]

Even in the Mafia, the rise of this ignorant peasant boy was spectacular. At twenty-one—barely two years after appearing on the scene—he had acquired fame, money, status, and scope. The fact that Leggio had been a fugitive since his first murder did not seem to get in his way. No Corleonese would turn him in; he had them scared witless. (He is said to have walked into a local barbershop once, wearing dark glasses. After removing the glasses to shave him, the barber saw who it was and fainted.)[15]

Leggio's affairs prospered. Piano della Scala made an ideal operative base. Masses of stolen cattle could be slaughtered in privacy there, for sale to the wholesale markets just thirty-four miles away in Palermo. Soon he was shipping black market beef to the city on an industrial scale. Caravans of trucks made the run for him nightly, with his own Corleonesi riding shotgun.

Leggio was barely twenty-three when police found his private cemetery—a chasm fifty yards deep and a yard wide in the wilds of Rocca Busambra, strewn with skeletons whose number is still unknown. One perilous descent was enough for a rescue team of firemen, who refused to make another. They brought up the remains of only three men, including the one police were looking for. He was identified by his belt buckle and rotting gum boots as Placido Rizzotto, Corleone's lone labor agitator, chained, shot, and tossed down to be gnawed by rats.[16]

Rizzotto had been an aggravating presence in Corleone. Apart from generally stirring up a wretchedly deprived peasantry, he was a vigorous opponent of the Mafia's flourishing trade in stolen cattle. Furthermore, he had taken to hounding Leggio in public for having altered the Belice River's course and stolen its waters. Worse, he was actually pressing for expropriation of Leggio's Piano della Scala property.

There was no mystery about his death in 1948. A twelve-year-old shepherd, paralyzed with fright, had seen Leggio with two accomplices, dragging Rizzotto up the fateful slope. By the time the boy got home and told his mother, shock had brought on a high fever and disquieting symptoms described later as "hallucinations." He was taken to the local hospital, whose director personally gave him an injection, whereupon he died in a matter of minutes.[17]

The hospital director, a physican of Old World charm named Michele Navarra, happened to be Corleone's resident Mafia chief.

Despite having gotten the hospital post by murdering his predecessor, Dr. Navarra was far more polished than his younger subalterns. President of the local Landowners' Association, member of a dozen civic-minded boards, and the recipient of many communal honors, he and would later be decorated by the Italian Republic as a Knight of Merit.[18]

The shepherd boy was said by Dr. Navarra to have died of "toxicosis," and was buried without an inquest. That should have been the end of it. But authorities were forced to intervene when a Palermo newspaper reported that the boy had identified Leggio and his two accomplices before dying. Both accomplices confessed; they actually led police to the body in the chasm. Nonetheless, Leggio was acquitted "for lack of sufficient evidence" by three judges in succession over the next thirteen years.

By the time Italy's Supreme Court handed down its definitive sentence confirming acquittal, Leggio had long since sent the two accomplices to their just reward and was wanted officially for murdering nine other people. One of these people was Dr. Navarra himself, Corleone's foremost Man of Respect, who turned out to have been one of Sicily's top ten Mafia bosses.[19] The recognition was posthumous. Italian authorities had no inkling of Dr. Navarra's place in the Mafia hierarchy when Leggio shot him in 1958. They did not know that there *was* a hierarchy, still less that it was ruled by a governing board called the Cupola. We also know now from judicial testimony that a dozen old-school dons in the Cupola summoned Leggio to account for the shooting of Dr. Navarra. Killing a boss without the Cupola's consent was unthinkable in those days; Leggio should never have gotten out alive. In the event, he merely assured his interlocutors that the whole thing was "a personal matter," and they agreed to forget it. So much for their old-fashioned moral values.[20]

It was inevitable that either Leggio or Navarra would eliminate the other. Though equally murderous and predatory, they were worlds apart in character and style. Leggio was brash, turbulent, insolent, inflamed by an unquenchable inner rage, and abrasively contemptuous of the law. His boss, Dr. Navarra, was the height of provincial *bon ton,* heavily dignified, outwardly obsequious to authority, and naturally disposed to discretion. Rather than alarm the public by shooting a policeman, he much preferred to buy one.

In 1958, after some fourteen years of working together, the pair had to part. Leggio was unmistakably preparing to take his boss's place, whereas Dr. Navarra had already concluded that he had had enough of his insufferable lieutenant. Incautiously, he sent fifteen gunmen after Leggio at Piano della Scala. They missed. Barely wounded, Leggio got away through a tunnel dug for such occasions and, shortly afterward, fired seventy-six bullets into Dr. Navarra.

Over the next months, Navarra's followers were hunted from house to house by Leggio's and shoved into waiting cars. Others were machine-gunned three or four at a time, at high noon, on Corleone's main street. Two rival gunmen renowned for their marksmanship and vanity—both wore foppish black velvet suits—strolled casually toward each other in the central square, simultaneously drew from the hip, and shot each other dead.

Nobody saw anything. "Who was killed?" a reporter asked a weeping mother muffled in black, following a coffin in one of Corleone's frequent funeral processions. "Why, is anyone dead?" was her reply.[21]

The score when the shooting stopped was twenty-nine dead on Navarra's side and thirteen on Leggio's. Corleone has been Leggio's ever since, but it was too small even then.

Cosa Nostra has always been amenable to change, and Sicily underwent two exceptional changes after the war. In 1947, it became a self-governing, autonomous Region of the Italian Republic. In 1950, land reform broke up the island's huge baronial estates.[22] The first change offered fabulous opportunities to manipulate politics and get at the public till. The second shifted Cosa Nostra's attention from the countryside to the cities.

Rural felonies still paid off—they do to this day—but the big landowners and *gabellotti* forming the Mafia's power base were gone. Hundreds of thousands of peasants were leaving the land as well, in search of work and a better life. Most were converging on Palermo, capital of the new Sicilian regional government. The city was also starting to pull in hundreds of millions of dollars from Rome in subsidies, special credits, and allocations from the *cassa per il mezzogiorno,* Italy's multibillion-dollar fund for the depressed south. This was the place to make money.

A magnificent city dating back to 600 or 700 B.C., Palermo lies like a tarnished gem on Sicily's northwestern shores. A splendid carpet of orange, lemon, and olive groves stretches out behind it on the Conca d'Oro plain. Once the city was a mecca for philosophers, scientists, and poets; the sonnet was invented there. Six emperors and kings are buried in its twelfth-century cathedral. Luxuriant water gardens graced their royal palaces. Stupendous traces remain of Byzantine, Arabic, and Norman architecture, overlaid by extravagant baroque and the elegant Liberty villas of the *Belle Epoque.*

Much of this is lost to view today in a landscape of concrete and rubble. After centuries of neglect and several decades of Mafia rule, Palermo is indescribably derelict.

Nearly a million Sicilians were crowded into the city and its environs by the 1950s. They had to be housed, and a third of the living space in the decaying old quarter was uninhabitable.[23] They needed to be clothed, fed, employed, or otherwise sustained. Their streets had to be lit, their water supplied, their sewage, garbage, and taxes collected. Their every daily need meant doing battle with a titanic bureaucracy, whether it was for a driving license, a peddler's permit, a pension, a seat in a classroom, a burial, or a hospital bed.

What Sicilians needed was a *sistemazione,* that untranslatable Italian word meaning, in effect, that somebody had to take care of them. Since a succession of inept governments couldn't or wouldn't, or at any rate didn't, the Mafia did, in its fashion. It delivered the vote for compliant politicians, imposed its own kind of order, and plundered the city.

When Leggio descended upon Palermo, around 1955, the city had long been held by some of the toughest Men of Honor extant. These were the *mammasantissima,* literally "Holiest of Mothers," biggest of Mafia bigshots in Sicilian parlance. Their territories quartered Palermo and its outlying province, interlocked with Mafia strongholds throughout western Sicily. Now that they are gone—those who didn't die off were killed off—they are spoken of as the old Mafia, representing order and moderation. Actually, they were the new Mafia of their day, the most degenerate yet.

There have been old and new Mafias in every generation, each set looking worse than the last. Writers in 1880 described a "legitimate" old guard challenged by younger "radical and openly criminal elements."[24] By 1900, the criminal elements had become Don Vito Cascio

Ferro's old Mafia. Though this Mafia ransacked the island and killed about once a day, it is remembered as a rock of tradition compared with the next one.

The new Mafia appearing around 1920 killed *twice* a day. Veterans of World War I, its men were said to "care only about getting rich quick." Their raw violence "hit everyone and everything as never before in the memory of man. No rules, no respect for anyone. . . . The old Mafia had no more power; the *picciotti* no longer obeyed," wrote Mussolini's Iron Prefect, Cesare Mori.[25]

By 1944, the *picciotti* of those days had turned into the old Mafia of Don Calogero Vizzini. Portrayed on his tombstone as "A Man and a Gentleman," the patriarch of Villalba is still held up as an old-fashioned Man of Honor—exemplary for his wisdom and restraint, the model surrogate for an absentee state. Ten thousand people attended his funeral in 1954; Villalba's public offices and Christian Democratic headquarters were closed for eight days to mourn his passing.

Yet Don Calò's Mafia had been a nightmare for ordinary Sicilians since the first postwar days. Shifting from rural to urban crime, the bosses he led had graduated from the *lupara* to the Beretta and tommy gun. Their methods were crude and their greed apparently bottomless. From 1944, these bosses' kill rate averaged three a week for sixteen years.[26] Scarcely a shred of their knightly code of honor remained by the end of Vizzini's reign, and he knew it. "Morto io, morto la Mafia" ("When I die, the Mafia dies"), he remarked to a distinguished visitor.[27]

These were the bosses in command when Leggio settled in Palermo, shortly after Vizzini's death. There was little difference between his designs on the city and theirs. They all meant to squeeze every last lira out of it. The difference lay mostly in Leggio's demonic ability to frighten the rest of them.

Leggio had grown sleek in his thirties, with money and good medical care; some found him rather handsome. But his deathly pallor, the bland smile he favored, the eyes glinting with malice, were inexpressibly disturbing. Unlike most Men of Honor, he did not always bother to hide his feelings. A judge who angered him once, and would be killed for it, was startled to see him literally foam at the mouth.[28] Later, Leggio would be caught by television cameras with his eyes rolled to the whites in sudden, blinding fury.

His eyes in particular could hold an audience frozen. Lazily amused or openly menacing, they stirred instinctive fear, unease, foreboding. The effect was heightened by his fame as a really gifted murderer, the most accomplished the Mafia had produced in a century. A confidential warning to this effect had followed him to Palermo, sent to the Carabinieri there from their opposite numbers in Corleone:

Luciano Leggio is naturally violent in character and criminal by constitution and tendency, habitually guilty of homicide, theft, extortion and violence, odious to the people of Corleone for the mourning and evil he has spread, held in horror for the cold determination and ferocity of his character, author of countless grave acts of bloodshed which none of his victims dares to denounce for fear of incurring his vengeance.

He has now seen fit to live in Palermo, seemingly extraneous to the Mafia there. . . . Actually, he is extremely active among Palermo's Mafia chiefs . . . bound not so much by his friendship with them as his ascendancy over them.[29]

For all the police knew about Leggio, they could not lay a finger on him. Corruption, complicity, the complexities of Sicilian thinking, the cowardice he unfailingly aroused, and a curiously hypnotic effect on the beholder kept him safe from the law. A presumably hunted man throughout his decade in Palermo, Leggio was in hiding but scarcely on the run.

"He moved around all the time; he was sure of himself," said Sicily's assistant police commissioner, Angelo Mangano, whose pursuit of Leggio cost him his career and very nearly his life.

He traveled in a procession of expensive cars, one ahead and another behind, each carrying rich and respectable Palermitani. They would be saluted with deference at police blocks, and stop to chat, while Leggio got away.

Once we got a tip that he was in a de luxe clinic. We mounted a huge top secret operation; a hundred men closed in on the place—and he was gone. He had woven a huge web of informants, held together with the spittle of gold and blood. He imprisoned thousands of consciences through corruption and fear. He paid to have the most illustrious physicians, the most beautiful women, the ablest killers.[30]

Leggio's days were taken up with business, for which he went about the city disguised as a monk, a police officer, a woman, or an American tourist hung in cameras. His evenings, undisguised, were spent in social conquest.[31] He no longer did much killing himself, leaving that to the fifty or so Corleonesi in his entourage. Hand-tailored suits encased his now bear-shaped form. He smoked eight-inch cigars, and caused a pleasurable *frisson* among the ladies as he drifted like visiting royalty from one elegant villa to another. The more haughtily titled the lady, the more pleasurable the *frisson,* it appeared. Countesses and baronesses vied for his amorous favors, he claimed. "My life as an outlaw was spent in Palermo's salons," he would say in prison.[32]

Leggio's relations with Palermo's Mafia bosses were less cordial. The bosses had no reason to welcome a new face, especially his. They were just taking over the city's wholesale produce market when Leggio got there in 1955: everything from production to transport to sales of fruit, vegetables, staples, fish, and meat. Every *cosca* in town—thirty-nine, in carefully staked-out districts—had fought to get a piece of the market. A lot of killing went on, but the profits were gratifying. The cost of living shot up to 70 percent above the national average in Palermo that year, thanks largely to a sudden jump in food prices.[33]

The protection racket was sewn up also. The *pizzu* had tightened around Palermo like a noose. Practically every kind of business—bars, hotels, construction firms, garages, insurance companies, ports, cemeteries, funeral parlors, nightwatchmen, florists—had to pay up every month or be bombed, vandalized, burned down, or shot.

Leggio was not altogether a newcomer; he had dominated Palermo's black market meat for some time. Now, he strong-armed his way into the grain market, collecting a 10 to 20 percent cut on sales. Then he got a corner on billiards and pinball machines. "He ran thousands of them, all over the province, cranking out money without a break, day in, day out, an income of maybe a billion lire a year," said Police Commissioner Mangano.[34] (That would have come close to $2 million.) "He wasn't just rich himself," added Mangano. "Everybody who worked for him, covered for him, sheltered him, nursed him, was rich. The source of his power from the start was that fatal, lightning readiness to kill. But in the end, it was money too. The man *gushed* money."[35]

Leggio dispensed largesse: lavish tips for waiters, flowers and perfume for nurses, candles for nuns to use to say mass, a testamentary gift of his eyes for an orphan child, expensive automobiles for members of his family and the swelling ranks of his retainers. He bought a millionaire's villa for himself and, providentially, large tracts of real estate.

These were the days of Palermo's colossal building boom. Starting in the late 1950s, a contractor with the right connections could graduate from a pushcart to a million-dollar line of credit overnight.

The governing Christian Democratic party had slipped quietly into partnership with the Mafia right after the war. All the Mafia notables were card-carrying party members, from Don Calogero Vizzini down. By the late 1950s, they had formed a particularly fruitful partnership with two Christian Democrats in Palermo: incumbent mayor Salvo

Lima and his public works assessor, Vito Ciancimino (from Corleone, as luck would have it). These men were the supreme rulers of Sicilian politics, then and seemingly forever after.

Under their supervision, the city issued 4,205 building permits in the space of four years. And 4 out of every 5—3,364 in all—went to just four Mafia frontmen: a bricklayer, a charcoal vendor, a manual laborer, and a worksite guard.[36] These four, all illiterate, jobless, and destitute, were authorized to build almost anything anywhere on behalf of un-named third parties.

Meanwhile, the third parties acquired more and bigger cars, cabin cruisers, and villas up and down the coast, while their wives took to ordering designer clothes from Paris. In exchange, they demolished Palermo's handsome Liberty mansions, bulldozed parks and gardens, threw up institutional cement boxes to house the city's offices at exorbi-tant rents, and built mile upon mile of instant-slum high-rise ghettos for the lower classes. They also picked up city contracts for garbage collec-tion, street lighting, and public works, and packed their own personnel into banks, government boards, and every corner of the public services.

By the end of the 1950s, according to a subsequent report to the Italian Parliament, the Mafia controlled "all activities in Palermo prov-ince: from building sites and construction to hiring labor, to granting sub-contractors' licenses, to credit, to wholesale produce markets, to irrigation waters for fruits and vegetables, to cattle rustling and slaugh-terhouses, to tobacco smuggling, to drug smuggling, to clandestine emi-gration, to cemeteries, to tomb-building, to licenses for gas stations."[37]

The Italian Parliament had no way of knowing that the Mafia was preparing to move out far beyond Palermo and all Italy. This plan, decided upon in 1957, was restricted to an inner circle dealing secretly with its Cosa Nostra counterpart in the United States. Leggio was not then a member of this circle. Though a formidable power in Palermo, he was not really a company man; not yet.

It was the old boys who made the deal for control of the world's heroin trade: Men of Honor wedded to tradition, who deplored the drug traffic but were up to their necks in it. Later, when they had lost the whole colossal venture to Leggio, they would blame him for all the nightmares that resulted. No wonder he saved his most savage mockery for the man who became his most implacable accuser—the last of the big losers, Tommaso Buscetta.

3

Don Tommaso Buscetta, the Last of the Big Losers

or his many admirers, Tommaso Buscetta is the last of the great Mafia dons. He speaks quietly, with consummate authority, in a velvety baritone. He is faultlessly dressed, from navy blue blazer and gray flannels to sober tie. His manner is courtly, his tone measured, his code stern—order, tradition, restraint. His very presence seems to emanate magnetic force: "my legendary aura," he calls it.

Hunted for years around the globe, Buscetta has captivated the hunters. The fugitive Buscetta was known to his hunters mainly as a black-hearted scoundrel. The man they met at last was the first of his kind to ever cross over to the outside world, the cream of the cream, the "gray eminence" of Sicily's Cosa Nostra, in his words.

American and Italian authorities have praised Buscetta's exceptional dignity and intelligence. A director of the FBI has wished aloud for "a thousand Buscettas" to rid the planet of organized crime. The Sicilian magistrate who knows him best, Giovanni Falcone, has described him as "a complicated man of rare qualities, a very elegant man, with a striking ascendancy over Mafiosi everywhere."[1]

Some have gone further. A famous Italian columnist, Enzo Biagi, has compared Buscetta to "a personage out of Shakespeare," deeply marked by love and death. "Is there such a thing as a good, gentle, and sentimental Mafioso?" he once asked the personage, without irony. "I am one," was the unblushing reply. Biagi appears to believe this; his prize-winning best-seller in Italy is subtitled "The true story of a true godfather."[2] Doubtless many others believe it as well. Buscetta has gone far to persuade a rapt audience that there really is such a thing as a good Mafia, locked in combat with its malevolent counterpart.

By the bad Mafia, he means Luciano Leggio's. Such is its genuine awfulness that Buscetta has had little trouble in laying all the latter-day horrors of Cosa Nostra at Leggio's door: the heroin, the piratical greed, the reckless killing of judges, policemen, and politicians, the systematic annihilation of Mafia opponents, the whole riotous breakdown of law and order in the ranks. It was to fight the "tremendous reality" of this new Mafia that Buscetta turned to the state in 1984, he explains. The tremendous reality of the old Mafia was not his concern. He sees nothing wrong with it. "I am a Mafioso; I have never done anything to apologize for," he tells the press.

Rather than probe in this delicate area, authorities have preferred to take him at his word. A man of his mold may be allowed his conceits, the reasoning goes. He is still the biggest Mafia boss who has ever turned on Cosa Nostra.

Buscetta was assuredly the most devastating witness against the Mafia in his day, though not necessarily the most informative—by the time he talked to Italian and American authorities, they already knew much of what he had to say. In contrast, they had known next to nothing when the only defector who approached him in importance— Joe Valachi—appeared before Senator McClellan's Subcommittee on Investigations two decades earlier.

Valachi was the first man who ever admitted to being a member of an organized, hierarchical, secret criminal society known as the Mafia. He was the first who even revealed its real name to an incredulous public. "What I am telling you, what I am exposing to you and the press and everybody, this is my doom. This is the promise I am breaking. Even if I talked, I should never talk about this," he said.[3] He despaired of ever getting the truth across, however. "What good is it, what I'm telling you?" he would say. "Nobody will listen. Nobody will believe. You know what I mean? This Cosa Nostra, it's like a second government. It's too big."[4]

While Valachi testified, in October 1963, he held the nation riveted;

he was "the biggest star of the biggest color television spectacular ever seen in America," reported a veteran Italian correspondent from Washington. He exposed a vertically structured, internationally connected, multibillion-dollar crime syndicate flourishing in America since at least the 1930s. He described its blood oath and rules, its lucrative operations in gambling, labor racketeering, usury, extortion, and narcotics, its methodical resort to murder. (Only seven mob killings had been solved in the United States up to then, out of nearly eight hundred during and since Prohibition. Valachi alone had taken part in thirty-three murders on order, that he could recall.)[5]

Why was he telling all this to forces of the law? The answer he gave the McClellan Committee was almost identical to Tommaso Buscetta's two decades later:

"No. 1, it is to destroy them."
"Destroy who?"
"The Cosa Nostra leaders, the bosses. The whole—how would you explain it—that exists."
"You want to destroy the whole syndicate, the whole organization?"
"That is right; yes, sir."
"You don't think such an organization should be permitted to operate, or to exist?"
"That is right."[6]

In the end, though, Valachi was not wrong about what would come of his testimony: nothing came of it. Nobody was arrested after he testified; people did not believe. By and large, American law enforcers could not conceive of a secret criminal society so powerful, pervasive, and hermetically sealed. Skeptics dismissed him as a liar or nut case, and went right on denying Cosa Nostra's existence.

But Joe Valachi was just an illiterate, low-grade enforcer and hit man. Don Masino Buscetta could not be brushed off so easily. His credentials as a ranking Mafia leader were established by thick police dossiers dating back twenty or thirty years, in Italy, Brazil, Mexico, Canada, and the United States. He had traveled everywhere, read books, and was articulate in three languages. Where Valachi had seen Cosa Nostra from the ground up, Don Masino had known it from the top down since the last world war.

His credibility was dented by a flattering self-portrait that would hardly bear close inspection. (It was not inspected closely, under the circumstances.) He claimed to have spent a lifetime in the Mafia without sin: the only Sicilian Man of Honor who had never trafficked in drugs, or been self-serving, or wronged anybody, or hated anybody, or yearned for vengeance. He even denied that he had ever killed anybody (except a few German soldiers, when he was a lad of fifteen). He was almost as flattering about his former inner circle, a failing that bent his whole picture of the Mafia out of shape.

Buscetta also held things back; the gaping holes in his story were nearly as instructive as what he disclosed. Though he was plainly using the law to strike at his enemies while sparing his friends, much of his reticence was a matter of vanity and pride. He could not bear to admit that he had ever trafficked in drugs. Nobody who does it likes to admit it; for a don of his pretensions, the admission would have been intolerable. On his insistence, therefore, a discreet veil has been drawn over that side of his past.

In 1984, Buscetta agreed to talk to both Italy and America in return for his freedom in the United States. As a result, charges related to the biggest international heroin ring that has ever been broken—his own Sicilian-Corsican ring, uncovered in 1972—were withdrawn. Tommaso Buscetta did serve time in Italy on those charges; but he will never be called to account in a U.S. court for his part in spreading the heroin habit across America. Nor has he yet revealed the role played by his allies and accomplices.

In fact, the Americans can hardly be said to have gotten their money's worth out of Buscetta. His help in New York's Pizza trial was markedly selective; the defendants he identified as made Sicilian Mafiosi had all gone over to Leggio's side in the Great Mafia War. On the other hand, he assured the New York court that the alleged head of the entire Pizza ring—Gaetano Badalamenti, his old-time ally—had never trafficked in drugs. (Badalamenti was sent up for forty-five years anyway.)

Even so, Buscetta made signal contributions to an understanding of the whole Mafia phenomenon. Indeed, he revealed enough to alter worldwide perceptions of Cosa Nostra. What's more, he did it in court. He opened the American government's case against 22 Sicilian defendants in New York's Pizza Connection trial, the biggest drug case ever to come before an American judge and jury. He spent a week on the witness stand in Palermo to testify against 464 other Sicilian Mafiosi— in a bomb-proof courthouse encircled by armed troops, he in a bullet-proof glass booth facing the judge, the defendants ranged in steel cages behind him.

Just to have him in a Sicilian courtroom was "incredible, stupendous," says a prosecutor in Palermo's anti-Mafia pool. So it was, considering the life he had led.

o‿o

Tommaso Buscetta's entrance into the world was scarcely more auspicious than Luciano Leggio's. Born in the back streets of Palermo just three years after Leggio, Buscetta was the fourteenth child of a glazier. (He has forgotten the names of the twelfth and thirteenth.) No omens attended his birth, nor could a shade of his later polish be discerned for some time. After quitting school in the fifth grade, he was "dedicated to a dissolute and idle life," according to an older brother, Vincenzo.

Neighbors remember him as a teenaged *picciotto* swaggering around the dismal slum quarter of Oreto: streetwise, pug nose at an insolent tilt, pomaded hair and pencil mustache, distinctive Mafia strut. "I was a Mafioso by nature long before being made. Everything they told me to do was already part of me," he has said.

For an ambitious youth in Palermo's poorer quarters, the Mafia offered a fast social fix. Its members were the lords of the *borgata,* their neighborhood, arbitrating quarrels, administering rewards, punishments, and patronage, protecting the most sacred of Sicilian institutions: the honor of women, the bonds of marriage, the integrity of the family. They could show off their manliness and bravado, commanding respect and envy. Elders deferred to them. They basked in the roseate glow cast by their favorite poet, Pitrè, who depicted the "Mafiusa" embodying beauty, grace, and excellence, an object of superior quality.

But Cosa Nostra's headiest attraction was its superb indifference to the law. Its members had only to keep faith with one another. They could rob, fleece, cheat, bully, blackmail, and lie to anybody else without a stain on their honor. They could kill lesser mortals, inferior beings, without a twinge of guilt. They could suborn juries, corrupt or intimidate judges, murder witnesses, buy politicians, or use any other measures to evade punishment by the state (whose authority they did not recognize). "The code of Cosa Nostra would fully support such activities," Buscetta said.[7] (The code of America's Cosa Nostra was identical, as FBI undercover agent Joe Pistone has reported. "As a wiseguy, you can lie, you can cheat, you can steal, you can kill people— *legitimately.* You can do any goddamn thing you want, and nobody can say anything about it. Who wouldn't want to be a wiseguy?" observed a soldier in the Bonanno Family.)[8]

The sense of being above all laws save their own was a source of intense, intoxicating pleasure for Mafiosi. It was worth dying young for, a fate they accepted as part of the bargain. Questioned about the murder of Salvatore Inzerillo in 1981—a *Capo-Mafia* much admired by Buscetta—a Sicilian Mafioso responded in this way:

> JUDGE: Totò Inzerillo was killed. He was only thirty-seven years old. Isn't it a pity to die so young? There are so many important experiences to have at that age. . . . So many things to do and see . . .
>
> MAFIOSO: Inzerillo died at thirty-seven, agreed. But his thirty-seven years were like eighty years for an ordinary person. Inzerillo *lived well*. He had a great many things from life. Others wouldn't have a hundredth of those things. It isn't a pity to die at that age if you've done, had, and seen all the things Inzerillo did, saw, and had. He didn't die tired or dissatisfied with life. He died *sated* with life. That's the difference.[9]

Buscetta was barely eighteen when he was sworn in to the Porta Nuova clan. The oath he took in Palermo in 1945 was exactly like Valachi's in New York in 1930: "rather ridiculous," he finds it now. Blood from his pricked finger was rubbed on a paper saint's image, which was set on fire in his hand. As it burned, he repeated the ancient vow: "May my flesh burn like this holy image if I am unfaithful to this vow."[10]

With these words, he crossed the threshold into an arcane world. His rights and duties no longer resembled a normal citizen's. A whole way of life had to be taught by word of mouth. "No one will ever find any written code of Mafia ethics. . . . But the rules are rigid and firm and universally accepted," he explained to Judge Falcone, his main questioner in Sicily.

Mafia ethics covered love, lust, marriage, fidelity, pride, envy, revenge, ambition, avarice. Gallantry had little to do with it; Buscetta, when asked by a New York judge if the Mafia had ever lived up to its pretensions of defending the poor and weak, drily answered, "No." The integrity of the family (small "f") was high on the Mafia's list. A Man of Honor was expected to keep up appearances as a husband and father. Maintaining a mistress was practically compulsory; but a member could be expelled for deserting or divorcing his wife, and summarily executed for sleeping with the wife of another member. Otherwise, the code was a martial manual, bristling with death penalties, designed to safeguard the secrecy and internal order of a tightly structured underground state.

Once in, never out; that was the first thing Buscetta learned. A member had to obey his *capo-cosca* blindly, wherever he was, for the rest of his life. "He never stops belonging to the Family. . . . It is not possible to lose that status spontaneously," Buscetta informed his questioners. ("The only way out is in a box," is how Lucky Luciano once put it.)

Every *cosca,* or clan, was defined by precisely drawn boundaries; there were thirty-nine in Palermo, a hundred-odd more in the rest of Sicily. The *cosca* could impose its will within its perimeters, but not beyond. A made member could only address someone from a different clan in the presence of a third made member, lest two alone might conspire together. Switching to another clan, or invading another's territory for whatever purpose, was punishable by death.

A made member could not lie about "Mafia business" in the presence of two or more members. Lying to just one or to outsiders didn't matter; but a *tragediaturi* (who lied to the *Mafia*) was liable to be shot. "Unless you understand this, you can understand nothing," Buscetta cautioned Judge Falcone.

Prostitution, pornography, and drugs were banned: they damaged the image and drew the police, the detested *sbirri.* Apart from these restraints—widely honored in the breach—members could go into any business, provided it was legitimate in the Mafia sense. "If I want to deal stolen checks, I tell my *capo,* and the *capo* tells me, 'Do it. But set something aside for our people in prison, and the lawyers.' Then it's legitimate," Buscetta said. (The something set aside was the *capo*'s cut. His permission was always needed, so that the cut was always paid.)

The rules for killing were elaborate and inflexible, in Buscetta's account. Men of Honor were forbidden to kill a woman, or anybody who was not a member of Cosa Nostra, or anybody at all for advancement, power, or profit. They could only kill with their *capo*'s consent, on their own clan's territory, and solely on honorable grounds. Thus, they could kill a fellow Man of Honor for lying, or committing adultery (within the Family), or getting *posato* (expelled) for misbehavior, or betraying Mafia secrets, or committing what Sicilians call *uno sgarro*—an unpardonable personal offense, however slight.

In practice, most of the strictures on killing had been disregarded as long as anyone could remember (although killing a woman was still a disgrace in the 1950s). But one rule was unfailingly enforced. "Every

Man of Honor must have killed at least once for Cosa Nostra before becoming a member. Every Man of Honor must become an assassin," Buscetta told an American debriefing team.[11]

Such was Don Masino's image of rectitude, when he crossed over to the law, that admitting to murder jolted his hearers. "Who was it, Tommy? Who did you kill to get in?" a U.S. attorney asked with a flicker of malice. Only some German soldiers in World War II— enough to prove his valor, he answered. Actually, he had killed rather often, as he confessed afterward to his unquestioning Italian biographer, Enzo Biagi. "A few times I did it myself; many times, I ordered it," he said, naming no names. All the victims deserved to die, he added, if for no other reason than that they were "wrong, irrefutably."[12]

In reality, Buscetta's murders were no more or less virtuous than most during his swift rise to the top. Judging from the evidence, he killed for advancement, power, and profit like everyone else.

In 1963, in Italy, by rare chance, an eyewitness testified to a double murder for which Buscetta was convicted *in absentia* and sentenced to fourteen years (see chapter 8). The victims were abducted and never seen again, a customary exercise in Mafia ethics known as "white death." The incident took place in 1960, when Buscetta's own Porta Nuova clan was fighting the old Mafia establishment for control of Palermo's building trades. The witness had seen Buscetta and his *capo-cosca* grab two of the opposition's men, hustle them into a car at gunpoint, and drive off. "Acqua in bocca," the witness had been warned— "Keep your trap shut"—which he did, until the killers were all out of Sicily or dead.[13]

Buscetta had long been moving in the best Mafia circles by then, though how he got there is still a mystery. His early life as a made member is a blank.

Sworn in just a year after Leggio, he moved in different spheres altogether. Leggio was a country boy, Buscetta a city brat. Leggio had only to kill a few people to become the focus of all eyes in Corleone; young *picciotti* like Buscetta were always killing people in Palermo. It was not just a killer's instinct that he needed to get ahead; it was also polish, composure, a certain gravity, judicious posture, and quick wits.

With such assets, Buscetta could be upwardly mobile more easily and less noticeably. Palermo was the Mafia's capital. His Mafia sponsors, an aggressive pair of brothers named Salvatore and Angelo La Barbera, were enterprising in business and enmeshed in Christian Democratic politics. Money, clothes, women, travel, political connections, were all more accessible.

A dapper young man, unexpectedly short but spruce and self-assured, Buscetta quickly picked up the urbanity of a well-to-do city dweller. He went to the theater and opera, frequented the right social clubs, cultivated influential Christian Democrats, and courted women, so he tells us. (An incorrigible womanizer, he was a husband at sixteen, a father by seventeen, and an assiduous adulterer ever after—his biggest problem as a Man of Honor.)

Buscetta has never said what he did for a living, though. A first hint of his Mafia connection appeared only in 1957, when a Palermo builder incautiously approached him for help in getting a construction license. Buscetta, said to be a good friend of Mayor Salvo Lima's, procured the licence and named his price: "not with open threats, but using an obscure and contorted language, apparently inoffensive, whose sinister meaning could not escape the interested party."[14] Buscetta wound up with two newly built apartments, a contract for his brother Vincenzo's window factory, a foreman's job for an associate, and cash payments "for friends at City Hall." The payoff came to around 25 million lire in all, close to $50,000.

Two years later, Buscetta was caught with nearly four tons of contraband Chesterfield cigarettes fresh off the boat, loaded onto a couple of old Dodge trucks.[15] He got away with a fine; it was his first arrest and trivial at that, he says. But he would never again be far from the thoughts of the Sicilian police.

The Chesterfields had come from Tangiers, a conveniently situated free port on the north African coast facing Gibraltar, favored by spies, smugglers, money changers, fugitive crooks, and other assorted villains. This was the seat of a Corsican buccaneer named Paolo Molinelli, whose private fleet plied the Mediterranean with contraband tobacco for all Europe.

Black market cigarettes were still a gold mine in 1959: the price went from 28,000 lire ($55) a case in Tangiers to 210,000 lire on the streets of Rome or Paris. Molinelli worked with a Corsican ring in the French port of Marseilles, the Camorra brotherhood in Naples (a secret criminal society older even than the Mafia), and the Mafia in Sicily. Apart from Chesterfields, Camels, and Pall Malls, his fleet carried morphine base from Lebanon to Marseilles, and refined heroin from Marseilles to Sicily for forwarding to Cosa Nostra in America. This was where the international heroin network got its start, and where master traffickers like Buscetta got theirs.[16]

The Guardia di Finanza, Italy's crack financial police force, was just getting interested in these shipments around the time of Buscetta's "trivial" arrest. Agents expert in contraband knew that heroin from Marseilles was landing in bulk along the Sicilian coast between Palermo and Castellammare del Golfo, a jagged line of sandy coves and sheer rock face forming a smuggler's paradise. They were beginning to identify a big Sicilian ring working with Molinelli and his Corsicans.

Sixty-odd Sicilian Mafiosi were under surveillance over the next six or seven years. A dozen, including Buscetta, were watched especially closely "in their mysterious comings and goings, from city to city and meeting to meeting . . . in luxurious hotels, with their girlfriends of the moment."[17] The investigation got almost nowhere until long after Buscetta had fled abroad, in 1963. By that time, he was wanted on two continents as a major heroin trafficker, and much more besides. For Italy's Parliamentary Anti-Mafia Commission, he was one of Sicily's top ten Mafia bosses: a "qualified killer . . . wicked, aggressive, engaged in a vast criminal activity . . . a Mafioso of the highest level who moves with the big shots of the American underworld."[18] Some even thought he was bigger than Leggio, but nobody in the early 1960s knew of his long-standing relations with the biggest Mafia boss in the world—Salvatore Lucania, a.k.a. "Charlie Lucky" Luciano.

oⒸo

Lucky Luciano had arrived in the northern Italian port of Genoa aboard the *Laura Keene* on February 9, 1946. He was appalled to hear that he was being shipped back to the Sicilian village he was born in. "I started to yell, 'Do you mean to say I gotta live in Lercara Friddi for the rest of my life? What the hell's goin' on here?' " he recalled long afterward.

A request to keep him under close surveillance had come from the head of the U.S. Narcotics Bureau, Harry Anslinger (habitually referred to by Luciano as "the dirty son of a bitch Asslinger"). "Washington has the crazy idea that you had yourself paroled to Italy so you could supervise the drug traffic from this side of the Atlantic," he was told, to his outrage.[19]

Lercara Friddi gave him a grand welcome. Hundreds of people waited in the square with banners and small American flags. A four-piece band played "The Stars and Stripes Forever" as the mayor, draped in a red sash, ushered him out of a police car. Gangster or no gangster, he had left poor and come back exceedingly rich.

Luciano soon talked or bought his way out of Lercara Friddi. By the summer of 1946, he had moved to Palermo, then Rome, and finally Naples, where he held court until his death in 1962.

Despite Luciano's unceasing complaints of police harassment in

Italy, he continued to be the most powerful of all Mafia leaders to the end. Couriers brought a steady flow of information and money from New York (a basic $25,000 a month plus), and carried back his orders. Dozens of American Mafia bosses voyaged to Naples to see him.

"There is no question that [Luciano's] power was so great that even in Europe he could exercise it," testified the intelligence chief of the New York Police to the McClellan Committee.[20] "No important decision that might affect the future of organized crime in the United States, he said, was made without his consultation and advice," wrote Martin Gosch and Richard Hammer, Luciano's biographers.

Few realized then—few do now, for that matter—how deeply Luciano affected the Sicilian Mafia's future as well. The legend of "Charlie Lucky" magnified everything he said or did or touched. Everybody in the Mafia, and a great many outside it, dreamed of getting near him somehow when he got to Italy. Apart from taking over Vito Genovese's black market, he was assailed with business propositions from a criminal fraternity whose hold on the country astonished him. "Half the people I met in Sicily was in the Mafia, and by half the people, I mean half the cops, too," he told Gosch and Hammer. "Because in Sicily, it goes like this: the Mafia is first, then your own family, then your business, and then the Mafia again. You might say it's like a private club that a lotta people belong to."[21]

One of his early Sicilian business partners was the *capo di tutti capi,* Don Calogero Vizzini. They opened a candy factory in Palermo together in 1949, importing "specialized" Sicilian workers from America and exporting to Germany, France, Ireland, Canada, and the United States. Some mystery surrounded the operation, since armed guards barred entrance to the room where the candy was made. When the Socialist daily *Avanti!* reported this in 1954—implying that the candy was laced with heroin—the factory shut down overnight.[22] It was the first time, and last, that Lucky Luciano and Don Calò were linked in the press. (A photographer who surprised them together in Palermo's Albergo del Sole was beaten up badly and had his camera smashed. He withdrew charges after receiving an expensive new camera and a comforting sum in cash.)

Apart from a natural reluctance to be identified publicly with the Sicilian Mafia, Luciano did not hold the organization in high esteem. He thought the old Mafia of prewar days "lacked the mental elasticity for the complex and delicate problems of the drug traffic," wrote Michele Pantaleone, dean of Italy's Mafiologists. On the other hand, the group emerging after World War II was "too noisy, quick on the trigger, undisciplined."[23]

While respecting Don Calogero Vizzini, Luciano had no use for his second-in-command and eventual successor, Giuseppe Genco Russo, known as "Zi Peppi Jencu" (Uncle Joe the Little Bull). "Peppi isn't even a rooster, let alone a bull. He's just a big fat hen," he observed. Accordingly, Luciano took only a handful of bright young Sicilian *picciotti* under his wing. Among the few admitted to his home—all to become notorious heroin dealers—was the fledgling Tommaso Buscetta.[24]

Buscetta was still in his teens when the two met in 1946. "Luciano was a myth for me. He took to me at once, and was affectionate until he died. I went to see him every month," he told his biographer, who then asked:

"What dirty business did Luciano do in America?"
"Nothing. All he did was smuggle whisky."
"What was he like?"
"He was very serious. Ugly in photographs but handsome inside, because everything about him was extraordinary. . . ."
"What was inside?"
"A great magnanimity. Even if he was a murderer. He killed to defend himself, not out of cruelty. . . . He didn't like injustice, and he didn't recognize the laws of the state, only his own."[25]

Luciano might have been surprised at this spirited endorsement. "Killing—I hadda lifetime of it," he remarked in his autumnal days, looking back at a long line of those who had fallen after getting in his way. But he did have a kind of magnanimity. I had a personal glimpse of it when *The Reporter* magazine sent me to interview Luciano in Naples in 1957. A deported hood in Rome gave me a note of introduction: "Hello Charlie. This little lady wants to talk to you."

The hood was one of some five hundred Italian-born racketeers, dope traffickers, and all-purpose mobsters shipped back from New York in the wake of Senator Kefauver's 1951 hearings. Half of them were in Naples, desperate and broke.

"Some of them would break your heart," Luciano told me. "They come around, been in stir for two months, in again, out again. I give 'em a thousand lire and tell 'em to get a shave and a bath and a meal, but if there's five hundred of 'em in Italy, four hundred come to me. I'm no bank. Sometimes I tell 'em, why don't you clear outta this place. But where would they go? To their hometowns? They'd die."[26]

We talked for an hour or so, sitting on a flowered cretonne couch before a low table in walnut veneer, with a vase of artificial flowers on a doily. Luciano's sweet-faced wife, an Italian ballet dancer named Igea, brought us coffee. My attention wandered from the wristwatch Luciano wore—platinum encircled in diamonds—to his eyes behind professorial, rimless glasses. The eyes were pools of cold indifference, utterly expressionless, unforgettable.

Otherwise he looked like any retired businessman, which he claimed he was. He spoke of the candy factory he had opened (and closed) in Palermo, a pharmaceutical supply company he had subsequently formed, and a factory he now owned in Naples that made hospital beds. The police would never let up, he complained; they were sure heroin was going out in the legs of the beds. As usual, they couldn't prove it. "They been watchin' a long time; let 'em watch," he said as he walked me to the door.

The police never did pin a heroin charge on Lucky Luciano, but they had no doubt of his guilt. His nemesis in Italy was Charles Siragusa, sent over by U.S. narcotics chief Harry Anslinger in 1951. "Mr. Anslinger, with his usual keen foresight, saw an influx of heroin coming into the United States when World War II ended," Siragusa said. "I was sent to Europe to corroborate our worst fear, that Luciano was responsible for the flow of heroin coming through the port of New York." For Siragusa, Luciano was "nothing but a pimp and a dope peddler which, ironically, are the two things no gangster wants to be considered. It was my duty to do everything legal to neutralize this man."

Siragusa went under cover in Naples, only to be spotted by Luciano's spies within hours of his arrival. "He no more 'n opened his mouth in Naples when I knew all about it. I thought to myself, when the hell is that fuckin' Asslinger gonna leave me alone?" Luciano said.

Eventually, Siragusa connected Luciano to a huge heroin shipment—nearly half a ton—diverted from a Milan pharmaceutical company and shipped to New York. The circumstances were highly compromising but, as always, not enough to stand up in court.[27]

The Italian authorities were finally ready to indict Luciano in 1965, after the Guardia di Finanza's exhaustive six-year investigation into Sicilian heroin trafficking. But by then he was dead.[28]

o◯o

There is nothing of this sordid side in Buscetta's account of his friendship with Lucky Luciano over a span of sixteen years. They talked of this and that, he says—racing, old times, Lucky's nostalgia for

New York—but never of dope. After 1951, indeed, they were forbidden to speak of any Mafia affairs at all.

The Kefauver Committee's relentless investigation in 1951 had upset Cosa Nostra in America. Among other precautions, it had decided to sever all ties with what Senator Kefauver had referred to as the "mysterious international criminal organization going under the name of 'Mafia.'" According to Buscetta, the first to disclose the fact, all communion between the two Mafias was banned for the next six years.[29] Then, in 1957, Lucky Luciano brought them together again and set them on a new course.

The U.S. narcotics agent who had dismissed him as "nothing but a pimp and a dope peddler" had greatly underestimated his quarry. Luciano was a clear-sighted corporate executive with a rare gift for rational organization, the Lee Iacocca of organized crime. He understood the laws of supply and demand, the benefits of scale, the advantages of a transcontinental operation joining raw material procurement to manufacturing to transport and marketing. He was the seminal force behind what became the biggest commercial enterprise in the world: the multinational heroin conglomerate.

The first prerequisite for this enterprise was an efficient working relationship between the Sicilian and American Cosa Nostras. It could not happen while the two were scarcely on speaking terms, nor was it enough to just start talking again. The Sicilian side was not in a position to carry out its end effectively. While Don Vito Cascio Ferro had introduced many ceremonial innovations at the turn of the century—complicated initiation rites, theatrical trials, ritual meetings in ancient vaulted caverns[30]—such things were no substitute for a competent modern government. And the island's clans were perpetually at one another's throats over territories and spoils. Their *capo di tutti capi* seemed to reign mostly by sheer force of personal magnetism, while a shadowy tribunal dealt with grave infractions of the code. The Sicilians had nothing like the ruling Commission that Luciano had invented for their American offspring as far back as 1931.[31]

Upon eliminating the rival Mafia chiefs behind New York's calamitous tribal war—Joe "The Boss" Masseria and Salvatore Maranzano—Luciano had laid down the law to the survivors. "I explained to 'em that all the war horseshit was out," he said afterward. "I told 'em we was in a business that hadda keep movin' without explosions every two minutes; knockin' guys off just because they come from a different part of Sicily, that kind of crap, was givin' us a bad name, and we couldn't operate until it stopped."[32]

The Commission Luciano had created was much like a company board of directors. Twelve Mafia bosses sat on the board, with Luciano in charge: "the Boss of All Bosses under the table," as Joe Valachi put it, since Luciano disliked the title. The Commission was designed to set policy guidelines, fix territorial boundaries, settle intramural disputes, and rule on in-house killings. Every Family undertook not to add more members or import trained soldiers from Sicily without the others' consent. (The first boss to break the rule was executed; no others did so for twenty years.)[33] Henceforth, "every outfit in every city could be independent," in Luciano's words, *provided it followed the Commission's rulings.*

A similar Commission was Luciano's gift to the Sicilian Mafia, through Buscetta. Sometime in 1957, Luciano suggested to his protégé that the Sicilians ought to have one, and Buscetta undertook to help set it up. The decision became official that October at a historic summit meeting of American and Sicilian Mafia leaders, a meeting that was to be the subject of mystified speculation for the next quarter of a century.

The Deal

The Grand Hotel des Palmes (Albergo e delle Palme), palms long gone and facade blackened with city soot, is now a chain hotel frequented by tourists in drip-dry garments. Taxis, scooters, buses, hurrying cars, and grinding trucks pound past its plate-glass doors. Fast-food counters sprout at its flanks.

Apart from its popular barman, Toti, not even the staff seems aware of the hotel's glories during the *Belle Epoque.* Once among the grandest of Palermo's private mansions, it was transformed and embellished in extravagant art nouveau style in the late nineteenth century. Europe's most elegant aristocrats stayed there. No opera star appearing at the celebrated Teatro Massimo would be caught staying elsewhere. Famous men of letters strolled through its luxuriant gardens. Renoir came to paint a portrait of Richard Wagner, who orchestrated his opera *Parsifal* in a sumptuous suite on the mezzanine.

The suite, now used only on high ceremonial occasions, is still called the Sala Wagner. Splendid antique mirrors reflect its vaulted ceiling of gilt and cerulean blue. Several of its original divans and armchairs are ranged along the walls: plump, gilt-legged baroque, covered in faded red and gold damask.

It was in the Sala Wagner that the American and Sicilian Mafias met, from October 10 to 14, 1957. The Hotel des Palmes had become their hangout after World War II, and all the big bosses were at home there. Lucky Luciano had his own screened-off corner of the lounge, known as the Little Red Room, Toti recalls. (It is the Little Blue Room now.) Most of the thirty-odd delegates to the summit were habitués. From Luciano down, they were among the most powerful criminals on two continents.[1]

The American delegation was led by Joe Bonanno of Castellammare del Golfo and Brooklyn. The most indomitably Sicilian of all the New York fathers—he allowed only the Sicilian dialect to be spoken in his Family—he described himself as the American Mafia's "chairman of the board." A red carpet was rolled out for him at Rome's Fiumicino Airport; Italy's foreign trade minister, Bernardo Mattarella (also from Castellammare), waited to embrace him. In Palermo, Bonanno was treated like a lord. A hush would fall over the city's most exclusive restaurants as he entered. Proprietors kissed his hand and asked for his blessing; "Vossia mi benerica," they would say, a phrase commonly addressed to titled noblemen.

Nearly everyone Bonanno brought to the summit from America had been born somewhere around Castellammare del Golfo, and most were related to one another. They included Carmine Galante and John Bonventre (respectively Bonanno's *consigliere* and *vice-capo*); Frank Garofalo (his "number two"); Antonio, Giuseppe, and Gaspare Maggadino (his cousins, whose Family ran Buffalo, New York); John Priziola (who ran Detroit); and Santo Sorge (whose cousin headed the Mafia in Sicily).

Sorge's cousin Don Giuseppe Genco Russo led the Sicilian contingent. Reigning overlord since Don Calogero Vizzini's death in 1952, "Zi Peppi Jencu" was a coarse, sly, half-illiterate ruffian loved by none. Nevertheless, he had superb political and financial connections. With him at the conference table were a dozen of the island's biggest *mammasantissima*. Among them were Salvatore "Cichiteddu" (Little Bird) Greco, scion of the Mafia's mighty Greco Family and leader of Palermo's old-school dons; Calcedonio Di Pisa, Greco's number two; and the La Barbera brothers, Buscetta's patrons.

Every man in the Sala Wagner was a drug trafficker. Some years later, an Italian judge would indict them in a body for "organizing the drug traffic to the United States via Sicily." The exquisitely genteel Joe Bonanno would head the list of the accused. "Bananas was very big in junk," noted Lucky Luciano, who was even bigger according to the judge.[2] For all that, the summit drew none of the attention then that it would generate later. American authorities did not even learn of the summit until long after the thirty-odd men in the Sala Wagner had set a juggernaut in motion.[3]

The Sicilian climate was hardly conducive to intense vigilance in 1957. Palermo's clans had all but completed their takeover of the city. Don Giuseppe Genco Russo, often photographed with bishops, bank presidents, civic functionaries, and party leaders, was the arbiter of island politics. Such was the Mafia's weight that no Sicilian newspaper dared refer to it by name. The law took its course accordingly.[4]

A few cops kept an eye on the big get-together at the Hotel des Palmes. They had only to sit in the lobby to learn who was there, but that was all they learned. The extreme secrecy surrounding this high-powered meeting underlines its extraordinary importance: not one of the players has ever uttered a word about it.

Lucky Luciano, whose confidences to authors Martin Gosch and Richard Hammer filled 450 printed pages, said nothing about this meeting. Bonanno, describing his trip to Palermo in his autobiography, *A Man of Honor,* did not mention it either. Instead, he expostulated at length about joining up in the Sicilian capital with "my former deputy Frank Garofalo" and "Uncle John Bonventre," and having a great time. Old friends—"men of my tradition"—took Bonanno around proudly "to show me all the new boulevards and office buildings." Accompanied by these Men of Honor, he dined in a "fine restaurant on the Piazza Politeama," where he threw a pitcher of ice water at the head of a waiter who had "trifled" with him. "The fellow cowered before me. In a way, I had taught him a lesson," Bonanno reported. He claimed to have devoted the rest of his visit to sight-seeing, visiting the renowned Teatro Massimo opera house, and dedicating an orphanage, an expedition for which he was given a police escort. "They would never believe this in New York," he noted, rightly.[5]

Buscetta, questioned nearly three decades later, stated flatly: "I know nothing of a meeting of Italo-American Mafiosi in the Hotel des Palmes in October 1957."[6] There had simply been a dinner party on or around October 12 of that year—a memorable evening he had spent with Lucky Luciano and Joe Bonanno.

The dinner had lasted twelve and a half hours, in a closed-off section of Spano's seafood restaurant on the Palermo waterfront, a quietly elegant establishment now boarded up and humped in sand. There, over starched linen and tasseled menus, chilled white wine and candles, *pasta alle sarde* and *pesce arrosto,* the Sicilian Mafia's own Commission—the Cupola—came into being.

According to Buscetta, Lucky Luciano had arranged for Bonanno to come over for the occasion; and he asked Buscetta to bring along half a dozen select Sicilian colleagues, including Salvatore "Cichiteddu" Greco, the La Barbera brothers, and a *mammasantissima* by the name of Gaetano Badalamenti, who would one day head the Sicilians' Pizza Connection network.[7] Joe Bonanno arrived with his *consigliere* and his underboss, among others. He addressed Buscetta as the natural leader on the Sicilian side, said Buscetta: "I was a rising star, shrewd, sharp, who knew how to talk a little, and I had the habit of reasoning."[8]

The chairman of the board had once likened the American Mafia's Commission to "the stars in the firmament by which a mariner plots his course." Now he sang its praises to the Sicilians. "Bonanno drew me aside and told me how the Commission prevented murders committed in ignorance," Buscetta explained to American investigators. "He said that, since its inception, the U.S. Commission had approved of all murders of Men of Honor in the U.S., and the system seemed to work. . . . I liked the idea; Greco and Badalamenti did too. . . . Bonanno instructed me on how to do it, and we went ahead."[9] It was that simple. The Cupola, destined to become a multibillion-dollar heroin consortium, was in business within a couple of months.

This was the first account ever of the Cupola's origins, one of Buscetta's more valuable contributions. But for all that, his omissions might have embarrassed a man of less aplomb. Obviously the big shots converging on Palermo were there for more than the dinner at Spano's; they were holed up at the Hotel des Palmes for four days. Indeed, the Sicilians' Cupola was hardly a matter for formal negotiation between the two Cosa Nostras. It was something for the Sicilians to decide on themselves, if perhaps with a word of fraternal advice from their American *compari.*

Although there is no firsthand evidence of what went on at the four-day summit itself, what followed over the next thirty years has made the substance clear. Authorities on both sides of the Atlantic are persuaded by now that the American delegation asked the Sicilians to take over the import and distribution of heroin in the United States, and the Sicilians agreed.

The one phrase that has come down to us, overheard by a waiter serving drinks, suggests that the bargaining must have been fierce.

"Blessed is he who is far away when a hundred dogs fight over a bone," murmured Sicily's Mafia overlord, Don Giuseppe Genco Russo, to Bonanno's *consigliere,* Carmine Galante. In fact, the Americans needed the Sicilians, and it was going to cost them.

oᗧo

The brilliance of Lucky Luciano's plan lay first in getting the American Cosa Nostra off the hook. By the time he suggested the visit to Sicily in 1957, the organization he had built up so skillfully in America was in deep trouble.

One in every three members of Joe Bonanno's Family in New York had been arrested on drug charges, as had one in every three in the Colombo Family; one in every two in the Genovese Family; two in every five in the Gambino Family; and three in every five in the Lucchese Family.[10] Altogether, New York's five Families and their satellites were bringing in 95 percent of all the heroin entering the United States.[11]

This was awkward for men of Joe Bonanno's "Tradition," who "shunned drug peddling" as an "immoral" and "unmanly activity." "My Tradition outlaws narcotics. 'Men of Honor' don't deal in narcotics," he wrote.[12]

It was not really necessary, either, as Lucky Luciano claimed to have warned before things got out of hand:

There was so much dough to be made in everythin' else we had, why ruin it with the dangers of playin' around with junk?

I tried to make 'em understand that . . . we was businessmen runnin' businesses and givin' people what they wanted in a way that didn't hurt nobody. People wanted to gamble, we helped 'em gamble; they needed booze, cigarettes and meat durin' the war, we took care of that.

Sure, here and there we would squeeze some guys, but look at all the money we was puttin' in circulation just from other good businessmen buyin' our protection. I said there wasn't a politician or a cop who could hold on to none of the money we paid him off with, that they spent it as soon as they got it, and that was very good for the American economy—to put money in circulation. [Here, he] looked right at Meyer Lansky and we both couldn't hold back laughin'.

But it didn't mean a fuckin' thing. On the subject of narcotics, I could see I wasn't gettin' through. All the time I was talkin', most of 'em had stone in their faces.[13]

By 1957, however, the American Mafia had cause to think again. For one thing, Cosa Nostra had struck it rich in the U.S. labor movement. This was a field for all-around racketeering that brought in billions of dollars, and yielded legitimacy and enormous political influence at virtually no risk. Meanwhile, dealing in drugs was getting very dangerous. The U.S. Congress had passed a severe Narcotics Control Act in 1956. Drug traffickers caught in America could be sent up for forty years. Before long, 206 big Mafia gangsters would wind up with stiff sentences for drugs.[14] Carmine Galante would be jailed for twenty years—this after replacing Bonanno as head of his Family. Vito Genovese, heading another New York Family, would get fifteen. Two ranking lieutenants in the Lucchese Family would get forty each.[15]

This clamping down on drug traffickers was largely the work of Senator Estes Kefauver, whose 1951 investigation had jolted Congress into passing the narcotics bill. The Democrat from Tennessee and his crusade against the Mafia had touched a deep, popular chord. Ordinary Americans, tightening their belts to pay for the Korean War, were incensed by a steep rise in political corruption and criminal violence. Kefauver's Special Committee on Organized Crime exposed not only the connection but the primary source: "a sinister nationwide crime syndicate known as the Mafia."

The Senate committee had held a hundred hearings and interrogated six hundred witnesses—live, in history's first television spectacular. Scores of humiliated Mafia bosses had taken the Fifth Amendment on camera: Frank Costello, who succeeded Lucky Luciano as Boss of All Bosses; Albert Anastasia, head of what became the Gambino Family; Gaetano Lucchese, head of his own Family; Meyer Lansky; and Joe Adonis, who ran Luciano's affairs in New York ("the most sinister of them all," maintained Senator Kefauver).[16]

They came out looking terrible. Every repellent crime was heaped on their heads, and dealing in drugs was the worst. The Mafia "specialized in the sale and distribution of narcotics," the committee said.[17] Furthermore, it was tied directly to the Sicilian Mafia through its ineffable leader in exile, Lucky Luciano, "the brains in an international drug ring running between Italy and the United States."[18]

Luciano was indignant. "Them investigations, when they was all over, didn't make a dent in nothin' back in the States. But every time my name got mentioned, the Italian cops kept pullin' me in for questionin', makin' my life miserable."[19] He was right about America. In the end, the Kefauver hearings did not make a significant dent in the Mafia. American justice was no more of a match for it in the 1950s, or 1960s or 1970s, than Mussolini's had been in the 1920s. Democratic Italy did no better, either.

One reason, perhaps the decisive one, was that the two Mafias could use their countries interchangeably without fear of detection. U.S. law enforcement agencies were accustomed to thinking of "the Mob" or "the Outfit" or "the Organization" as local pockets of crime. Their Italian opposite numbers thought of the Mafia as a natural emanation issuing from millennial history, uniquely Sicilian, impossible to export. By and large, therefore, the American and Italian police went their own ways. With few exceptions, they did not tell each other anything, or look for connections, or even keep track of their own Mafiosi very far beyond their borders. Certainly they were unaware of the ceaseless comings and goings across the Atlantic, and that was their big mistake.

Men of Honor had been commuting freely between Italy and America since the days of the Black Hand. Largely unnoticed by police other than their own, they could find sanctuary and sustenance on either side of the ocean. Despite membership restrictions on each side over the years, they were all members of "a private club that a lotta people belong to," as Luciano remarked.

Many were also blood relations. He was a rare Mafioso in Castellammare del Golfo or Brooklyn who did not have a brother or uncle or cousin, or several of each, in the Mafia across the water. There was no beating that combination for secrecy and mutual trust. Sicilian family ties, tightly interwoven and practically indestructible, have always been the Mafia's most priceless asset.

In effect, the two countries offered alternate life supports. A Man of Honor might drop in to one or the other for a weekend to transact some business, or stay for years to dodge arrest warrants and a long stay in jail. Many maintained two households. Some had trouble remembering the names in their assorted passports. "We used to buy them like other people buy shirts," admitted Gaetano Badalamenti long afterward at the Pizza Connection trial.[20]

Eventually, members lost some of their old visiting privileges, but they still belonged to the club. In moments of adversity, the two Mafias have always pooled their forces to outwit the law.

Thus, Joe Bonanno and his colleagues took Luciano's advice in the autumn of 1957 and made the pilgrimage to Palermo. The American Families were anxious to live down their public disgrace and get the law off their backs. Sicilian Mafiosi, slipping in and out of the country unobserved, were practically free of such worries. They had no police records in the United States, for the most part: no case histories, no fingerprints or mug shots on file. What went on in Sicily rarely came to be known in New York, and vice versa. The Sicilians could run the heroin in and distribute it far from home; the Americans could provide the leasehold on the marketing territory and collect the rent, without appearing to be in the business at all.

ᴏᴄⒶᴏ

The two Mafias had been out of touch for six years—the result of the calamitous Kefauver hearings—when they met at the Hotel des Palmes. They had a lot to talk over besides drugs.

First, they had to redefine their formal relations. There was no going back to the old days, when a made member of one was automatically accepted into the other. The two brotherhoods were going to be separate and distinct. A Man of Honor from one country might be welcomed in the other as a guest, but was forbidden to work there (in the Mafia sense) without a *Capo-Mafia*'s approval. Indeed, neither Cosa Nostra was allowed to do business on the other's soil without permission, on pain of death.

These rules, crucial to understanding what happened later, were perfectly concealed from the outside world for nearly two decades. By now, Buscetta has spelled them out in detail, but the first inkling of their nature was picked up by the Royal Canadian Mounted Police in 1974, in a tape-recorded conversation in a bar.

The speaker was Paul Violi, boss of the Mafia in Montreal, the Canadian arm of the Bonanno Family. Talking things over with a visitor from the *cosca* in Agrigento, Sicily, Violi said:

> Let's say, you need something, we're at your disposal. *But you aren't part of us.* . . . If you belong over there, you can't just come over here. . . . You can't talk about your Family here. You can't talk about *anything.* . . . Let's say you take it into your head to do something on your own . . . something heavy . . . and you don't say anything to anybody and something happens to you. . . . Tell me, how do you get out of it then? Do you see how things stand, Carmelo?[21]

Later, the "Sicilian faction" in Montreal murdered Paul Violi for taking the edict too literally. The Americans had grown powerless to stop them. Apparently, those attending the summit in 1957 had failed to foresee the treachery of their Sicilian partners.

Apart from working out protocol, the delegates needed to settle the fate of a disconcerting character called Albert Anastasia. Born in Calabria, on the southern Italian coast, Anastasia had been at Lucky Luciano's side in New York from the earliest days. Always a psychopathic killer, he had headed Murder, Inc., the killing arm for both Mafias during the 1930s. But by 1957, he was running amok. Even

Luciano had to admit that "Albert was really off his rocker, and he just wanted to kill anybody who came to mind that he got mad about."

It is generally accepted now that Anastasia was sentenced to death by the two Mafias in Palermo. The verdict was carried out in New York as soon as the American delegation got home. The more far-reaching decision made at the summit—the heroin deal—was ratified in the United States just a few weeks later. The sequence of events was as follows.

Ten days after the conference adjourned at the Hotel des Palmes, Anastasia was gunned down in a barber's chair at Manhattan's Park Sheraton Hotel. The *mandanti* in New York, those who gave the orders, were Vito Genovese and Carlo Gambino; a pair of *sicari* (assassins) were sent over from Sicily to do the shooting, however.[22]

Nobody at the time connected Anastasia's murder to the secret parley at the Hotel des Palmes. The American police had not even heard of it; the Italian police showed little interest. Later, when they looked in earnest at the Palermo conclave, Italian authorities concluded that "the elimination of Anastasia . . . was part of the program" decided on there.[23] The most important part followed swiftly.

Eighteen days after Anastasia's death—on November 12, 1957—an elite group of Cosa Nostra's policymakers in America met secretly in Livingston, New Jersey, from noon on November 12 until five the next morning.[24] Much as any political party might do on the eve of a national convention, they were making crucial decisions. Twenty-four hours later, a police sergeant in upstate New York named Edgar Croswell stumbled on the entire leadership of the American Mafia in the peaceful little town of Apalachin. The scene was so hilarious that its sinister implications were nearly lost on the public. Reporters had the time of their lives. The nation rocked with laughter.

The site was a spacious ranch house nestled among rolling wooded hills, owned by Joe Barbara of Castellammare del Golfo, Apalachin's wealthiest resident. A hundred or so bosses from New York, New Jersey, Philadelphia, Boston, New Orleans, Chicago, Cleveland, Tampa, Detroit, Dallas, Kansas City, Colorado, and California had descended upon his home. They were wearing silk shirts and pointed shoes, dark suits and fedoras, riding in dark chauffeur-driven limousines, with an entourage of meaty bodyguards.[25] Everybody who had attended the conference at the Hotel des Palmes was there. Several others, including Carlo Gambino, made a quick trip to Italy beforehand to consult with Lucky Luciano.[26] The men were in the process of consuming several hundred pounds of barbecued beefsteak when the police arrived, whereupon they scattered over the countryside in frantic disarray. According to the testimony of Joe Valachi in 1963, "Barbara had a cop that was after him through the years and that is how they got suspicious, because he ordered so many steaks and so many rooms, he was renting."

"It never would've happened in your place," observed Stefano Maggadino, boss of Buffalo, to Sam Giancana, boss of Chicago, over a tapped phone shortly afterward.

"You're fucking right, it wouldn't. This is the right territory for a big meet. We've got three towns just outside Chicago with the police chiefs in our pockets. We got this territory baled up tight," replied Giancana.[27]

In Lucky Luciano's account, the meeting place had been chosen by Vito Genovese, the ultimate proof of his stupidity. "What the hell did Vito think would happen when a bunch of guys from all over the country, dressed in fancy city clothes, come drivin' up some country road in their big Cadillacs like it was a fuckin' parade?" he observed when the news reached him in Naples. "I bet not one of them overfed fat guys runnin' through the woods for their lives had been off the city streets before. I could just picture 'em, being lost for days in the woods, maybe even starvin' to death and probably freezin' their balls off."[28]

Some forty got away, but sixty-two were rounded up: living (if stunned) examples of the Mafia whose existence would continue to be denied for years to come. Naturally the bosses denied it themselves. They were visiting a sick friend, they all claimed.

Law enforcers had never seen such a collection of "14-karat hoodlums," in Sergeant Croswell's words.[29] They had no idea that the hoodlums represented every Mafia Family in America, not to speak of its ruling Commission. Joe Valachi's testimony was still years away, and the state of police intelligence in 1957 was deplorable.

"There was no such thing as organized crime charts or rosters of Families," Croswell has explained. "You didn't have computer checks where you can get information in three minutes. Then it would take you days—you would probably never get it—it would get lost in the files or the mail. Each individual policeman who was interested in organized crime was a voice in the wilderness and that worked both ways: there was nobody to listen and he didn't know what he was talking about."[30]

Thus, the most momentous American Mafia meeting of the century was virtually lost on forces of the law. Having nothing to pin on the captured delegates—visiting a sick friend is not a crime—they let the whole bunch go.

Though the press referred to Apalachin merely as a "gangland gath-

ering," it was a full-dress national convention of the American Cosa
Nostra, the first and last of such perilous size. "Men in my world were
in a tizzy over the upcoming convention," wrote Bonanno. "All the
people who mattered from the whole country had been invited. Everyone was talking about the Big Barbecue at Apalachin. Those privileged
enough to attend . . . anticipated it with the same glee as do Republicans
or Democrats when they meet every four years."

But not even Apalachin could induce law enforcers to believe that
there really was a Mafia in America. It remained for Senator McClellan, six years after the event, to see a national syndicate behind "this
surreptitious conclave of the high and mighty in the underworld's domain."[31]

By 1963, the McClellan Committee had heard of the 1957 conclave
in Palermo as well, and made the vital connection. Running down the
list of known narcotics traffickers present at Apalachin, the committee
noted: "Immediately prior to the Apalachin meeting of 1957, Carmine
Galante had appeared at Palermo, Sicily, with underworld leaders Joe
Bonanno and John Bonventre. It is believed that the meeting set the
pattern of the Apalachin meeting which followed shortly afterward."[32]
In Italy too, law-enforcement agencies agreed by then that the two
meetings were "interdependent."[33]

∘⊖∘

The long-accepted explanation of these extraordinary concomitant
gatherings had to do with domestic Mafia politics. Vito Genovese had
shot his Family boss, Frank Costello, six months before Apalachin. He
and Carlo Gambino had jointly directed the shooting of Gambino's
boss, Albert Anastasia, just three weeks previously. Both were anxious
to be ordained as the new heads of their respective Families. Yet big
Mafia chiefs had been killed before. Anastasia himself had murdered his
predecessor, Vincent Mangano, and had been ordained by the Commission afterward.[34] Fanatically discreet and jealous of its prerogatives, the
Commission customarily handled such matters *in camera.*

Crime experts also agreed that the "narcotics issue" was to be discussed at Apalachin as well. But most of them, not knowing that the
American Cosa Nostra had brought the Sicilians into a secret partnership, concluded that the Mafia banned all drug traffic at the conference.

According to Buscetta, the ban was severe enough to endanger the
life of Angelo La Barbera, the *capo* of his own Mafia clan. La Barbera
had tried to bring five kilos of heroin into New York in 1960, and Carlo

Gambino had hit the roof, Buscetta told the DEA: "Gambino said that if La Barbera crossed the U.S. border with drugs, he would be obliged to forget his friendship with La Barbera and have him killed."[35]

Buscetta's account was in direct contradiction to what is known about Carlo Gambino now. In 1960, he was about to open up his Family's main enclave in Brooklyn to Sicilian heroin traffickers. In another decade or so, they would be in charge there.

Joe Valachi seemed to be confirming what crime experts believed, when he revealed the Mafia's new policy for the first time. The policy was tough, he told the McClellan Committee in 1963:

All Families were notified: no narcotics. That was a rule that was discussed by the bosses themselves. . . . You are in serious trouble if you were arrested for narcotics. You had to prove to them—you have another trial after having a trial with the Government. . . .

In Chicago . . . they gave their soldiers $200 a week to stop selling narcotics. . . . While I was in jail I heard that they raised it to $250. . . . I was told that Chicago was taxing certain businesses . . . that helped to pay these members to keep them out of the narcotics. Now, if they were caught after getting that kind of payment, there was no chance at all for them. They would pay with their lives.

The Genovese Family had the same penalty. If you were caught and they had the evidence on you, you were dead.

Yet Genovese, Valachi's Family boss, had rebuked him sternly even as they worked a heroin deal together:

He said, "Did you ever deal in junk?" I said, "Yes." He said, "You know you ain't supposed to fool around with junk." And I said, "Yes," and he looked at me and he said, "Well, don't do it again," and I said, "OK."[36]

Obviously, the new policy was ambiguous, as Valachi promptly conceded:

"Is the narcotics rule carried out? Well, it is supposed to be carried out, but there is always somebody sneaking."

"You mean there were lots of people in business?"

"That is right."

"Did even some of the bosses violate the rule? Did they get some of the profits even though they themselves may not have been involved directly?"

"Well, certainly. . . ."

"In other words, they entered into an arrangement, the soldiers would handle the narcotics and make the purchases, and have the deal, and they would get the profit?"

"That is right."[37]

If the ambiguities were plain, however, the policy set at Apalachin still looked like an all-American policy from the outside. The American Mafia had to be *seen* to be out of drugs; and, not without difficulty, this was arranged.

Incorrigible traffickers like Vito Genovese and Carmine Galante, ungovernably greedy and too arrogant to be discreet, had become a serious hindrance. In fact, Genovese was removed in short order. The arrest and conviction of this formidable father were so unusual that everybody in Cosa Nostra thought he was framed—which, apparently, he was.

"I decided that the best and easiest way to get Genovese out of everybody's hair without knockin' him off was to let the U.S. Government do the job," said Lucky Luciano to his biographers. "All we hadda do was frame the evidence and we could hand Vito over on a silver platter. . . . But we hadda send him to a federal prison, because in a state pen that little bastard would be runnin' things in a week."

The plan was made barely a year after the Palermo and Apalachin summits. Carlo Gambino, summoned to meet Luciano in an Italian seaside resort, agreed to help. Genovese was tricked into making an undercover heroin buy of 160 kilos, and went to jail for the rest of his life.[38] "I don't know whether the Narcotics Bureau really knew that Genovese was a gift, and I don't give a shit," Luciano observed. (Carmine Galante and twenty others were also caught in the trap set for Genovese, an accidental bonus, according to Luciano. Accidental or not, Galante spent almost the rest of his life in prison and was shot dead after getting out.)

Next, Mafia members at lower levels who were dealing in drugs had to be *seen* to be outside the Family fold. "They didn't say that nobody could do it," explained Ralph Salerno, former head of New York's police intelligence unit and longtime expert on organized crime. "What they said at Apalachin was: 'If you do deal, *you must warn your friends, relatives, and associates to stay miles away from you, under penalty of death.* If you implicate others, that's it.' I have it on a bug," Salerno continued. "The fellow says: 'Holy Mackerel, these guys are in trouble. They were dealing *and they never told nobody.*' Then his *capo* says:

'Look at the newspaper, the date. They did it before Apalachin. It's okay.' "[39]

A good many went on doing it long after Apalachin, but they were simply thought to be bucking the system. By and large, the myth prevailed that Cosa Nostra was essentially "out of narcotics."

It was Tommaso Buscetta who ultimately exposed the Apalachin hoax, though that was hardly his purpose. Intent on incriminating his Sicilian enemies, he was no less resolved to protect the American Mafia's good name.

Buscetta intended to live in America after his defection, a consideration that affected everything he chose to say or hold back. Not only did he want no enemies in the American Cosa Nostra, he *liked* the organization. "The Americans don't know the phenomenon as it is among us," he explained. "Their Mafia is made up of people who follow their fathers' tradition without using it for inhuman crimes. . . . In America, Cosa Nostra's activities are true commercial enterprises that shun publicity and strive constantly for silence and discretion."[40]

Consequently, Buscetta presented his questioners with an extraordinary revelation, half of which was missing. "As for drugs, I can say that while I was in the U.S. it was strictly forbidden for the American Cosa Nostra to take part in such activities," he declared. *"Everybody involved in the drug traffic in America was a Man of Honor in the Sicilian Cosa Nostra"* (my italics).

Asked what relations the Sicilians had with American Families, he said they had none. He himself had been instructed to "keep out of U.S. Mafia business" within a week of reaching New York, he testified. "When the old ties were in effect, a Sicilian Man of Honor emigrating to America could enter Cosa Nostra there at once. But when I was in the U.S. . . . I saw that a Man of Honor like me had no such possibility. The only courtesy they showed me was to indicate where I could get a job as a manual laborer, and that applies to anybody in my position. . . . It is absolutely out of the question that a Sicilian Man of Honor could join the American Cosa Nostra."[41]

In that case, the Sicilians had to be running in several tons of heroin a year on their own: breaking the American Mafia's rules and offending its sensibilities, using its premises without its knowledge or consent, amassing billions of dollars in profits and sending it all home. This certainly strained belief, and indeed proved wildly untrue. Buscetta himself specified that the Sicilian Cosa Nostra could not do business on American soil without the Americans' permission. Carlo Gambino in person—the Boss of All Bosses at the time (1965)—had warned him "to commit no crime without their approval." If he did, it would "cause some problems for the Mafia Family here, but for me it could mean my death."[42]

There were no deaths, however. Sicily's Men of Honor were bringing heroin into the United States with the full knowledge and consent of Cosa Nostra's hierarchy in America. "They had the sanction of the American Mafia . . . all the way up to Paul Castellano, the most powerful member of the American Mafia Commission," declared U.S. attorneys at the Pizza Connection trial.[43] And it was an exclusive concession. "We've got the license to bring it in; nobody else has it," said Gaetano Badalamenti, directing the Sicilians' Pizza Connection network, in a tapped phone call from Rio de Janeiro to the boondocks of Oregon, Illinois.[44]

By the time the Pizza Connection was broken in 1984, the authorities had finally figured out what had happened at the Grand Hotel des Palmes in 1957. "Everybody involved was a narcotics track star," said Assistant U.S. Attorney Louis Freeh, who led the government's team at the Pizza trial. "Buscetta claims that they met in Palermo to set up the Commission; but they really met to set up the Sicilian Mafia's heroin franchise for the United States."[45]

5

Exodus from Palermo

vents after World War II unfolded as if in some satanic plot. Everything seemed to be pushing the Sicilian Mafia toward its maleficent destiny: the distractions and indulgences of the Allied Military Government; Lucky Luciano's deportation to Italy; the accommodating posture of Italy's postwar politicians and a suddenly inquisitorial U.S. Congress; the conclave at the Grand Hotel Des Palmes. Only the final touch was lacking—a primal upheaval that would scatter Sicily's Mafiosi to the ends of the earth—and that came next.

A preternatural calm followed the Palermo summit in 1957. After Buscetta and Cichiteddu Greco took Lucky Luciano's advice and formed a Commission, the Cupola, Greco himself became president, as was only right.

The Grecos were royalty in Mafia circles. Denizens of Ciaculli, a verdant strip of coast on the outskirts of Palermo, their Men of Honor went back several generations, each worthy of the last. In 1921, a Greco who had suffered a *sgarro* (a personal affront) killed two shepherds along with their whole flock of sheep. In 1929, a Greco fired twenty bullets into an enemy's great casks of wine and then sat down amid the foaming splinters to smoke his pipe. In 1939, a Greco set fire to the home of a newlywed couple on their wedding night. In 1947, a Greco avenged his murdered son by annihilating an entire family of ten.

Cichiteddu Greco was therefore a natural choice to head the Mafia's first formal government. A small and birdlike don of imperious will and infinite rapacity, he was "feared and revered" by all in his purview, noted a judge who kept trying in vain to send him to jail.[1]

The Cupola consisted of twelve *capi-mandamento,* each speaking for three Palermo Families. Several other provincial commissions were formed, notably in the major drug-smuggling regions around Trapani and Agrigento, but the one in Palermo ran the show. Most of its twelve original members were loyal followers of Greco's, including his underboss, Calcedonio Di Pisa, and Gaetano Badalamenti. A brash younger set was represented by Buscetta's Family *capo,* Salvatore La Barbera.

Buscetta himself preferred to stay out: "I loved life too much, and they did whatever I told them to do anyway," he explained later to the DEA in New York. Nevertheless, he devoted himself "exclusively to Mafia business" for the next six years.[2]

In the course of these years, Palermo enjoyed a brief interlude of peace. Killings over territorial disputes, the produce markets, the *pizzu,* the building trades, tapered off. "The Cupola worked so well that I cannot recall any Man of Honor being killed between 1957 and early 1963," Buscetta said.

During the same years, the wholesale price of heroin nearly doubled in New York—from $12,000 to $22,000 a kilo. Sicily's Men of Honor, selling it there for four or five times what it cost them in Marseilles, were getting their first heady taste of the profits to come. By 1963, Sicily was already the world's biggest staging area for drugs.[3]

Not that the entire Sicilian Mafia was jumping into the heroin business. Many were not told of the secret covenant agreed upon at the Hotel des Palmes. Those who were in on it were not eager to spread the wealth around. A number of fastidious dons would have disliked the idea of dealing in drugs anyway.

Palermo pulsed with opportunity in the late 1950s. Mountains of money could be made in ways less revolting than heroin, and less likely to draw police attention. As Lucky Luciano once said—or said that he had said—why ruin everything else by playing around with junk?

Italy's Guardia di Finanza was just becoming aware of the heroin traffic in 1957. Its agents knew nothing of the newly created Cupola, but they began to keep a close watch on the Cupola's president and most of its members during the very year it was formed. Cichiteddu Greco and his aides were high on the list of some sixty Mafiosi suspected of running the first big drug ring ever detected in Sicily. Agents followed them, tapped their phones, and tried, largely in vain, to keep track of their excursions abroad. These Mafiosi traveled continuously, everywhere, with disconcerting ease. One of the Ciaculli Grecos owned three different passports, out of a batch of twenty-five stolen from Palermo's Questura (police headquarters) in 1957; alternately cleanshaven, mustached, and bearded, he used them for trips to Britain, France, Spain, and Tangiers.[4]

Cichiteddu Greco had a passport in his own name, as many others did. Getting a letter of recommendation as "a person of good moral, civic, and political conduct" was no trouble for a Man of Honor in 1957 (or 1967, or 1977). A close colleague of Buscetta's got his Italian passport renewed after Mexico had actually shipped him home for dealing in drugs in 1959. His reissued passport was valid not just for Mexico but for the United States, Canada, Argentina, Cuba, Cyprus, Lebanon, Libya, and Japan.[5] (Later, he was granted a gun permit on the grounds that "his work required him to travel often with large sums of money.")

Buscetta himself managed to retrieve the passport taken from him after his arrest for smuggling tobacco in 1957 by presenting a note to the Questura:

Dear Dr. Jacovacci:
    I heartily entreat you to renew the passport of Signor Tommaso Buscetta, a person who is of very great interest to me. Confident of your personal concern, I thank and cordially salute you.[6]

The note was signed by Francesco Barbaccia, a Sicilian "friend of the friends" in Parliament.

These were still early days. The American heroin market was very small: perhaps fewer than fifty thousand addicts in all. Major traffickers like Vito Genovese and Carmine Galante, both behind bars and out of business by 1958, had been enthusiastic but haphazard. They had simply bought the heroin where they found it, to meet existing demand.

The Sicilian Mafia was going to *create* demand. Once its network was in place, the American addict population would increase to five hundred thousand.[7] Not all, but a good part, of the increase would prove to be the Mafia's doing.

Here again, Lucky Luciano set his young Sicilian protégés on their way. The important thing was to organize supply, he observed, after sending Vito Genovese to jail and taking over his drug network in Europe.[8] "All them guys like Vito found it so easy to buy junk that they never gave a thought to organizin' anything but the sales; they always figured the suppliers couldn't live without 'em," he said. "That's the first lesson I was gonna teach 'em—that without the supply they could have all the demand in the world and it wouldn't do 'em no fuckin' good." Luciano himself intended to "tie up the junk supply in Europe. . . . If they wanted to make a buy, they was gonna have to come to me." He sent agents scouting around France, Germany, Lebanon, Turkey. The message—for poppy growers, small boat owners, smugglers, and refiners—was that "Charlie Lucky wanted to organize." He offered them "the same protection and bargaining strength as those who created the demand."

The response was gratifying. "Half my life, the name Charlie Lucky was supposed to carry a lotta weight, but I never gave it much thought. This time, the guys kept reportin' back that the minute my name was mentioned, them guys in Turkey and Italy and Egypt and Germany practically scraped the ground."[9]

All the same, tying up the supply was not easy, even for Charlie Lucky. Unlike cocaine, whose raw material is grown only in a small mountainous patch of South America, the opium poppy needed for heroin grows all over the place: Burma, Laos, Thailand, Afghanistan, Pakistan, Turkey, Bulgaria, Lebanon, Mexico. Until halfway through the 1970s, furthermore, four-fifths of the heroin refining was done by the Corsicans in Marseilles. It would take many years for the Sicilians to establish their dominion.

But since negotiating their heroin franchise in 1957, they had a captive market in the United States. The advantage was enormous; it made them the Corsicans' most privileged customers. By the time Lucky Luciano died in 1962, Sicilian Mafiosi were head over heels in the junk business. They had cut out all middlemen, dealing directly with the Corsicans' Pascal Molinelli. They acquired their own fleet; a cousin of Cichiteddu Greco's by the same name—Salvatore Greco, "the Engineer"—had an especially fast ship plying the Mediterranean under a Honduran flag. They invented radio silence at sea, among dozens of superbly sophisticated ways to elude the police.[10] The heroin reaching Sicily from Marseilles was moving regularly to Havana, Tampa, St. Louis, Kansas City, and New York, in false-bottomed trunks, cans of sardines, wheels of *caciocavallo* cheese, and barrels of olive oil, long before the Sicilians themselves were in place at the other end to receive it.

Despite Apalachin, at least three of New York's five Families went right on dealing heroin until 1963, the year the McClellan Committee investigation frightened them off for a while. Sicilian shipments were going to a number of American fathers in the food-importing business, from Joe Bonanno down. Joe Profaci, an old sidekick of Lucky Luciano's, ran the Mamma Mia Import Company in New York, mostly importing oranges from Sicily. Half of the oranges were made of wax and stuffed with 110 grams of heroin each, when Italy's Guardia di Finanza came across them in 1959. A case of these "pregnant" oranges was worth $1 million in New York.[11]

In Palermo, the first serious symptoms of heroin fever were setting in by the late fifties. Though the Mafia's code decreed death for trafficking in drugs, the offense was now common and the punishment rare. (Nobody was punished, in fact.) Both the old and new Mafias were involved, but the old was by far the more egregious offender. Indeed, the president of the Cupola was among the worst. There was no uproar in the ranks over the fact that Cichiteddu Greco was breaking what purported to be one of the Mafia's sternest moral laws. Morality was the least of their worries where heroin was concerned. The problem was rampant greed.

Men of Honor were lying to, cheating on, and stealing from one another to lay hands on this lucrative commodity. "Thieving from a thief who is more of a thief than a thief is not thieving," a Mafia saying goes. Soon they were killing in earnest for primacy in the heroin business. One side in this struggle was headed by the Grecos of Ciaculli, the reigning establishment. They were the old boys, who had the indispensable connections in New York. Most of the *mammasantissima* were aligned with them. Luciano Leggio, making deep inroads in Palermo, had made it a point to become a particular friend of Cichiteddu's; Buscetta, once part of the younger troops, was now the Little Bird's inseparable companion.

The other side was led by Angelo and Salvatore La Barbera and their new New Mafia. Their methods were extremely crude. They had beaten out the Grecos in the building trades, using dynamite, arson, Berettas, and machine guns. Now they were muscling in on the heroin trade.

The two factions managed to work together until the autumn of 1962, when avarice got the better of Cichiteddu Greco's underboss, Calcedonio Di Pisa. Formidable in his own right, and a member of the Cupola, Di Pisa was not just a confirmed trafficker but a blown one: he had already been tricked into making a two-kilo heroin buy from a U.S.

narcotics agent. In consequence, American and Italian agents were watching him when he undertook to send a large heroin shipment to New York on behalf of both Mafia factions. Despite the surveillance, he was not caught. Unwisely, however, he kept a sizable portion of the proceeds for himself.[12]

The Greco faction voted to spare his life, but the La Barberas killed him anyway, or were thought to have done so. (They had been set up, it turned out.)[13] A heated confrontation ended in excommunication for the La Barberas' central Palermo *cosca*. "Who do you think you are?" the insolent Salvatore La Barbera demanded of the Cupola's president, Cichiteddu Greco. "Who am I? I am your GOD!" Greco shouted, and slapped his face.[14]

There followed the worst shooting war in memory. The Grecos killed Salvatore La Barbera, his brother Angelo killed in return, the Grecos shot but failed to kill Angelo, and so on without cease until the two sides had reached a murder a day by June 1963. Then came an incredible accident that scattered members of the Sicilian Mafia to the four winds, carrying the plague of heroin with them.

A bomb was planted in the heart of Ciaculli, a Mafia demesne where the streets have no names and the houses no numbers, and ranking bosses live with killer guard-dogs behind steel gates and ten-foot walls. Although the bomb's final destination has never been established in a court of law, almost any of Ciaculli's residents might have been the target: Leggio for one (he was sheltering in a secret compartment above a ceiling panel in an elegant Ciaculli villa). But the likeliest objective was Cichiteddu Greco.

The bomb was packed with two hundred pounds of dynamite and tucked into the trunk of a stolen Alfa Romeo. A flat tire had sent the car's occupants into headlong flight, and an anonymous caller had asked the Carabinieri to tow it away. Seven officers rushed to the scene, and saw a dummy liquid gas bomb with a spent fuse, plainly visible on the back seat. One of them opened the trunk. A tremendous explosion sent flames fifty feet into the air and altogether destroyed a nearby villa. In the crater where the car had stood was all that remained of the seven men: a pistol, a finger with a wedding ring, and an officer's beret.

Accustomed to a passive public and a tactfuly dormant state, the bosses of Palermo were stunned by what followed. Italy rebelled. "Get everybody with a criminal record and throw them into jail, on my orders," thundered the regional army commander for Sicily, General Aldo De Marco. "Torture them and see what they let out. Or shoot them on sight. I'll go to prison. But we can't, we can't go on like this."[15]

Year after year of funerals and mourning, grief, fright, shame, dishonor, trickery, exploitation, and suffocating silence were too much at last for ordinary Sicilians. Even Rome appeared to have had enough.

Men who had ordered death routinely for a good two decades in Sicily were flaunting their lawlessness like a pennant. Few had so much as set foot in a courtroom. Nearly all could cause incriminating evidence to vanish at will. Most had permits for the guns they carried openly on the streets, in bars and restaurants, and in the corridors of the Regional Sicilian Assembly. Their arrogance had grown immeasurably since Mussolini claimed to have wiped them out nearly half a century before. Indeed, the Mafia's advance since then had been inexorable, unarrestable. For all those who had succumbed to its insidious powers of intimidation and corruption—businessmen, bankers, editors, magistrates, senators, even cabinet ministers—Italy's young republic was itself advancing too rapidly to tolerate such a state of affairs. Or so it seemed.

Certainly the law came down hard. Ten thousand police and *carabinieri* spread out through Palermo and its suburbs with helicopters and parachute squads, armored cars and man-hunting dogs. Whole blocks were cordoned off in the deep night and plunged into bright light. Platoons armed with grenades and machine guns searched from house to house, from cellar to roof.

Weapons of every size and make were confiscated: revolvers, sawed-off double-barreled shotguns, hand grenades, plastic explosives, knives, bayonets, machine guns, millions of cartridges. In all, 1,903 arrests were made. A single police raid in Palermo yielded 731 court orders for special surveillance. A dozen Mafia chiefs of the highest rank—*mammasantissima* all—were sent into guarded exile on the Italian mainland or some remote and inhospitable island.[16] An inflexible Sicilian judge named Cesare Terranova opened an investigation that would eventually bring 114 elite Mafia leaders to trial.

Moreover, Parliament was stirring. The first Anti-Mafia Commission in the Italian Senate's history had begun and ended a brief existence the previous year without ever meeting. Now, a fresh commission met *within five days* of the Ciaculli disaster, and proposed the republic's first anti-Mafia law, which was approved barely six weeks later.

That summer—1963—a committee of six Mafia wise men gathered to reflect on the crisis. Cichiteddu Greco and Leggio were among them. Wisdom in their circles meant bowing like reeds in the wind until the storm passed. "By common agreement, these six decided to suspend all criminal activity that might confirm the perils of organized crime," wrote Judge Terranova.[17] Actually, they decided to dissolve the Cu-pola—in effect, to disband, the only known occasion when the Mafia ever did so.[18]

Nearly every Mafioso known to the police and still at large dropped out of sight. Leggio and some of his followers retreated to Corleone. Other Mafiosi took to ground farther away on the Italian mainland, but for many more that was not far enough. They did what Sicilian Men of Honor have always done in troubled times. Starting in the autumn of 1963, they fanned out into an unwary world.

The position of the planets had never been so favorable. Sicily's Mafiosi had privileged access to the world's biggest heroin suppliers, a lock on the world's biggest potential market, and now, the men to organize the traffic at strategic points around the globe. The ablest of them settled in Montreal, Caracas, São Paolo, Mexico City, and New York; and the drugging of America, which had been going on for six years, now began in earnest.

Starting Up:
North America

ommaso Buscetta, sharing pride of place with Luciano Leggio as Italy's most wanted fugitive, slipped out of Italy in 1963 and made his leisurely way to New York. Traveling with a new girlfriend, soon to be his bigamous second wife, he stopped off in Switzerland, West Germany, Great Britain, Paraguay, Mexico, and Canada. When he finally entered the United States in 1965, he was Manuel Lopez Cardena, with a nearly impeccable Mexican passport.

Settling down in Brooklyn, Buscetta commanded the respect due the most powerful Sicilian don in New York—Don Masino, the Man of Honor who had consorted with Lucky Luciano and set up the Mafia's Commission in Palermo, the "gray eminence" behind it, in his words.

Carlo Gambino, Boss of All Bosses in America, sent for Buscetta within ten days of his arrival. He was welcome, Gambino said, but he mustn't operate on the Americans' territory without permission, a rule Buscetta claims to have "followed to the letter." Gambino threw a banquet in Buscetta's honor, as befits visiting royalty, and the two became close friends. "I'd go to his house, he'd come to my house, we'd go to restaurants. . . . We'd have lobster, spaghetti *con vongole,* wine, champagne," Buscetta recalls. "The FBI was watching his front door, but I'd go through another house in another street, and get in through a secret passage. . . . We were like father and son."[1]

One wonders what they had to say to each other in all their evenings together, the virile, full-blooded Buscetta in his prime and Gambino, the bloodless, shrunken little man of sixty-five—"a servile, cringing, fawning" hypocrite, in Joe Bonanno's view. Whatever they talked about, it wasn't business, as Buscetta tells it. Asked what the head of America's Cosa Nostra did for a living, he answered long afterward: "I wouldn't know what Carlo did: legitimate activities, but I don't know which ones."[2] (Carlo Gambino was "in gambling, shylocking, labor racketeering, vending machines, extortion, and criminal receiving," reported the McClellan Committee in 1963. He had been arrested sixteen times and had six convictions.)[3]

Paolo Gambino, Carlo's younger brother, was another close crony. Buscetta, who had played cards with Paolo every weekend when they were neighbors in Palermo, took to doing so again. "Paolo was into everything—meat markets, gambling, the numbers, everything," he conceded, failing to mention that the younger Gambino was also running a huge Sicilian alien-smuggling ring in New York.[4]

Starting just around the time Buscetta arrived in New York, America was "flooded with Sicilians departing Italy."[5] Mingling with honest immigrants, several thousand made Men of Honor and *picciotti* were slipping over the borders and spreading out across the country like KGB moles. Among the many flocking to Brooklyn were some of Buscetta's best friends, most of whom gathered in two Mafia enclaves where no New York cop was likely to winkle them out.

Knickerbocker Avenue, in the Bushwick section of Brooklyn, was the Bonanno Family's territory. This long street of unrelieved squalor is mostly Hispanic now. A Chinese fast-food take-out place occupies the premises of Joe and Mary's, where Carmine Galante was gunned down in 1979 while lighting up a cigar after lunch. Here and there, a fading sign or grimy plate-glass window recalls the past: Vito's Pizzeria, La Bella Palermo, Cafe Sport, Cafe Viale. But in the 1960s, the avenue was a Sicilianate oasis in an alien desert. The dialect spoken there, the fragrant scent of cannoli issuing from pastry shops, the family bonds and rituals, the intricate code of behavior, had been transported intact to this sanctuary four thousand miles from home.

Knickerbocker Avenue was where a fellow fugitive of Buscetta's, a certain Salvatore Catalano, anonymous and unobtrusive, opened a little newspaper-souvenir shop in 1966. It was just opposite the Cafe Viale, a hangout for the Bonanno Family's nascent "Sicilian faction," which Catalano headed.

Buscetta himself was installed in the Gambino Family's enclave, around 18th Avenue in Bensonhurst. Here too was a solid piece of the Old Country. Threaded among the caterers for weddings and saints' days, the marbled funeral parlors, the *pizzicherie* (delicatessens) with their ropes of sausage and wheels of *parmigiano,* and the *macellerie* (butcher shops) displaying miraculously cheap (hijacked) cuts of veal were the Sicilian Mafia's other branch offices in Brooklyn. They were unpretentious cafés with thick walls and tacky formica tables: the Valentino, the Mille Luci.

The Cafe Valentino belonged to John, Rosario, and Giuseppe Gambino, a trio of interesting provenance. Today they are known as the Cherry Hill Gambinos, for their country seat in the New Jersey town of that name. Though Carlo Gambino was their uncle, they did not owe him allegiance. They were *Sicilian* Mafiosi, made men from Palermo whose father had brought his family to New York in 1964.[6] They could not have been made in the American Cosa Nostra, whose books had been closed almost uninterruptedly since 1931.[7] In any case, they would not have been free to join; they were accountable solely to their own *cosca* at home for life.

The Cherry Hill Gambinos were the pivot of Sicilian Mafia operations in the United States. Nearly all the exiles who would dominate the heroin consortium over the next fifteen years were clustered around them. The future heroin king of Palermo—Salvatore Inzerillo, who would make them billionaires—was their inseparable companion.

Buscetta gravitated naturally toward their inner circle.[8] It was Rosario Gambino who took in Buscetta's estranged first wife and daughter after he had them smuggled into the country.[9] Buscetta's older sons, Benedetto and Antonio, were put to work in a New Jersey pizzeria owned by the three Gambino brothers. The Gambinos' ace heroin courier, Emmanuele Adamita, set up Buscetta's letter drop in Manhattan. (The mailing address was 205 Allan Street, where an uncle of Emmanuele's lived.)[10]

But it was another member of the inner circle who had most to do with Buscetta in the United States. He was an old-time Sicilian associate of Lucky Luciano's by the name of Antonino Napoli.[11] This was the same Napoli who, with his brothers Vincenzo and Gaetano, became the obsession and affliction of Detective Douglas Le Vien in New York ten years later.

Interred among Detective Le Vien's reports on the Napoli case, forgotten or never read, were documents foretelling two decades of anguish for millions of people—the beginnings of the Sicilian Mafia's silent invasion of America.

o⊂⊃o

In 1966, the U.S. Bureau of Narcotics and Dangerous Drugs (BNDD) opened a confidential correspondence with Italian authorities concerning an "aggravated criminal conspiracy to smuggle narcotics in and out of Italy." The bureau believed that "a new group of Mafia traffickers was emerging," led by Tommaso Buscetta, and requested information about a dozen suspected accomplices, including Antonino Napoli. The Guardia di Finanza replied:

We advise that . . . Antonino Napoli [is] involved in the trafficking of narcotics between Italy and the United States. The illicit activity is disguised by regular exports to the U.S. of wigs for women. The wig factory, which is owned by Antonino Napoli, is located at Barcellona (Messina-Sicily), and is called Industria Siciliana Parruche Ltd. . . . Vincenzo Napoli, residing in Brooklyn, N.Y., is a partner in the enterprise.[12]

The wig factory in Sicily was founded on September 13, 1963, scarcely three months after the Ciaculli bomb disaster. A month later, the Lisa Wigs and Wiglets Company opened for business at 11 West 42nd Street in New York. Its imports, thought to contain heroin hidden in human hair, came mostly from the Sicilian factory. Antonino Napoli was its president, his brothers Vincenzo and Gaetano respectively its vice-president and treasurer.

The BNDD had too few agents for too many cases to keep track of Antonino Napoli, or any Napoli, for that matter, and so the trail petered out. But Lisa Wigs and Wiglets thrived as long as Antonino Napoli and Buscetta were in the United States. The company was a million-dollar-a-year business; human hair from Sicily was apparently in abundant supply. Among its eight employees were Buscetta's first wife and daughter, hired as soon as they got to New York.[13]

Buscetta himself had gone straight onto Antonino Napoli's payroll upon his arrival. Every Sicilian alien had to be seen to have a job, whether he needed one or not. For the record, Buscetta became an apprentice pizza maker at La Dolce Vita in Brooklyn,[14] one of several pizza parlors owned by Napoli. Within a year, Buscetta was his partner in at least three: the Pizza Den in Brooklyn, Pizza Masters in Jamaica, and Pizza City on 42nd Street and 8th Avenue in Manhattan.[15]

Pizza City was a collection depot for gambling and loan-shark money, mainly from the Napoli brothers' own gambling clubs. Enzo ran a smart club on the East Side, the Murray Hill Town House, where he charged a staggering 5 percent weekly vig on loans. Antonino ran another in Brooklyn where the Sicilian cheese king, Joseph Falcone, was said to have dropped half a million dollars one night. (According to an FBI informant, Falcone reportedly was forced to burn down his cheese factory in Alburg, Vermont, for the insurance money to square the debt.)[16]

All three of the pizzerias owned by Buscetta and the Napolis were infested with Sicilian heroin traffickers. Those known to the police at all were on the books as mere low-grade hoods, picked up (and regularly released) for assault, gambling, extortion, or running porno films or massage parlors. Nevertheless, their names kept cropping up in Narcotics Bureau files, including those on the Napoli brothers and Buscetta.[17]

Another name that kept cropping up was that of Filippo Casamento, a native of Palermo who had stowed away on a passenger liner in Genoa and simply walked off the ship in Philadelphia. "Tizio" to his friends, he looked like anybody's twinkly blue-eyed uncle. He was an "affable, outgoing, joking, lovable" shopkeeper, according to his lawyer. In February 1968, Casamento opened a modest store on Avenue U in Brooklyn called the Eagle Cheese Company, with shop windows that displayed inviting piles of mozzarella and provolone. Heroin and cocaine entered and left at the back. Within a year, he was handling narcotics by the ton.

The list of Casamento's associates read like a Sicilian Mafioso's family album. All the low-grade hoods identified with the Cherry Hill Gambinos, the Napolis, and Buscetta were in federal agency files on Casamento as well. All three Napoli brothers were listed as Casamento's "close associates." Antonino himself was down as Casamento's partner in Eagle Cheese. Buscetta was frequently sighted at the store, and actually worked there for a while.[18]

Regally indifferent to legal niceties, the whole crowd ran around loose in New York for years. Information from Italy, where they were wanted for more parlous crimes, either did not reach America or failed to register. Buscetta himself seemed invisible to the authorities, notorious though he was. The Italians had been signaling his presence somewhere in Brooklyn since he arrived, to no effect. The U.S. consulate in Mexico received a message about him in 1967 from the French Côte d'Azur: "An Italian named Tommaso Buscetta is commuting between Mexico and Brooklyn, New York, with drugs. He's a South American, although he is actually a Sicilian from Palermo."[19]

In fact, Buscetta was tied in to the hottest narcotics crowd in Mexico City. A fellow Palermitano who had settled there, Giuseppe "Pino" Catania, was his connection. The two had been *compari* since Buscetta first stopped off on his way to New York from Sicily. Catania was the godfather of a daughter born to Buscetta in Mexico, his trusted friend, accomplice, and confidant.

They had traveled from Mexico City to Canada together, linking up with the Mafia's emerging Sicilian faction there in 1964.[20] Moving on to New York with Buscetta, Pino Catania had made another indispensable link, with the new Sicilian faction in Brooklyn, after which he became a fixture of the Sicilian Mafia's expanding heroin routes to the United States via Mexico and Canada. "Call Pino Catania in Mexico. Tell him to start a new company that needs sardines, tomatoes and pasta. . . . We'll send him a hundred kilos of macaroni every month," ordered the unobtrusive Salvatore Catalano of Knickerbocker Avenue, on the phone from Milan in 1970.[21]

It was Pino Catania who presented Buscetta to the overlord of Mexico's heroin and cocaine trade, Jorge Asaf y Bala, while they were in Mexico. Their first deal was for twenty-five kilos of heroin, shipped to Brooklyn in March 1969. But the heroin was of poor quality, and Buscetta refused to pay up. (He sent it on to the Mafia in Montreal for whatever it might bring.)

Next came a whopping eighty-nine kilos, in February 1970; and here the story grew more tangled. Buscetta flew into Mexico City from Madrid, on a Canadian passport issued to "Adalberto Barbieri" (in which he had made himself six years younger). He had procured the heroin from Corsican suppliers in Marseilles, and shipped it airfreight to Mexico City. He wanted Asaf y Bala's couriers to deliver it to Brooklyn, which they did—but not to Buscetta. The shipment went to a certain Carlo Zippo, who sold it to the Eagle Cheese Company.[22]

Carlo Zippo was just "a refined and *simpatico*" Neapolitan who had befriended Buscetta's family, Buscetta said later. Actually, the two made a terrific team. In another year or so, they would be bringing in about a third of the heroin reaching the streets of New York.

○⊂⊃○

Shortly after the eighty-nine-kilo deal—in June 1970—Buscetta suspended operations in America for a while. There were big decisions to be made in Palermo, and he was needed there. "It's necessary to know who I am," he explained to Enzo Biagi.

I'm a normal person, but Mother Nature gave me charisma; I have something extra.

When I'd go to a *fèsta,* or a wedding, or a baptism, all the women would receive the men with affection and respect, and as soon as I came in, they'd close up like clams. Nobody wanted to say hello first. . . . I enter a restaurant, maybe a hundred people are there, and ninety look at me. . . .

I'm a very authoritative figure in Cosa Nostra. They come looking for me when there are difficult questions to settle, because if I pronounce an opinion, it's the right one, and they'll be forced to admit "Tommaso said this."[23]

Buscetta had already made one of these decisions from New York in 1969, thereby shattering the longest peace Palermo had known.

The kill rate had hovered around zero in the city after the Ciaculli bomb disaster of 1963. Then, in 1969, the Mafia inflicted the most inglorious defeat ever suffered by the Italian judiciary. A succession of trials, mounted after the Ciaculli crackdown, ended in an incredible succession of acquittals. Hundreds of the island's feistiest Men of Honor were released from jail, and promptly began to even old scores.

The killings were not too noticeable until a massacre in grand style hit the headlines. On a mid-December evening in 1969, six Mafiosi wearing police uniforms burst into a construction office on Via Lazio, a busy shopping street in Palermo. Even as they shouted "Police! Open up!" their machine guns were firing. In three minutes, they left three men dead and two badly wounded, carrying off a dying man of their own. Another of their men had his head blown away before he reached their car.

Their target was a devious boss on the Mafia's old Cupola named Michele Cavatoio. He too had barely gotten out of prison, and he had much to answer for—specifically the shooting war between Mafia factions in 1963. The Grecos of Ciaculli had blamed the outbreak on the insolent La Barbera brothers for murdering Cichiteddu's lieutenant, Calcedonio Di Pisa. In fact, Michele Cavatoio had murdered Di Pisa, framed the La Barberas, and taken over their territory.[24]

"We decided he had to die: as we walked down the street, in America," Buscetta told his biographer, ". . . I and a certain Antonino, who came to find me in a pizzeria. I took care of it, through someone going to Palermo. . . . 'Tell them it would be a good thing if Cavatoio were killed in the utmost secrecy,' I said. And in the utmost secrecy, it was provided for."[25]

If this was Buscetta's idea of a secret, it was nobody else's. The massacre in Via Lazio caused a furor in Italy, brought out the police in force once again, and ended the *pax Mafiosa*. By the summer of 1970, Men of Honor were luxuriating in their renewed freedom to kill, and Buscetta had to come back to restore the peace.

He left New York for Italy in early June, accompanied by Cichiteddu Greco, who was living in Caracas. In Rome, they met secretly with two other Mafia power brokers to revive the Cupola, dormant for seven years. One of the men was Gaetano Badalamenti, rough and untutored but "revered as a god on earth" in their circles, according to Buscetta. The other was Stefano Bontate, son of a renowned old Mafia don. Young, rich, personable, intelligent, and judicious by Mafia standards, Bontate was emerging as the Sicilian Mafia's acknowledged leader. He was perhaps the only Man of Honor who had Buscetta's honest admiration.[26]

The four of them agreed that the new Commission would have to include Luciano Leggio. The boss of Corleone had become an uncontainable force in Palermo while others waited out the crisis abroad. In any case, they weren't *against* him—he was godfather of Badalamenti's youngest child, and Greco was an old friend—and he was indispensable to imposing order.[27]

So in June 1970, Buscetta and his allies brought the man who would destroy them into their innermost councils. Luciano Leggio got a foot in the door of the Mafia's Cupola for the first time. A Commission of ten was formed, ruled by a triumvirate: Stefano Bontate, Gaetano Badalamenti, and Leggio's surrogate, Salvatore Riina, known as "the Beast." It would last just long enough for Leggio to get more control over the next Commission.

Before returning to New York, Buscetta was nearly captured in a curious episode. A routine police patrol stopped his Alfa Romeo near the northern Italian border. With him in the car were Greco, Badalamenti, another member of the new Cupola, and a chronic drug trafficker—"a tireless fabrics salesman," according to Buscetta—who would be in charge of all the heroin refineries in Sicily a few years later.[28] Buscetta displayed his Canadian passport as Adalberto Barbieri and Greco presented a Venezuelan passport as Renato Martino Caruso. The police took their names and waved them on.[29] Afterward, the Carabinieri placed Buscetta in Zurich, a day's drive from the Italian border, around the same date. He was seen at the hotel where "the most important Mafia Bosses in the world were meeting to divide up zones for the drug trade over the incoming decade," the Carabinieri reported.[30]

Buscetta was scarcely back in New York when his luck ran out. Driving across the Brooklyn Bridge in a white Thunderbird one day in August, he was stopped by New York state trooper Mike Minto. "He gave me some phony ID and I told him, 'Mr. Buscetta, don't fuck with me,' and he said, 'Okay, I'm Buscetta.' It was so easy," recalls Minto.[31]

Minto, a large, paunchy cop who knew his business, was detailed to a special unit keeping an eye on what he called the "Mob biggies." His biggy of the moment was Carlo Zippo, known to be planning a two-hundred-kilo heroin shipment to New York. (It was supposed to arrive from Brazil in wooden "Christ of the Andes" statuettes.)[32] Minto had caught up with Buscetta while keeping Zippo's safe house in Rosedale, Queens, under heavy surveillance. When Buscetta came out the door that August day with his twenty-two-year-old son Benedetto, one of the cops surrounding the place had an old Interpol flier with Buscetta's picture. Minto happened to know a little about him; the Narcotics Bureau was just getting on Buscetta's trail. So he followed the white Thunderbird—Zippo's, it turned out—to the Hotel Woodstock in mid-Manhattan, where Zippo was waiting. After a long coffee with Zippo, Buscetta was driving back to Brooklyn when Minto arrested him.

The Interpol flier, deplorably out of date, did not tell Minto what a formidable figure he had collared. The whole machinery of law enforcement was out of date, all over the globe, where the subterranean world of his captive was concerned.

The police had been watching Carlo Zippo for a solid year. They had observed nearly all of Buscetta's in-group making contact: obscure Sicilian aliens drifting back and forth to Montreal and Mexico City, dodging in and out of hotel rooms and parking lots, swapping cars. (Buscetta used Zippo's Thunderbird; Zippo used Antonino Napoli's rented gold Cadillac.) In October 1970, the U.S. narcotics agent running the investigation wrote of a "multi-facet, highly organized and diversified smuggling conglomerate . . . that utilizes front companies and false travel documents, furnishes total identities, and extends to and from Italy, France, Canada, Brazil, Argentina, Mexico and the United States." He called it "the Carlo Zippo organization."[33]

Such a conglomerate did exist, but it was the Sicilians', not Zippo's.

o⊖o

Buscetta's arrest, in August 1970, caused a flurry in his circles. Carlo Zippo disappeared for a while; so did the co-owner of Eagle

Cheese, Filippo Casamento's brother Franco. All things considered, though, Buscetta got out of his scrape very well.

The New York courts did not know that an Italian court had convicted Buscetta *in absentia* in 1968 for criminal conspiracy and multiple murder.[34] The Italians, inexplicably, did not ask for his extradition. The BNDD knew he was trafficking in drugs, but lacked the proof that would stand up in a courtroom. The United States had nothing on him except illegal entry, by means of his nearly impeccable Mexican passport.

Buscetta was ordered to leave the country, so in the spring of 1971, he moved to Brazil, taking along his oldest son Benedetto and Carlo Zippo but leaving both wives behind. Here again, the ease of their travel was disconcerting. These were two of the most renowned and gifted drug traffickers on the international scene. Their photographs and fingerprints were in Interpol's files, circulated in some 150 countries. Yet they drove undisturbed down through the United States to almost the bottom of the Western Hemisphere: from New York to Mexico, Guatemala, Honduras, Nicaragua, and Panama, on through Colombia, Peru, and Ascension, Paraguay—where Buscetta bought himself citizenship and a new passport as Thomas Roberto Felice.

On the way, they stopped by to see Pino Catania in Mexico City. It must have been an exhilarating encounter, judging from Catania's testimony later. "Buscetta gave me $10,000 as a bond of friendship, and told me they could send merchandise if we could find buyers in Mexico City," he declared. "I spoke to Asaf y Bala, and he said he had a good client who could take any amount of heroin. I gave Buscetta and Zippo our agreement and told them I had a good contact at the airport to smuggle the stuff in."[35]

A good client in Mexico was not the half of it. Buscetta and Zippo were about to play a major part in igniting the great heroin epidemic of the early 1970s, the first explosion of heroin addiction in the United States.[36]

Buscetta and Zippo were in a holiday mood when they rolled into Rio. Few cities are more seductive. The long Copacabana strip, all white sand, palm trees, and sapphire sea, is an invitation to indolence and romance. Buscetta was in town for barely two weeks when he met a gorgeous blonde on the beach and really fell in love.

Maria Cristina Almeida de Guimaraes, twenty years his junior, was slender and elegant, intelligent, educated, rich, and well connected. Her father, Homero Guimaraes, was a prominent lawyer moving in an influential set; Brazil's former right-wing president, Joao Goulart, was among his intimates. Buscetta was taken into the family. Maria Cristina became his cherished companion and, eventually, his third and lasting wife. Buscetta moved out of the apartment he had taken with Zippo, and set up house with Cristina: a seafront apartment on the Copacabana strip, a weekend home on the coast at Ilhabela, and a huge *fazenda* 250 miles south of São Paulo. Cristina's father went into the insurance business with him in São Paulo, Buscetta says. They went into the drug business together as well, according to the Brazilian police.

The whole Guimaraes family was believed to be dealing in narcotics, reported the FBI from Brazil in 1972: Homero, Sr.; his sons Nadar and Homero, Jr.; and Maria Cristina herself.[37] All were arrested with Buscetta that year, as Cristina and her father would be again a decade later. (Homero, Jr., vanished in the meanwhile, a victim of what the Mafia calls "white death.")

o⊂⊃o

Brazil was not just another place to hide for men like Buscetta. Italian immigrants had settled there in the millions—four million in the city of São Paulo alone. Every wave of Mafia migration from Sicily inserted another Mafia wedge into this hardworking and prosperous émigré population. In consequence, Brazil was one of two nations in South America with a regular chartered branch of Sicily's Cosa Nostra; Venezuela, next door, was the other. Both were recognized by America's Cosa Nostra but accountable solely to Palermo—we have Buscetta's word for it.[38] (Doubtless there were more branches of this kind, but we have nobody's word for them.)

Brazil was also the country chosen by the Corsican Union—and Buscetta too, some say—as a new South American base for transshipping drugs to the United States. While customary transatlantic routes to New York were closely watched in the early 1970s, the BNDD had only one agent assigned to all of South America. Brazil's vast open territory—unending seacoast, innumerable little islands, virtually inaccessible Amazonian jungle—looked ideal. Consequently, the country became the base for the biggest heroin-smuggling ring ever uncovered anywhere, then or since. When seven of the ring's members confessed after the network was smashed in the autumn of 1972, they revealed a far greater narcotics traffic than the Pizza Connection's a decade later. That ring was bringing some 120 kilos of heroin a year into New York in 1984. The ring in Brazil was preparing to ship 300 kilos a *month* to the United States by 1972,[39] a time when the entire American addict population was consuming only 90 kilos a month. Thus the traffickers in Brazil were not just feeding a habit; they were creating it. By the summer of 1972, when they were caught, America's addict population had jumped to a staggering 720,000—this from under 50,000 less than a decade before.[40]

It is not fashionable to cite such figures. The raging controversy over epidemic drug use today has tended to exonerate the suppliers. They simply provide what people want, the argument goes: without demand, there would be no supply. Yet the evidence shows overwhelmingly that supply creates its own demand.

American soldiers who got hooked on heroin in Vietnam were not users before they got there and had it thrust upon them, deliberately, massively. Their suppliers were at cross-purposes. Communist China wanted to undermine U.S. troops; the CIA wanted to undermine the communist Pathet Lao, by helping the opposing opium-growing hill tribes in Laos. From opposite ends, however, both created a huge demand that had not been present before. Countries lying in the traffickers' path have been victimized also, deliberately and still more massively. India, a major transit point from southwest Asia in the 1980s, had barely a handful of heroin addicts before then and is thought now to have around three-quarters of a million. Thailand, the main passageway from Southeast Asia and a producer in its own right, has about half a million.[41]

Pakistan is an especially instructive case. Though long a big producer of opium, the country had many opium users but practically no registered heroin addicts until the neighboring state of Afghanistan was occupied by Soviet troops. Afghan hill tribes, growing opium in twelve of the nation's twenty-five provinces, are among the world's biggest heroin producers. Unable to export over their western borders after the Russians came, they shifted to routes through Pakistan and to an increasing amount of refining there. The heroin addict population of Pakistan thereupon shot up from nearly zero in 1981 to around a million in 1989.[42] Almost half the heroin passing through the country was used to hook the Pakistanis themselves. Islamabad's *saqui khanas* (heroin dens) would offer two or three free fixes, and that was it. The traffickers were "load shedding": generating enough profit to cover any losses for cargoes spotted at the airport.[43]

Every country with a drug problem knows about the free fix today. It is practically infallible, provided there is a copious supply behind it.

o◯o

The ring broken up in Brazil was run by Corsicans, but they could not get along without the Sicilian Mafia. While the Corsican Union had

Don Giuseppe Genco Russo, *capo di tutti capi* from the late 1950s through the 1960s, led the Sicilian delegation at the Hotel des Palmes in Palermo in 1957, when agreement was reached with the American Cosa Nostra to let the Sicilians run the heroin trade in the United States. The incumbent *capo di tutti capi,* Luciano Leggio, has run his fearsome Corleonesi from his prison cell since 1974 (ANSA).

Birthplace of Luciano Leggio and home of the murderous Corleonesi, Corleone, population 11,000, sits at the foot of a rocky Sicilian outcrop crowned by an abandoned prison (opposite, top, ANSA). Thanks in good part to the Corleonesi's conquest of the Sicilian Mafia, the mayor of Palermo, Leoluca Orlando, travels with an armed bodyguard (opposite, below, Lucky Star). Two star Mafia defectors who turned state's witness in the 1980s and testified against Leggio at Palermo's maxitrial in 1986 were Tommaso Buscetta (right, ANSA) and Salvatore Contorno, shown with his wife and children (below, ANSA).

Once a favorite haunt of the Sicilian Mafiosi operating in America, the Cafe Mille Luci (above) in the Bensonhurst section of Brooklyn was named in the Pizza trials as a heroin depot and hangout for Mafia hit man Luigi Ronsisvalle (below) and the Cherry Hill (New Jersey) Gambinos, John, Rosario, and Giuseppe (opposite, counterclockwise from top left). Ronsisvalle, who admitted to thirteen hits in Brooklyn, turned himself in to the FBI in 1979, the only Sicilian Mafioso who ever did so. The Cherry Hill Gambino brothers, John especially, were prime figures in the Sicilian Mafia's U.S. heroin network. John Gambino is still at large.

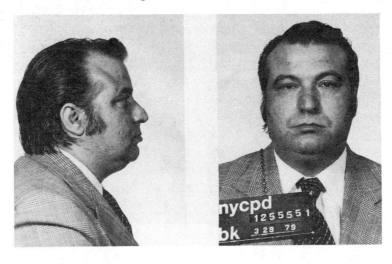

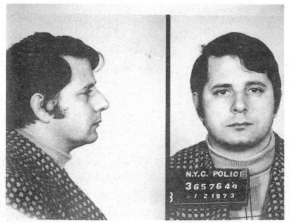

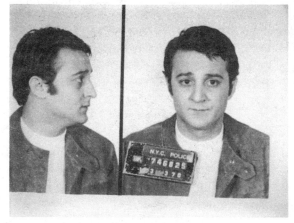

NYPD undercover agent Douglas Le Vien (left), posing as a gangster in a daring masquerade, uncovered Vincenzo Napoli (below), a Sicilian heroin kingpin in New York. Sentenced to thirteen years in prison in 1977, Napoli was released after four years and is now free and living in Brooklyn. Le Vien ran his sting operation out of a van on the Manhattan waterfront (opposite, top). (Inset is a 22-caliber assassin's weapon sold to him by Napoli, who assured him, "It's nice, it's quiet, it don't make problems." Clad with a silencer, the gun reputedly can "hit" someone two blocks away from the tenth floor of a building and not be heard in the apartment next door.) In another sting operation, in Philadelphia (opposite, below), DEA undercover agent Frank Panessa, right, makes his first heroin buy from Sicilian trafficker Paolo La Porta, center—$85,000 in cash, in a bag, for ten ounces.

K38 QY
80119033

Giuseppe Bono, shown with his bride (left), celebrated his wedding at a $65,000 reception at the deluxe Hotel Pierre in New York City. The wedding pictures, including likenesses of Cesare Bonventre (below, in dark glasses) and Baldo Amato (standing behind him, left), two young Sicilian Mafiosi in New York, became the international guide to the Sicilian underworld.

a corner on raw materials and refineries, the Sicilians had a corner on the U.S. market.

Buscetta and Zippo had hooked up with the Corsicans in 1971, within forty-eight hours of checking in to the Copacabana Palace Hotel in Rio. There, they went into conference with the Corsican Union's representative, Michel Nicoli, underboss for the man who ran the whole French Connection operation in South America: Lucien Sarti.[44] The Corsicans were a lethal crew of gangsters and mercenary killers, wanted in France for murder, armed robbery, and chronic drug trafficking. (Sarti would later be accused of accepting an American Mafia contract to kill President Kennedy, though this has not been proved.)[45] Buscetta's conference with the Corsicans lasted several days, and reportedly settled on the future staging area: the tiny Brazilian resort island of São Sebastiao, some two hours by launch from the coast near São Paulo.[46] With the Corsicans supplying the goods, Buscetta's inner circle in New York took it from there.

The Eagle Cheese Company was the hinge of the operation in the United States. Indeed, it was the wholesale outlet for much of the heroin entering New York over the next two decades. During the autumn of 1971, Eagle Cheese bought 440 kilos of heroin in just six weeks from Buscetta's ring in Brazil.[47] In the course of that one year, the company bought 980 kilos of heroin—2,156 pounds, 45 million fixes—through Carlo Zippo.[48]

Staggering quantities of heroin and cash changed hands across oceans and continents between June 1971 and July 1972. The heroin flowed westward from Marseilles, usually via Sicily, by plane, cargo vessel, yacht, and parcel post; the cash flew eastward to Rome in tourist luggage. Pino Catania alone described six deals involving 330 kilos, worth half a billion dollars on the street.[49]

Catania, Buscetta's trusted *compare,* was only one of several accomplices who confessed to these dealings, including Buscetta's son Benedetto (who conceded that his father was "a big man in the narcotics traffic").[50] The confessions were "precise and circumstantiated, specific down to the smallest details with regard to time, methods, and participants," said an Italian court. But Catania's evidence was the most damning.

Later, for the Italian authorities, Catania "refused to confirm or deny" what he had told a Brooklyn grand jury. Having agreed to collaborate with justice in America—where he walked free in exchange—he was under no obligation to tell the Italians anything. Nevertheless, an Italian court of appeals found his American testimony to be "perfectly true and reliable . . . rich in details, particulars, and information that could not possibly be the fruit of fancy." All of Catania's charges were "corroborated by the various protagonists," the court declared.[51] This was the burden of their testimony:

A few days after Buscetta and Zippo met with the Corsicans at the Copacabana Palace Hotel in June 1971, Zippo ordered fifty kilos of heroin from Michel Nicoli, which were then smuggled up from Rio by car, and delivered to Eagle Cheese. A month or so later, Buscetta and Zippo ordered another fifty kilos, offering to help arrange shipment to Mexico City via Milan, by trunk. In August, they sent Pino Catania to Italy to meet Nicoli and expedite the matter. Two trunks arrived in Mexico City in September. Buscetta's share of the money was sent to him by courier in Rio.

Things moved at an ever-faster clip over the next few months.

October 1971: Lucien Sarti offered another 120 kilos "to the Buscetta-Zippo organization" provided Buscetta agreed to a price increase (from $6,500 to $7,000 a kilo). Buscetta agreed.

November 1971: A small private plane landed the cargo at an abandoned military airport in Mexico City. Jorge Asaf y Bala shared the profits with Catania, Buscetta, and Zippo.

December 1971: Lucien Sarti sent 46 kilos more from Rio to Mexico City as commercial cargo. Buscetta, Zippo, Asaf y Bala, and Catania once again shared the profits.

January 1972: Sarti told Pino Catania that he was expecting 300 kilos for Carlo Zippo; an Italian was bringing it by yacht from Marseilles.

April 1972: Michel Nicoli told Buscetta he could have another 60 kilos. Buscetta replied that he was ready to finance "any amount of merchandise" if Nicoli could find a way to get it from France to New York.[52]

July 1972: Nicoli ordered another 180 kilos for Buscetta from a Corsican refiner in Marseilles, but time was running out.

In a single year, the Corsican ring had shipped 266 kilos of heroin to New York through Buscetta and Zippo, and had transacted for over half a ton more.[53] The ring had sent another 440 kilos to Eagle Cheese through a pilot for the Portuguese Airlines, TAP. As Lucien Sarti had confided to Catania and Zippo, it was preparing to ship *three and a half tons a year* when the Sicilian-Corsican venture in Brazil came to a sudden end.

Sarti, the Corsicans' leader, was arrested in Bolivia and bought his way out, settling in Mexico City. There, in April 1972, he died in a shootout with the police when they approached his car. His girlfriend, a Brazilian prostitute named Helene Ferreira, was arrested and talked.[54] Several other of the gang's girlfriends followed suit.

The Brazilian police, and the lone agent of the U.S. Narcotics Bureau in South America, had already been keeping an eye on the Corsican ring anyway. In October 1972, they arrested Michel Nicoli. Some days later, they seized sixty-one kilos of heroin aboard the ship *Mormac-Altair* in Guanabara Bay, off Rio de Janeiro's northern shore.[55] A chain of arrests followed, twenty-five in all, including the entire Guimaraes family.

Buscetta was caught with his son Benedetto on a remote *fazenda* near the Uruguay border. Pino Catania was taken in Texas.[56] Carlo Zippo was captured in Salerno, Italy. Filippo Casamento was arrested in New York. His brother Franco and Antonino Napoli got away, a jump ahead of the law; Napoli fled to Venezuela. (Both were "John Does" in the New York indictment.)

All those arrested in Brazil were tortured. Michel Nicoli was hung upside down over a steam pipe with his ankles shackled, while a cattle prod was applied to his genitals. When U.S. agents took him off the plane to stand trial in New York, he could hardly walk. Another member of the ring slashed his wrists to get into the prison hospital. Later, fearing more torture in the United States, he swallowed razor blades. (He had panicked upon seeing two battery cables under a table in New York.)[57]

Buscetta was given electric shocks on his genitals, anus, teeth, and ears; his nails were torn out; he was hung from a beam for hours under a hot sun, with a hood over his head. He insists the police didn't get a word out of him, but they did.

The FBI's agent in Rio de Janeiro at the time reported that two U.S. Customs agents were present during "the delicate and pressing interrogation" of Buscetta. He added:

Brazilian authorities believe that Tommaso Buscetta is the ringleader in the drug traffic between Europe and the United States.

Buscetta and his son Benedetto are wanted for murder in Italy and fear for their lives should they be returned to that country. . . . In this regard, Buscetta has made a tentative deal with the Brazilian police. He has expressed a desire *to tell all he knows concerning narcotics dealings and dealers and the location of laboratories.* . . . In return, [he wants] a promise that Brazilian authorities will not expel his son, who has obtained Brazilian citizenship under a false name. (My italics)[58]

The bargain apparently ended in a compromise. Benedetto was shipped to America. Buscetta was deported to Italy; the information he gave in exchange for the favor to his son was "not outstanding." Even so, the deal would have warranted a Mafia death penalty when he was extradited to Italy, had the word gotten out. It has never gotten out.

Apart from Carlo Zippo, also imprisoned in Italy, Buscetta was the only one who served much time in jail. Those who confessed pleaded guilty in New York and got off lightly, or were not prosecuted at all. Filippo Casamento, who denied everything, fared miraculously well. After a New York judge sentenced him to fifteen years in 1973, the judge began to receive moving letters. Casamento wrote of delivering milk in Palermo at the age of seven to "bearly eak [sic] out a living for my large family. . . . All that life has permitted me to have, I acquired by means of my honest efforts and sweat." His brother Franco wrote that the punishment of this innocent man "drives me crazy." The pastor of Our Lady of Grace Church in Brooklyn said he had "a worthy sense of honesty and decorum," and enjoyed "the high esteem, respect and confidence of our community." The family's parish priest in Palermo affirmed that Filippo Casamento "could never have been involved in such criminal acts." Amending his sentence, the judge wrote: "I have been impressed by the sincerity of the letters. . . . [They] make me think that the prospects for rehabilitation are good, and that justice does not require the maximum sentence which was originally imposed."[59] Casamento was released after serving seven years.

No sooner was he back on the street than he was off and running on the same old track. Eagle Cheese would continue to be the Sicilian Mafia's wholesale outlet in New York until Casamento went to jail again with the whole Pizza Connection crowd in 1984. The cozy family store was open to the end. Casamento, draped in a striped apron, sold me some very superior mozzarella while I was covering the Pizza trial and he was free on bail.

Fate was less kind to Buscetta. After being deported to Italy, he seemed to face an eternity behind bars. During his absence abroad, he had been sentenced to fourteen years for "criminal conspiracy" and "the unlawful continuing detention" of two men. (These were the two "white deaths" he had been accused of a decade earlier.) A year after his internment in Italy, the United States brought massive drug charges against him. Rather than extradite him to New York, a court in Salerno tried and convicted him of these charges, and added ten years to his sentence.[60]

The punishment said much for his glittering criminal fame. Hardly any Sicilian Men of Honor were going to jail in the 1970s for very long, if at all. But Buscetta was still the Mafia's role model then—an arch villain for the state, a hero for his fellow sinners. Neither side would have dreamed that he would turn on his own kind one day, to become the most devastating Mafia defector of all time.

Indeed, Buscetta received a royal welcome at Palermo's Ucciardone prison. A "legendary aura" had preceded him, he told Judge Falcone long afterward:

I did nothing to create the undoubted ascendancy and prestige surrounding me. . . .

Unfortunately, my strong and proud personality created a myth around me as an international drug trafficker and violent, ruthless Mafia boss, which was not true at all. . . . The more incredible fact is that this myth influenced not just the press and police but the criminal underworld itself. . . . In prison, I was regarded with fear and respect, enhanced by my reserve, which was taken for Mafia power derived from illicit gains and crimes I never committed. . . . And it was perfectly useless for me to try convincing them that I wasn't the monster they thought, because they always laughed when I protested my innocence.

Starting Up:
South America

nlike Brazil, which had its ups and downs, Venezuela offered a charmed life to Sicily's Men of Honor. There were no big drug busts in its sunlit capital, Caracas, during the 1960s, 1970s, or 1980s. Indeed, nothing untoward has ever happened to the Sicilian Mafia in Venezuela. Venezuelan politicians generally look surprised if the subject of the Mafia comes up. "The Mafia as such does not exist in Venezuela; a few Mafiosi just come here for rest and recreation," concluded a commissioner of DISIP, the national intelligence service, after investigating the matter in depth.[1]

In reality, an exceptionally sinister wing of the Sicilian Mafia has operated out of Caracas since the great flight from Sicily in 1963. This regularly chartered branch, recognized by the American Cosa Nostra but accountable to Palermo, plays a master role in assuring a copious flow of narcotics to the United States and Europe.[2] Its members are impregnable, untouchable. No matter how many tentacles of the Octopus may be lopped off elsewhere, nobody gets near enough to lop this one.

The Venezuelan branch has organized heroin deliveries to the

United States by the ton—three tons a year by 1982, half the total
entering the country, according to the FBI.[3] It brokers, or washes the
money for, nearly two-thirds of the cocaine passing through Venezuela;
and 80 percent of the cocaine leaving Colombia now passes through
Venezuela.[4] It launders drug money for Colombians and Sicilians both.
Billions of narcodollars have been recycled through its colossal financial empire—an estimated $2 billion or more in 1983 alone.[5]

To look back at its beginnings is to watch dark lines slowly spreading over a huge canvas. This was where the heroin delivery system to
America was perfected, where the earliest failsafe methods for washing
drug money were devised, where cocaine was brought into the equation
with heroin to supply both sides of the Atlantic, where the two giants of
the worldwide narcotics trade—the Sicilian Mafia and what became the
Medellin cartel—formed their working alliance.

Probably the Men of Honor who first settled in Venezuela had nothing so ambitious in mind. The Cupola had been disbanded in Palermo
when their advance guard arrived. There were no traces of a grand
design until the Cupola was revived in 1970, and even that took another
half-decade to mature.

Nevertheless, Caracas was a magnet from the start. The Cupola's
first president, Cichiteddu Greco, chose to settle there when he slipped
out of Italy with Buscetta after the Ciaculli bomb disaster. Written off
as dead by the Italian police, Greco lived on as Renato Martino Caruso,
a kingpin of the international drug trade for the next sixteen years. (He
died in his bed from cirrhosis of the liver in 1979.)

Antonino Napoli, dodging arrest in New York when the Brazilian
drug operation came to an end in 1972, also took cover in Caracas. He
was a very big fish, and the United States knew it. Detective Le Vien,
stumbling on the Napoli brothers a few years later, was told as much by
his boss at the Eastern District Strike Force, U.S. Attorney Tom
Puccio. Antonino Napoli was "the biggest mover of junk into the U.S."
and "one of the major narcotics dealers in the world," said Puccio; *he*
was the Napoli brother to go after.[6] But American agents at that time
presumed that Napoli was just away from New York on business. Once
they learned that he had moved to Caracas, they forgot about him.

In fact, in Venezuela, Antonino Napoli was helping to set up the
Mafia's main narcotics terminal in the Western Hemisphere. The orga-
nization rotated around three brothers who have come to head the
Sicilian Mafia's most powerful constellation abroad. They are the
Cuntreras: Pasquale, Paolo, and Gaspare. A fourth, Liborio, died in
London some years ago (also of cirrhosis). The Cuntreras might be

nobodies, for all that is known of them in the outside world. Inside Venezuela, they are known too well in certain quarters to be talked about. The wedding of Paolo Cuntrera's daughter in Caracas did make a splash; her marriage—to one of the most notorious drug traffickers anywhere—was a national television event.[7] Otherwise, the Cuntrera brothers live tranquilly in palatial twin residences called "Mary" and "Dalila" on the Calle Terepaima. Heavily curtained and guarded, abounding with electronic equipment, shielded from view by tall pine trees, they are sealed off as if in a finespun silken cocoon.

My own questions about the Cuntreras brought blank looks in Caracas. The head of the Anti-Narcotics Squad in the Ministry of Justice gave me to understand that he had barely heard of Paolo Cuntrera, and this only in connection with illegal gambling in the city. He knew nothing about any Cuntreras in drugs, still less of repeated Italian requests for their extradition as master operatives in a colossal narcotics enterprise.[8] (The latest of these requests was an arrest warrant issued October 1984 for the Palermo maxitrial.) He seemed astonished by the lengthy police printouts I had brought over from Italy. So, unaccountably, did the DEA agent at the U.S. embassy.

The Venezuelan minister of justice, Jose Manzo Gonzalez, was not just amazed but perturbed. He had put his life on the line to fight the drug traffic during his three years in office, he assured me. How could the biggest traffickers of all have operated under his nose throughout that time—since 1970, in fact—without his knowing anything about it? A possible answer was suggested some months after my last interview with the minister. He resigned on March 29, 1988, "amid allegations that he operated a secret police force deeply involved in drug running," according to the *International Herald Tribune.*[9]

Like Luciano Leggio and Tommaso Buscetta, the Cuntreras are part of the Mafia generation that came of age in Sicily just after World War II. Unlike both, however, they have never set foot in a courtroom, or gotten their pictures in the papers; the police don't even have their mug shots.

Their power rests on a personal fortune estimated at around half a billion dollars, and an imperial family dynasty: some twenty relatives by blood or marriage, including two sons, a son-in-law, and a brood of cousins wedded into the group, named Caruana. Singly or in pairs, they have been positioned strategically over the years in London, Geneva, Malta, Montreal, and Miami as well as Caracas. In the process of moving drugs, they have grown into kingpins of international finance.

The Cuntreras were all born in or near Siculiana, a rocky, white-washed hamlet of five thousand inhabitants on the southern Sicilian coast near Agrigento. This was a singular stroke of luck from their point of view. Agrigento, a glory of Greek antiquity, is today a godforsaken town of fifty thousand with the lowest income in Italy, one tired and bored Carabinieri station, two unconscionably overworked investigating magistrates, and a single copying machine for its entire courthouse.[10]

The Mafia had no fear of being watched there. The courts had pinned nothing on a Man of Honor in Agrigento for half a century. The Cuntrera brothers grew up in enviable liberty. Starting out as *gabellotti,* like Leggio, they were no less cruel and grasping if perhaps a degree less homicidal. Moldering police records cite them for systematic theft, extortion, arson, bombing, and multiple murder, for which they were periodically arrested and released.

Even the Cuntreras felt the pressure of the Ciaculli bomb disaster, however, and directly after it happened in 1963, they cleared out of Siculiana. They were eluding a long stay in *soggiorno obbligato:* guarded internal exile, an expression of Italy's helplessness to convict the Mafia in a court of law.[11]

They had an excellent patron for their wanderings abroad. The boss of Agrigento province, Don Giuseppe Settecase, was a man of exceedingly high respect. He had traveled to the United States for the historic Apalachin conference, to New York for talks with the Gambino Family, and to Canada for a conference with Mafia chiefs there.[12] His *picciotti* had worked with Lucky Luciano since the 1950s. Most important, he presided over a corner of Sicily's notorious drug-smuggling triangle—Agrigento-Trapani-Palermo—which had moved heroin since the earliest postwar days. But none of this was known to the police until decades later. The Mafia's secrets were safe in Agrigento even after they were revealed—as they were, by astonishing chance—in 1974.

In the spring of that year, the Royal Canadian Mounted Police taped the illuminating conversation in a Montreal bar that revealed the Sicilian Mafia's tight hierarchical structure (see chapter 4). The dialogue, between Montreal's Mafia boss, Paul Violi, and a certain "Carmelo" on a visit from Agrigento, had to do partly with a nephew of the Cuntreras', Giovanni Caruana. Carmelo wanted Giovanni to have full working privileges in Montreal while living in Venezuela, and Violi said no: "You people in Italy have bad habits. . . . He was made in Siculiana, now he's in Venezuela, suppose he wants to go back to Siculiana, then he wants to come here. . . . You people want your own law here, but it's different here."[13]

The rest of the conversation laid out the Sicilian Mafia's working rules and structure, its island-wide hierarchy, and its entire chain of command in Agrigento province. The Canadians sent the transcript to the judiciary in Agrigento, where it remained at the back of a desk drawer for the next eight years. It turned up after Don Giuseppe Settecase was murdered, aged eighty, in the Great Mafia War of 1981–83.[14]

Only through this transcript did the Agrigento police finally discover who had headed the Mafia in their province. They had not known that Don Giuseppe was actually holding his Mafia meetings daily, in full view, while playing cards in his favorite café; they had thought he was senile.[15]

The Cuntreras, formed under Settecase's paternal eye, had returned to Siculiana just once while he was alive, for a family wedding in 1973, decked out in pin-striped suits and violent oversized ties. By then, an Agrigento court had dropped all charges against the senior Caruana, Leonardo, pronouncing him "no longer capable of subverting the property of others by force and violence."[16] Upon leaving again, the Cuntreras donated a fund for the local soccer team, and ordered the construction of a million-dollar villa, "American style." Ugly and empty, rusting and cracking in the salty air, the villa now stands on a mountaintop overlooking the village—a perpetual reminder of their presence.

In 1963, after leaving Siculiana, the Cuntreras went first to Brazil for a year or so, and then headed for Montreal, whose branch of the Mafia had been set up by Joe Bonanno (just after World War II) and then led by Carmine Galante. The men in charge now were handpicked old-timers who had dealt for years with Lucky Luciano and Sicilian traffickers in Europe.[17] Nevertheless, Sicilian interlopers in their own organization were something else. The Cuntreras and Caruanas were told that they would have to wait for permission to operate in Canada, as protocol demanded, but they didn't.

The Montreal Mafia and its new "Sicilian faction" were soon on a collision course. Sporadic killing went on for some time; the Sicilians did not take over altogether until they gunned down the Montreal boss, Paul Violi, in 1978. Though many outsiders worked with them—local Mafiosi, independent hoods, Corsicans, Neapolitans in the Camorra— the Cuntreras and Caruanas were unmistakably in command. By 1970, they were already "the biggest exporters of heroin to the U.S. from Canada," concedes Buscetta, who spent a month with the Cuntrera brothers in Montreal that winter.[18]

Sometime in the same year, the Cuntreras moved on to Venezuela, leaving some Caruanas behind to mind the store. Montreal was now the

Sicilian Mafia's northern gateway to the United States. When Caracas was well in hand, the American eastern seaboard would be sewn up from top to bottom.

o◯o

Venezuela is a beautiful country with deep mountain gorges and towering peaks, majestic waterfalls, dense forests, virginal beaches. There are immense empty spaces, and 1,750 miles of inviting coastline along the Caribbean Sea. Some of the safest island sanctuaries in the hemisphere, such as Aruba and Curaçao, are a hop and skip away. Medellin is barely a couple of hundred miles to the east, across the Colombian border. It is a rich country as well, blessed with natural resources, especially petroleum and iron ore. The Venezuelans are the most prosperous people in South America, and among the freest.

Conditions were ideal in the country's modern, comfortable, easygoing capital for the Cuntreras and their friends. They could take out citizenship with little trouble, or buy a complete new identity from some obliging petty functionary for $500: birth certificate, passport, driver's license. As "naturalized" citizens, they could not be extradited under Venezuelan law.

There were also no exchange controls. Dollars could be bought and sold freely. Converted to Venezuelan bolivars, they could be deposited in local banks, used to underwrite ghost companies, and then withdrawn, reconverted to foreign currency, and exported. Or dollars could go into legitimate investments, for which there were splendid opportunities. Venezuela has excellent grazing lands, notably along the Colombian border, and builds many highways, dams, urban subways, and housing projects. Caracas is a sprawling metropolis of steel and glass high-rises, clover-leaf freeways, tourists, shoppers, and spenders.

The Cuntreras went into business in a big way, setting up dozens of companies with a fascinating team of partners. Registered formally as shareholders were Cichiteddu Greco, alias Renato Martino Caruso; Antonino Napoli; John Gambino, eldest of the Cherry Hill Gambinos in Brooklyn and New Jersey; Giuseppe Bono, later to be the Sicilian Mafia's top emissary to New York for the Pizza Connection ring; Nick Rizzuto of Agrigento, famed drug trafficker and future head of the "Sicilian faction" in Canada; and Nino Mongiovi, Paolo Cuntrera's son-in-law, rated by the DEA today as a super traffic manager for drugs of all kinds passing through Miami.[19]

The partners invested in real estate, construction, cattle raising, meat packing, agroindustry, furniture, interior decorating, travel agencies, oil, casinos, water, gas, car concessions, a shirt factory, a bed-spread factory, and a sizable maritime fleet. They all sat on one an-other's boards of directors, brisk men with expensive briefcases, occu-pying elegant office suites bearing innocuous company names: Agropecuaria Gas Michelin; Comercial Hotelera; Fábrica de Cubre-Camas Americanos; Corporación del Mueble Ris Mari CA.[20]

The Cuntrera brothers formed their own giant building trades com-plex, MAPLISA, in the northern Valencia region, and built all along the coast; three of their hotels—the Royal, the Terminus, and the Odeon—went up on the Sabana Grande, heart of the Caracas shopping district.

Several partners opted for the cattle trade, a strategic as well as profitable decision. Cocaine is often smuggled out of the region in cow bellies, hides, or cattle trucks crossing the border; the cattle smell stronger than the drugs do. (Fifteen tons of cocaine were smuggled out of Venezuela in cattle trucks in 1987, according to the head of the Venezuelan Parliament's Anti-Narcotics Committee.)[21]

John Gambino set up a cattle-breeding station in 1971, with his wife and his cousin Erasmus, in the Venezuelan state of Barinas near the Colombian frontier.[22] Cichiteddu Greco and Nick Rizzuto went into partnership with Gaspare Cuntrera to form a huge cattle company, Ganaderia Rio Zapa, in Barinas the same year.

Antonino Napoli also acquired a vast cattle ranch, along with sev-eral milk powder factories. By 1976, when Detective Le Vien was strug-gling to pierce the mystery of the Napoli brothers in New York, An-tonino was reported to be shipping heroin north in cow bellies, and was said to have already amassed about $100 million.[23]

In the space of a decade, the Cuntrera-Caruana group's investments in Venezuela swelled to four billion bolivars: a billion U.S. dollars at the time. This was not just an educated guess but a documented figure, arrived at by Venezuela's intelligence service, DISIP. Though an alarmed Parliament had demanded the investigation, the DISIP report was never published. Indeed, the most scorching portions simply disap-peared. Eventually, the two intrepid deputies who had turned over the scorching facts in the first place disclosed them.[24]

No legitimate enterprise in the country compared in size or capital with the Cuntreras' corporate complex, for good reason; the Cuntreras got their capital from illegitimate enterprises. They were doing what comes naturally to Men of Honor everywhere—gambling, loan-shark-ing, extortion, prostitution—but laundering drug money quickly be-came their specialty. They had the facilities, and there was a lot of money to launder.

In another decade, an unending river of dollars would flow from the United States to some small bank in Montreal, and from there by telex around the globe until reaching the Cuntreras in Caracas. Six or seven tellers would spend a full day counting bills, hand-carried by couriers for deposit in Canada.[25] Pickup trucks stacked with cash would sometimes draw up to the bank's front doors.

Canadian and Italian police tracking a small part of these narcodollars over a single year—$13 million in 1981—followed them from a suburban branch of the Montreal City and District Savings Bank in Canada to the Union Bank in Horgen, Switzerland; the Banco di Credito Commerciale e Mobiliare in Horgen (where one of the Caruanas, Alfonso, kept an account); the Union Bank of Switzerland in Zurich; the Banco de Maracaibo in northern Venezuela; the Banco Exterior in Caracas; and the Banco República in Caracas. There was no tracing the money once it crossed the Venezuelan frontier.[26]

It seems obvious now, so long after the event, that what went on in Venezuela in the early 1970s was a key to the Sicilian Mafia's entire heroin operation worldwide. Cocaine was always involved as well—Mafiosi could sell it wholesale in New York for $11,000 a kilo in 1970, nearly twice what they were getting for heroin then. But heroin would be selling for upward of $200,000 a kilo before long. The heroin market was growing rapidly in the United States—they were helping it grow—and that was plainly the focus of their attention.

The activities of the Cuntreras' shareholders made this clear. John Gambino, returning to the United States, became the prime associate there of the clans dominating Palermo's heroin consortium. Giuseppe Bono was sent up to New York to represent the entire Sicilian Mafia (after leaving a notarized power of attorney with Gaspare Cuntrera to handle his holdings). Nick Rizzuto returned to Montreal to complete the Sicilians' takeover of the Mafia there; this just after the Sicilian Cupola opened a regular heroin pipeline to New York through Montreal.[27]

The Cuntreras were also entwined with the Sicilian Mafia's other chartered branch, in Brazil. Its reigning patriarch, Antonio Salamone, was in and out of Caracas all the time. The Cuntreras spoke of him as "Il Vecchio," the Old Man, apparently a person of awesome authority. ("How can we let the Old Man know? I can't go to him, he isn't in that place . . . he's traveling," said a nervous Paolo Cuntrera when his brother Pasquale called to tell him that their phone calls to Italy were being tapped.)[28]

Salamone, a member of the Cupola on leave, had disappeared from Sicily after being acquitted of omnibus criminal charges there in 1974;

the Italian police had written him off as dead. Actually, he was living peacefully among São Paulo's four million Italian-born residents. Wispy and white-haired, a retiring elderly gentleman who never even got a parking ticket, he was utterly unknown to the Brazilian police.

Another intricate web linked the Cuntreras to the Neapolitan Camorra's sizable forces overseas. Members of the Camorra were consummate smugglers by vocation. Like their Sicilian opposite numbers, they went wherever the money was—which brought them into proximity not just with the Cuntreras but with practically every person mentioned in this book. Although the Camorristi of Naples were doing the same things in the same places as Sicily's Men of Honor, the two formations were not fighting over drugs; they were joining forces. There was no question about who gave the orders, however. The Sicilians did.

oⵀo

The Cuntreras had still another link that would jolt Scotland Yard when it finally came to light. In 1975, Liborio Cuntrera moved to London. He bought a mansion in Surrey, the stockbrokers' belt, for just under $1 million in cash, and made his discreet entrance into the City, the banking center of London.

The authorities showed no signs of knowing he was in London, still less what he was doing there, until a decade later, long after he had died and been shipped back to Siculiana for a suitable burial. In the course of that decade, a dramatic increase in domestic heroin use jolted the British public. Yearly heroin seizures in Britain rose from 20 kilos to 220 kilos: by the one-to-ten reckoning of narcotics agents everywhere, this meant an inflow of over two tons. The heroin addict population reached perhaps 100,000—reliable statistics are lacking—and was now increasing exponentially by 25 percent a year. Cocaine seizures rose from 7 kilos to upward of 110 kilos, and were also increasing by 25 percent a year. (The figure was 483 kilos for the last half of 1987 alone.)[29] Narcotics had become a terrifying problem in Great Britain.

It was tempting to put the blame on small-time operators, as many in authority did; body carriers bringing in a kilo or two apiece were overrunning the country like ants by the 1980s—Pakistanis, Indians, Vietnamese, Ghanaians, Nigerians. But body carriers are the mules of the trade. They could not conceivably have brought in *and distributed* the massive quantities of heroin and cocaine that first hooked, and then fed, Britain's addict population.

The Mafia did not move in on London halfway through the 1970s merely to peddle a few kilos of junk. The Cuntreras and Caruanas were coordinating the traffic: supplying the national market; financing enormous international transactions; using the United Kingdom as a safe haven for nine-digit money laundering and a free port for massive heroin transshipments from Asia's Golden Crescent to North America.

Even after the evidence was in, official Britain seemed unwilling or unable to grasp the fact that the Sicilian Mafia had successfully—triumphantly—invaded the country. Some of Italy's best cops tried repeatedly to tell their counterparts in London how things stood.[30] They came home baffled, as I did after spending a pleasant day with Scotland Yard's National Drugs Intelligence coordinator, Colin Hewett. "The Mafia did try to muscle in with gambling casinos in 1970, George Raft and that crowd, but we put a stop to that. We have no Mafia problem here," Hewett told me, just after Liborio Cuntrera's chief lieutenant was caught in the biggest heroin bust on record in Britain.[31] If Hewett had heard of Cuntrera's elaborate criminal establishment in London, he showed little interest in it in the course of my interview with him.

Yet Scotland Yard had been warned of a threatened Mafia invasion as early as 1974, by the head of its own International Organized Crime Squad. Detective Chief Superintendent Harry Clement, retired now, had turned in a thesis to that effect during a refresher course and gotten nowhere. "My tutor said he didn't understand it, and my superiors said and did nothing," he told the *Daily Express* later.[32]

Clement had only six men on his team when Cuntrera arrived in London. They tried to watch the organization's movements through Europe. To cut corners, his men bypassed Interpol and the usual diplomatic channels, keeping directly in touch with opposite numbers in the Paris Sûreté, Germany's BKA (Bundeskriminalamt), and the FBI. But Clement's team was disbanded before it could get very far, and Liborio Cuntrera went his way undisturbed.

Cuntrera set up a whole new extension of the Mafia's money-laundering system for Europe, through phony companies in London, headed where possible by compliant British frontmen. The system was ingenious, cranking out hundreds of millions of washed dollars yearly after a while. One particular arrangement worked like this:

In 1976, a Sicilian trafficker named Michelangelo Aiello—the former mayor of Bagheria, a Palermo suburb—formed an export company called IDA (Industria Derivati Agrumi). Its British customers were represented by a businessman in the City, one Raymond Michael Kingsland, who represented a company called Banderola Compania Naviera; several other fictitious companies also served as IDA companies—Kaymaritime, Laymaritime, Versola, and Amar. Through one or the other, oranges and lemons would be ordered from IDA. The bills would arrive punctually, though the fictitious cargoes did not. Kingsland would pay in a sequence of curious moves. He would transfer the money from his own account at the Banca Nazionale del Lavoro in Palermo to another account of his at Lloyd's in London. Then he would instruct Lloyd's to transfer the money to an account of Aiello's in Switzerland—the Kredit Privat Bank in Lugano, or the Unione di Banche Svizzere in Bellinzona. Aiello would then order his Swiss bank to telex the money to his account in Palermo.

The odd thing was that Aiello himself made the original deposit to Kingsland's bank account in Palermo. Thus, Aiello appeared to be paying for his own nonexistent oranges and lemons. Actually, he was depositing dirty dollars carried over in suitcases from New York, and getting them back clean.[33]

Aiello, laundering up to $12 million a year this way, was just one of many. Some 120 Mafia front companies like his turned out to have extracted $350 million in subsidies for citrus fruits from Italtrade, the financial arm of Italy's Fund for the South.[34] At least as much if not more was reportedly milked from the Common Market, for "destroying" the Mafia's spurious "surplus" fruits. When an Italian judge finally indicted Aiello, his fifty-three codefendants included big stars in the Pizza Connection ring—Salvatore Catalano of Knickerbocker Avenue and Filippo Casamento of Eagle Cheese, among them.

The London operation expanded rapidly after Liborio Cuntrera settled in there. Two Caruana sons, Pasquale and Alfonso, took to commuting from Montreal to London and Switzerland, while their father made extended visits to Palermo. Before long, the Caruanas settled in Britain too. Alfonso paid close to $1 million in cash for Broomfield Manor, a sumptuous estate in Godalming, Surrey, surrounded by eight-foot-high walls. Pasquale paid $800,000 for another estate with an indoor swimming pool, in nearby Hook Heath, Woking. The brothers ordered BMWs, and a Mercedes 500 SEL from Switzerland, where Alfonso eventually acquired a lakeside villa conveniently situated in Melide, near Lugano, the Swiss banking center on Italy's northern frontier.[35]

In 1976, a compatriot came out to join them from Altofonte, a small town halfway between Palermo and Corleone. His name was Francesco Di Carlo, and he was an expert mover of junk.

Several other Men of Honor drifted into London with Di Carlo. Flush with cash, the local proceeds of their work, they invested in hotels, restaurants, a wine bar in Streatham, three travel agencies, an antique shop, a sex shop, and two offshore companies registered in the Channel Isles. (Di Carlo himself bought a $50,000 Ferrari.) For the rest, they set up a string of dummy import-export companies.

Here, they enjoyed the courtesies extended to members of the British Commonwealth. Cargoes in transit from one commonwealth country to another are not cleared through British customs; and cargoes forwarded to Canada from Britain are not likely to arouse suspicion. So upon leaving Thailand, heroin was shipped in teak furniture to India and then to Britain, labeled for transshipment to Canada. A dummy company in London acted as forwarder. The labels had only to be switched while the cargo waited on dockside for the final lap of its journey. When it reached Montreal, its provenance was no longer Thailand but the British Isles.

Nobody knows how much heroin was fed into the Montreal–New York pipeline this way, still less how much the Cuntrera-Caruana ring brought in for British consumption. Its members worked in gilded obscurity for a full decade before they were noticed at all.

They finally attracted attention when Francesco Di Carlo and three accomplices were arrested for a sixty-kilo heroin transshipment to Montreal in December 1984. According to the British police, Di Carlo was "a boss sent from Palermo in 1976 to control the Mafia's financial interests in Great Britain."[36]

By the time he and his three accomplices were tried and sentenced, in 1987, four-fifths of the heroin flowing through the British pipeline was remaining in the United Kingdom for domestic use.[37] Sicilian traffickers still dominated the market, with perhaps fifty top-echelon men in place around the United Kingdom. As Palermo's Judge Falcone observed, "Di Carlo's operation was only part of one tentacle of the Octopus."[38] The Cuntrera-Caruana ring in London was also reportedly "funding and distributing" a multimillion-pound trade in cocaine, supplied by its old-time Colombian allies; and its money-laundering operations reached from London to the Virgin Islands, New York, Lisbon, Vienna, Hong Kong, and Tokyo.[39]

The Cuntreras had much to answer for to society, but there was little likelihood of their being called to account in Venezuela. It was the Mafia in Palermo they had to reckon with. Surprisingly, considering some of the company they kept, they had no cause for worry there either.

Few Men of Honor were so good at remaining above the fray. Where others were identified with one Mafia faction or another—old boys or new, haves or have-nots, Palermitani or provincials from the boondocks—the Cuntreras did business with everybody. More particularly, they had had the foresight to accommodate Luciano Leggio.

The boss of Corleone had hovered in the wings while preparations for the great heroin venture got under way. The planned routes, the deals with the Corsicans, the money-laundering grids, the men positioned from Montreal and Brooklyn to Mexico City, São Paolo, and Caracas, were not his; not yet. He did not really begin to move in until halfway through the 1970s.

One of his first strategic maneuvers was sending Francesco Di Carlo to join Liborio Cuntrera in London. Di Carlo *was* his. There hadn't been any Mafia clan in Altofonte, Di Carlo's hometown, until the Corleonesi created it. By dispatching this accomplished drug trafficker to be the Cuntreras' number two in London, Leggio was staking his claim. And, characteristically, he did it when nearly everybody in his own and the outside world thought he was done for: he had already been arrested, tried, convicted, and sentenced to spend the rest of his life in jail.

The Scarlet Pimpernel of Corleone

Don Luciano Leggio, a fugitive in a manner of speaking for over a quarter of a century, was finally led off to jail for good in May 1974. He smiled, waved, bowed, and posed genially for a swarm of cameramen as he was escorted from a luxurious penthouse in Milan to a waiting police car. He had become Italy's counterhero—the press called him the Scarlet Pimpernel of Corleone—and this was going to be his last sublime joke on the Italian state.

By 1974, Don Luciano was a symbol of everything that was wrong with the law where the Mafia was concerned. He had beaten the rap more often, and more outrageously, than any Man of Honor in the country. The courts had tried and acquitted him for multiple murder with depressing regularity: eleven times, mostly *in absentia,* for only a fraction of the murders to his credit. He could not be caught, though he lived in opulent quarters and rode around in a Rolls-Royce; or if caught, could not be held.

Now that he was caught and held at last, he would show how insubstantial prison bars could be. He had the money, the troops, the al-

liances, and the immense authority to win control of the Sicilian Mafia
from his cell.

Any resourceful convict can project himself out of a locked room.
Common criminals do it everywhere. Several American Mafia bosses
have kept their Families cowed for years from a federal penitentiary.
Italy's Camorra was actually created by convicts in the eighteenth century, illiterate derelicts whose secret brotherhood could reward and
punish, rob, blackmail, and kill from a distance, terrorize all Naples,
and dictate to its imperial rulers. And not even Leggio could hold a
candle in this regard to a Neapolitan contemporary who has spent
nearly all his grown life in jail. Convicted of murder in the late 1950s,
Don Raffaele Cutolo resurrected the apparently defunct Camorra with
his fellow inmates, and turned it into the even more deadly Nuova
Camorra Organizzata—the Organized New Camorra—which he ran
from prison for the next thirty years.

Where Cutolo's power base was in a single city, however, Leggio
was contending for an empire that now spanned two continents. Although the old Mafia establishment was still firmly in command, Leggio
had a strategic advantage over many of the old guard's leaders: he had
stayed behind when they fled after the Ciaculli bomb incident in 1963.
Though imprisoned for a while after that incident, he had nevertheless
managed to press deeper into Palermo with his Corleonese clan, pick up
allies in the outlying provinces, and penetrate the Cupola at last. His
encounters with the law had made him a legend besides—a criminal
mastermind who could outwit anybody and get away with anything, in
or out of jail.

Don Luciano was arrested for the first time in 1964. When the
police came for him, he was reading in bed. Tolstoy's *War and Peace*
lay on his night table, alongside a book of prayers and Kant's *Critique of
Pure Reason.* He didn't bother to pull his pistol out of the drawer.

The house in which Leggio was sheltering, scarcely two hundred
yards from Corleone's police headquarters, was surrounded by an army
of police and *carabinieri.* Two agents competing for the prize crashed
through his bedroom door. To one, a Carabinieri colonel, Leggio threw
a gracious accolade: "You fought me with honor and you should win
with honor." To the other—Police Inspector Angelo Mangano of
Palermo, his detested adversary—he threw a glance of flaming hatred.
"Your mission is over," he murmured. Mangano was shot and nearly
killed afterward.[1]

Don Luciano was not well. Medicine bottles, pills, and syringes littered the room. A heavy leather brace showed through his pajamas, supporting the spine crippled by Pott's disease; a spare brace in silver lay nearby. "What could you want with me? I'm getting old," he said almost gaily, struggling to his feet. (He was under forty.) "If you intend to keep me alive, you'll have to take me to a place in the sun. I need a lot of sun."[2]

He had been in the house for months, nursed and cherished by a woman whose fiancé he had killed some sixteen years previously—Corleone's lone labor leader, Placido Rizzotto. Once, the woman had vowed to eat the murderer's heart. Now, she combed his hair and wept.

Two husky *carabinieri* half carried their ailing prisoner down the stairs. A mob of reporters waited to see him off for Palermo, and one, a photographer, climbed into the ambulance with him. Leggio, prostrate on a stretcher, gave the man a kick that sent his camera flying and ordered the driver to move on.[3]

There went the last of the *mammasantissima,* many thought, as the heavy doors of Palermo's Ucciardone prison closed behind him. Doctors gave him just a few years to live. Wanted on fifteen charges of murder, he was bound to be kept in jail at least that long.

As far as investigators knew, Leggio had not been doing much before his capture, nor had his Mafia colleagues. Those who weren't dead or in jail were abroad or in hiding. Apart from a few stabbings or shootings for personal reasons—jealousy, adultery, seduction—hardly anybody was getting killed in Palermo. The city was having its most peaceful year since World War II. No movement had been discernible since the car bomb in Ciaculli had blown up seven *carabinieri* in June 1963. Police informants were saying that the organization had been disbanded. Later, Tommaso Buscetta would assert that the Mafia might actually have been put out of business altogether then, if the courts had been up to the strain. It was Italy's last chance, he added.

At the time of Leggio's capture, the prisons were already filled with his associates. Nearly two thousand Mafiosi suspects had been arrested between July and December 1963. Even their *capo di tutti capi,* Don Giuseppe Genco Russo, had been nabbed.

This was perhaps the one moment in a century when the Mafia's opponents seemed to have a chance. Sicily's Men of Honor were in severe public disfavor. Half of them were out of the country, waiting to see what Italian justice would do to the other half. For once, ordinary Sicilians seemed ready to set aside their millennial suspicions, if Rome proved it could stand up to the Mafia. Rome seemed ready to set politics aside and do it, for once. The attorney general of Palermo called the Mafia a "pathological phenomenon," and promised to "sink a surgeon's sanitizing scalpel" into it.[4]

Mussolini's Iron Prefect, Cesare Mori, had used almost identical words, but his fascist courts were rigged. Now the contest was real. This was the first time that a free society anywhere was preparing to prosecute the Mafia seriously, and by due process of law, which meant that a Mafioso had the same rights in a courtroom as anybody else. He was presumed to be telling the truth short of convincing proof to the contrary. Hearsay, anonymous tips, suspicious circumstances, and educated guesses could not convict him. To break these rules for a Mafia defendant would be to break them for everybody.

Applying the rules narrowly proved calamitous, however. No sooner did the big trials of the 1960s get under way than witnesses recanted or disappeared. Material evidence under lock and key vanished. Charges based on years of laborious investigation fell apart. Judges and juries were threatened physically, and overpowered politically. It was all right to go after the Mafia's foot soldiers, always expendable. But a phalanx of politicians formed a shield around dons of Leggio's caliber: Men of Honor who could make or break bank presidents, high public servants, members of Parliament and the government.

Appearing in the big trials of the 1960s, for instance, Don Giuseppe Genco Russo sent a thrill of nervousness through the island's establishment. Sicily's overlord might be fat, slovenly, violent, and vulgar—he used to spit on the floor, no matter in whose presence—but he was universally sought after and fawned upon. Upon showing up in court, he presented a petition from seven thousand prominent politicians, priests, bankers, doctors, lawyers, and merchants in Mussomeli, his hometown, who begged to testify on his behalf. "Il Signore Cavaliere Genco Russo enjoys the highest esteem of this population. . . . He has dedicated his life to our welfare. He has set an example in probity and rectitude," the petition read. To drive the point home, his lawyer threatened to publish telegrams from thirty-seven Christian Democratic deputies—one a cabinet minister—thanking the Mafia's *capo di tutti capi* for helping them get elected.[5]

As always in such delicate affairs, Italians watched for signals from the Palazzo, the voiceless and faceless command of Italy's governing class. Such signals are cryptic but rarely misread: a casual comment to the press, a few awaited words left unsaid, a ministerial presence bestowed or withheld. Jurists know when the Palazzo wants to press ahead or proceed with leaden feet. (Italy is no exception in that regard.) In this instance, the Palazzo let the Mafia trials happen, and that was all. There were no urgent signals of commitment. It was understood that the courts were on their own.

Italy had no *pentiti* in the 1960s to help out the state prosecutor, and offered no incentives for anyone to do so: no plea bargaining in exchange for a confession, no reduction in prison terms for information given, no Witness Protection Program. There was not even much chance of a sympathetic hearing. People were still incredulous about the Mafia's true nature. A witness turning state's evidence was likely to be dismissed as a liar or crank as well as a rat, before getting a bullet in the head.

(In 1973, a modest Man of Honor called Leonardo Vitale tried to tell an unbelieving Italian court about Sicily's Cosa Nostra—the first made member in Sicily who ever did so. He testified to its code and structure, meetings, methods, and unspeakable crimes. And he named those who were fast becoming its most sinister leaders: his codefendants, Luciano Leggio's men. Prominent among these was Giuseppe "Pippo" Calò, later known as the Mafia's treasurer and one of Leggio's closest allies. The court acquitted his codefendants and committed Leonardo Vitale to a criminal lunatic asylum. He was freed from the asylum in 1984, and shot dead in Palermo within a few weeks of his release.)[6]

Hauling the Mafia into court under these circumstances turned out to be worse than useless. In a succession of spectacular trials pitting Leggio and his fellow bosses against the state, the law in effect became the Mafia's accomplice.

The first of these trials, in 1967, was the first major drug trial held anywhere in the world. Leggio, though still in custody with his Mafia associates, was not a defendant in that case; he had played no major role in the drug trade up to then. But the outcome was crucial to the heroin consortium that he would head in years to come.

The investigating magistrate had enough in hand (he thought) to destroy the network. His information went back to the late 1950s, when the chief suspects—Cichiteddu Greco and Buscetta among them—had come under tight surveillance. He had visited the United States to get a deposition from Joe Valachi, and his archives bulged with voluminous police reports, including a lengthy one on the summit meeting at the Grand Hotel Des Palmes.

The judge indicted everybody alive who had discussed the Sicilian heroin franchise at the Hotel des Palmes. (Lucky Luciano was dead, to the judge's chagrin.) All the American delegates were cited, though none was extradited: Joe Bonanno, Carmine Galante, John Bonventre, the Maggadinos, Santo Sorge. The entire Sicilian contingent was named as well, starting with Don Giuseppe Genco Russo.[7] They were charged with "a criminal conspiracy to enrich themselves, not hesitating to kill and kidnap, and organizing the distribution of narcotics reaching the United States via Sicily." All were acquitted in the autumn of 1968 for "lack of sufficient evidence."[8] Italy did not have another big drug trial until 1983.

The truly calamitous confrontation occurred in December 1967, in a different trial, when Leggio made his first, clamorous courtroom appearance. He had been held in jail for three years—a form of detention that has since been abolished—and was finally being tried after a quarter of a century of unpunished larceny and homicide. This became known as the "Trial of the 114," a showdown between the Mafia and the judiciary that the press called "the impossible war."

The investigating magistrate, Cesare Terranova, was among the finest who have ever challenged the Mafia in Sicily. He took them all on at once—the biggest *mammasantissima,* the most degraded killers, the bosses with the highest connections in Rome. In particular, he went straight for Luciano Leggio.

These two men embodied the dramatic contest between a civilized society and the terrorist criminals preying on it. Leggio had no equal among Sicilian Mafiosi as a frightener and predator. Terranova, who had spent a lifetime fighting the Mafia on the bench and in Parliament, was the man he hated and feared above all others.

Terranova was just as Sicilian as Leggio, born with the same race memories, produced by the same tormented history, moved by the same ethnic heritage to become exactly Leggio's opposite—the kind of Sicilian who redeemed his people's name. Portly and dignified, with resolute features and a direct, clear-eyed gaze, the judge looked like a daguerreotype of somebody's favorite ancestor in the Italian Risorgimento. He was in fact a dedicated jurist of unusually lucid mind and inflexible principles, who was well ahead of his time. He was not taken in by the folklore, not half-fascinated, half-repelled, as so many others were by an ancient and mysterious clandestine order. He believed in none of the Mafia's myths, least of all its immunity to the law.

A judge for some years in the Mafia-dense town of Marsala, Terranova had sent fifty or so Mafiosi to jail by 1964, one or a few at a time, mostly of the lower orders. This was standard procedure everywhere, and about as effective as swatting flies. The age-old problem was how to reach those who ran everything, the untouchables. And now in Palermo, here they were, in police custody, from Leggio down.

On May 31, 1965, Judge Terranova had signed an order sending 114 Mafiosi to trial in a body. In reality, it was a trial of the Mafia itself, the first authentic one in the annals of justice anywhere. Italy had not outlawed Cosa Nostra yet, but there was a law against "organized delinquency." Terranova thought it was time to name names. The nation must "see the phenomenon as it is. . . . The Mafia is organized delinquency and the Mafioso is a delinquent," he wrote in his indictment.

The Mafia is oppression, arrogance, coercion, greed, self-enrichment, power, and hegemony above and against all others. It is not an abstract concept, or a state of mind, or a literary term. . . . It is a criminal organization regulated by unwritten but iron and inexorable rules . . . contaminating all Italy . . . with the tolerance and even passive acquiescence of the organs of the state.

The myth of a courageous and generous Man of Honor must be destroyed, because a Mafioso is just the opposite. A Mafioso stabs in the back, when he is sure the victim is at his mercy. He would sink to any compromise to save himself from danger.

The knowledge that nobody will dare to accuse him, that occult and authoritative influences will work on his behalf, makes a Mafioso haughty and complacent, defiant and overbearing—so long as he is not touched by a just and severe application of the law.[9]

More than a hundred of the haughtiest and most overbearing were now sent to face a judge and jury. Had they been dealt with justly and severely, their whole organization might have been set back twenty years. As it was, they gained as much and then some.

These were the men who had built up the Mafia's gigantic heroin network, mostly from the end of the 1960s on. Luciano Leggio, Tommaso Buscetta, and Cichiteddu Greco were named in the indictment as "promoters and organizers" of the whole criminal organization. Other defendants included Angelo La Barbera, Buscetta's former patron; Pippo Calò, the Mafia's future treasurer and underground ambassador to Rome; Gaetano Badalamenti, future leader of the Pizza Connection ring; Salvatore Catalano of Knickerbocker Avenue; Antonio Salamone, future Mafia patriarch in São Paolo; Gerlando Alberti, Buscetta's "tireless fabrics salesman," who would later supervise a dozen heroin refineries in Sicily; and many others on their way to underworld stardom.

Since nobody knew about their activities abroad, they were accused only of domestic crimes. The charges, running to 221 pages, dated back to 1957: extortion, kidnapping, theft, drug running, tobacco smuggling, public massacre (the Ciaculli bomb), multiple homicides for "cruel and abject motives," and "organized delinquency."

The trial was conducted in the Calabrian city of Catanzaro on the mainland. (Sicily was not considered safe.) Four schoolrooms and a gym had been turned into a courtroom, guarded by five hundred *carabinieri.* The defendants sat in a giant cage at the center. Twenty-five who had decamped in the meanwhile—Buscetta, Greco, Badalamenti, and Catalano among them—were tried *in absentia.* [10] The hearings lasted over a year. A single state prosecutor faced fifty lawyers for the defense. Just one family of a Mafia victim took part as a friend of the court: the parents of Captain Mario Malausa, one of the seven *carabinieri* blown up in Ciaculli. No government ministry held a watching brief, the Palazzo's signal. No politician named in the proceedings was called to testify.

All but 10 of the 114 defendants on trial were acquitted. The few convictions merely underlined the enormity of the Mafia's triumph. Buscetta and La Barbera were found guilty only of two "white deaths." (La Barbera got twenty-two years, Buscetta fourteen.)[11] Nobody was convicted for the Ciaculli bomb, nor did anyone spent much time in jail for organized delinquency.[12] The Mafia was home free, safe for decades to come.

The crowning victory went to Luciano Leggio, exonerated on all counts. Though still in custody pending appeal, he continued to be an honest citizen in the eyes of the law.

But Leggio the Honest Citizen was too much for Judge Terranova, who proceeded to dig deeper into the past, concentrating on Don Luciano's half-forgotten war for supremacy in Corleone. A court had already acquitted Leggio of putting seventy-six bullets into his former Mafia boss Michele Navarra. (Fragments of broken glass from Leggio's car headlights, the only material evidence, were inexplicably missing from a locked box under government seal.) But he had yet to account for the many followers of Navarra's who had also fallen in battle.

Two months after the Trial of the 114, Judge Terranova sent Leggio back to be tried for nine more murders, thereby signing his own death warrant.

Leggio had nursed an almost maniacal hatred for the judge since their first encounter at the Ucciardone prison in Palermo. At that time, he had refused to be interrogated, sending word that he was too sick. When Terranova insisted, Leggio showed up in a wheelchair convulsed with rage. He would not answer questions. When, in response to one of them, he replied that he could not even recall his own name, or his father's and mother's names, the judge instructed an attending clerk: "Write that Leggio does not know whose son he is."

"Leggio actually had foam on his lips; he would have killed me on the spot if he could," Judge Terranova told his wife that night. Later, Leggio admitted as much. "If I could have bitten him then, I would certainly have poisoned him," he testified at his trial for Terranova's murder—where he was acquitted for insufficient evidence. The judge had borne witness to his own approaching murder, in a way. "Yes, I know Leggio hates me; at worst he could kill me," he told a reporter in Palermo. "He considers me responsible for his ruin, and in fact, that's how it was. First I sent him to trial for a series of homicides. Then I went back to dig out old crimes for which he had never stood trial. And I indicted him for those too."[13]

The trial for Leggio's old crimes opened in a different court, in Bari, on the Italian mainland, in February 1969. The whole Corleone clan was in the dock with Leggio this time, sixty-four in all, including his trusted proconsuls Salvatore Riina and Bernardo Provenzano, known as "the Beasts." Leggio appeared in court alternately on a stretcher or on crutches. By now, he had been in jail five years awaiting trial. Life in a prison infirmary hadn't cured him, but hadn't been the death of him either.

With fresh eggs and milk, and expensive delicacies from the outside, he had grown sleeker and more bear-shaped than ever. He was faultlessly suited, and his hair, receding across the crown of his head, was neatly coiffed. At a distance, he looked like a college professor. But the same old Leggio showed through in his big white face, with its insolent smile and eyes spitting malice.

Two witnesses were supposed to testify against him. One, too frightened to take the stand, had been consigned to a lunatic asylum beforehand. (The court noted that he suffered from "a form of psychogenic reaction," meaning stark terror.) The other, a barber, was reduced to jelly by Leggio's freezing stare. ("Nienti sacciu!"—"I don't know a thing"—he shrieked at a reporter who came looking for him years afterward.)[14]

Leggio had always claimed to be a victim of communist persecution. Now he accused the police besides. "My vicissitudes began when a police officer begged me repeatedly to pleasure his wife; and I, for moral reasons, refused," he testified. "I had no relations with that lady. She did not try to lure me. Please don't ask me for names. I am a gentleman."[15]

He spoke of other sordid experiences with law enforcers. "During the war and right afterward, I dedicated myself to the so-called black market. . . . In fact, I made a pile. That attracted first the attention and then the greed of a Carabinieri officer, who asked me for money. I always refused such requests, and that was how I came to be persecuted by the police."[16]

As the trial drew to a close, the presiding judge and jury received identical copies of an anonymous letter signed with a cross:

To the President of the Court of Assizes of Bari and members of the Jury:
    You people in Bari have not understood, or rather, you don't want to understand, what Corleone means. You are judging honest gentlemen of Corleone, denounced through caprice by the Carabinieri and police.
    We simply want to warn you that if a single gentleman from Corleone is convicted, you will be blown sky high, you will be wiped out, you will be butchered and so will every member of your family.
    We think we've been clear. Nobody must be convicted. Otherwise you will all be condemned to death—you and your families.
    A Sicilian proverb says: "A man warned is a man saved." It's up to you. Be wise.[17]

The jury found Leggio guilty of stealing grain in 1948, for which he received a suspended sentence. All sixty-four defendants were pronounced not guilty on all other counts, Leggio included.

The presiding judge conceded that an "impenetrable wall of silence," made up of "fear and connivance," had blocked the state prosecutor at every turn. Nevertheless, the prosecutor had relied "exclusively on information from police informers who didn't want to be named, while direct evidence was scarce or nonexistent." There was no proof that Leggio's "florid patrimonial consistency . . . came from illicit sources," the judge observed. He appeared to have gotten rich through purely "commercial activities." The rest of the "vast material" submitted in evidence was useless. "The court cannot fill the gaps caused by *omertà* . . . overstepping the limits of juridical procedure," he concluded.[18]

This was the law, not to be confused with justice. The public was stunned; Leggio, making a regal exit from the courthouse, was amused. He had always said there was no such thing as a Mafia, he reminded reporters, and the verdict proved it. "If the Mafia is everything they claimed that I was—well then, the Mafia does not exist," he remarked, as he climbed into a luxurious Lancia and sped away.[19]

Leggio's five years in prison had been no hindrance—far from it. Events soon showed that he had become the most esteemed and privileged criminal in the country.

Officially, he was a fugitive upon leaving Bari's courthouse. For Palermo's chief of police ordered his immediate arrest once again, pending formal arrangements for his preventive custody. Unaccountably, Palermo's attorney general then ruled that he could be arrested only in Corleone.

Leggio told the press that he was not going to Corleone; he checked into a clinic on the southern Italian coast instead. The head surgeon advised the police of his presence at once, whereupon the Ministry of the Interior launched a nationwide "hunt" for him. This was the beginning of a protracted farce. People all the way up to the top were covering for him.

The object of this manhunt remained in the clinic for three months, enjoying good medical care and a tender affair with a widowed nurse. Then he moved on to a more deluxe clinic in Rome. His own lawyer told the police of his whereabouts this time. "Specialized personnel, intelligent, well-trained, and expert" were sent from Rome's police headquarters to guard him for the next two months.

When Leggio was quite well, he walked out to a waiting black Mercedes and vanished. (The Mercedes was laid on by Frank "Three Finger" Coppola, an old colleague of Lucky Luciano's deported from the United States, who thought Leggio was "a most exquisite person.")[20]

A couple of policemen, dropping by at the clinic two days later, were surprised to find Leggio gone.[21] They seemed unaware of another order for his arrest, just issued in Palermo for evading the first one.[22] With Interpol now helping to hunt him down in the United States and Venezuela, Leggio returned to the Rome clinic twice for a checkup. He was due back again in January 1970—seven months after the initial arrest order—when reporters finally got on to the story, after which he vanished in earnest.

The scandal shook Italy. Confused explanations issued from high ministerial quarters. The prefect of Palermo hastily sentenced Leggio *in absentia* to a year in jail for failing to turn himself in. (A general amnesty later canceled the sentence.) Thunderous statements were made in Parliament. Its Anti-Mafia Commission investigated "a series of incorrect and objectively illicit acts" on the part of public officials. The commission's report condemned officials' "unconditional surrender" to the most objectively vicious of Mafia chiefs. "Indolence, ingenuity, misplaced hopes for tranquillity and advantage, if not for money, have ended by favoring the rise of this terrible delinquent," the report declared. "How can it be that nobody has been able to cut out this noxious plant?"

No heads rolled. Nobody resigned. Eventually, the public officials under heaviest suspicion were promoted. The attorney general of Palermo, most suspect of all, was propelled upstairs to a mainland post. (The Mafia gunned him down before he could leave with his secrets. Leggio shot him personally, according to fellow Mafiosi in a position to know.)[23]

At the end of 1970, Bari's court of appeals reversed Leggio's unbroken string of acquittals. He was finally convicted—in absentia—of murdering his old Capo-Mafia Michele Navarra more than a decade earlier. But not because there was new evidence. He was found guilty because "no crimes of the Mafia type have been committed in Corleone since Leggio's arrest [in 1964]." The maximum penalty, life imprisonment, was imposed because "Luciano Leggio's sinister personality has been clear in these proceedings, and the fact that he is a Capo Mafia is absolutely beyond debate."[24] The Supreme Court upheld the verdict, but everybody knew it was based on the flimsiest grounds, just as everybody knew that Leggio was guilty. There was no other way to get him. Things had come to that pass.

Still at large when the verdict came down, Leggio entered upon his best years. He had taken to speaking of himself in the third person, lionized in Mafia (and not just Mafia) circles. A trail of expanding criminality suggested where he might be, or had been, no longer just in Sicily but up and down the mainland. A whole new center of Mafia activity grew up around him in Milan, northern Italy's industrial heartland: theft, extortion, building rackets, gambling casinos, a "muscle market" for immigrants from the south, kidnapping on a grand national scale.

Leggio became Baron Osvaldo Fattori, a rich jeweler, in Milan and roamed Europe on eleven other passports: as Pablo Villa, Antonio Tazio, Calogero Polla, and Sebastiano Tavola. In 1972, he was actually photographed at a restaurant in a small Swiss mountain town. "Certain Rome notables were furious at the mania we journalists have for finding hot coals in the ashes," wrote the Italian reporter who snapped the picture.[25]

The police finally caught up with Leggio in 1974 after tapping the phones of lower-cast Mafiosi transplanted to Milan, who would refer reverentially to a certain "Signor Antonio": "Baciamu li mmanu a vossia" ("We kiss the hand of Your Lordship"), the age-old Sicilian peasant's salute to nobility. "Antonio" was a wealthy, middle-class gentleman of stifling respectability, living with a rather plain Yugoslav refugee companion. When the *carabinieri* came for him, his greeting was affable, his smile radiant, somewhat at odds with the machine gun and automatic pistol found in the trunk of his car.

Finally behind bars in Sardinia, his final ascent to the top really began. The Mafia's old guard had never seemed so prosperous and secure, but new money was beginning to do its insidious work. The venture into heroin was about to pay off beyond the wildest expectations. The Corsican Union in Marseilles was breaking up under French and American pressure. The production side of the heroin trade, which it used to dominate, could be joined to the distribution side, now largely in Sicilian hands. The Sicilian Mafia was on the verge of capturing the entire worldwide market.

Accordingly, Men of Honor excluded from the traffic so far were clamoring for a share, while those who had a share wanted more, faster. Leggio, an aging and ailing convict in jail for life, would undertake to sort this all out, in his fashion.

9

Istanbul, Sofia, Naples, and the Golden Crescent

eggio was no sooner in jail than luck and larcenous instinct brought everything together for the Mafia bosses of Palermo. They hooked up with the *babas* of Istanbul and the Camorra of Naples, and the whole heroin cycle from raw materials to manufacturing to marketing came under their dominion.

The *babas,* bosses of what is known now as the Turkish arms-drugs Mafia, were the brokers for morphine base from all over southwest Asia—the Golden Crescent, embracing Iran, Pakistan, and Afghanistan, the largest opium-producing region on earth. The Neapolitan Camorra, engaged in every kind of international contraband, used the most extensive smuggling routes on earth. By 1975, the Sicilian Mafia had a lock on both, through an extraordinary conjunction of events beyond the Sicilians' control, in the United States, Brazil, France, Mexico, Bulgaria, Iran, and Turkey.

Providence, in the form of an insistent American president and a harried French government, knocked the Corsicans right out of the heroin game (the breakup of the French Connection). Strong on law and order (until his untimely political end), Richard Nixon declared war on drug traffickers soon after his inauguration in 1969. His Task Force One, guided by Henry Kissinger, made narcotics an issue of foreign policy. The Corsicans in Marseilles, the world's biggest heroin refiners, were first on America's hit list.

Pressed by the White House, Brazil smashed the Corsicans' enormous South American drug ring in 1972. France, under similar pressure, located and closed down eight of their refineries the same year. Finished in France for the moment, the Corsicans tried to move in with the Camorra in Naples and start again. Sicily's Mafia bosses promptly did what they had been preparing to do anyway. They came up to Naples in force, threw the Corsicans out, and moved in with the Camorra themselves.[1]

Meanwhile, President Nixon's crusade had reached into Turkey. In 1971, at his urging, the flourishing opium poppy was banned. Although the ban was lifted three years later, the *babas,* supplying most of the morphine base for the Corsicans' refineries, were obliged to look for their opium abroad in the meantime. From simple traders, they turned into brokers.[2]

The Golden Crescent, starting at Turkey's eastern border in Iran, was now bursting with opium. Iran, a natural conduit to the West from Afghanistan and Pakistan, had banned its own poppy crop in 1956 on the insistence of a previous U.S. president. But the shah had lifted the ban in 1968, and crops were soon bigger than ever. While much of the opium was going to the million users at home, many Iranian growers preferred to sell for hard currency.

The *babas* became the indispensable middlemen for these growers and others from the eastern Mediterranean to the borders of India. They bought up smaller opium stocks in Syria and Lebanon, and tied up the entire Golden Crescent. Crude labs on Turkey's Anatolian plains converted their opium to morphine base for the Corsicans' French refineries; tons were stockpiled when the bottom dropped out of the market in France.

By 1975, the Turkish Mafia was desperate to sell its morphine. Western addicts would not buy the low-grade Number Three heroin made in primitive quarters at home, mostly used for smoking. They wanted Number Four, to inject in the veins, requiring consummately skilled chemists and sophisticated laboratories—none in evidence since the Corsicans' fall.

The Sicilian Mafia was feeling the strain at the other end. There was not enough heroin to be had for its clients. Frantic American addicts were paying $300 for a fix, up 200 percent in a year, and even that price failed to stimulate production. Europe was refining next to no heroin. Mexico, once a provider for the American West Coast, had bowed to President Nixon's wishes as early as 1969 and destroyed its poppy crop. The Golden Triangle in Southeast Asia—Burma, Laos, Thailand—had plenty of heroin but no way in to the Western market.

Contrary to a popular view, the Golden Triangle was never the West's main source. Even as late as 1986, it was providing less than a fifth of the heroin reaching Europe and North America. Burma, exporting sixty-five tons worldwide in 1988, sent just one ton to the United States.[3] Nearly all the rest went to the proliferating addict population in Asia.

When the shortage was at its height, in 1975, the Golden Triangle was hardly supplying Western users at all. Some highly prized "China White" had gotten through to American addicts in body bags from Vietnam, but this was no substitute for a regular delivery system. "The major constraint seems to have been the lack of reliable connections," reported the DEA's John Bartels, Jr., a year or so later.[4] To make matters worse (for the addicts), the Golden Triangle in Southeast Asia suffered a severe drought in 1975. On the other hand, the Golden Crescent in the Asian southwest enjoyed a bumper poppy crop, and the Turkish Mafia had a corner on it.

In the autumn of 1975, the *babas* of Istanbul approached the Mafia in Sicily. An emissary named Sami Duruoz went ahead to sound out the Sicilians, while Turkey's top criminal bosses waited in a Yugoslav town near the Italian border. Displeased with the news Duruoz brought back, they beat him to death in a Yugoslav hotel room—their version of shooting the messenger—and sent a higher-ranking envoy in his place. Then the two bands got down to business.[5]

Long afterward, when tracking back on the murdered man's mission, Italian investigators realized that they had come upon a momentous happening. The Turkish Mafia was offering its Sicilian interlocutors an incalculable fortune. Together, they were going to build a broad, safe heroin highway from southwest Asia to the heart of Europe.

In the early 1980s, Judge Carlo Palermo uncovered a lethal, self-propelling arms-drug traffic of staggering international dimensions. The judge's investigation began with the discovery of 7.5 kilos of heroin in a northern Italian chicken coop, which led to another 200 kilos found buried in a snow-covered vineyard and finally to impenetrable thickets of international intrigue that were very nearly the death of him (see chapter 16).

Crashing through the thickets, Judge Palermo ran into too many secret services, powerful politicians and party financiers, corrupt public servants, bent bankers, and diplomats piloting their ships of state through tricky East-West waters. In consequence, he was banished to an obscure government office, and his investigation was never completed. The most scabrous testimony he gathered was commandeered by a parliamentary committeee and sealed for the next forty years.

The arms-drugs ring that Judge Palermo stumbled on went back to 1968, when the communist republic of Bulgaria formed a state corporation called Kintex. The PLO in Lebanon was just beginning to shop for arms at the time; and Turkey, a prime target of the Soviet bloc, was wide open for a terrorist siege. Kintex was meant to procure weapons for both the Palestinians and Turks in Europe. It became the only outfit in the world to offer drugs in payment.[6]

"The Bulgarians, primarily through an official government trading firm, Kintex, have an officially sanctioned program for selling illegal drugs to Western Europe and using the proceeds to finance illegal arms transactions and bankroll terrorist groups," said a spokesman expressing the U.S. State Department's belated concern sixteen years after the program began.[7]

The evolving pattern was described to a congressional committee by the DEA's acting director, John Lawn:

Our information indicates that Kintex was formed in 1968 by the merging of three export-import firms. . . . Knowledgeable sources consistently tell us that top-ranking members of the Bulgarian Security Service . . . comprise [its] directorate. . . .

The Bulgarians, through Kintex, became active in assisting the flow of illicit arms throughout Europe to the Middle East.

In 1970, they began to sell heroin and morphine base to European traffickers which had been seized by Bulgarian authorities.

Intelligence sources further indicated a plan by some Kintex directors during this time to import large amounts of opium into Bulgaria for conversion into morphine base and heroin, through selected Turkish traffickers in Sofia.

Two hundred kilos of Bulgarian-made morphine base had been seized in Frankfurt, West Germany, in December 1969, Lawn testified. German chemists had found chemicals in the substance that were only used around Sofia, the Bulgarian capital. The source of supply was identified as "a Turkish national based in Sofia," Lawn continued:

In virtually every report available to the DEA since 1970 about narcotics trafficking in and through Bulgaria, Kintex is mentioned as a facilitator of transactions. . . . Certain smugglers are permitted to conduct their activities within and through Bulgaria. In effect, Bulgarian officials, through Kintex, designate "representatives" to operate as brokers who establish exclusive arrangements with smugglers for a fee. These representatives are primarily composed of Turkish nationals . . . known as the "Turkish Mafia."[8]

The Turkish boss running the show was Abuzer Ugurlu, Turkey's most famous and frightening criminal. "Ugurlu! He's the biggest! He's the godfather!" exclaimed a former Turkish minister of the interior at the mention of his name. A hulking, shaven-headed, hard-eyed villain, Ugurlu kept a crew of professional killers and could buy or silence policemen, customs officers, secret service agents, and members of Parliament. In power if not formal rank—the Turkish Mafia has no structured hierarchy—he was the Boss of All Bosses. His connections were crucial to the phenomenal success of the joint venture with Sicily.

Later, Ugurlu came to be known abroad in another context. It was one of his young hoods, Mehmet Ali Agca, who shot and nearly killed Pope John Paul II in 1981. Ugurlu had not only arranged Agca's escape from an Istanbul prison the year before, but had sent him to shelter in Bulgaria under the wing of a certain Bekir Celenk. Both Ugurlu and Celenk maintained homes and offices in Bulgaria.

Mehmet Ali Agca may have made a convincing lunatic at the trial for the papal shooting—he had his reasons—but he was dead right about the Turkish Mafia's relations with Bulgaria. His story of the Bulgarian connection, much of which was never published, was told to Judge Palermo. Dozens of witnesses bore him out.

Ugurlu owned a Bulgarian passport, an apartment in Sofia, and a villa in Varna on the Black Sea. He had worked for Kintex since 1969, and for the Bulgarian secret service directly since 1974. (He admitted the first item in a Turkish military court; the second is reported in CIA files.)[9] His job was to gather intelligence and get the guns to the right places. In return, he was given a monopoly on the arms for Turkey—a billion-dollar concession.

There was a limit to how many guns could be sold even in Turkey, however. When the country was saturated with weapons, in 1975, Ugurlu moved into drugs as well.[10] From then on, as the DEA noted later, Ugurlu controlled "a multi-billion dollar contraband partially financed by the sale of narcotics."[11]

Ugurlu rarely strayed beyond Turkish-Bulgarian confines. Anywhere else was a risk, but he was almost as safe in his own country as in Bulgaria; no civilian government in Turkey had ever managed to jail him save once, for a week. (After a Turkish army junta took over in 1980, its only recourse was to have him kidnapped on Bulgarian soil and bundled over the border.)[12]

His compatriot, Bekir Celenk, kept a hotel suite in Sofia but dealt mostly with clients abroad. Smooth and worldly, fond of good cigars, sexy women, discos, and baccarat, Celenk was constantly on the move from Sofia to London, Zurich, Vienna, Milan, Damascus, and Beirut. He claimed to be exporting Bulgarian mineral water. In fact, he was trading drugs for arms in Western Europe, and arms for drugs in the Middle East. He had worked for four different Bulgarian agencies in this regard, according to what he told Judge Palermo.

Agca, the pope's would-be assassin, had heard about the two-way trade while working for Ugurlu in Turkey, and seen it firsthand during a summer he spent in Sofia.[13] "The arms would come to Bulgaria from Belgium, Italy, Czechoslovakia, Hungary, Poland, for shipment to Syrian and Lebanese terrorists," he told Judge Palermo. "The trucks would arrive in Sofia, with pistols and machine guns for Arab rebels, Iranians, Iraquis . . . and clients would come from the Middle East, with cash, or smuggled gold, or drugs."

Bekir Celenk had many Turks running the arms into Bulgaria, and moved in and out of the Middle East to swap them for drugs, continued Agca. "Celenk often went to Syria, Lebanon, and Cyprus to buy heroin and morphine from terrorists and Palestinian extremists; he would ship it to Sofia, and bring them arms." Celenk was "a famous personage in Bulgaria" for such swaps, agreed an inside source in the Turkish Mafia, an observation amply confirmed by others.[14]

For all his standing in Sofia, nonetheless, Celenk was just a subaltern. It was Abuzer Ugurlu who presided over the Turkish Mafia in Bulgaria, probably the most privileged and cosseted band of drug runners ever turned loose on the world.

Sofia was their sanctuary, the place they could always run to when the cops were on their heels, the one place where they were never bothered. Many with a price on their heads in Turkey settled in as permanent residents. Big shots were assigned to comfortable villas; others were put up in government guest houses. "These drug dealers resided openly in Sofia, maintaining flamboyant and free-spending lifestyles," testified the State Department's spokesman to the same congressional committee. "Their presence was so obvious and their deals so flagrant that it was impossible not to conclude that they were enjoying official protection."[15]

Though perhaps not everybody's favorite city—it is scarcely the

gayest and freest of world capitals—Sofia was a mecca for the traffickers' clients: "one of the principal meeting points for suppliers of drugs
and arms," according to Judge Palermo.[16] With or without valid passports, clients were waltzed through the airport and lodged in the best
hotels. Later, the Japanese-built Hotel Vitosha became their hangout.
This modern white, thirty-stories-high tower boasted a bowling alley, a
sauna, a king-sized swimming pool, a reflecting lily pond in the land-
scaped garden, several bars and a panoramic restaurant, chic boutiques
charging Paris prices, a naughty nightclub floor show, prostitutes "licensed for foreigners," and a gambling casino featuring blackjack and
roulette. Kintex, just down the road, would frequently pick up the
clients' tab.[17]

(In 1982, a Sicilian delegation arrived in Sofia to map out the movement of huge morphine shipments. Kintex blocked off an entire floor of
the deluxe Park-Hotel Moskva for the conference, and ordered immigration officers not to stamp the Sicilians' passports so as to leave no
trace of their visit.)[18]

While traffickers sported in the Bulgarian capital, Kintex would
take their cargoes in charge, provided they were screened and approved. "Kintex is immensely powerful in this country," said a Turkish
drug smuggler in 1974. "It's not just a government agency. If Kintex
decides not to let you smuggle through Bulgaria, you can have a tough
time here." On the other hand, added his companion, "if you've got the
right connection with that agency, you can pass morphine base through
Bulgaria without the slightest ripple."[19] The smugglers had only to say
when and where the goods were waiting for "controlled entry." Kintex
would collect its cut—15 to 30 percent—and the cargo would roll.

Bulgaria was uniquely placed for the purpose. Sharing a long and
notoriously porous land border with Turkey, the country was the smugglers' bridge from Asia to Europe and vice versa. Fifty thousand trucks
a year crossed over, going or coming. Half of them were transcontinental TIR trucks (Transport International Routier), which could be cus-
toms-sealed by international agreement and travel freely across borders
in transit.[20] Thus, Bulgarian and Turkish TIRs would simply take off
from Sofia with false cargo documents for fruit, chickens, or soft drinks.
"Beaucoup de bonbons," said one driver with a wink, handing over a
bill of lading for cocoa beans at a European border crossing.

Nearly three-quarters of the morphine base reaching the West was
soon moving this way; and the drugs were bankrolling the biggest illicit
arms traffic ever uncovered.

Whole armies could be equipped with the weapons returning eastward through the same channels: Kalashnikovs and Tokarevs by the ton (fifty-six tons in a single shipment to South Yemen from Poland), millions of rounds of ammunition, land mines, grenades, infrared night sights, 105-millimeter cannons, ground-to-air missiles, Cobra helicopter gunships, Leopard tanks. The weapons came from factories and military depots all over East and West Europe: Italy, Spain, Belgium, West Germany, Hungary, Rumania, Czechoslovakia, and Poland.[21]

Huge shipments went to Turkey's right-wing and left-wing terrorists, found to have nearly a million guns between them when the army took over in 1980. Some four-fifths of the PLO's armament also traveled the Bulgarian route, half of it paid for in drugs. The PLO placed Usama Abdul Madir Adim, the organization's former liaison with the Libyan army, in the Turkish Mafia's Rome office to expedite the exchange.[22] The remaining arms went on to trouble spots around the Middle and Far East. Massive cargoes reached Kurdish insurgents in the Turkey-Iran-Iraq triangle, Kosovo's dissidents in Yugoslavia, President Assad's brother Rifat in Syria, and various customers in Saudi Arabia, Kuwait, South Yemen, Pakistan, India, Thailand, the Philippines, and China.[23]

A striking singularity of this two-way trade was the extreme reluctance of any country concerned to do anything about it. Eastern Europe certainly didn't mind the drugs going west; the more the better. Less understandably, Western intelligence services learned of Kintex and the arms-drugs exchange in 1970 but never lifted a finger to stop it.[24] Both sides had an urgent interest in the arms, whether to sell them as a purely commercial proposition, to get them secretly to a chosen destination, or to gather intelligence through the circuit. To go after the drug runners in the same circuit was to disrupt the whole covert operation. By and large, nobody went after them.

All of this was built into the Turkish Mafia's proposal to Sicilian Mafiosi late in 1975: assured morphine supplies, protected delivery routes, and immunity or something close to it. The Sicilians had already taken the Camorra in charge the year before. Now they controlled everything.

The Camorra had established its own delivery routes, in every direction, for every kind of contraband. Cocaine and heroin were regular items, cocaine especially. But tobacco, an old Camorra standby, could give the Sicilian Mafia what it needed most in 1974—money. Setting up a vertical, multinational heroin conglomerate was exceedingly expensive. Thousands of menials had to be hired; there were five thousand on the personal payroll of one egregious Sicilian trafficker alone, Tommaso

Spadaro. Every consignment of raw materials or finished goods had to be paid for on the spot as well, in cash.

In the early 1970s, for reasons still unclear, contraband tobacco was suddenly bringing in that kind of money. Where five hundred cases of foreign cigarettes at a time had been a big deal a few years before, the Camorristi were handling shiploads of thirty-five thousand or forty thousand cases by 1974. Their extravagant leader, Don Michele Zaza, known as 'U pazzu—Michael the Madman—boasted of doing even better.

Sly and falsely humble, illiterate, shifty, garrulous to the point of sounding as crazy as he hoped he looked, Zaza had grown filthy rich on smuggling tobacco. (He smuggled drugs too, but he hated to talk about it.) He kept a Rolls-Royce in Italy, a million-and-a-half-dollar mansion in Beverly Hills, a $13-million-dollar bank account at Mitsui Manufacturers Bank in Los Angeles for spending money, and a quintal of gold (220 pounds) in a Swiss bank vault for a rainy day. He liked to say he had worked his way up in the business. "I worked and saved," he told a quizzical Italian magistrate:

> First I'd sell five cases of Philip Morris, then ten, then a thousand, then three thousand, then I bought myself six or seven ships that you took away from me. . . .
> I used to load fifty thousand cases a month. . . . I could load a hundred thousand cases, $10 million on trust, all I had to do was make a phone call. . . .
> I'd buy $24 million worth of Philip Morris in three months, my lawyer will show you the receipts. I'm proud of that—$24 million![25]

Zaza did not say, though it would be nice to know, where he had bought $100 million worth of Philip Morris cigarettes in the course of a year.

Zaza, a leading boss of the Neapolitan Camorra, became a made member of the Sicilian Mafia in 1974.[26] Several other high Camorra dons were sworn in at the time, binding them to Palermo for life, on pain of death. The two brotherhoods were going to be earning the stakes for the entire heroin enterprise; the Sicilians wanted no doubts about who was in charge.

Their pact was sealed at a summit meeting near Naples, on the sprawling estate of the Camorra's notorious Nuvoletta brothers. The outcome was "an extremely dangerous Mafioso consortium which does not tolerate insubordination," the Carabinieri of Naples reported. "It is dedicated mainly to smuggling tobacco but also to the drug traffic . . . and its members are accountable solely to the biggest Sicilian bosses."[27]

The Grecos of Ciaculli, Gaetano Badalamenti, and the rising young Stefano Bontate were all in on the deal. Leggio was represented by his Corleonese proconsuls, the Beasts. The Cuntreras' partner in Venezuela, Giuseppe Bono, flew over to visit Italy often—he was a particular friend of Don Michele Zaza's—as did their lieutenant in London, Francesco Di Carlo. The Mafia's patriarch in Brazil, Antonio Salamone, kept in touch through a brother.

Sicilian Mafiosi began to commute to Naples. They liked the city, the next best thing to Palermo. Business could be done here in much the same way, in homey trattorias like 'U Cafone, over mounds of mussels and platters of spaghetti *marinara,* served by deferential waiters who had long since learned to be deaf and dumb.

Several Mafiosi moved to Naples bag and baggage, and the Cupola sent an accredited ambassador, Gaetano "Tanino" Fidanzati, a voracious dealer in junk.[28] One of the hundred-odd Mafiosi who had walked free in the Trial of the 114, Fidanzati had been consigned to guarded exile in northern Tuscany, but that was no problem. He merely asked for and received permission to take a "temporary thermal cure" of long duration—in Naples, where he roomed with Don Michele Zaza.[29]

The sealing of the Mafia-Camorra pact in 1974 produced a couple of riotous years. The port of Naples got so choked up with contraband ships that the Cupola arranged to off-load the cigarettes in turns. Zaza's ship came first, the Cupola's next, another Sicilian ship third, the Nuvoletta brothers' last. But '*U pazzu* didn't have an honest bone in his body. Such were his cunning antics at the others' expense that the Cupola was finally obliged to call the whole thing off.

It no longer mattered, anyway. The boom in contraband tobacco was subsiding, the Mafia and Camorra were both heading for the real money, and heroin was building into a great tidal wave.

o◯o

Early in 1976, Abuzer Ugurlu and his biggest drug partner in Istanbul, Huseyn Cil, sent a relative of Cil's to Italy to tie up the Sicilian deal. That done, the Turkish Mafia stationed a go-between in Milan to deal with its new associates. His name was Salah Al Din Wakkas, and he "answered to Ugurlu," according to the DEA.[30]

Heroin refineries sprouted in Italy overnight. They were well equipped, abundantly supplied, manned by superb chemists who used to work in Marseilles, and capable of producing far more than Marseilles ever did. One alone, in the seaside and gambling resort of San Remo near the French border, could turn out fifty kilos of high-grade heroin a week—two and a half tons a year, 112 million fixes—for customers in northern Italy, France, Switzerland, Holland, and West Germany.

By agreement with the Sicilians, when the Turkish and Sicilian traffickers carved up Europe together, Abuzer Ugurlu was given his own heroin territory as well. The Turkish Mafia thereupon hired its own Marseilles chemists and opened heroin refineries in West Germany and Holland, working in tandem with the Sicilians for distribution.

Between them, the Sicilian and Turkish dealers had a devastating impact. Holland became not only Europe's number two heroin supplier but its number one heroin victim, with the worst addiction problem on the Continent. West Germany, with only twenty-five known heroin addicts in 1975, reported 623 deaths from heroin overdose just three years later.[31] Spain experienced an explosion of heroin addiction starting in 1977. In Great Britain there was a "sudden steep rise" around the same time. West Berlin's deaths from heroin overdose shot up from almost zero in 1973 to 84 by 1977. France, with no hard drugs in evidence up to 1973, registered a "dramatic increase of epidemic proportions" starting in 1977. The same thing happened in Greece and Portugal.[32] Italy, with just one overdose death in 1973, was turned into Europe's most intractable case.

In Italy, the northern labs supplying Europe were small change compared with those in the south supplying America. The first two refineries found in Palermo could produce fifty kilos a week *apiece*— five tons a year, far more than American addicts could absorb at the time—and at least a dozen refineries were operating on the island before long. The refineries were never short of basic ingredients. Ugurlu's man in Milan, Salah Al Din Wakkas, saw to that. Much of the morphine base came by sea in the early days, as he later told Judge Palermo:

Turkish fishing boats would load up at Varna [on Bulgaria's Black Sea coast]. . . . They'd take on arms, like Kalashnikovs, and a lot of cigarettes made in Bulgaria. When they got past the Straits of Dardanelles, they'd off-load the cigarettes and some arms onto other fishing boats, and take on the morphine.
Then they'd head for Cyprus. . . . A Sicilian from Catania would be waiting there. . . . A group of Sicilians would transfer the drugs and arms to their own fishing boats.[33]

Overland, TIR trucks would rumble into northern Italy from Istanbul, via Bulgaria and Yugoslavia, with fifty, a hundred, two hundred kilos of morphine base at a time. Some turned north toward Munich and Berlin. The rest proceeded from Trieste, near the Yugoslav frontier, to staging areas all over the Italian north: Trento, Bolzano, Verona, Milan. About a third of the morphine went to the northern refineries. The rest was for Sicily.

Wakkas, coordinating the inflow, dealt with the highest Mafia echelons in Palermo. Most members of the Cupola were on his list, starting with the *mammasantissima* just chosen to head it, Gaetano Badalamenti. A major client was Gerlando Alberti, the "tireless fabrics salesman" who was in charge of Sicily's proliferating refineries. The Cupola's traffic manager for heroin shipments to New York, Francesco Mafara, was another. Ambassador Fidanzati's numerous brothers were among those shipping the morphine to Palermo from Milan.[34]

By the end of 1976, Sicilian Men of Honor were in a state of euphoria. Twenty years after acquiring the American heroin franchise, they were ready to launch the world's biggest commercial enterprise. All the pieces had fallen into place, by chance and through their own intuitive gift for raising a nose in the air and sniffing out where the money was.

They were in the clear. No police force anywhere appeared to have an inkling of what they had been doing over the previous twenty years. The few who had been noticed were seen through the optic of some local or national crime scene. The fact that they were now part of a criminal fraternity girdling the planet—that the Sicilian Mafia had gone international—was wholly unknown.

10

The Heroin Pipeline

he Sicilians' extraordinary international organization came close to discovery in 1979, when an insignificant Sicilian hood in Brooklyn turned himself in to the FBI. Absorbed in the local crime scene in Brooklyn, law enforcers never noticed a human speck there who hand-carried more than a ton of heroin—over fifty million fixes—in 1977 alone. And he continued to be invisible even after he turned himself in, the first and last Sicilian Mafioso in America who ever did so.

The FBI's report gave this description:

Name	Luigi Ronsisvalle
Date of Birth	Oct. 1, 1940
Place of Birth	Catania, Sicily
Alien Registration No.	A14 784 513
	Entered US at New York
	City, March 16, 1966
Build	Fat

Occupation	Five years ago Luigi was a waiter. He stated that he kills people for a living.[1]

Actually, Ronsisvalle did other things for a living as well, which, since the FBI did not ask about them, he did not mention. Aside from killing thirteen people (eleven for business and two for pleasure), he had sold hijacked meat, collected illicit gambling debts, put shylock money out on the street, torched pizzerias, kited hot checks, passed counterfeit money, stolen a million dollars' worth of diamonds, and moved more heroin than almost anybody would find conceivable.

Carrying the heroin drove him to drink, but not to the FBI. He gave himself up because the last crime he had committed was, in his opinion, "the worst thing a man can do." He had robbed a lady.[2] Not until he held her up (for the $2,000 in her briefcase) did he feel that he had lost the last shred of his honor. "In Sicily, if a man belongs to the Mafia, even if a million dollars in a lady's pocketbook, he don't touch the lady," he tried to explain in his strangled English.

A saddened, seedy, overweight, middle-aged hood, Ronsisvalle could not shake off childhood memories of the manly figure he had longed to become. Growing up in Sicily, he had been fascinated by the Mafia's image of knightly gallantry and insolent villainy, by the mystery surrounding this secret brotherhood, the fright it inspired, and respect it commanded. He could hardly wait to be a made Mafioso. "At age ten, eleven, twelve, like American kid falls in love with baseball, I fall in love with the Mafia," he said.

Thirteen years in Brooklyn had turned him off its American counterpart. "In America is no Mafia. They don't even got no idea what is Mafia," he declared.

The real Mafia never deal with heroin. Man of Honor no go killing kids around the world. Mafia never do that. I never hear this when I was in Sicily, never.

There is only one Mafia, Sicilian, only one. Because these people who come from Sicily . . . they come here and they rob their own people, go around pick up money every week, killing Italian people. . . . They call themselves a Mafia. But in Sicily today they no have nobody.

Alas, in Sicily they had everybody (in the Mafia, that is). Ronsisvalle always assumed that he was working for Americans in Brooklyn.

In fact, his bosses in Brooklyn were working for Sicilians in Palermo.

When he got to New York in 1966, several thousand men under the Sicilian Mafia's command were slipping into the United States and fanning out across the country unobserved. "They were setting up a heroin net, all through the sixties and seventies, right under our noses," said the FBI's Mafia expert in New York, James Kallstrom.[3]

"The first we ever heard of the Sicilian Mafia here was the Pizza Connection case in 1984," added Louis Schiliro, in the FBI's Brooklyn-Queens office. "The New York Police Department doesn't even acknowledge the Sicilian Mafia *now* [1986]. . . . The Pizza case opened all sorts of windows for us, but we never really understood where the American Mafia's five Families fit in. We termed it 'the Sicilian faction of the Bonanno Family,' but now we see it was mislabeled. The informants we developed laughed at our theories. 'If you're made in Sicily, your allegiance is to Palermo,' they told us."[4]

Luigi Ronsisvalle might have told them that and much more. If nothing else, he could have alerted them to the staggering dimensions of the drug traffic. At the time he turned himself in, 1979, the biggest heroin seizure on record anywhere was of eighty-six kilos, in New Jersey in 1971.[5] Ronsisvalle had moved fifteen times as much in 1977, personally. He could have identified the Sicilians running him in Brooklyn, and the head of what was thought to be the Sicilian faction of the Bonanno Family. He had actually seen Salvatore Catalano take over the Bonannos' enclave on Knickerbocker Avenue late in 1976.

Ronsisvalle had also served a Sicilian faction in the Gambino Family—a still more subterranean formation that mattered far more. He used to deliver to its enclave on 18th Avenue, where one or another of the Cherry Hill Gambinos was usually on hand. He had watched them all fraternize with mysterious Men of Honor just in from Palermo, and had even attended a sit-down with colleagues of theirs from Caracas.

These were the everyday facts of his life. An unwitting conscript in the Sicilian Mafia's silent invasion, he had no idea of its magnitude. Like a man going deaf, he could hear these people talking but could not make out what they were saying. All he did was carry out their orders.

Thus, Luigi Ronsisvalle never really knew how much he knew. His interrogators could not imagine that he knew anything whatever.

o⊙o

He was just another number in a federal penitentiary until Detective Douglas Le Vien found him there in 1985, six years after he settled in. Attached to President Reagan's Commission on Organized Crime by then, Le Vien had long since abandoned his luckless pursuit of Enzo Napoli. To have known Enzo Napoli was to understand Ronsisvalle, however.

Ronsisvalle had been one of Napoli's *picciotti.* He had stolen the diamonds for Napoli, kited his checks in Miami, bought in on a couple of his heroin deals. Almost certainly, he had also killed for Napoli. His regular partner for contract hits, a humble Sicilian tailor who crossed the Atlantic on demand, was one of the people Napoli called most often in Palermo.[6] But Ronsisvalle had done odd jobs for several others in Brooklyn as well. Passed from hand to hand, he had gotten a vivid panoramic view of the local crime scene from ground level.

His customary hangout was the Cafe Viale on Knickerbocker Avenue. At the back of the café was a round table favored by a forgotten generation of Mustache Petes, hunched in their overcoats under broad black felt hats. Upstairs was a floating baccarat game raided periodically by the police. Here, or at the Cafe Sport down the street, newly arrived fugitives from Italian justice would sit around by the hour, hoping to make contact with the Mafia in New York.

These were Mafiosi of no account, who were held to the standing rules; they could not work in Brooklyn without some Family's permission. Higher-ranking Sicilian Mafiosi appeared to have no such worries—Buscetta, say, or the Napoli brothers. Rules or no rules, such men were encamped all over the Americans' turf: in the five boroughs of New York, in New Jersey, Delaware, and Pennsylvania, in Texas, Florida, Virginia, Massachusetts, and Vermont, in Michigan, Illinois, California, Arizona, Maryland, and Washington, D.C.[7] Singling them out was not easy, because so many in both the Sicilian and American Mafias bore the same names, shared the same relatives, and spoke the same undecipherable jargon. Ronsisvalle could no more tell them apart than the police could; the Americans' Sicilians and the Sicilians' Sicilians all looked alike to him.

He had arrived in 1966 with only a vague introduction from his *Capo-Mafia* in Catania. "If you go to Brooklyn, to Knickerbocker Avenue, mention my name," advised the boss. The name, mentioned over a cup of coffee at the Cafe Viale, established his credentials for one of a dozen hit men who had come over from Sicily a couple of years before. Soldiers in the the Buccellato Family of Castellammare del Golfo, these men had been sent to give Joe Bonanno a hand. Bonanno had brought over scores of Castellammaresi in the past. But he was in fresh trouble in 1964, having put out contracts on three fellow members of Cosa Nostra's Commission, starting with Carlo Gambino.[8] Expecting all hell to break loose when he was found out, he had sent for reinforcements.

It did not take Ronsisvalle long to perceive that the Bonanno Family owned Knickerbocker Avenue. The *capo* in charge of the street, invariably a Bonanno man, reigned supreme. "Anything moving in there, even a tree, they got to say to him, I want to move the tree," Ronsisvalle said later.

His new career began with a modest proposition from a fellow Sicilian named Paolo La Porta, who would unknowingly provide the first breakthrough in the Pizza Connection case. Later, La Porta would brag to an undercover DEA agent that "his people" were laundering $5 million a day in drug money.[9] Even so, he was a small-time punk when Ronsisvalle first met him. "Say, you're from Sicily. Can you show us some guts?" La Porta asked him. Ronsisvalle was game. "I just got to United States. This is Mafia American, let's go, let's do it."

He was given a .45 and sent to rob a drugstore. The till contained less than $50, and the druggist shot Ronsisvalle besides (whereupon La Porta ditched him and drove off at high speed). Wounded in the leg but still game, he got himself home.

When he recovered, La Porta took him to Niagara Falls. The two of them crossed the bridge into Canada, furnished false passports to six waiting Sicilian aliens, collected $500 a head, and brought everyone back in under an hour.

Ronsisvalle was told only that La Porta "had some kind of connection to get passports." In fact, he was helping to run the Sicilian Mafia's underground railroad. Several thousand of its troops were being ferried in this way, to the mystification of American officials.[10]

(U.S. authorities were making "seemingly fruitless efforts" at the time to understand the cause of an influx of Italian aliens "in unprecedented numbers," noted a New York State Police report. "Most of [those] entering the U.S. illegally between the mid-1960s and early 1970s were fugitives from Italy on charges ranging from murder to narcotics trafficking," stated an FBI report later.)[10]

The trip to Niagara Falls settled Ronsisvalle's future. Whatever he had expected of America, he was hopelessly entrapped. All but illiterate, he had no money or conventional skills. He couldn't get used to the country, couldn't master its language, couldn't even communicate in anything but an unintelligible Sicilian code. He could only take what the Mafia had to offer in Brooklyn, like it or not. (We don't know which.) He was never altogether broke from then on, though he appears to have been cheated so methodically that he didn't get rich either. As the occasions arose, he worked as a gofer, an armed burglar, an enforcer, a contract killer, and a truly prodigious heroin courier.

Murder was easier in the United States than in Italy, he found, because "in New York we have five Families, and if I kill somebody—is more easy to fix." Sometimes he chose his own victim. One was a Mafia loan shark who had lent him $5,000 to put out on the street. When a fellow in the Bronx failed to pay up, the loan shark wanted Ronsisvalle to break the man's legs. In a reassuringly human flare of temper, he shot the loan shark instead.[11]

Otherwise, the contracts were farmed out so many times over that he could hardly tell who sent him. Some he would willingly have murdered without pay: a gambler who had staked his own wife in a poker game, for instance. (The man had offered a night in bed with her, to raise the ante when his money ran out. He lost the hand; she acquiesced that night, but told her brother in the morning. Her brother happened to be a cop on a Brooklyn beat.)

Toward the end of his career, Ronsisvalle was in prime demand as a hit man. A go-between offered him two contracts on behalf of the renowned Italian financier and swindler Michele Sindona, God's Banker and the Sicilian Mafia's, about whom more later.[12] The go-between, a boon companion of Enzo Napoli's named Mario Maimone, wanted Ronsisvalle to eliminate a U.S. attorney in New York and a lawyer handling the receivership of Sindona's bankrupt bank in Milan. The conversations went like this, according to Ronsisvalle:

He say, "Luigi, you want to make $100,000?" I say, "Whoa, no ask." He say, "The D.A. is too much on Mr. Sindona's back. They want to kill him. They pay the money in Switzerland." I say, "Whoa, you are talking about something heavy. . . ."
Before that, he said to me: "Mr. Sindona wants you to go to Italy, and the name is Mr. Ambrosoli. They pay you $100,000 in Switzerland." I say, "No kill no people in Italy. The law is too tough for me over there."

Ronsisvalle eluded that job—Sindona found somebody else to take care of Mr. Ambrosoli in Milan—and failed to catch up with the federal attorney.[13] But he did agree to silence another inconvenient witness:

Mr. Maimone say to me: "We have a gentleman from Milano who make settlement with FBI, testify against Mr. Sindona." I go in office of gentleman,

101 Wall Street, and I say: "You better no testify no more, or I will kill you, your wife, and your kid." That was the end of these people.

Long ago, in Catania, he might have flinched at the thought of killing a wife and child. Once he had slipped into the junk business, however, his meager store of Mafia honor was fast running out.

o⊂⊃o

Ronsisvalle had gotten into junk when Salvatore Catalano took over Knickerbocker Avenue, in the late autumn of 1976. Catalano, arriving a decade earlier from Ciminna, Sicily, had opened a modest newspaper-souvenir shop opposite the Cafe Viale. Taciturn and watchful, he had kept himself to himself. "Nobody knows him. Some people, they know him, but he was very, very quiet man," said Ronsisvalle.

In those days, the Bonannos' *capo* on the street was an obstinate old-timer called Pete Licata, who would not allow narcotics in his territory "He say, 'I want no drugs on Knickerbocker Avenue, no heroin. . . . You start selling wholesale, and then you start to sell retail, and then we are going to ruin the Italian people here.' They say, 'Okay Don Pietro,' and after, they kill him," Ronsisvalle explained.

Licata was murdered on November 4, 1976. Three days later—without a murmur from the Bonanno Family—Catalano became Knickerbocker Avenue's new *capo*. Several fresh faces from Sicily promptly appeared. In particular, two strangers from Castellammare del Golfo took over the floating baccarat game at the Cafe Viale, possibly worth half a million dollars a week. They were Cesare Bonventre and Baldassare "Baldo" Amato, who became Catalano's inseparable companions and formed a trio that dominated Knickerbocker Avenue for the better part of a decade. Together, they took over the American Mafia's entire Bonanno Family for a while.[14] Together, too, they wielded iron control over the heroin entering and leaving the Bonannos' Brooklyn enclave.

Baldo Amato would wind up in the dock with Salvatore Catalano eventually, for the Pizza trial. Cesare Bonventre would have done the same had he not met his end in three fifty-gallon drums at a glue factory in Garfield, New Jersey. (His head was in one and assorted limbs in the others.)

Though Ronsisvalle never thought of this new regime as the "Sicilian faction," he had good reason to remember its ascent. He began to move heroin in a matter of days after Salvatore Catalano took command of Knickerbocker Avenue. "I feel so bad, I have to load my belly with scotch," he said. (Testifying at the Pizza trial in 1985, he was asked whether he had begun to drink heavily because he was "so morally disgusted" by his heroin deliveries for the Mafia. "Well, I've got to see you with forty pounds of heroin in a bag and see how you feel," he replied.)

Ronsisvalle's first cargo of heroin was uncut, plainly just in from abroad, and he only had to carry it a few miles across Brooklyn: from Knickerbocker Avenue in Bushwick to 18th Avenue in Bensonhurst. Why two American Mafia Families, the Bonannos and the Gambinos, should be sending cases of pure heroin to each other—as he thought— was none of his business; he just made the deliveries. In the course of the next twelve months, he made fifteen trips from the one avenue to the other, each time with a 40-kilo load. That came to 600 kilos of heroin in all, 1,325 pounds, perhaps half the annual supply for the growing addict population of greater New York.

The Sicilian running Ronsisvalle was one Felice Puma, who owned the Cafe Scopello in Bonanno territory. Ronsisvalle would pick up the crated shipment at Puma's café on Knickerbocker Avenue, ride shotgun in the van with a double-barreled *lupara* on his knees, then drop the crate off at Enzo Napoli's café on 18th Avenue—the Mille Luci.

The work wasn't hard. It wasn't even very dangerous. The Brooklyn Narcotics Squad was going after pushers selling fractions of an ounce in little glassine bags. It wouldn't have occurred to a cop in 1976 to look for over half a ton of heroin moving from the Bonannos' territory to the Gambinos'. Nobody in law enforcement had any idea that so much heroin could have entered the country.

Ronsisvalle was paid $5,000 a load, about a hundredth of 1 percent of its value on the street. He had no complaints so long as the work lasted, but it came to a sudden stop early in 1977. They were in for "a dry spell," Felice Puma told him. "You got to relax a little while. I am waiting . . . I don't know when."

Then, that August (when a dozen refineries in Sicily came on stream), Puma gave him the good news. "He say: 'We are in business again. . . . Do you know the pipe from Canada into the States, the one that brings oil? We have same thing with heroin coming to U.S. from Sicily.' "

This was what Sicilian traffickers had worked toward for twenty years. Their heroin pipeline to America marked their rise to the heights of the international underworld. They were the biggest manufacturers in the West now, allied to the biggest raw material suppliers (the Turkish Mafia), assured of privileged access to the biggest market, served by their own intercontinental distribution system, the largest ever mounted for narcotics.

Strictly speaking, the Sicilian Mafia did not quite have a monopoly; there would always be independents making and selling heroin. From here on, however, most independents would have to use the Sicilians' distribution channels, or broker their deals through Palermo, or close shop.

The inauguration of the pipeline in 1977 brought an irruption of heroin such as America had never seen. Sicilian traffickers were thrusting the drug into pushers' hands, offering prodigal quantities on a buy-now-pay-later basis, a practice unheard of up to then. "But I don't have the cash!" protested a DEA undercover agent when several kilos, worth perhaps half a million dollars wholesale, were pressed upon him by Paolo La Porta. "Who's talking about cash?" replied the agent's smiling, friendly mark.[15]

By the end of 1977, the U.S. heroin addict population had shot up to 750,000, almost twenty times what it had been when Sicily's Men of Honor began their invasion in 1963.[16]

o⊂⊃o

Forty-eight hours after Ronsisvalle got the good news about the "pipe from Canada," he noticed a stranger in close conversation with Salvatore Catalano at the Cafe Scopello. This was Giuseppe Ganci, the Sicilian Cupola's new overseer in New York. Ten days later, Ronsisvalle was back at work.

Now he was getting out of Brooklyn. Puma sent him to Los Angeles twelve times by plane, and to Chicago fifteen times by train. He carried some twelve kilos of heroin to the one city and three hundred kilos to the other. Twice, he brought hundred-kilo loads up from Florida to New York without turning a hair; they might have been cartons of breakfast cereal or detergent.

On one of those occasions, Puma phoned and told Ronsisvalle to hop a plane for Miami. Puma himself was waiting on a downtown Miami street in a red Porsche the next morning. A *lupara* and a .38 were on the seat next to him, and 100 kilos (220 pounds) of heroin were in the trunk. The pair then drove nonstop from Miami to Knickerbocker Avenue. When they drew up to the Cafe Scopello, Ronsisvalle recognized the man waiting outside; Salvatore Catalano in person. The state would be heavily indebted to Ronsisvalle for this testimony one day; he was the only witness in the seventeen-month Pizza Connection trial who had actually seen Catalano awaiting a 100-kilo heroin consignment.

At that time, 1977, the Brooklyn police had never heard of Catalano; and the Italian police had lost sight of him since he walked free in the Trial of the 114. In his own realm, however, the self-made *capo* of Knickerbocker Avenue had become an imposing personage.

A mere street-level boss, Catalano mingled with the highest Men of Respect in both the Bonanno and Gambino Families. Ronsisvalle kept running into Catalano on Gambino territory, mixing with the Mafia gentry. Some were American bosses; Aniello Della Croce, the Gambinos' mighty underboss, was a regular crony. But most were the Sicilians' Sicilians: John, Rosario, and Giuseppe Gambino of Cherry Hill, Enzo Napoli, and so on.

It did not occur to Ronsisvalle that he was privy to a chillingly dangerous secret. Watching the Sicilians' Sicilians drift back and forth daily between the two U.S. Mafia enclaves—even shifting their incredible cargoes of heroin from the one place to the other—he could hardly help noticing the deferential treatment reserved for the Sicilians. A brighter fellow might have realized that they were a group apart, engaged in a very particular mission. Luckily for Ronsisvalle, he didn't give the matter a thought.

In April 1977, Ronsisvalle was given an unusual glimpse into the complicated relationships between the Sicilian Mafiosi in Brooklyn and their American hosts. It happened during the heroin "dry spell," when he pulled off a million-dollar diamond heist for his personal patron, Enzo Napoli.

Napoli had had the job all figured out. Ronsisvalle and an accomplice were in and out of a shop in the heart of New York's diamond district within ten minutes. After giving them $25,000 on account, Napoli took the diamonds to sell—he threw them on the table for Doug Le Vien the next night—while Ronsisvalle withdrew to Chicago until the heat wore off.

He had barely settled into a Chicago hotel when two hit men came looking for him. "They open the door and start shooting my bed and then go inside the toilet, shooting inside there. Mr. Enzo Napoli tried to kill me to no give me my share," said Ronsisvalle later. He escaped unharmed, having moved in with a lady upstairs who had a tower suite and color TV. But he went back to New York "with something on my mind. I want to kill Mr. Enzo Napoli."

Unfortunately, word of his intentions got back to Knickerbocker

Avenue, whereupon Salvatore Catalano stepped in. "He said to me: 'Luigi, I hear Mr. Vincent Napoli never take care of you. I am going to make sure you get whatever coming to you.' I say: 'I don't want that. I am going to take care of him personal.' He say: 'No, that is not the way . . . I take care of everything.' "

A classic Mafia sit-down followed at Da Cesare, an exclusive East Side restaurant in Manhattan. Gathered around the table with Luigi Ronsisvalle and his fellow burglar was an array of big shots who would not ordinarily put themselves out for a nobody like Ronsisvalle. Enzo Napoli was there, flanked by an emissary sent up from Caracas by his brother Antonino "to cool the beef. That's my purpose." A cousin of Salvatore Catalano's with important heroin interests in Venezuela had come along. Catalano himself presided, presumably representing the Bonanno Family. Next to him was the *consigliere* of the Gambino Family, Joe N. Gallo, representing America's most powerful Mafia leader, Paul Castellano.

It was quickly apparent that cooling the beef was not their only purpose. They were there to talk about a million dollars' worth of diamonds. Enzo Napoli was plainly entitled to their protection from a miserable low-grade contract killer, but he had his obligations too. He had mounted the heist on American Mafia territory. Apart from paying off his own Sicilian superiors, he would have to offer the Americans their due.

As things worked out, Ronsisvalle and his partner got an extra $30,000 apiece. Everybody else got a diamond. Napoli then produced a glittering four-carat gem and directed Ronsisvalle to take it "in appreciation" to Paul Castellano, reigning chief of the Gambino Family and America's Boss of All Bosses. Thus, on Salvatore Catalano's orders, Ronsisvalle was obliged to shake Enzo Napoli's hand instead of putting a bullet through his head. "I went out with my tail between my legs," he said.

(Was it true that Catalano had "interfered with your desire to kill a man named Napoli?" defense counsel asked him at the Pizza Connection trial. "Yes," he replied, explaining that Napoli had cheated him of his share in a robbery and then tried to kill him. "I believe if you were in my place, you would have done the same thing," he added, "evoking loud laughter from jurors as well as spectators.")[17]

Ronsisvalle's career in America came to an end in the spring of 1979, when he robbed the lady. He had been told the bearer would carry a payroll of $30,000—it was only $2,000—but had not been told that the bearer was a lady. Ronsisvalle was arrested and managed to pay the

$500 bail, but didn't see how he could pay a lawyer. "Because I have robbed a woman, I can't go on Knickerbocker Avenue and say I need some money," he explained.

He also feared the Bonanno Family's wrath. Visiting Sicilian Mafiosi around Knickerbocker Avenue were not supposed to go around stealing without consulting the Family. "They are going to spit in my face. Those people are going to shoot me in the head," he declared, not realizing that "those people" were his own people.

There were other reasons for Ronsisvalle to give up his freedom, betray the brotherhood he had revered since childhood, and put himself in the hands of the detested *sbirri* (cops). He was tired, fed up with the company he kept, and filled with self-loathing. "How do I face it, what I have done with my life—everything in the drain?" he exclaimed.

Whatever his faults, he had the virtue of simplicity. Before going down, he tried to blackmail the biggest Mafia man he knew. He sent a letter to Don Michele Sindona, asking for $20,000 in remembrance of things past. "I say, if he no give it to me by tomorrow night, six o'clock, I will turn myself in to the FBI and I will go in prison. I don't know how much I am going to get, but he will go with me."

Sindona did not go with him. (He went separately.) But Ronsisvalle turned himself in anyway. He just walked into police headquarters on 5th Street in Brooklyn and said, "Please call the FBI. My name is Luigi Ronsisvalle. I want to give up myself."

He might have amazed the FBI agents who questioned him, as he would one day amaze a spellbound judge and jury. He was an unexpected miracle for U.S. attorneys in the Pizza Connection trial, once Doug Le Vien had found and deciphered him. But the sodden hood who presented himself to FBI agents in 1979 was unlikely to stir their fancy. Ignorant of the yawning gaps in their knowledge, he poured out a confused and disjointed tale. They got him for murdering a cook and attempting to murder a federal attorney, and he vanished behind prison walls.[18]

From the Pipeline to the Pizza Parlor

uring the year when Luigi Ronsisvalle was hand-carrying over a ton of pure heroin around Brooklyn—1977—Detective Douglas Le Vien discovered that Enzo Napoli had opened a pizzeria in Virginia Beach, Virginia. It was called the Little Sicily, and Tommaso Buscetta's sons Antonio and Benedetto were his partners. Not even Le Vien could have imagined where the discovery might lead, in the unlikely event of his having a chance to pursue it. Here was a vital clue to the Sicilian Mafia's underground delivery system for heroin—the Pizza Connection in all its enormity, which nobody to this day has ever pursued to the end.

The Pizza Connection uncovered in a New York courtroom in 1986 was only a segment of the connection that is still in place. After six years of crushingly difficult and often brilliant investigation, the FBI and DEA failed to close down one suspect pizzeria. They succeeded only in exposing a faction in a single American Mafia Family, working with thirty-odd men in a single Sicilian heroin ring, involving deliveries to a single corner of the United States, amounting to no more than 150 kilos a year.

But the Sicilian Mafia was bringing in three or four or even five tons of heroin a year by the mid-1980s.[1] There were a number of intersecting rings—nobody knows how many—directed by hundreds of Men of Honor, employing thousands of menials and associates, delivering heroin to every corner of the country, in collusion with several American Mafia Families, the seemingly untouchable Gambino Family in particular.

Big cases, big problems. No U.S. agency was equipped, or prepared, or remotely imaginative enough to investigate anything that big. None is even now. So the Little Sicily Pizzeria in Virginia Beach was left in peace.

To the Virginia State Police, the only people who noticed, the joint looked shady. It "opened and closed more or less at will," wrote a sergeant in police intelligence, and the management was thought to have burned down twenty-two buildings in the vicinity within two months.

Detective Le Vien had discovered the pizzeria by pulling the records of Enzo Napoli's long-distance phone calls. The Little Sicily's number was among the six that Enzo called most often. He would ring somebody there once or twice a week, and somebody there was spending around $5,000 a month on phone calls to hundreds of pizzerias throughout the United States, as well as Milan, Palermo, and Caracas.

In July 1977—it took six months of pestering—Le Vien persuaded U.S. Customs to run an international computer check on calls made from Enzo Napoli's six favorite phone numbers, the Little Sicily's included. The computer turned up two hundred phone numbers of known major traffickers in drugs and weapons, from Miami to New Orleans to San Diego, Dallas, Detroit, Chicago, Seattle, Washington, D.C., and strategic points in Europe and South America.[2] What Le Vien had in his hands was almost certainly a blueprint of the Sicilian Mafia's point-to-point circuit for marketing heroin nationwide. The Little Sicily had to be a major money-laundering center if not actually a staging area, linked by phone to several hundred pizzerias across the country and their managerial personnel. Le Vien had it, but nobody seemed to want it. "Washington didn't know what it meant," he said.

o◯o

The Sicilian Mafia did not invent the pizza, but made richly inventive use of it. Sooner or later, from 1963 onward, nearly all Cosa Nostra troops in America got into the pizza business, sheltered behind it, washed their drug money through it, skimmed the cash take, worked it to extort payoffs by arson, acid, bombing, and murder, pulled a thousand scams on its customers, and passed dope on from one of its kitchen doors to another. Two decades passed before the FBI discovered that Sicilian Mafiosi were running "a sizeable portion of the heroin importation business to the United States" through these pizza parlors.[3] The violence and extortion had attracted some attention, but the names and faces had not.

Mafiosi usually muscled their way into the business. The Cherry Hill Gambinos picked up the pizza franchise at the Cherry Hill Mall in southern New Jersey by burning the place down, firebombing the manager's car, and then giving him a call. "What I did to your car, I'm going to do to you if you don't do what you're told," said the voice on the phone. "I'm gonna take a gun in my hand and blow your face off. Get wise. Get smart. Close up. Turn your keys in."[4]

Not that they were necessarily averse to peaceful surrender. The Sicilian Mafia's branch manager in Washington, D.C., a convivial host named Luciano Fiumefreddo, claimed to have acquired his nicest pizza parlor in Prince George County, Maryland, merely by asking. "I couldn't sleep one night, so I drove over there and saw the Landover Mall. I was so overcome by its beauty that I waited in the parking lot all night, and then went in to ask if I could rent the place," he explained.[5]

Fiumefreddo, who owned six more pizza parlors around the nation's capital, had bought a dozen others up and down the eastern seaboard since arriving from Sicily in October 1963—three months after the Ciaculli bomb. Fellow fugitives were doing the same from coast to coast. They worked hard, sifting flour and kneading dough, hauling cartons and swabbing floors, opening early and closing late. To outsiders, they were indistinguishable from thousands of honest Sicilian immigrants in the trade.

There was nothing like hiding in full public view. All America could watch them at work without a twinge of suspicion. The public loved these new Sicilian-run eateries, springing up like mushrooms after rain. They were fast—that was probably the secret of the traffickers' unique success in devising just this system for just this country of fast-food fans—as well as cheap and less poisonous than many. The pizzeria run in Oregon, Illinois, by a Pizza Connection defendant was missed after his arrest. "He used to put real bacon in his pizzas—not bacon bits," a customer recalled.[6]

The police rarely bothered these establishments, and then only because of so many illegal Sicilian aliens in their employ. Nine out of every ten deported by the U.S. Immigration and Naturalization Service were found working in pizzerias.[7] The phenomenon puzzled law enforcement agencies. As time went by, they began to think that drugs might have something to do with it, but that was as far as they got.

All the big Sicilian Mafia players on the New York scene were helping to smuggle the aliens in: the Cherry Hill Gambinos, Emmanuele Adamita (their main heroin courier), Salvatore Inzerillo (Palermo's future heroin king), Enzo and Antonino Napoli, Buscetta, and the whole crowd of their close associates.[8] For agents accustomed to minding their own backyard, however, these were just the "geeps," or "zips," the "fucking siggies" who didn't count. It was taken for granted that some American Mafia Family must be running the aliens in; probably the Gambino Family, since Carlo Gambino's brother Paolo was clearly in charge.

"I came to New York in 1970, and was put on a special squad to cover the Carlo Gambino Family," said James Kallstrom, the FBI's crack Mafia watcher in New York.

We had a case on his brother Paolo then. Paolo was very rich, but not from their normal activities. He was bringing in the aliens.

We saw the whole network; they were setting up the heroin net all through the sixties and seventies, right under our noses. They were all in cheese—making mozzarella and selling to pizzerias that were popping up everywhere. . . . I followed their cheese trucks to pizza parlors in New York, New Jersey, Connecticut. They had hundreds of pizzerias, all run by illegal aliens just in from Palermo. . . . We thought the Gambino Family must be bringing in hundreds of Sicilian illegals, paying them a little and forming an army—but what for?

We thought it could be drugs; enough dope was seized in casual arrests to suggest a drug ring. But the association wasn't clear.[9]

The New Jersey State Police had assembled many more facts by 1973, but hardly gotten closer to the truth. The exceptional influx of Sicilian illegals was "harder to comprehend from one day to the next," the police intelligence analyst observed.[10] Several thousand aliens were now known to have come through. Though many were under indictment for murder and mayhem at home, they were "unidentifiable in the U.S.": nonpersons with no fingerprints or Social Security numbers on file. Obviously they could serve some criminal purpose. But which?

Sicilians appeared to have no trouble getting into the country. A good number used throwaway forged passports and lied their way in on their own. Thousands more were ferried in smoothly by an organized international ring. As the New Jersey police described it, a certain travel agent in Sicily would collect $500 a head, sell the customers an airline ticket to Montreal, and give them a business card for the Laurentian Hotel there or the Royal Motel in Lachine, Quebec. Upon checking in, they would be told to wait for "Salvatore" (or "Paolo" or "Giuseppe"), who would collect another $500 and take them over the border.

The Canadian–U.S. border below Montreal runs for 1,200 miles from the Atlantic Ocean to the Great Lakes, with dozens of small waterways and backwoods roads in between. Only a hundred border guards were stationed on the U.S. side in those years, from Maine to Erie, Pennsylvania; and fewer than twenty were on duty at any given time.[11] Eluding them was child's play.

Once across, the illegals would scatter according to their means. Those with the right connections took over pizzerias, usually with start-up money from fellow Mafiosi already settled in. The others worked in the pizza shops as slave labor. They would be paid a few dollars a week and be bedded down in a dormitory or on the shop floor. Without papers, or knowing a word of English, they were prisoners.

Eventually, deserving illegals would get a *sistemazione,* as Italians call it; the Mafia would arrange to make them legal. The methods varied from simple forgery or fraud to methodical bribery on Capitol Hill. One way was a quickie marriage to an American girl; the groom would get naturalized citizenship in six months followed by divorce, the bride $1,500. Another was the falsification of petitions for residence permits. Cheese makers were given a much higher priority on the waiting list than manual laborers, for instance. Thus, by faking his employment references—among other things—a prime Sicilian trafficker and pizza franchiser, Michael Piancone, became a lawful resident of the United States. According to the New Jersey Police report:

In preparation of his petition for permanent status, a fourth application listed his occupation as a cheesemaker even though the first three applications listed his occupation as a salesman.

The petition was accompanied by several Italian language documents with English translations, indicating extensive experience as a cheesemaker. A close examination of the documents determined that . . . information not contained in the documents was added to the translation. Piancone had worked for a cheese company, but as a laborer. . . .

In acting on Piancone's petition, the Immigration and Naturalization Service inspector, according to intelligence reports, was ordered against his will to approve the petition even though it was a known fraud. Despite illegal entry and fraudulent applications, Michael Piancone was granted permanent residence on November 8, 1966.[12]

An office calling itself the International Institute of Jersey City took care of such things, the report continued.

The International Institute of Jersey City . . . originally started in 1936 at a YWCA as a center for cultural exchange. It soon began English and Citizenship classes and then provided assistance in legal and technical work for aliens.
. . . The Institute has been a major contributor in submitting petitions for immigration preferences for illegal aliens. The Institute, according to intelligence information, is a tool used by perpetrators of the alien-smuggling operation as a legitimate go-between from the illegal side of the operation (smuggling, hiding out, etc.) to the attempt at legality (preference petitions, Congressional bills, etc.). It is alleged by some that the Institute is a conduit for payoffs by aliens to the mob, Congressmen and attorneys.

A number of the aliens in question were major Sicilian criminals now running pizza parlors, added the report.

A great number of private bills sponsoring aliens for citizenship are introduced in Congress; [one congressman is reported to have] introduced 39 private bills for citizenship in one day [and] a total of 111 such bills during the 91st Congress [1969–1971].
[Another congressman is said to have] sponsored 26 private bills for citizenship. . . .
New York Congressman Mario Biaggi and his predecessor . . . have also introduced many private bills sponsoring Italian aliens for citizenship. . . . Biaggi has been known to sponsor known criminals for citizenship with a private bill.[13]

Congress did not even have to pass such a bill, provided it was reintroduced regularly. Under U.S. law, an alien could not be deported while his bill was pending—and could no longer be deported at all if he could hold out for seven years. This was something an accommodating congressman could easily manage for his clients, as the New Jersey report explained:
"A check of private bills by New York Congressmen has shown a pattern of passing the alien bills around. One will sponsor a certain alien in one session and it will be introduced by another Congressman in the next session. The bills are passed around and traded off in this way."[14]

Nothing of this got into the press, still less into court. Those were the days of the Italian-American Civil Rights League, when no public figure in his right mind would have broached the subject.

The flamboyant Joe Colombo, heading the New York Mafia Family of that name, had created the league in the late sixties to distract the FBI. "They were always watching you, taking your pictures, following you everywhere," explained an aide. "This made it hard for Colombo to conduct his illegal business because all his mobster friends did not want their pictures taken. There came a point when Joe Colombo Jun. got picked up for melting down silver coins, so Joe Snr. said: 'This harassment has to end. I am going to form the Italian-American Civil Rights League.' "[15]

The league became a formidable electoral weapon. Millions of decent Italo-Americans were conned into identifying with the Mafia in the belief that an attack on it was an attack on them. Joe Colombo harangued them daily, as a guest star on prime time television: "The president is knocking us down; the attorney general hates our guts," he would thunder.

Eventually, the Italo-American community realized its unhappy mistake, especially when Italo-Americans like U.S. Attorney Rudolph Giuliani became the nation's most effective Mafia bashers. Throughout the 1970s, however, politicians were frightened stiff. The word "Mafia" disappeared from public print. The FBI, picketed by outraged citizens, was actually forbidden to use the word in 1972 and for more than a decade thereafter.

In the course of that decade, the Mafia-run pizza empire expanded into a huge conglomerate, reaching into the remotest boondocks, from Niles, Ohio, and Aurora, Colorado, to Temperance, Michigan, Pinellas Park, Florida, and Wyomissing, Pennsylvania; the Pennsylvania Crime Commission found the empire implanted in fifty-four towns and cities in that single state by 1980.[16] By 1985, state and federal authorities around the national capital reportedly agreed that

organized crime controls over a hundred restaurants in Virginia, Maryland, and the DC area alone. . . . Investigations over the past two years have focussed on restaurants whose operators and employees tend to be recent immigrants, most of them young Sicilian or Italian males. . . . Some came directly to jobs in established pizzerias, or moved in as cooks and managers. . . . The number has grown remarkably in the past five years. . . . Officials are concerned about the narcotics moving through these places, but more concerned about skimming and money laundering. . . . The amount of money is astronomical.[17]

The pizza circuit used its own suppliers, with a monopoly on all the necessities for the pizza industry—ovens, oils, tomato sauce, meat, mushrooms, mozzarella cheese. ("How come you don't make mozzarella?" the FBI's James Kallstrom once asked a Kraft Cheese Company officer, who winked in reply.) Supplies were "totally controlled, from the time they are contracted for in a foreign country to the time they are delivered to the ultimate consumer in the United States," stated a U.S. Customs report on the West Coast.

Many American Mafiosi had been taken into partnership, joining forces with their Sicilian counterparts much as two corporate giants might do. Joe Bonanno, a pioneer in the field, was locked into the circuit with his Grande Cheese Company in Wisconsin (a manufacturer of national importance) and an intricate web of subsidiaries. His sometime partners, the Falcone brothers of Sicily and Brooklyn, ran an elaborate network of dairies as well as an interstate King of Pizza chain.

Carlo Gambino's brother Paolo and nephew by marriage Frank Ferro owned another cheese-making network, Ferro Cheese, covering a territory from Virginia to Maine. Carlo Gambino's brother-in-law and future successor, Paul Castellano, was a major meat supplier.

All crossed paths with a singular outfit called Roma Foods, which did business in cash with 650 pizzerias from South Plainfield, New Jersey, to Jacksonville, Florida, and Dallas, Texas.[18] Its Sicilian-born owner was Louis Piancone, one of two brothers of unusual interest in this story.

The Piancones came from Carato Bari, Sicily. Louis had married (and later divorced) an American tourist overseas; his brother Michael, the illegal with fake cheese maker's credentials, had slipped into the United States in 1963. Early partners in the pizza business, they had branched out in different directions by the end of that decade.

Michael Piancone owned a four-state chain of Piancone Pizza Palaces, sold franchises for others, and hired more illegal Sicilian aliens than anybody in the state of New Jersey. Several of his pizza parlors were notorious heroin bases. The biggest heroin seizure on record up to 1971 was made that year in one of his New Jersey Pizza Palaces: eighty-six kilos, shipped from Palermo by Gaetano Badalamenti. The biggest heroin merchant in New York was arrested in another Piancone Pizza Palace two years later: Filippo Casamento of Eagle Cheese, rounded up in the international drug bust that snared Buscetta in Brazil.

Dozens of other renowned Sicilian traffickers held the franchise for one or another Piancone Pizza Palace: two of Badalamenti's nephews by the name of Sollena; the fugitive boss of Trapani, Antonio Minore;

Emmanuele Adamita, who ran heroin in bulk for the Cherry Hill Gambinos from the early 1960s until his latest arrest in 1988.[19] Eventually, Michael Piancone wound up in jail for trafficking in heroin himself.

Louis Piancone founded Roma Foods, the sole East Coast distributor for Joe Bonanno's Grande Cheese Company, and that was just one of the his holdings. He controlled bakeries, fancy groceries, specialty shops, a frozen food company, a pasta company, and an all-purpose Piancone Distributing Company supplying everything to meet a pizzeria's needs. The pizza distributing company gave him a corner on supplies for the entire industry. He was famous as the sugar daddy of the pizza world, loaning millions of dollars in start-up pizzeria money to newly arrived Sicilian émigrés. He dealt with all the cheese, dairy, and meat companies in the Bonanno and Gambino Families, and had an inside track to the Colombo Family besides.

Salvatore Profaci, son of the Colombo Family's founding father, had come over to Roma Foods from Bonanno's Grande Cheese Company in 1971. From then on, he worked out of an office in a Roma Foods warehouse as Louis Piancone's full-time "consultant," labor relations adviser, and territorial enforcer.[20]

To round out the picture, Piancone Pizza Palaces, Michael Piancone's company, set up the Caribbean Management Corporation in 1972. Its company seat was Georgetown, Grand Cayman Islands, British West Indies. Though it may be pure coincidence, the Grand Caymans are widely known as among the freest money-laundering centers in the world.

There things stood as the Sicilian Mafia's golden decade drew to a close. Not until 1980 did the FBI begin its investigation of what came to be known as the Pizza Connection. The agents who finally cracked the case, earnest, dedicated, and able, thought the pizza trail began when they first detected it.[21]

Could American authorities really have learned so little, or forgotten so much, about the previous quarter of a century? Apparently they could. On April 12, 1988, the U.S. secretary of commerce, William Verity, actually went to Moscow with Louis Piancone of Roma Foods for the signing of a contract that would spread a chain of Piancone pizza parlors across the face of Soviet Russia.[22]

The Senate Judiciary Committee had long since identified Louis Piancone by then as "a soldier in the Colombo crime family," for his connections with Salvatore Profaci. The FBI, the New Jersey State Police, and the Pennsylvania Crime Commission had further identified him as "one of the principal figures in organized crime's pizza network." All this had been reported in the *Washington Post.* [23]

Yet nobody complained of the commerce secretary's monumental forgetfulness, or suggested that the U.S. government might be helping inadvertently to implant the Sicilian Mafia on Soviet soil. Nobody even seemed to notice: not in the FBI, the DEA, the CIA, the Department of Commerce, the Department of Justice, or the Department of State.

Michele Sindona
and the Billion-Dollar
Blackmail Scam

By the close of the 1970s, Sicilian traffickers were sending somewhere around $1 billion yearly from America to Palermo by way of Switzerland, Liechtenstein, London, Caracas, and the Cayman Islands. That kind of money needed managing, and the most renowned international banker-swindler of his day, Don Michele Sindona, was entrusted with its management. Unfortunately, he lost a substantial part of it on his way to jail in 1979.

This gave rise to an epic intercontinental scam in the brief interlude between his indictment and imprisonment. If the Sicilian Mafia had outgrown Sindona already by then—it has certainly done so since—there was still a way to shake some money out of him.

The "kidnapping" of Michele Sindona in August 1979 had its comic side. Free on bail, he was slipped out of the United States in shrieking disguise: dark glasses, wig, false beard, yellow chicken skin pasted on his cheeks. (He was sweating so hard at the airport that the chicken skin began to peel off.) Preposterous communications from his "kidnappers" were signed by a "Proletarian Committee of Eversion for a Better Life." The whole plot fell apart because the Italian postal service, an early victim of postindustrial decline, was incapable of delivering a letter on time.

Nevertheless, the conspiracy behind this C-movie scenario was murderously real; and the police, uncovering it, got their first significant break in twenty-five years. Following the leads in Don Michele Sindona's simulated kidnapping, they finally found out about the Sicilian Mafia's heroin network and who was running it.

o☉o

Sindona, an impeccably turned out gentleman of steely purpose and contained inner fires, was a financial genius. Born in Messina at the eastern end of Sicily—where the Mafia was not believed to exist, though it did—he was spotted by his local bishop at an early age. The bishop recommended him to Cardinal Giovanni Battista Montini, then papal secretary of state and later Pope Paul VI. Sindona was also in contact during his youth with the Mafia's incomparable black marketeer Vito Genovese, for modest postwar dealings in lemons and wheat.[1] These two introductions gave Sindona the beginnings of a lifelong connection to the governing Christian Democratic party, the Catholic church, and the Mafia.

Settling in Milan as a corporate tax lawyer in 1948, Sindona rose to giddy heights over the next three decades. The "Gruppo Sindona" came to include six banks in four countries, the international CIGA Hotel chain, Libby Foods, and some five hundred other corporations. He became the Holy See's appointed banker under Pope Paul VI, with full control over its foreign investments on behalf of the Vatican's bank, the IOR (Istituto per le Opere di Religione, Institute for Religious Works).[2]

Sindona controlled the stock market in Milan, where 40 percent of the shares traded on any given day were under his direct or occult command. His capacity to influence the nation's finance was such that former prime minister Giulio Andreotti once called him the "savior of the Italian lira." His capacity to blackmail Italy's financial establishment and governing class could be measured accordingly.

The biggest blackmail potential was built into Moneyrex, his international currency brokerage firm. Formed in 1964, Moneyrex claimed 850 client banks throughout the world and did some $200 billion worth of business yearly.[3] Through Moneyrex, Italy's rich and powerful could squirrel away enormous fortunes illegally and safely in foreign bank accounts. Sindona did them this favor but kept a secret ledger incriminating the five hundred richest and most powerful. The "List of Five

Hundred" was meant to be his lifesaver when the ship went down.

In addition, Sindona invested funds for two sinister and deeply sub-terranean organizations that proved to be working hand in hand. One was a wildcat Masonic lodge calling itself Propaganda Due, known as the P-2, later disowned by the Masonic movement. Sindona, a member since 1964, was an intimate of the P-2's *Maestro Venerabile,* the im-penetrably mysterious Licio Gelli. The two of them juggled astronomi-cal sums together.

Sindona's other underground client was the Sicilian Mafia. Some say he was present at the historic Hotel Des Palmes summit meeting in 1957.[4] At any rate, he was flagged by Interpol a decade later as number one among bankers allegedly working with the Mafia in the interna-tional drug trade.[5] Later, he was found to be paying generous kickbacks or "black interest" to Sicily's top Mafia bosses. His go-between, caught in the act, was a Christian Democratic senator heading the island's State Mining Corporation.[6] Insistently toward the end, 1979, various official sources reported that Sindona was using fiduciary accounts in Switzerland to launder the Sicilian Mafia's heroin money.[7]

Sindona's troubles began when he bought the Franklin Bank in New York with money he didn't own, siphoned off from his banks in Italy. The Franklin was the eighteenth largest bank in America, and among the healthiest. By October 1974, when he had emptied its coffers for his own uses, he managed to borrow $1.7 billion from the Federal Reserve to save it. The Franklin Bank went bankrupt anyway six days later, marking the biggest bank crash on record in America. Four other banks of Sindona's collapsed in Europe within another week: the Banca Privata Italiana, Finabank, Amincor, and Bankhaus Wolff of Ham-burg.[8] Uncounted billions of dollars went down the drain, the Mafia's and Licio Gelli's included.

Sheltering from Italian justice in New York, Sindona finally came to the end of the road. In March 1979, a U.S. indictment cited him on ninety-nine counts of fraud, perjury, and misappropriation of bank funds.[9] He faced twenty-five years' imprisonment in America, and per-haps as much again in Italy if and when the courts there could lay hands on him.

The two countries compared notes through their respective repre-sentatives: Assistant District Attorney John Kenney in New York and a fearless lawyer in Milan, Giorgio Ambrosoli, handling the receiver-ship of Sindona's Italian banks. It was then that Luigi Ronsisvalle was offered $100,000 apiece to get rid of them.

A month after the U.S. indictment came down—in April 1979—the

Cherry Hill Gambinos began to prepare Sindona's fake abduction. John Gambino, eldest of the brothers, procured a false passport for Sindona in the name of Joseph Bonamico, and consultations with Palermo got under way.[10]

Many have long believed that John Gambino was doing this for the *American* Mafia; he was thought to be a mere appendage of Carlo Gambino's New York Family. Actually, his true role came to light in this very case. Italian magistrates found him to be the Sicilian Mafia's "converging point" for all its operations in the United States.[11]

"Johnny" Gambino's friendship with Sindona went back a long way. They dined together often and openly: at the discreetly luxurious Hotel Pierre on Fifth Avenue, Sindona's New York residence, or at the Gambino brothers' Cafe Valentino on 18th Avenue in Brooklyn. He was a frequent guest at New York dinner parties in Sindona's honor; "This is Carlo Gambino's nephew," Sindona would proudly inform the others.

Sindona was the "financial consultant" for Johnny's G and G (Gambino and Genovese) Concrete Company, and had "lent" him money for several other companies besides (mostly nonexistent). When solicitous Italo-Americans raised funds for Sindona's legal fees, he would split the take fifty-fifty with Johnny Gambino's inner Mafia circle.[12]

Gambino's people used to fawn upon Sindona, his son Nino told biographer Luigi Di Fonzo. "Don Michele, you are the greatest of all Sicilians," they would say. "Let us help you with your problems. Tell us whom you want killed. Tell us who these bastards are."[13] But the fawning stopped when it was clear that he had lost billions of dollars irretrievably: his and theirs. "Sindona can be considered a dead man," they informed his family's lawyer when the U.S. indictment came down.[14] Indeed, he had outlived his usefulness.

Here was a banker who was incurably light-fingered with other people's money, who depressed the stock market and destabilized currencies, who took insane risks and moved in a cloud of lurid scandal— in a word, who was too much of a shifty crook. He was no longer the kind of banker to handle one of the world's fastest-growing fortunes. The model banker in the Mafia's future would have to be cautious, conservative, strictly professional, committed to orderly capitalist growth, radiating probity and integrity in the outside world. Scores of such people must be working for the Mafia today.

Nevertheless, Sindona still had one last, precious asset, and his friends in Johnny Gambino's inner circle intended to exploit it.

On August 2, 1979, Sindona walked out of the Hotel Pierre in his chicken-skin disguise, and vanished. An anonymous caller informed his secretary that he had been abducted. In fact (after hiding out for a while at the Hotel Tudor on East 42nd Street), he was on his way to Sicily under close escort of the Mafia and the Masons answering to Gelli. An old *capo-cosca* from Catania, Joseph Macaluso, traveled with him from New York. They were joined during a stopover in Athens by an enigmatic Sicilian physician, Dr. Giuseppe Miceli Crimi, a thirty-third-degree Mason in Palermo's covered CAMEA lodge. (A covered lodge reveals nothing about its activities or members to any other lodge.) With him was a fellow Mason responsible for getting Sindona safely into Palermo, who was also a brother-in-law of Stefano Bontate, by then the Sicilian Mafia's reigning prince.[15]

Several others from the CAMEA lodge took care of the logistics, and a half-dozen local Men of Honor shared the burden. Later, John Gambino flew over personally to round out the party. Whether Sindona was their precious charge or their prisoner, he was never out of their sight for a minute.

It seemed an odd time to bring him to Sicily. The atmosphere was incandescent there in August 1979. The chief of the civilian Judicial Police (Squadra Mobile), Boris Giuliano, had been gunned down a few weeks before; tipped by the FBI, he had been tracking Mafia heroin money through Sindona's banks.[16] He was the first to fall in a relentless Mafia war on the forces of law and order, and the island was crawling with nervous policemen.

Sindona himself was perhaps the world's hottest fugitive at the time. By early 1979, he had ruined thousands of depositors and investors, convulsed international money markets, and sent tremors through the austere corridors of the Holy See. (Not long afterward, the Vatican's IOR was found to have covered a $1.4 billion loan that disappeared after passing through Panamanian banks owned by Sindona, Licio Gelli, and the Vatican itself.) Now, Sindona had not only jumped his $3 million bail in the United States, but eliminated his implacable adversary in Milan. The valiant Giorgio Ambrosoli had been shot to death on July 11, the day after signing a deposition concerning Sindona's multibillion-dollar swindles. All Italy believed Sindona had hired the killer—as he did, it turned out.[17]

Even so, Sindona spent seventy days in Sicily without once being spotted. Shedding the beard, wig, and chicken skin, he moved freely around Palermo, talking to scores of people and maintaining "intense relations" with heavyweight Mafia bosses.[18] John Gambino, who never left his side, would whisk him off in a black Mercedes for secluded talks with the bosses, some lasting seven or eight hours, and then take him to dinner at the favorite restaurants of the rich and famous, the Charleston in downtown Palermo, for instance.

To say the police never knew he was there is to simplify an unspeakably complex affair. *Most* policemen didn't know it. One who certainly did was Palermo's new state police chief—the murdered Boris Giuliano's successor—who proved to be a member of Licio Gelli's P-2 Masonic lodge. The higher-ranking police superintendent *(questore)* was a member also.[19] Their *Maestro Venerabile,* Licio Gelli, knew all about Sindona's kidnapping because Dr. Miceli Crimi made two trips north to Gelli's home in Arezzo to report and get his orders. Miceli Crimi himself was the chief police surgeon of Palermo. Furthermore, Gelli maintained a direct line to Sicily's aforementioned reigning Mafia prince, Stefano Bontate, found to be the *Grande Sacerdòte* (high priest) of another covered lodge.[20] (The Sicilian Mafia and a wing of the Italian Masons were on much more intimate terms than anyone realized at the time. As an authoritative Mafia defector disclosed later, Stefano Bontate was already in "advanced negotiations" by 1977 to create a secret covered lodge specially for top-flight Mafia bosses.)[21]

Revelations like these, coming one on top of another, would have a numbing effect on the public afterward. The script was so deliberately bewildering, the players so daunting, the stakes so enormous, the investigation so laborious and prolonged, that very few were able to follow the whole story. Merely to read the judicial records, filling shelf after shelf in the archives, took inhuman effort. Even now, the ascertained truth is largely unknown to the public.

The reasons for Sindona's kidnapping were buried under mounds of verbal rubbish. The first version, backed by heart-wringing letters from Sindona and his "captors," claimed that he was held by pitiless communist terrorists. To strengthen the claim, he enlisted the help of his Masonic guardian, Dr. Miceli Crimi. Sindona leaned over a table while Crimi's girlfriend pulled down his pants and injected a light anesthetic. Then, as John Gambino held him by the shoulders, Miceli Crimi fired a Colt .32 at a few inches' range into his thigh. When the wound looked angry enough, and Sindona tormented enough, they snapped some Polaroid pictures for public consumption, with the warning "WE will conduct the right trial" scrawled across.

Hardly anyone believed this first version, but the next, told by Sindona to the FBI after he surrendered, did rather better. Sindona assured the bureau that he had gone to Italy to lead a popular uprising for an independent Sicily. He wanted to save the island from communism, he said. The Masons had joined him because they hated communism as much as he did. John Gambino had helped because he was "an Italian patriot who hated communism" too. The American government was "completely aware of the plans and encouraged him."[22]

This manifestly silly story was dismissed by the FBI as "implausible and improbable," and by Italian magistrates as "decidedly unbelievable." Nevertheless, it is still resurrected occasionally as an example of nefarious plotting on the part of Sindona, the P-2, the Mafia, and the CIA. Indeed, Tommaso Buscetta gave the tale new life seven years after the event. Asked in court about Sindona's lengthy encounters with Stefano Bontate in Palermo, Buscetta replied: "I heard that Michele Sindona met Stefano Bontate and Salvatore Inzerillo while he was in Palermo. Bontate told me, directly. He said Sindona was crazy, and wanted help for an armed uprising in Sicily, or better yet, a revolution. Since Bontate had no interest in such a proposition, he preferred to cut off all relations with Sindona."[23]

This was as patent a fiction as the whole revolutionary plot had proved to be long since. It was a matter of court record that Sindona had no plans for an armed uprising. He had cooked up the cover story in New York, but debunked it himself before he even got to Sicily. His Masonic escort, Dr. Miceli Crimi, admitted as much to Judge Guido Viola, who wrote:

Miceli Crimi has declared that already from June 1979, Michele Sindona told him in the U.S. of his intention to mount a fake kidnapping permitting him to go to Italy to recover some documents which he considered essential for his defense in New York. He had also said that he meant to organize the separation of the Sicilian Region from Italy, which would be a first step in the fight against communism. In Greece, said Miceli Crimi, Sindona informed him . . . that the separatist "coup" was no longer realizable. At this point, he recognized that the story of a coup was a pretext, and that Sindona, in reality, intended only to retrieve some documents he considered very important.[24]

By the time these few enlightening lines of testimony were available, the Italian police had made far more stupendous discoveries. There was no longer much doubt of Sindona's real intentions, or those of his fellow conspirators. The Mafia and the Masons were not trying to subvert Italy's democratic order (not this time, anyway). They were just trying to get their money back.

From August until early October 1979, the Mafia proceeded to shake down Italy's political and financial rulers on a breathtaking scale: "Il Grande Ricatto," the Great Blackmail, Judge Viola called it. Messages went out by letter, phone, or courier to selected individuals who were bound—*instructed*—to pass them on to the press. No intended victim could have missed them; the contents were "veiled but not too veiled," the judge observed.

Sindona possessed documents that could destroy untold numbers of influential people in Italy—this was the message between the lines. He could turn the material over to "communist terrorists" under duress, or use it himself. Either way, the influential people would have to pay for silence. They might get off lightly if they could manage to quash pending charges against Sindona in New York and Milan, in which unlikely event he would have a chance to recoup his fortunes. Failing this, they could contribute to his "defense fund," or make the payoffs to the "Proletarian Eversives" holding him, or leave the money somewhere in a shoe box, for that matter. They would be told where to pay when the time came.

The stunning implications of the blackmail operation emerged in a letter from the "Proletarian Committee of Eversion for a Better Life," which announced that Sindona would be held until he yielded up the following information:

1. The "List of Five Hundred" and their secret bank accounts abroad. "Even ten would be enough, if they are important in politics or finance."
2. The names of foreign companies in the "Gruppo Sindona" whose funds were available to the Christian Democratic party.
3. The same for the Socialist party (PSI) and Social-Democratic party (PSDI).
4. Records of payments made by Sindona's banks to political parties and personalities.
5. Records of "irregular operations" of Sindona's on behalf of "important clients" such as the Vatican, the Agnellis (Fiat), Montedison (chemicals), Snia Viscosa (textiles), and half a dozen other huge industrial conglomerates.[25]

Sindona wrote carefully drafted letters of his own—alternately pitiful, petulant, peremptory, and coldly menacing—in which he let it be known that he would be killed if his jailors' demands were not met. Lest that solution should appeal to his intended victims, he added that he had told the "Eversives" plenty already. "They think I know everything about everybody," he noted slyly. He also hinted that there were some things he might keep back. One was a "special book" he had hidden away, matching names to the numbered foreign bank accounts of 530 very special clients.[26] "The blackmailing potential was enormous," Judge Viola wrote.

Few italians doubted that Sindona had the goods on the Palazzo. The shadowy group of men who really ran Italy had made him and covered for him right up to the end. His "rescue operation," an outrageous plan to foist his crooked debts on the public, had been endorsed by the governor of the central bank and practically the entire cabinet from Prime Minister Andreotti down.[27] The Bank of Italy's director of vigilance had been arrested and then fired for opposing the plan. Ambrosoli, its most stubborn opponent, had worked and died alone; not a single member of the government attended his funeral.

A governing class that would go to these lengths had to have something to hide. To all appearances, Sindona could make them all pay, and pay, and pay. Nobody but the players knew that the Mafia and Gelli's Masons planned to do the collecting.

By October the blackmailers were ready to cash in. Sindona and his "Eversives" were to meet in Vienna with his lawyer, who was supposed to bring "the documents." But the whole purpose of the meeting, allegedly to "negotiate" Sindona's "liberation," was merely to transmit the final signals through the TV evening news. "It didn't really matter if the lawyer brought the documents to Vienna," wrote the judges who signed the Italian indictment. "What Sindona wanted was that potential victims of the Great Blackmail should get the message."

The meeting date was fixed for October 10. A letter notifying Sindona's lawyer in Rome was mailed from Milan on October 2. This was an unfathomable error; no Italian should have expected the letter to get there on time. On October 9, the lawyer received a phone call informing him that a courier would arrive with a copy of the letter. But the phone was tapped, and the courier was intercepted. Sindona, already waiting in Vienna, hopped on the next plane for New York; Rosario Gambino waited at Kennedy Airport to hustle him off. Soon after, Sindona surrendered to the FBI. John Gambino, on his way to join Sindona in Vienna, was back in New York within forty-eight hours.

Once the courier was identified, the whole course of Mafia and anti-Mafia history took a turn. "The Mafia, seen through the [judicial proceedings] that followed, appeared before me as an enormous world, boundless, unexplored," remarked Sicily's celebrated anti-Mafia judge, Giovanni Falcone.

The courier was Vincenzo Spatola, a seemingly sound Sicilian citizen. His brother Rosario was an apparently irreproachable figure moving in the highest spheres. From peddling watered milk in his youth, Rosario Spatola had risen to become the biggest taxpayer in Sicily and fifth biggest in all Italy: a multimillionaire building contractor, a public benefactor, and a power in politics. He had just assured a landslide electoral victory for a a potent Christian Democratic cabinet minister in Rome, a nephew of Sicily's cardinal primate. "Now go home and tell your friends, *and the friends of the friends,* that they must support this man of integrity and honor," was his toast at a campaign dinner he threw for the minister.[28]

No whiff of "Mafiosita," the vapor of a Mafioso, had touched the Spatola family. Now, police concluded that the damning letter to Rome was a Mafia ransom note, and Rosario Spatola was arrested on charges of kidnapping Sindona.

It soon developed that he had been Sindona's friendly host instead. Sindona had spent weeks at Spatola's father-in-law's villa in Torretta, not far from Palermo, where the friends of his friendly host had obligingly shot him in the thigh.

But Spatola was in much deeper than that. He was John Gambino's cousin, business partner, and prime accomplice. He had phoned Gambino incessantly in New York on the eve of the "abduction," and had actually picked up Sindona at the Tudor Hotel on East 42nd Street when the operation began. Furthermore, he was laundering and reinvesting an astonishing amount of heroin money, and John Gambino was sending it.

In the next two or three years, the Spatola case grew and grew, spanning Western Europe and the Atlantic, spinning off in a dozen directions. Investigators turned up over a hundred Sicilian traffickers operating between Palermo and New York, all locked into a single criminal organization—something law enforcers everywhere had obstinately refused to believe. In the end, the case furnished certifiable proof that the Sicilian Mafia had become an enormous international heroin cartel.

The same cast of Mafia characters behind the farce of Sindona's abduction proved to be heading the cartel on both sides of the ocean. The discovery of their intricate relationship was spectacular—amazing.

The Spatolas were found to be one of four Mafia Families forming a transatlantic colossus. The Cherry Hill Gambinos were another. The Inzerillos, closest of all Palermo's clans to Stefano Bontate, were a third. The fourth, related to the other three by blood and marriage,

were the Di Maggios of Palermo and southern New Jersey. Their intercontinental family ties resembled the Hapsburgs' or Hohenzollerns',
the marriages arranged to strengthen dynasties and preserve the blood
royal. There were six Spatolas involved, five Gambinos (three brothers
and two cousins), four Di Maggios, and fifteen Inzerillos. The Gambino
brothers' mother was a Spatola. The Inzerillos' father had married a Di
Maggio, whose brother had married a Spatola.

Salvatore Inzerillo, the biggest heroin broker of all, had been chosen
to head the Family's clan by his retiring uncle, Rosario Di Maggio. (A
true *mammasantissima,* Di Maggio died of a heart attack when police
came to arrest him in 1980; he thought they were Mafia killers in disguise.) Inzerillo was married to a Spatola. His sister was married to a
Spatola. His uncle Antonio in New Jersey was married to a Gambino.
His cousin and namesake in New Jersey was married to a Gambino. His
cousin Tommaso was a brother-in-law of John Gambino, who was married to a different Gambino. His cousin Maria Concetta was the wife of
John Gambino's younger brother, Guiseppe.[29] All the American-side
members of these families were made Men of Honor from Sicily; and all
had homes in or around Cherry Hill.

Describing their dimensions, the prosecutor in the Spatola case,
Giusto Sciacchitano, wrote:

These four Families, living partly in Sicily and partly in New York, form a
single clan unlike anything in Italy or the United States—the most potent
Family in Cosa Nostra.

John Gambino is the converging point in the United States for all of the
group's activities in Italy, and the final destination for its drug shipments.
Salvatore Inzerillo has emerged as the Gambino brothers' principal interlocutor, the central personage in Sicily, with myriad interests and heavy capital
investments. . . . Rosario Spatola is just below them in the structure.[30]

Like most of their fellow Mafiosi in America, the Gambino brothers
were sending their heroin money back to Sicily. It was going to Inzerillo
and Spatola, to be invested in legitimate business: bathroom fixtures,
building materials, construction, real estate. By 1982, the Gambino-
Inzerillo-Spatola holdings in Palermo alone were found to be worth
around $1 billion.[31]

Finally, also in 1982, seventy-nine Sicilian Mafiosi went on trial in
Palermo, and warrants of arrest were out for another fifty-odd. Among
the full roster under indictment were six Spatolas, five Gambinos (in-

cluding John, Rosario, and Giuseppe), four Di Maggios, fifteen Inzerillos, and Sindona (although he was by then involved with American courts). Several future defendants in the Pizza Connection case were on the list as well. To top it off, the billion-dollar Gambino-Inzerillo-Spatola holdings were seized by the state. (Some years later, the city of Palermo put some of this confiscated property up for public auction at bargain prices. There were no bids. The Inzerillos might be dead, the Spatolas in hiding abroad, the Gambinos far away in Cherry Hill, but the fear lingered.)

○⊂○○

So ended the Great Blackmail scam. Judging from the wreckage, it was a miserable flop. Sindona received twenty-five years in New York and a life sentence on top of that in Italy, where he died of strychnine poisoning the day after his trial. Whether he took or was given the strychnine, he had been squeezed dry and tossed away.

Licio Gelli appeared to get nothing but grief from his part in the scheme. His P-2 lodge had been deeply hidden until Dr. Miceli Crimi's testimony brought police to search his villa in Arezzo. There they found a stupefying list of P-2 members: seventeen army generals, four air force generals, nine Carabinieri generals, eight admirals, all three heads of the secret services, thirty-eight deputies and senators, fourteen magistrates, three cabinet ministers, and five prefects, among others.[32]

The Mafia must have hated the exposure of its anomalous Masonic ally, whose capacity for corruption and political intrigue had afforded priceless protection. The exposure of its own tremendous secrets was far worse—and for what? All for nothing, or so it seemed.

Sindona, cracking up, had appeared hysterical, if not deranged, at the end. The plot had been botched so badly that he had no chance to recoup his fortunes or collect a dime. Sicily's Men of Honor had lost not only face but, apparently, their last chance to get any money out of him.

Yet the Mafia came out of it all improbably well. Rivers of heroin continued to flow from Palermo to New York. The same cast of Mafia characters continued to direct the traffic. The courts on both sides of the Atlantic seemed incapable of using the extraordinary knowledge they had gained.

Rosario and Giuseppe Gambino were acquitted in New York, and John Gambino was not even arrested there, still less extradited to Italy at Judge Falcone's request. Spatola was jailed for a while in Palermo, but was released provisionally on a technicality and vanished. Inzerillo and Bontate went right on about their business. More than enough money poured in to make up for whatever they might have lost at Sindona's hands.

Italy's investigating magistrates still don't know whether any money changed hands during or after Sindona's simulated abduction. Nevertheless, as they observe: "The presence of John Gambino at Sindona's side [in Palermo] leads to the belief that Sindona's fake kidnapping was part of a broader project. It was elaborated, yes, in Sindona's interest but also in the more general and converging interest of Mafia power."

The implications seem plain. Mafiosi of John Gambino's metal would not put themselves out as they did for nothing more than an IOU from a failed banker-swindler. They would almost certainly have demanded usable information, in the form of a down payment in advance and further installments as the plot unfolded. If that was the case, the Mafia has been in a position to blackmail an unknown number of Italy's big wheels ever since.

These things happen, but the public rarely gets to know about them. Sindona died revealing nothing, and Sicilian Men of Honor don't talk about such matters. Buscetta, who did talk of other things, put this succinctly when he was asked in court about the Sindona affair: "Sindona's secrets! They were a feather compared with Bontate's secrets!"

Bontate, the personable, rich, and comparatively judicious leader of the Mafia's old boys then, took his own secrets with him when he died in 1981. And they were a feather compared with the secrets of Luciano Leggio, who had him killed and replaced him.

13

Palermo's
Great Mafia War

he Great Sicilian Mafia War
broke out in March 1981. The Mafia was awash in money, and drunk
with greed. The bestiality of the struggle to conquer a fabulous empire
was in keeping with the prize. It was an atrocious war, lasting two years
and leaving a thousand dead.

Luciano Leggio's men had all the appearance of right (in the Mafia's
sense) on their side. Those in command on the other side—the widely
admired Stefano Bontate and his closest ally, Salvatore Inzerillo—had
incautiously stolen several million dollars from the Mafia's own till. It
was like stealing petty cash at that stage, but history is full of wars
waiting to start over such trivial affairs.

The Mafia's till, a revolving fund for quick turnaround expenses in
the heroin business, to which all the clans contributed, contained some
twenty billion lire, around $15 million in 1981. The whole venture was
organized on a corporate basis, paying dividends of 1,600 percent.[1]
Indeed, the Mafia was issuing heroin shares like a company on the stock
market's big board.

The work was parceled out among the clans. Some procured morphine base, and heroin occasionally, through the Turkish Mafia. Others were linked up directly to suppliers of refined heroin in Southeast Asia: pure China White from the Golden Triangle, coming to Sicily in massive shipments of two hundred, three hundred, and even five hundred kilos. Different clans ran the refineries in Italy, while still others were in charge of the transporting, distributing, marketing, and money laundering. The product was available to everyone in the consortium. Orders could be placed overseas as if from a Sears catalogue; the merchandise would be shipped in bulk with special markings for individual customers.

Made Men of Honor had considerable latitude. They could cross Family boundaries for the heroin business, and use outsiders—chemists, couriers, launderers—for many chores. They were able to take part in the production process or just buy some points in it. They could invest individually or in a group. They might take their quota of the product and get it to market, or wait until it was sold abroad and paid for. Those preferring this last got a higher cut, since they shared the risk of police seizures.[2]

A flourishing cottage industry in body carriers was spreading the wealth to whole villages. In Torretta, a hamlet of three thousand off the main Palermo-Trapani road, humble stone farmhouses were found to have mother-of-pearl floors and gold bathroom faucets. Peasant housewives and grandmothers who might never have seen a city would make a few trips a year to New York. They would carry four kilos of heroin at a time in special girdles, drenched in perfume to put drug-sniffing dogs off the scent. In return, they received ten million lire a trip and a free week at the Sheraton Hotel.[3]

By now, the Sicilian consortium was dealing in multiples of a billion dollars. It had been supplying most of the heroin sold in the United States since 1975, as FBI director William Sessions testified later.[4] (Mexican heroin accounted for the rest.) By official count, some six tons a year were entering the country to supply half a million American addicts. But this was mostly a head count of *known* users, those seeking public assistance or dying of an overdose. There were no numbers for addicts opting out of the system in the United States, and virtually none for the rapidly swelling market in Western Europe.

Judging from what Sicilian traffickers could now *produce,* they were creating as well as feeding the West's heroin habit on a terrifying scale. Some fifteen refineries were tracked down during the early 1980s, in Sicily and on the Italian mainland.[5] One of the first discovered, on Palermo's waterfront, could produce 50 kilos of pure refined heroin every ten days, 1.8 tons a year.[6] A lab in Varese, near Milan, turned out 3 tons of heroin by 1981.[7] The Alcamo lab, near Castellammare del Golfo in Trapani province, was making 1.6 tons a year and preparing to triple production when it was discovered.

A sophisticated electronic pressure pump recently installed at this lab would have raised its production capacity to 80 kilos a week—a staggering 4.5 tons a year from this single source. The pump, made in Bulgaria, suggested that there had been continuing Bulgarian involvement since the Sicilian-Turkish Mafia deal of 1975.

(According to Italy's investigating magistrate, the Alcamo lab was not only equipped but also "supplied with morphine base from East European countries, more precisely Bulgaria." Among other things, he cited the discovery of twenty-two jute bags hidden under a nearby haystack, bearing traces of morphine and "stamped in Cyrillic writing used in certain Slav languages including Bulgarian." A northern Italian newspaper lying among used coffee cups was opened suggestively to an article headlined "From Bulgaria with Arms and Drugs.")[8]

To all appearances, the refineries were working to capacity. They were usually in use until hours or minutes before the police arrived—they would reek of freshly cooked heroin—and there were no stockpiles around.

Pure uncut heroin was selling for $250,000 a kilo wholesale in those days: a quarter of a billion dollars a ton (one thousand kilos). American authorities thought that about $300 million a year was going back to Palermo, but it had to be much more. In the United States alone, Sicilian traffickers "had the facilities to launder $5,000,000 a day," as Paolo La Porta confided to DEA undercover agent Frank Panessa.[9]

The money was enough to assure an interlude of peaceful coexistence in Palermo between Luciano Leggio, on one side, and Stefano Bontate and Salvatore Inzerillo, on the other. By the early 1980s, the Cupola was directing the entire heroin consortium.[10] Spheres of influence were determined by tacit agreement. Leggio's men sat in board meetings with Bontate and Inzerillo, dividing up profits and discussing investments.

Then both sides started scheming to grab all the money available. "L'appetito viene mangiando," Italians say; eating gives you an appetite. The richer they grew, the hungrier they grew.

For all that has been written about their war, the wholly compelling and irreconcilable interests that made it inevitable—foreordained—have never been pieced together, to my knowledge. Perhaps this was a failure of historical memory, a constant in dealing with Mafia affairs.

Partly, at least, it was the result of self-serving versions offered by the war's losers and accepted at face value by the authorities. Certainly, the victors were so spectacularly vicious that the vanquished escaped the censure they deserved.

According to the losers, Buscetta in particular, the war had nothing to do with drugs; it was purely a struggle for power. In reality, the two were indivisible. Even if Leggio cared nothing for money—a ridiculous idea—he could certainly have wielded no power over the Mafia by 1981 without controlling the source of its sudden, unimaginable wealth. For that if nothing else, he had to eliminate Inzerillo and Bontate.

Leggio had left them for last. After being jailed for life in 1974, he had taken his time to tighten a cordon around the Mafia establishment in Palermo. The Corleonesi had worked in from the outermost provinces, courting the envious, the voracious, the upwardly mobile. Now, they had secret allies from Trapani to Agrigento to Catania to the heart of Palermo. Buscetta's own Porta Nuova Family was in Leggio's hands.

The clans in his camp were doing very well in heroin, but their strength was largely on the raw material supply side. Catania was the key port in Sicily for off-loading morphine base, and Leggio's allies controlled it. Other allies of his, old-time smugglers working with the Camorra, had opened up channels from Southeast Asia's Golden Triangle around 1978. Leggio himself, in business for years with the Camorra's famed Nuvoletta brothers, had excellent access to the Middle and Far East. What he did not have was access to the market in the West. The money in procuring ingredients was nothing compared with the money in sales, solidly in the hands of Inzerillo and Bontate.

These two men represented the old boy network, embedded in Palermo for generations and firmly entrenched in New York. Bontate was "the Prince" in the Sicilian Mafia's hierarchy; Inzerillo was "the central personage in Sicily" for its intercontinental superclan—the Inzerillos, Gambinos, Spatolas, and Di Maggios. Together, they controlled all the heroin marketing arrangements in the Western Hemisphere.

They had the franchise deal with the American Mafia. They controlled the heroin pipeline through Canada, the Canadian Mafia's Sicilian faction, Salvatore Catalano's Sicilian faction in Brooklyn, the Cuntreras and Caruanas in Venezuela, and the Mafia branch in Brazil. The Cupola's marketing manager in Italy, Francesco Mafara, was theirs.[11] The boss of Palermo's crucial Punta Ráisi airport, Gaetano Badalamenti, was theirs. The director coordinating Palermo's refineries was theirs, as was the clan behind the enormous Alcamo refinery.

This particular clan, based in Trapani province, was a disconcerting example of the many hidden tentacles issuing from the more visible body in Palermo. Working independently of Palermo, the Trapani clan was "above all others, the most important clan for its ties to America," wrote the judge investigating the giant Alcamo lab. The earliest heroin refineries in Italy had been based on its territory. For forty years, the Trapanesi had been "transforming and selling heroin to the U.S., silently, intensively, and continuously, investing huge sums and amassing enormous riches." Their heroin was going directly to the Gambinos of Cherry Hill; Rosario Gambino would be caught red-handed eventually with part of a seventy-five-kilo shipment from Trapani. Their fugitive boss and "diamond point" in the United States, Antonio Minore, was sheltering with the Gambino brothers in southern New Jersey.[12]

For all these reasons, Bontate and Inzerillo held the high ground in Palermo. While the truce lasted, they were designated to supervise operations on behalf of all the others. They were entrusted with the revolving heroin fund; represented the Sicilian Mafia in contacts with the Camorra, the Calabrian 'Ndrangheta, and other crime syndicates abroad; and handled grandiose joint ventures on behalf of the consortium in Venezuela, Brazil, North Africa, and the United States.[13]

Even as calamity struck, Bontate and Inzerillo were planning to transform Atlantic City, New Jersey, into the Las Vegas of the American East Coast, with gambling casinos, hotels, discos. The Cherry Hill Gambinos had worked out the deal with the American Mafia boss of Philadelphia, Angelo Bruno, with whom they had a special relationship. (The two groups had divided up Philadelphia; the Gambinos were installed in the northern half, Bruno's people in the south.)[14] The Atlantic City project was going to bring in 130 billion lire for the Sicilian Families—$100 million—and Salvatore Inzerillo personally was going to hold 20 percent.[15]

These alignments might shift—practically all the survivors did shift, overnight—but only when Bontate and Inzerillo were seen to be finished. There, Leggio got unexpected help from the two men themselves.

In February 1981, Bontate and Inzerillo were summoned to a meeting of top Mafia bosses to account for "large" missing funds. They had been skimming for years: selling the consortium's heroin in New York, pocketing part of the proceeds, and claiming that American customers were paying less because the heroin was no good. Some of their couriers were bringing back a few kilos of low-grade junk to prove it.[16] On this particular occasion, Inzerillo had sold fifty kilos of heroin for Leggio's

Corleonesi, and kept the money, which probably came to a good $10 million. He said the Americans hadn't paid up yet, and promised to produce the money at another Mafia summit in March. In fact, he and Bontate meant to kill Leggio's surrogates on the Cupola when the March meeting convened.[17]

Leggio had already begun to crowd the pair to the wall, demanding a bigger share of the heroin money, enticing and corrupting their allies, using every devious trick to harass them. In 1978, the Corleonesi had framed Inzerillo for murder by killing the boss of Riesi, Giuseppe Di Cristina, on Inzerillo territory. (Previously, they had framed the boss of Riesi by killing the boss of Catania on *his* territory.)[18] They had also grievously insulted the proud Stefano Bontate: though kidnapping inside Sicily was strictly forbidden by the Cupola, they had kidnapped and killed the father-in-law of a powerful financier under Bontate's protection. (Bontate, asked to intervene, made them reduce the ransom from $6 million to $3 million, but failed to save the father-in-law. Afterward, he ordered eighteen Corleonesi and their helpers shot.)[19] Furthermore, the Corleonesi had not only dislodged Gaetano Badalamenti as head of the Cupola but expelled him from Cosa Nostra altogether, for reasons still unknown. As a *posato,* an expelled member, he was supposed to be shot on sight; he continued to handle heroin for everybody, however.[20]

War was in the air. Both sides were arming to the teeth, with pineapple bombs, bullet-proof vests, M12 machine guns, night sights, Kalashnikovs shipped from Lebanon in cargoes of morphine base. (Three Mafia runners admitted later that Palestinians in Lebanon were selling the Mafia morphine base and Kalashnikovs "to finance their war in the Middle East.")[21]

Surprisingly, it was the moderate and judicious Don Stefano Bontate who decided to break the truce and strike first—all the police informants agreed on this—and not just in self-defense. He and Inzerillo (and Badalamenti, who was consulted secretly) intended to shoot Leggio's proconsul in the Cupola, Salvatore Riina, capture the Cupola, and "take direct control of the heroin traffic."[22] Leggio heard all about the plot in prison; Bontate's and Inzerillo's would-be successors both ratted on them.[23] Nobody of importance in Leggio's camp showed up at the March summit, where Inzerillo was supposed to produce the $10 million. Instead, underlings were sent to witness the equivalent of his confession; he brought no money.

The tactical war gave way to a shooting war. "The Corleonesi, learning that Bontate, Inzerillo, and Badalamenti were plotting to eliminate them, killed first," wrote the informants' confidant in the Squadra Mobile, Commissario Antonino Cassarà, in a landmark report to the judiciary.

Bontate was ambushed and murdered a month after the March 1981 summit, on April 2. He had just celebrated his forty-third birthday at the family's villa in town, a million-dollar home with closed-circuit television, a failproof electronic alarm system, and an opulent boardroom whose refrigerator was packed with Dom Perignon champagne. Driving off to spend the night at his country house, Bontate was stranded at a traffic light while his armed escort drove on. The gunmen drew up beside him with a Kalashnikov and shot half his head off. His own underboss had signaled them by walkie-talkie. (Nobody but his family went to the funeral, though five truckloads of wreaths were sent.)

Inzerillo thought he was safe because of the $10 million he still owed Leggio, but he was wrong. He was cut down by the same Kalashnikov that got Bontate, a month later, on May 11. The gunmen fired through the sealed window of a new bulletproof Alfa Romeo; they had tested out the weapon on a jeweler's bulletproof showcase beforehand and found that a concentrated spray of fire on a small patch of glass worked very well.

A relentless strategy of massacre followed, spreading from Palermo across Sicily, and from there across Europe to the United States and South America. Police were finding a corpse a day, sometimes four or five daily: shot, strangled, burned, beaten, dismembered, hacked, tortured, trussed. They could not keep track of the dead, especially victims of the *lupara bianca* (white shotgun), whose bodies were never found. Some victims were identified only when a mother or wife appeared outdoors wearing black. Several became known when their severed heads were found on the seats of parked cars.

Twenty-one Inzerillos were wiped out. Salvatore Inzerillo's fifteen-year-old son had his right arm cut off to teach him not to try avenging his father, after which he was shot to death anyway. Inzerillo's brother Santo was lured to a meeting carrying (belatedly) a suitcase full of money owed to Leggio, and never came home; nor did the Di Maggio who went with him. An uncle of Inzerillo's, Antonio, walked out of his house in Delran, New Jersey, and failed to return. Another brother, Pietro, was found in the trunk of a New Jersey Cadillac belonging to Erasmus Gambino, cousin of John, Rosario, and Giuseppe. The body was wrapped in a plastic bag and handcuffed behind the back, with dollar bills stuffed into the mouth and crotch. (Money in the mouth stood for greed, in the genitals for being less than a man.)

Stefano Bontate's clan of 120 made members was decimated. Those who weren't turned were executed. Everyone else suspected of loyalty to Stefano Bontate was killed, if and when found. The man he had picked in advance to head the Cupola was stabbed thirty times in the prison yard of the Ucciardone.[24]

Gaetano Badalamenti lost eleven relatives. A nephew was tortured, shot, and cut into pieces in West Germany. A brother-in-law was dumped on a Palermo side street. Two other nephews, Salvatore and Matteo Sollena, were exterminated in New Jersey. Salvatore's body was found in a car trunk, wrapped in a green trash bag with his hands tied behind his back; he had been shot several times in the head.

Other bosses associated with the old regime were slaughtered methodically. The Cupola's heroin-marketing manager was shot dead, as were the Buccellatos of Castellammare del Golfo, close to the Bonannos in New York; the Rimis of Alcamo ("the nightmare of Alcamo," police had called them); two Catania bosses close to Bontate;[25] the octogenarian boss of Agrigento, Don Giuseppe Settecase; and a Caruana rash enough to be seen around Palermo. An entire buried car cemetery was dug up later in Agrigento province, with the charred skeletons of other bosses shot and burned before burial.

Though the massacre went on for three years, the Corleonesi suffered no casualties. Once Bontate and Inzerillo were cut down, the old guard submitted meekly to slaughter—an extraordinary and still inexplicable phenomenon—or switched sides.

o⊝o

In 1983, in Palermo's bunker-courthouse, a witless and hapless youth named Vincenzo Sinagra described the horrors of those killing days. He had taken part himself, in a place that came to be known as the Death Chamber of Piazza Sant'Erasmo.

This was a squalid cement stall in a junkyard, squatting behind dusty reeds and a torn wire fence near the old Palermo port. Beyond lay crumbling eighteenth-century palaces, blind-eyed warehouses, rusting trucks, a discouraged café. The stall consisted of one room with a small grimy window, a table and a couple of chairs, chains, ropes, and a metal drum for acid baths. The table was used for interrogations; the chains served to bind and the ropes to strangle, usually with two men pulling at opposite ends. The acid took fifteen to twenty minutes to dissolve hair, teeth, nails, flesh, bones—everything except the victim's watch, Sinagra said. Sometimes the bodies were simply chopped up and thrown to the pigs, or weighted and dumped in the sea.

Sinagra, who had worked in the stall for a pittance, could not explain its reasons for being, but he could describe what went on there. It took him twenty-one sessions to tell the story to a Sicilian judge.

He was merely a *manovale,* literally an unskilled laborer, in Mafia usage an indentured servant. A foolish mistake had delivered him into Mafia hands. he had robbed a household in his neighborhood, a prerogative reserved for the local Mafia clan. He might have gone into the acid tub head first for that—he saw it, done to others afterward, for the same offense—but the local Mafia boss offered to let him work for them instead. "They were going to kill me; I was afraid. So I went with them," he explained.

Any stealing Sinagra indulged in after that, in fact everything he did, was for them, not him. They paid him 400,000 lire ($300) a month, on and off, and he was their property. He might be told to hold up a jewelry store, connect with a drug courier, collect his *capo*'s monthly payoff from a building site, savage a recalcitrant client, or kidnap somebody. Mostly, though, his job was to find and deliver candidates for the bloodstained shack.

There, he would hold the victim's legs while somebody tied the noose. Or he might keep one quiet while another screamed under torture, shoot one in the head or pull an end of the rope, stuff a corpse into a car trunk or drop it off a fishing boat. Once, he had to pull a half-decomposed body out of the acid and hustle it off the premises because of a police helicopter hovering overhead.

Sinagra was too clumsy and dim to be good at his work, and was soon caught in the act of murder at another location. The Mafia ordered him to pretend to be crazy to avoid life imprisonment, but he was no good at that either. "I never tried to be a lunatic before. How do you be a lunatic?" he asked the lawyer bringing him instructions in jail. He was advised to walk around naked; flood his cell and demand to go fishing; grow a beard and eat filthy bread plucked out of the garbage; sit on a piece of rotten meat to make doctors think he didn't wash. He could cut his veins or hang himself if all else failed, the lawyer said.

"I don't want to be a lunatic anymore; I want to serve my time in prison," he informed Mafia higher-ups eventually. But he could not be trusted to keep quiet in prison. "You will get yourself into an insane asylum or die trying," he was told. Before arrangements could be made for him to die trying, he talked.[26]

Sinagra's employer was the dread boss of Palermo's Corso dei Mille clan, Filippo Marchese, who would sniff cocaine and masturbate during torture sessions in the Death Chamber.[27] Marchese ran with a pack of others who clearly enjoyed their work—Pino "Scarpuzeddu" (Old Shoe) Greco of Ciaculli, for one. But those in command of their advancing army were not necessarily sadists or perverts. The wholesale, brutal slaughter was deliberate, impersonal terrorism: Mafia warfare carried to the highest state of the art.

By the autumn of 1981, the victors were already beginning to divide up the spoils. In October, twenty of them had gathered in an elegant Palermo villa and were haggling over the dead Stefano Bontate's territory when the cops broke in. Most shot their way out, but those left behind were the first clue to the Sicilian Mafia's new chain of command.

They were a roomful of traitors, a host of whom throughout Sicily had already gone over to the winners; and the winners, emerging from their Black Hole—the Sicilians' word for all Mafia mysteries—came as a stupendous surprise.

"First among the firsts" in Palermo was Don Michele Greco, head of the Cupola since Badalamenti's expulsion in 1978. Known as "the Pope," Greco was a figure of such daunting social prestige and duplicity that police had had no inkling of his Mafia connections for twenty years. Though a Ciaculli Greco, he had not been identified with Salvatore Cichiteddu Greco, a distant relative and bad hat. This Greco was a country squire of solid wealth and reputation, who sat on the boards of fifteen or twenty companies and frequented the city's smartest salons.

Silver-haired, dignified, tweeded, and devout, Michele Greco kept open house at La Favarella, his sprawling estate, an easy six-mile drive from Palermo. Politicians, bankers, and titled aristocrats went to hunt there and lunch outdoors on roasted artichokes and game. Friends fond of shooting pigeons were given keys to the gates, including policemen and *carabinieri*. None seemed aware of the Cupola meetings held at his home, still less the heroin lab hidden on his grounds.

The village of Ciaculli and the bordering Croce Verde Giardini (Green Cross Gardens) were Greco's personal barony. This lush crescent of citrus groves curving down to the sea was silent and deserted even at high noon. Miles of underground passageways linked cellar to cellar, assuring Don Michele's soldiers a fast getaway. "We knock, give them one minute, and kick down the door, or they'd be out through the tunnels and gone," said a detective who took me on his rounds.[28]

Nobody of less than proved loyalty was allowed to live in Ciaculli. Cruising empty streets and knocking at unnumbered doors, detectives found a hundred vacant homes whose residents were forced to move away; none had complained to the police.

Later, when Don Michele Greco was tracked to an isolated farmhouse serving as his hideout, he emerged Bible in hand. "Violence is foreign to my dignity. I am the most slandered man in the country," he said. Indeed, it was not necessary for him to murder in person. Next to Don Luciano Leggio, he controlled the choicest crew of psychopathic killers in Sicily, led by Scarpuzeddu Greco, Don Michele's nephew and protégé.

Even so, Michele Greco was not really in charge. He had been installed as head of the Cupola by Leggio's men, gradually becoming their subaltern. It was Leggio who ran the war.

Leggio's strategy, brilliantly conceived and punctually executed, brought all of Sicily's Mafia clans under the rule of the Corleonesi—an unprecedented feat in Mafia history. "The Corleonesi are the global point of reference for all the emerging groups operating in the various Sicilian provinces. The groups in each zone of influence are local delegates or representatives of the Corleonesi, especially in regard to the drug traffic," wrote the High Commissioner to Combat the Mafia some years later.[29]

From the time he went to jail, Leggio had gulled the police into blaming all the Mafia's excesses on his adversaries. Everybody in law enforcement was sure that the Bontates, Inzerillos, and Badalamentis were killing each other off. Carefully planted cadavers and anonymous tips kept them looking that way, while the Corleonesi did as they pleased.

This was Don Luciano Leggio's supreme joke on the state. No longer hunted or watched, half-forgotten once the courts had finally put him away, he was freer than ever behind bars. Only a sick mind—as he would say—might imagine that this aging, invalid lifer could conquer the Mafia from his cell.

But a lifer like Leggio had notable advantages. Where Mafiosi walking free had to keep clear of the cops and mind their backs, he could rule over a prison kingdom undisturbed. No monarch is so absolute as a reigning *Capo-Mafia* in jail. Leggio, the most potent and frightening *Capo-Mafia* in any Italian jail, could order the lives of his subjects at will. He had "the Respect," together with an uncanny ability to inspire instant, abiding terror. "I've been a great power in prison for years; I'm a myth," he would boast to a Palermo court one day. Fellow convicts schemed desperately to meet him, just so they could say, "I have met Leggio," he declared.[30]

All he had to do was map strategy; everything else was done for him. Doctors looked carefully after his health, prison guards curried his favor, menials of every description waited on him. Obviously he could get instructions out, and expect to be obeyed. His Corleonesi, faithful for well over a quarter of a century, were unlikely to do otherwise.

Those on the outside understood as well as those on the inside that Leggio could have anyone killed from his cell, anywhere. In-house killers were no problem. Italy does not have a death penalty; multiple murderers jailed for life are easily recruited for such work. He chose the best to head his prison death squad, a calloused knife-and-gun man from Catania.[31] "Uncle Luciano sends his best regards," the knife-and-gun man would write, to remind certain unimprisoned associates of Leggio's continuing interest.

Outside, there were his proconsuls in the Cupola, Salvatore Riina and Bernardo Provenzano, the Beasts. Aside from the victims of a roving squad of handpicked hit men at their disposal, they had personally racked up some forty murders apiece.[32]

The kill rate within the Mafia was high, but not necessarily too high for public tolerance. So long as Sicily's Men of Honor merely killed off each other, people were inclined to let them get on with it. But Leggio was also waging a parallel war against the state—a terrible, anguishing war that shook the country. Contrary to sacrosanct custom, the Mafia was killing judges, prosecutors, police officers, politicians, and journalists in what became an unmistakable pattern. "The Mafia would no longer permit anyone to oppose its hegemony over all Sicily," wrote the Palermo judges who convicted 342 of its members some years later.[33]

The immediate consequences looked disastrous for Leggio himself. The law bore down harder than ever before; the Mafia's tremendous secrets came out; Leggio stood revealed; the heroin consortium he had just taken over was exposed and presumably wrecked. Some even thought the Sicilian Mafia was finished, but it wasn't.

Distinguished Cadavers

The first cop to fall in the Mafia's war against the state was the head of the Squadra Mobile in Palermo, Boris Giuliano. He was drinking a *cappuccino* at a bar on a hot summer's morning in 1979 when someone walked in, shot him four times in the back, and walked out. According to the bartender, the gunman's hands were shaking. Giuliano was so fast on the draw that people called him "the Sheriff." Had he turned around, the gunman might have fallen instead.

Giuliano, a full-faced, sad-eyed man with a flowing black mustache, was a superlative cop. Sharply intelligent and intuitive, he had an extra professional edge. He had attended the FBI's academy in Quantico, Virginia, and was on close terms with the DEA. In fact, a new era in Italo-American collaboration began with him.

Sensing what he could not yet prove, Giuliano was homing in on the drug traffic. Where others merely went after couriers, he was watching the men with the money, trying to get at their bank accounts, investigating their own banker, Michele Sindona. He was also exchanging information with the Americans, an exhilarating experience on both sides.

A yearlong joint investigation with the DEA convinced the Americans as well as Giuliano that he was right in his suspicions: "The fact is emerging, as long suspected, that the Sicilian Mafia has reentered the international drug traffic with plentiful men and means, using the big old tobacco networks in the south of Italy and the islands, under the iron guidance of big Mafiosi," he reported shortly before his death.[1] Giuliano had even begun to find proof. At Punta Ráisi Airport, he came upon an unclaimed suitcase on a moving baggage track that had traveled on a flight from New York and contained half a million dollars in small bills. Here at last was material evidence of a massive traffic in drugs between Sicily and America. Two weeks later, Giuliano found four kilos of fresh heroin and a stash of guns in a Palermo safe house— evidence that the drug was *produced* in Sicily.[2] Within another week, he was dead.

Two months later, on September 25, 1979, Judge Cesare Terranova was shot dead with a Kalashnikov as he walked out of his doorway. He had been in Palermo for just two days, after serving on Parliament's Anti-Mafia Commission in Rome for seven years. Convinced that Sicily's Mafiosi were immersed in drugs, he was returning to the Sicilian bench to take them on again. "Don't worry, they don't dare touch judges, they won't touch me," he had assured his wife.

Fear and foreboding spread across Sicily as the list of "distinguished cadavers" lengthened. The Christian Democratic president of the Sicilian Region, the party's most outspoken opponent of the Mafia, was shot dead in broad daylight on a downtown street. The commander of the Carabinieri station in Monreale, five miles from Palermo, was shot dead as he walked to a town fair with his wife, carrying his four-year-old child; he had been investigating the Corleonesi. ("The son of a bitch was creating an uproar" in high Mafia circles, said a bent colleague of his to an equally bent officer of the Italian secret service.)[3] A state prosecutor who had just signed warrants of arrest for Salvatore Inzerillo, John Gambino, Rosario Spatola, and fifty of their followers was shot dead as he browsed at a bookstall. The regional secretary of the Communist party was shot dead as he drove through the center of town; he was sponsoring a bill in Parliament to confiscate illicit Mafia profits and outlaw the brotherhood by name. Finally, the new prefect of Palermo, General Carlo Alberto Dalla Chiesa, was shot dead, and the Mafia's vicious terrorist strategy was all laid out.[4]

Men of Honor had often killed cops and politicians, but they did not make a habit of it. The Mafia, which had its own pretensions as a force for law and order, had always preferred courtship and corruption to head-on confrontation. Now, with a heroin conglomerate spanning the earth, Cosa Nostra was openly proclaiming its dominion over Sicily. Money was power, and the money in this enterprise bordered on absolute power. The police, the courts, the government, would no longer be permitted to get in the way. Whoever did would be executed, period.

The Mafia must have thought it would be a pushover. Kill one, frighten ten thousand; that was how it should have worked.

What happened instead was a continuing collective act of rare courage. A small group of policemen and judges kept pressing deeper and deeper into forbidden Mafia territory: like-minded men in the Squadra Mobile, the Carabinieri, the Guardia di Finanza, the state prosecutor's office, the Investigating Magistrates' Office. They were all Sicilians, with an intimate understanding of the enemy and no illusions about their probable fate. The enemy picked them off one after another. "The message was unequivocal. We knew that the more seriously we investigated the Mafia, the more our lives were in danger," says Giovanni Falcone, who came to lead the judges' anti-Mafia pool. Nevertheless, as each went down, a colleague took his place.

The pressures were grinding, and the solitude oppressive. To upset the Mafia was to jar the sensitive mechanisms that kept Sicily in some kind of political and economic balance, for what that was worth. Many were inclined to see these few obstinate men more as troublemakers than heroes. Sicilians in particular seemed to regard them with skepticism and mistrust. *Palermo-bene,* the city's upper crust, was distinctly cool. (The "other" Palermo, more honest, had yet to speak its mind.) No comforting signals came from the intangible center of power in Rome that Italians call the Palazzo. On the contrary, the absence of signals implied displeasure, if not active disapproval. And something close to hostility emanated from colleagues in Palermo's courthouse. "First they ignored me; then they treated me like a rare animal; then came the poisoned arrows. Finally they established formal relations, without a spark, without sympathy," Judge Falcone recalls.[5]

Yet by the summer of 1982, these determined investigators had found out almost everything that dozens of Mafia defectors would be saying two or three years later. The sum of their knowledge was submitted to the judiciary that July by Commissario Antonino Cassarà of the Squadra Mobile, in a confidential report that proposed the arrest of 162 Mafiosi mostly for heroin trafficking and multiple murder. Entitled "Greco + 161," the report became the working premise for the most devastating judicial assault on the Mafia in its history.

Antonino "Ninní" Cassarà, deputy chief of Palermo's civilian po-

lice force, was young and deceptively relaxed in manner, tall and casually elegant, and his men loved him. His office, a cramped and sunless
box in the decrepit palace housing the force, was a center of running
excitement in the hours I spent there: chain-smoked cigarettes, whiskey
in paper cups, shrilling phones, exhausted detectives huddling over al-
bums of villainous mug shots.

Cassarà had pulled together an extraordinary team of plainclothes
cops. They were underpaid (less than $1,000 a month) and incredibly
ill-equipped. The Squadra Mobile had no computerized data bank, and
indeed no computers. Its Mafia files were ten or twenty years out of
date, and useless anyway; whatever might have been of interest had
been removed long since. Barely half a dozen unmarked cars were available to cruise Palermo's Mafia-infested quarters, overaged rattletraps
whose two-way radios kept breaking down. Security conditions were
dismal. The Squadra Mobile's headquarters had no back door; any
loiterer in the little park facing the entrance could instantly report who
went in or came out. A large bronze plaque in the dusty archway bore
the names of colleagues who had been ambushed and murdered so far.

In spite of these conditions, the team cracked some of the Mafia's
best-kept secrets. For once, the Mafia's own people helped. Cassarà
recruited several remarkable informants. One, code-named "Prima
Luce" (First Light), was Salvatore "Totuccio" Contorno, a Man of
Valor (killer) who had worked for Stefano Bontate since 1975 (see chapter 16). A dozen of his relatives had been killed in the Mafia's ongoing
war, and he had escaped death himself only because he was a faster and
better shot than his would-be assassins. (The doctor who treated his
bullet wounds was killed next.) Arrested on a drug charge in March
1982, he turned on the winning clans with deadly venom.[6]

Another source, code-named "Ambrosiano," was Ignazio Lo Presti, related by marriage to the multimillionaire Nino Salvo, one of the
island's mightiest financiers. The Salvos, licensed to collect all of
Sicily's taxes—from which they creamed 10 percent—were deeply sub-
merged Men of Honor. They were Bontate's and Inzerillo's respectable
front, the main conduit to what Cassarà called "a vast and indefinable
gray area" linking the Mafia to the Italian establishment. Lo Presti,
arrested briefly after Inzerillo's murder, was part of the Salvos' inner
circle. (He vanished forever soon after his release, in August 1981.)[7]

If not for the savagery of their opponents, sources like these would
never have talked. As it was, they provided explosive information. By
the summer of 1982, Commissario Cassarà knew about the heroin consortium, the irreconcilable forces in the Cupola, the shifting alliances,

and the reasons for Stefano Bontate's fall and Luciano Leggio's relentless ascent.

It is questionable whether anything in a quarter of a century so enraged the Sicilian Mafia as the Cassarà report. The mighty Salvos were exposed, facing prison and ruin. (They accused Cassarà himself of being a "new Mafioso" fifteen days before they were arrested.) Don Michele Greco's cover was blown, forcing him into hiding. Leggio's demonic role was revealed. The Corleonesi emerged as the Mafia's new rulers, and new lethal allies of theirs appeared out of nowhere in Catania.

This was perhaps the most dangerous secret of all. Catania's million-odd inhabitants had always been considered lucky, enjoying as they did a marvelous climate, miraculous soil, soft white beaches, an excellent harbor; and by all accounts, they were Mafia-free. Actually, the Mafia had been installed there for sixty years—Catania was second only to Palermo in the drug traffic, among other things—but nobody in authority was allowed to know that.[8]

The city was Sicily's Milan, a center of big business, big money, and big politics. It was the seat of famous international entrepreneurs, the Cavalieri di Lavoro (Knights of Labor, an honorary title bestowed by the president of the Italian Republic). These men lived in their own enclaves; Cavaliere Carmelo Costanzo and his sons owned a compound of twelve villas with an Olympic-sized swimming pool and a private football field. Their cars flew the family flag, and all traffic stopped when they passed. The whole city came to a halt when they threw their annual parties, at which little gold elephants nestled under the ladies' plates and hundred-thousand lire notes were earmarked for the local cops.[9]

The Cavalieri di Lavoro contributed generously to all of Rome's governing parties, especially the Christian Democrats and Socialists. Their political influence was enormous. Nobody had dared to suggest that they might have dealings with the Mafia, whose existence in Catania was unfailingly denied. "The Mafia is a pure invention, a product of fantasy," said the city's leading Christian Democratic deputy, loyal to the end, long after all Italy knew of its presence.[10]

The Cassarà report was the tightest of secrets for a while. It was addressed to Palermo's chief investigating magistrate, Judge Rocco Chinnici, an upright jurist so haunted by its contents that he would trust nobody around him. A copy went to General Dalla Chiesa, who did not trust many around him either.

Dalla Chiesa was designated as the state's reply to the Mafia's in-

sufferable insolence, and there could have been no worthier choice. The
Dalla Chiesas came from the nation's political shrine: the Piedmont in
the far north, home of the House of Savoy and the fathers of the Risorgimento, birthplace of modern Italy (1865). Generations of Dalla Chiesas had served with distinction in the Carabinieri since that gallant
force was formed to protect the young nation's heads of state. The
general himself, a solid and erect figure with a soldierly panache, embodied the values, honor, and dignity of the nation's finest public servants. It was impossible to doubt his loyalty and courage. At the start of
the 1980s, Italy had been faced with the world's worst terrorist assault,
apart from Turkey's; Dalla Chiesa had turned the whole calamitous
situation around. By 1982, he was a legend in the ranks of the
Carabinieri and a national hero.

Approaching retirement age, the general was then set decorously on
the shelf as the Carabinieri's second in command, where he was wasted
and depressed. When the government asked him to leave his cherished
Carabinieri and take on the emergency in Sicily, he agreed, though not
without misgivings. "It surprised me, it almost frightened me . . . once
again I was becoming an instrument of a policy that leaked on every
side," he wrote in his diary.

Dalla Chiesa reached Palermo on April 30, 1982, in a flare of popular excitement. To many Italians, he looked ten feet tall. The most
intrepid of Mafia bosses appeared to have much the same impression;
they were genuinely afraid of him, and had been from the time he had
commanded the Carabinieri's legion for western Sicily a decade earlier.
I had met him at that time, a dashing officer in impeccable uniform and
white gloves, very polite and unnervingly clever, a remorseless Mafia
hunter even then.

The Anti-Mafia Commission's archives were full of the general's
warnings about the growing drug traffic in those days; this at the start of
the 1970s, when the traffic was passing almost unnoticed. Worse, he had
submitted merciless reports on the Mafia's political allies. There, he was
cutting to the bone.[11]

The Sicilian Mafia could never have grown into the colossus it was
without the collusion of certain Christian Democratic leaders. Not all,
by any means: mainly those embroiled in Sicilian politics. Dalla Chiesa
had singled out the most compromised among them as authentic Mafiosi, providing circumstantial facts and dates. The men he named—up
to the rank of cabinet minister—had assured the Mafia's security, profits, and privileges throughout the postwar years. And the same politicians he had denounced in the early 1970s were running the island in

Luciano Leggio, later to be *capo di tutti capi,* is taken away to prison for life on May 16, 1974 (above). While in prison, he conquered the Sicilian Mafia in the Great Mafia War of 1981–83. Salvatore Inzerillo, the heroin king of Palermo, and Stefano "the Prince" Bontate (left and right, below) were murdered in early 1981, inaugurating the slaughter (ANSA).

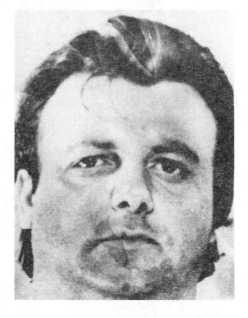

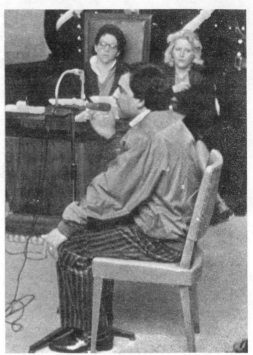

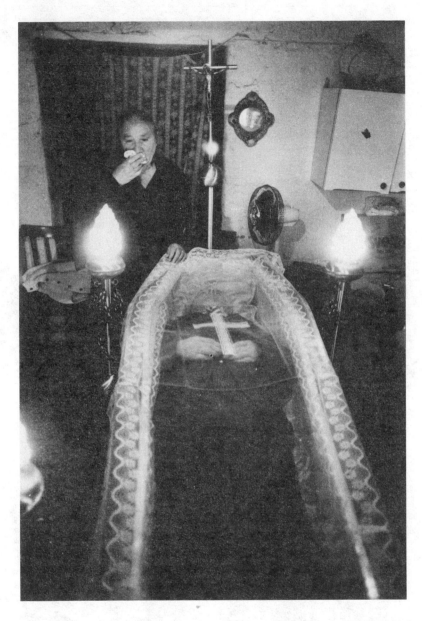

Vincenzo Sinagra (opposite, top right, ANSA), a hapless youth, exposed the horror of the Sicilian Mafia's death chamber (opposite, top left, Lucky Star) at Palermo's maxitrial. Scores of Mafiosi died in the chamber, their remains dissolved in acid, dumped at sea, or fed to pigs. Other Mafia victims are mourned by widows at Palermo's municipal cemetery (opposite, below, ANSA) and by a mother attending her son's wake (above, Lucky Star).

CHINNICI

Preparing for the Great Mafia War of 1981–83, the Corleonesi turned their weapons on the Italian state. Among those murdered were Judge Rocco Chinnici (opposite, lower left), who was drafting an indictment of 464 Mafiosi for Palermo's maxitrial when he fell victim to a radio-activated car bomb (opposite, above); General Carlo Alberto Dalla Chiesa (opposite, lower right), prefect of Palermo and scourge of the Sicilian Mafia, who was shot in ambush together with his young wife; Boris Giuliano (above), commander of the Squadra Mobile of Palermo, another ambush victim; and Cesare Terranova (right), an investigating magistrate and Leggio's implacable accuser, who was gunned down in front of his house (ANSA).

The maxitrial opened in February 1986, in a $22 million bunker built onto Palermo's Ucciardone prison (opposite, above, ANSA). It featured 464 Mafia defendants, 200 defense lawyers, 1,337 witnesses, and 8,607 pages of indictment. Michele Greco ("the Pope"), head of the Cupola, shown in his defendant's cage (opposite, below, ANSA), said when captured, Bible in hand, "Violence is foreign to my dignity. I am the most slandered man in the land." His accuser Tommaso Buscetta, his face altered by plastic surgery and partially hidden by dark glasses (above, AP/Wide World), testified for the prosecution when he turned informer after the Corleonesi murdered two of his sons and five other relatives.

Detective Douglas Le Vien (above) at work in Washington, D.C., with the President's Commission on Organized Crime in 1986. Ten years earlier, Le Vien began an investigation that would prove to be the key to the Sicilian Mafia's secret invasion of the United States. Antonino Cassarà, deputy chief of the Squadra Mobile (left), filed the report to the judiciary that led to the maxitrial indictments. Designated enemy number one by the Cupola, he was ambushed by ten men firing Kalashnikovs on August 16, 1985. No man was more instrumental in bringing the Mafia to the bar of justice, but four years after his death, leading forces of the Italian judiciary were again denying that the Mafia even existed (ANSA).

the early 1980s: the new president of the Sicilian Region, Mario D'Acquisto; the incumbent mayor of Palermo, Mario Martellucci; the most notorious of former mayors, Salvo Lima and Vito Ciancimino.[12] (Lima was mentioned 163 times in the Anti-Mafia Commission report of 1976; Ciancimino took up seventy full pages.)

These were the men who delivered the vote for several powerfull Christian Democratic politicians, and especially for the most powerful of all, Giulio Andreotti. A strong part of Andreotti's electoral base was in Sicily, representing nearly a quarter of his party's electorate there. The Christian Democrats could not do without Andreotti, who could not very easily do without politicians like Salvo Lima.

That was the trouble with Dalla Chiesa's mission. He had always been close to the Christian Democrats, his staunchest supporters up to now; Andreotti personally had admired and endorsed him. Where Sicily was concerned, however, the two were bound to collide.

People still argue about what happened between the two men. Nothing happened, according to Andreotti. Nevertheless, Dalla Chiesa did have an awkward conversation with him before going to Sicily. "I made it very clear to him that I would have no special regard for that part of the electorate associated with his Grand Electors," the general wrote in his diary. "My father mentioned the meeting to the family," wrote his son Nando, recalling the general's words: "I've been to see Andreotti, and when I told him everything I know about his people in Sicily, he went white in the face."[13]

Whatever the tenor of their talk, Dalla Chiesa plainly expected no help from that quarter. Certainly, none was forthcoming from the Andreottiani presiding over Palermo. The general had predicted "a subtle and brutal local resistance if not outright rejection" by the Sicilian establishment, and that is what he got.

This was a much different war from the one he had led against the terrorists. The Mafia was no longer just the scourge of Sicily. It was an international crime syndicate menacing the entire country and a good part of the West—an incomparably graver threat to a free society than the Red Brigades. But Italy's governing class did not mobilize to fight the Mafia as it had done to fight the terrorists. Sending Dalla Chiesa to the front again was little more than a gesture. Perhaps the saddest part of his tragic story was that ordinary Sicilians were with him, and the state was not.

As prefect of Palermo, the general was the state's chief envoy. The cabinet had voted to give him broad powers to "coordinate the fight against the Mafia nationally and locally," without which he would have turned the mission down. He wanted his powers "declared and codified," he wrote to the prime minister before leaving, "because experience has shown that every promise is forgotten, every guarantee bogs down, everything is suffocated, once certain interests are touched."[14] But in fact, the promise was forgotten; the powers the cabinet had voted to give him were never codified. Withholding them was exactly the kind of message from the Palazzo that Sicilians watch for.

From the first, Dalla Chiesa was snubbed by the island's rulers and cheered by the public (to the astonishment of many). "I found myself in a situation where miracles were expected of me on one side, while the other cursed my arrival," he wrote in his diary.

The public gave me the oxygen of its esteem; and the state staked its existence not on a will to combat the Mafia, but on the use of my name to silence the irritation of political parties. . . .

I, certainly the most informed depositary of everything that has happened in the recent past, find myself with a task that is truly unendurable and—why not?—dangerous too. Promises, guarantees, expressions of support, all come to nothing. The truth is that I have been catapulted into untrustworthy surroundings . . . with no one around me, without the help of a friend.[15]

Dalla Chiesa was anguished by the dangers for his second wife-to-be. Wellborn and sheltered all her life, a volunteer Red Cross nurse, she was a beautiful woman half his age. He did not want her to join him in Sicily, but she persisted until he gave in. They were married in a setting of nightmare violence.

The bloodletting was then at its height in Palermo. Killers roamed the streets on big motorbikes at high noon, firing almost casually. Beheaded corpses were left in cars at the railroad station, dead men were burned on downtown streets, bodies were dumped at the door of police headquarters. "The atmosphere was pitiless, terrible in its arrogance," wrote the presiding judge in Palermo's maxitrial.[16]

As the judge noted also, a prefect who was a "man of action" like Dalla Chiesa could not help but generate "elements of friction, dissatisfaction, and intolerance. . . . The further he went ahead, the more bureaucratic obstacles he ran into." There were less innocent obstacles as well. The more Dalla Chiesa learned about the Mafia of the 1980s, the more he felt surrounded and trapped. Like Judge Chinnici and Commissario Cassarà, he could only feel safe within a small circle. Beyond, he sensed the Mafia's invisible presence at every turn.

The general discovered Mafia moles in high public office and others whose presence disturbed him in his own Prefettura.[17] Cassarà's report had told him something about certain men of the highest repute—the Salvos, the Costanzos, the island's untouchables—and he was learning more as the weeks went by. (Barely twelve days after he reached Sicily, fifty of the Guardia di Finanza's agents raided the Salvos' offices and carted off ten cases of documents.) Every social invitation seemed to hold a hidden snare; he turned nearly all of them down. Shortly before his death, he confided to Italy's leading political columnist, Giorgio Bocca:

The Mafia is cautious, slow, it takes your measure, it listens, it makes sure about you from a distance. . . .

For instance, a friend who has done business with you or worked in your office says as if by chance: ".Why don't we go and have a coffee with so-and-so?" The name is illustrious. If I don't know that heroin is flowing in rivers through that house, I'll go, and serve as their cover. If I know it and go, it's a signal that I'm prepared to give my sanction.

Scurrilous rumors dogged Dalla Chiesa. He was said to be "criminalizing all Sicilians," "undermining Sicily's autonomy," scheming to become another "Iron Prefect" like Mussolini's Cesare Mori. A fashionable Palermo lawyer declaimed:

General Dalla Chiesa can be a disaster for Sicily. If he gets to be a superpoliceman against the drug traffic, he'll end by ruining this city. Imagine everybody who lives off drugs being thrown out of work. They'd sack our homes. They'd hold us up, break into our stores and offices. Restaurants wouldn't be safe. Our wives couldn't go out in furs. We couldn't go out at night. There'd be no more peace, believe me. No, beware of what he does, this Piedmontese General.[18]

The general's best defense was the common public. He would drop in at a high school unannounced for a talk with the students, and draw heartening applause. He visited union halls, spoke at labor rallies, and even invited a group of small-town mayors to Corleone for a refreshing exchange of views. His message was simple: "To be able to look at our interlocutor without lowering our eyes, to be able to laugh, talk, listen, face our sons and their sons without self-reproof, to be able to pass a life on to the young made up of sacrifice and renunciation—but clean—we can do that if we are together."[19] The response belied the most enduring of typecast Sicilian clichés. Decent Sicilians were eager to fight the Mafia, given the chance. They didn't trust the Palazzo, but they trusted the legendary Carabinieri general from the Piedmont.

Nevertheless, the fact remained that Della Chiesa was horribly exposed. The silence in Rome, the barbs in the progovernment press, the icy hostility of local politicians, made it plain that the state had cut him off. Whether this was a result of indifference, incomprehension, political expediency, or bureaucratic torpor—the courts have ruled out anything more sinister—he was left in the classic position for a Mafia kill: standing in the middle of an empty space.

Dalla Chiesa knew that, as he revealed in an interview with Giorgio Bocca at the end of a nerve-racking summer: "I have been studying this new fact: the Mafia that kills the powerful, that raises its sights to the gentlemen of the Palazzo. I think I've understood the new rules of the game: the powerful man is killed when a fatal combination comes about, when he has become too dangerous but can be killed because he is isolated."

When did a powerful man become too dangerous? When he insisted on enforcing the law, or proposed to strengthen it, or investigated the Mafia's "accumulation of capital [and] elaborate network of controls," or threatened to expose thunderous secrets. The general mentioned a few of these secrets in the same interview: the Mafia in Catania and the Cavalieri di Lavoro, for instance.[20]

The prefect of Catania promptly rushed into the breach. There was not now, nor had there ever been, a Mafia in Catania, he assured the press. The mayor of Palermo deplored such allusions. "Mafia, Mafia ... how people talk!" he exclaimed. The president of the Sicilian Region demanded clarification of the general's remarks. "If these things are true, we must take the consequences. If they are not true . . ." He left the phrase unfinished.

On Dalla Chiesa's 127th day in office, he met secretly with the U.S. consul in Palermo, Ralph Jones. The general was deeply distressed by the Italian cabinet's failure to keep its word, the ominous behavior of local political leaders, and, above all, the Christian Democrats' flagrant complicity with the Mafia. Regardless of protocol, he was appealing to the United States to intervene. "He believed that only the U.S. Government could do something at the highest level to bring movement," Jones revealed afterward.[21]

Jones also spoke of a story General Dalla Chiesa had told him that day:

While a Carabinieri commander in Sicily in the mid-1970s, he said, he received a call from the force's captain in the west Sicilian village of Palma di Montechiaro, who had been getting threats from the local Mafia boss.

General Dalla Chiesa drove up to the village. It was the time of the late afternoon stroll. The general took the captain's arm, and began walking slowly with him up the main street, then down it, then back up again. Everyone was looking at them.

Then this strange couple stopped outside the house of the village Mafia boss. They stood there until the point had been made that the young captain was not alone.

"All I'm asking for is somebody to take my arm and walk with me," the general said.

Dalla Chiesa told this to Jones on September 3, 1982. He was murdered that same evening. His new young wife had come to call for him at the Prefettura, and they had left for home in her small car. Two big motorbikes followed them from headquarters. Eight men in all—four on the motorbikes, the others in backup cars—ambushed them in Via Carini, in the old quarter, along with their bodyguard in the car behind. The gunmen emptied a Kalashnikov first into the wife and then into the general, who had flung himself across her. Then someone got out of a BMW and fired again to make sure.

"Here lies the hope of honest Palermitani," wrote an anonymous mourner who left flowers on the spot where he died.

The general's solitude had made him vulnerable, wrote Judge Falcone afterward. "Carlo Alberto Dalla Chiesa was flung into the land of Sicily in less than ideal conditions to *appear* to be the expression of an effective will to [combat] the Mafia. He did not personify the authority of the state, as should have been the case. Thus, Cosa Nostra believed it could strike with impunity, because he personified only himself."[22]

The Kalashnikov that killed him was the same one used on Salvatore Inzerillo, so there was really no mystery about who had sent the killers. The decision could only have been made by the Sicilian Mafia's new high command.

This time, Leggio and his men appeared to have gone too far. The popular reaction was overwhelming, and the government moved. A new prefect was sent to Palermo with many of the powers that Dalla Chiesa had been denied. A new Anti-Mafia High Commission was set up in Rome. The Italian Parliament passed the toughest law of its kind in the world in a matter of weeks. The bill was cosponsored by the Christian Democratic interior minister, Virginio Rognoni (the original sponsor, the late communist leader Pio La Torre, had been assassinated in Palermo on the day General Dalla Chiesa arrived).

The Rognoni–La Torre law made membership in the Mafia a criminal offense, punishable by lengthy prison terms. It abolished bank se-

crecy where suspect Mafia funds were concerned. Any assets gained
through violence or fear were subject to government seizure—cash,
jewels, yachts, cars, real estate, securities, commercial companies,
whether owned by the Mafioso or his wife, fiancée, or mistress. Agents
of the Guardia di Finanza began to work their way through a maze of
camouflaged bank accounts. The Salvos were stripped of $30 million
within a month. Any Mafia boss could find himself poor overnight, a
fate he might well consider worse than death.

Yet none of this frightened them off. Men of Honor did not hump
and run in 1982 as they had done after the Ciaculli bomb incident two
decades earlier. Relations between the Sicilian Mafia and the state had
changed, or so Palermo's jubilant Mafiosi believed; "any effort to
weaken it from now on will be cut off by armed attack," informants told
the police.[23]

The next attack came barely four months later, in January 1983.
The victim was Judge GianGiacomo Ciaccio Montalto, machine-
gunned at one in the morning as he drove up to his door. An investigating magistrate in Trapani for thirteen years, Ciaccio Montalto had "an-
noyed a lot of people," according to a high government official.[24]

Trapani, with a population of eighty thousand, had the highest concentration of banks in Sicily,[25] the highest accumulation of bank deposits in all Italy, and Sicily's highest concentration of Mafiosi per capita.[26]
Judge Ciaccio Montalto was sure that tons of heroin had gone to the
United States from this province over the years. He himself had tracked
shipments worth a third of a billion dollars from Trapani to Paris to
Montreal in the space of a few months.[27]

On the trail of the drugs, he had been exchanging information with
Judge Carlo Palermo, who was investigating the Turkish arms-drugs
Mafia in northern Italy. Ciaccio Montalto had recently turned up sizable dollar deposits in Trapani's banks, and signed forty-one warrants
of arrest. Above all, he was hunting intensively for refineries in the
city's environs. The biggest refinery in all Europe—the one in Alcamo,
preparing to produce four tons of heroin a year—was found shortly
after his murder.

Ciaccio Montalto was another of those dangerous, isolated men.
The state would not lift a finger against the Mafia in Trapani. The
subprefect of Trapani had warned General Dalla Chiesa "not to crimi-
nalize this serious and hardworking city." The state prosecutor stationed there had never been able to mount an anti-Mafia case for lack of
investigative police. The local courthouse had been closed altogether,
after a piece of ceiling fell into the library. Ciaccio Montalto, one of only

two investigating magistrates for all of Trapani, could not extract so much as a personal computer from the state to make up for having no personnel. Prominent citizens accused him of "exasperated personalism" for pursuing the town's biggest Mafia bosses. "Whoever did this should be sent into exile!" someone shouted on the sole occasion when the judge managed to drag one into court. "My son told me many times that he felt alone, that only a very few in his office understood and helped him," his mother told the press. "He had the sensation that those surrounding him were trying to create an empty space round him," added his wife.[28]

So it went. The killing did not let up, and heroin flowed more copiously than ever; indeed, shipments to the United States reached an all-time high. The Italian government did not launch a renewed assault. The Sicilian establishment continued to drag its feet. The same small band of judges and cops pressing into forbidden Mafia territory was left to carry on more or less as before.

Then, in the summer of 1983, the Mafia proclaimed its sovereignty over Sicily once more. Judge Rocco Chinnici, working in obsessive secrecy along the lines traced in the Cassarà report, completed his massive investigation of Mafia crimes going back to 1975. That July, he signed warrants of arrest for the Salvos; the head of the Cupola, Michele Greco; Leggio's proconsuls, Salvatore Riina and Bernardo Provenzano; and some two hundred other Men of Honor. On July 29, a hundred-pound radio-controlled car bomb blew up Judge Chinnici, his driver, two bodyguards, and the *portiere* of the apartment house he lived in, while his wife watched from a window.

Chinnici was the last judge who would work alone. The terrible secrets haunting him were passed on to an anti-Mafia pool of ten judges and prosecutors, led by Giovanni Falcone. Henceforth, they would share the secrets and risks. All criminal investigations involving the Mafia on the island would pass to or through them. Killing one would still leave nine others to keep going until they had sent the whole murderous pack of Mafia bosses into the dock.

The Octopus Emerges

he Great Mafia War caused little stir abroad. People in law enforcement elsewhere tended to think it was no business of theirs, and many Italians were inclined to agree. The Sicilian Mafia still seemed to be their own peculiar national, even regional, affliction.

Nevertheless, the Mafia was operating now not only in Italy but throughout the world. A multinational of this size could not be hidden forever. Any of a thousand crisscrossing trails could lead back to it eventually, as some finally did.

The time came, in the 1980s, when traces of the Mafia turned up in Great Britain, France, West Germany, Belgium, Holland, Spain, Switzerland, Greece, Kenya, Thailand, South Africa, Canada, Venezuela, Brazil, Haiti, the Dominican Republic, Puerto Rico, even Aruba and the Seychelles. The United States in particular found enough evidence by 1984 to break up one of its more impressive operations—a huge drug ring bridging three continents.

Through an extraordinary concomitance of events, the United States and Italy penetrated the Sicilian Mafia's protective cover independently of each other, during the same years. American investigators began to discover its presence on their territory in the early 1980s, just when the Italians were starting to crack its secrets at home.

The Americans worked differently and certainly thought differently. Cosa Nostra in America did not kill judges and cops, or its own members at the rate of one a day; not even Al Capone had managed to kill more than seventy-five a year when he was the crime lord of Chicago in the 1920s. Heavy corruption and paralyzing official inertia were the worst the Americans were up against. They were not under the suffocating pressures familiar to their Italian counterparts, nor did they have anything like the Italians' experience of Mafia duplicity and camouflage.

Actually, they knew very little about the Mafia at all until 1980. Early investigations—Senator Kefauver's, Senator McClellan's—had generated practically no motion. Local cops continued to think of organized crime as the local Mob. Narcotics agents were collaring small dealers, who made small problems. The FBI was almost wholly engrossed in hunting subversives. J. Edgar Hoover would not hear of a "national conspiracy" in the criminal underworld; the bureau was forbidden to look for one until he died in 1972. In any case, there was little chance of getting anywhere during Hoover's reign. FBI agents had a mike planted for three years in the office of Boston's Mafia boss, Raymond Patriarca, but could not use the evidence in court. The United States had no laws for such situations. "We just got the sick, the lame, and the unlucky in those days," says Steve Ryan, former counsel for the President's Commission on Organized Crime.

Congress had remedied the situation by 1970. Wiretaps were legalized under Title 3 of an omnibus act authorizing controlled electronic surveillance. RICO, the Racketeer-Influenced and Corrupt Organizations Act, made it possible to prosecute a continuing criminal enterprise; two or more people committing two or more crimes in a racketeering pattern could be sent up for life on the drug kingpin statute. These were revolutionary provisions, reversing long traditions in law enforcement, and they would hit Cosa Nostra with punishing force—but not until another decade had passed.

The decisive change came at the beginning of the 1980s, with President Reagan's war on organized crime. It was America's first concerted nationwide assault on Cosa Nostra, devastating largely because of a determined, spirited, and persuasive young Italo-American named Rudolph Giuliani. Assistant secretary of justice under the incoming Republican president, Giuliani cut through bureaucratic sludge, banged some official heads together—the FBI's and DEA's, most notably—and went for Cosa Nostra from the top down. First, he set up an Organized Crime Drug Enforcement Task Force, pooling the personnel and resources of the FBI and DEA, along with the Justice Department's federal attorneys, customs, the Immigration and Naturalization Service, the Internal Revenue Service, and metropolitan and state police. A dozen regional task forces carpeted major crime cities. These strike forces had money, agents, government backing, all the ingredients for a major offensive. The purpose was no longer to make low-level piecemeal arrests, but to nail entire Mafia Families starting with their ruling bosses.

So, in the course of nailing the Bonanno Family, the Americans came upon the Sicilian Mafia's secret army. They did it the way Americans do such things best, with an array of trained manpower, cross-pollinated data banks, superb electronic gear—the most formidable intelligence-gathering apparatus in the world. A million man-hours went into what became the Pizza Connection case. The New York Task Force ran forty-seven wiretaps in the city and sixty nationwide. A hundred agents worked two shifts daily for eighteen months on physical surveillance. The agents collected a dense mass of information, not all of it useful and much of it incomprehensible. The Pizza trial was already under way before they realized what they had uncovered.

Even then—as late as 1985—the FBI had accumulated "positive data" on only twenty made Sicilian Men of Honor in the entire United States. Two years later, the list was up to a thousand.[1] The truth was so far from the perceived wisdom on Mafia matters that it took a long while to sink in.

∘◌∘

The Pizza Connection case really began with the man who had been Detective Douglas Le Vien's discovery and affliction—Enzo Napoli. Very few were ever aware of his role; Napoli certainly wasn't. I learned of it myself only while writing this chapter. My source was the DEA's brilliant intelligence analyst Mona Ewell, the first to detect and pursue the Sicilian Mafia in America.[2] "We were getting Enzo Napoli's direct phone calls in Danbury [Connecticut] prison. In all honesty, that's how it started," she told me. Napoli had been in jail for two years on a one-kilo heroin rap when the DEA decided to take a closer look at him. Between 1980 and 1982, agents listened in on hundreds of his phone calls, and Mona Ewell tried to discern some pattern in them.

After a while, a pattern did emerge. Enzo's brother Antonino would phone from Caracas to their younger brother Gaetano in Brooklyn. Gaetano would at once call Enzo in Danbury, whereupon Enzo would make further outgoing calls. The man he called regularly was a fellow Sicilian by the name of Domenick Mannino, who owned a chain of twenty-six pizzerias in north Philadelphia called Mimmo's Pizzas. "The Napoli brothers were the key. When the calls went from Venezuela to Gaetano and at once to Enzo in Danbury, I knew something had to be going down. The Napolis got us to Philadelphia, to Domenick Mannino—that's how it all began," Ewell told me.

By 1982, Enzo Napoli's name was the first circled on Mona Ewell's file card for Caracas, and the DEA was intrigued enough to send an ace narcotics agent named Tom Tripodi to Venezuela. Tripodi, who had worked with Police Chief Boris Giuliano in Palermo four years earlier, knew something about the Sicilian Mafia. Even so, he was staggered by what he discovered in South America. "He came back with the whole thing," said Ewell:

We had it all; we knew it completely. Antonino Napoli was a partner of the Cuntreras. We saw the Cuntreras, and the Caruanas. The security around their homes was incredible. . . . They had control in Venezuela like you wouldn't believe.

We saw their businesses, all fronts for paper-shuffling. What these people handled was the money. Their names had been coming up for years on the money. *Historically,* they worked the money.

They did it for cocaine as well as heroin: the money was coming in, and the cocaine was going out to Europe. There was a huge Sicilian cocaine pipeline to Europe that went back at least to 1978—the year cocaine *burst* on Europe. . . .

It was a tremendous operation, and it was going on a long, long time. . . . In my opinion, that's still the key. They're the people with the money; they've been in the business of narcotics the longest.

The DEA could do nothing in Venezuela. Neither could the Italian police, who had begun to mount a massive investigation of the Cuntreras around the same time.[3] Venezuela had no extradition treaty with either country and showed no disposition to be helpful in any case. But even at DEA headquarters in Washington, Tripodi and Ewell ran into a stone wall. "It was a long and hard struggle to get people in law enforcement to believe this," she said. "It was very frustrating for us; nobody here believed it. The Italians knew, but our own people wouldn't go for it."

Nevertheless, her superiors did go for the fellow Enzo Napoli kept calling in Philadelphia. Late in 1982, a DEA undercover named Frank Panessa was sent into Philadelphia for a try at Domenick Mannino. He didn't get Mannino—nobody has yet—but he got what thousands of wiretaps in New York's Pizza Connection case could never produce: "the powder," the Sicilian Mafia's heroin.

A tall, amiable, laid-back agent who had been working narcotics for twenty years, Panessa inspired instant trust, enhanced by exceptional access to ready cash. The DEA, which had never laid out for a whole kilo of heroin before, could do so now; Rudolph Giuliani's new OC-DETF (Organized Crime Drug Enforcement Task Force) was putting up the money. Therefore, Panessa was able to make six heroin buys of a kilo each, for which he forked out close to $1 million.[4] (He had to fight off buying still more, he told me. "They pushed the heroin at me, three to five kilos at a time. 'I'm not asking you for the money,' the supplier would say. 'Does it make sense for me to carry this all the way back to Brooklyn?' ")

The Philadelphia traffickers Panessa dealt with, all made-in-Italy Sicilian Mafiosi, took him to their bosom; anybody shelling out $1 million for their goods couldn't be a government agent, they figured. Artlessly, in all innocence, they confided more to Panessa than any of their kind ever did to the FBI. (Apart from Luigi Ronsisvalle, who failed to make a deep impression, not a single Sicilian Mafioso in America had ever talked to the FBI.)

Panessa's best informant was Paolo La Porta, a made Man of Honor from Palermo, the Philadelphia ring's main supplier. (It was La Porta who had taken the newly arrived Luigi Ronsisvalle in hand on Knickerbocker Avenue in 1965.) They ate sumptuous meals together, exchanging gift-wrapped "presents" at the table: the heroin and the money. La Porta felt comfortable enough to offer advice on marrying off Panessa's teenaged daughter, and even to borrow $100,000 from him. (The bearer bonds he gave in exchange were redeemed later at a Puerto Rican bank, and paid 13 percent interest tax free.)

La Porta used to travel down from Knickerbocker Avenue in Brooklyn, home of Salvatore Catalano's people. The New York Task Force knew them as the Sicilian faction of the Bonanno Family; but La Porta was in a position to know better. The "Sicilian faction" was in fact the Sicilian Mafia, he told Panessa; and its territory was not just a Bonanno Family enclave but all of Brooklyn.

Judging from what La Porta said, the American Mafia appeared to have *given* Brooklyn to its silent Sicilian partners. As Panessa testified later to the President's Commission on Organized Crime:

We had many conversations relative to Brooklyn. Brooklyn meant the Sicilian Mafia, as distinguished from the Italian-American La Cosa Nostra in the United States. There was a distinct difference. . . .

Brooklyn controlled all the heroin in the United States, La Porta told me. . . . The Sicilians used the Italo-Americans to distribute the heroin, and that was the extent of it.[5]

La Porta himself moved among the Sicilian Mafia's top men in the drug trade. Salvatore Inzerillo had been his great friend; he was very close to Gaetano Badalamenti; he did business with (and introduced Panessa to) the Cherry Hill Gambinos; and most of his heroin came from Salvatore Catalano's closest aides, Cesare Bonventre and Baldo Amato. He also got cocaine in bulk from these fellow Sicilians. Once, he laid out thirty kilos of it on the table for Panessa, who was startled. "What's to be surprised? Our guys in Brooklyn control cocaine too," La Porta explained.

Bonventre was cheating on his own fellow Sicilians, cutting the heroin himself and sending down low-grade junk. When Panessa grumbled about the quality, La Porta told him bluntly: "Look, this is the Mafia! You don't complain. There is nothing we can do about it. These come from Sicily. When we get the consignments, we have to accept what it is. . . . But a couple of people will pay for this. . . . Everyone will get their due reward in time."[6] There was "a power struggle going on in the Sicilian Mafia over heroin distribution in the U.S.," La Porta continued. Thus, in due time, the severed parts of Cesare Bonventre turned up in Garfield, New Jersey, in three fifty-gallon drums.

La Porta was planning to bypass Bonventre anyhow. He and a long-time partner—Filippo Ragusa, a big man in the future Pizza case—had just brought over a forty-kilo heroin shipment from Palermo packed in crates of ceramic tiles. (FBI agents caught up with the heroin in Buffalo but failed to catch Ragusa. Unaccountably, they ignored his partner in Philadelphia.)

La Porta had also visited Bulgaria and Yugoslavia. He and some fellow Mafiosi were going to buy the liquid morphine base manufactured there, bottle it at his family's bottling plant in Marsala, Sicily, and ship it to the Dominican Republic, where "his people" were setting up a refinery. "We own the Dominican Republic," he told Panessa.[7]

The liquid morphine gave Panessa an incredible chance to meet La Porta's home team in Palermo. The bottled dope was going to be shipped on a trial run through Panessa's dummy (DEA) export-import company in Frankfurt, West Germany. He was actually on his way to

Sicily with La Porta's brother to set up the deal when La Porta abruptly summoned him back. "He told me that his people over there had to kill a judge," Panessa testified afterward. "He said that now was not the time to try to move heroin through Italy because the Italian police were grabbing everyone to find out who did it to the judge." The judge was Rocco Chinnici.

The magnitude of the intercontinental operation was hard to take in. Once, when Panessa offered to wash some of the Philadelphia ring's drug money, La Porta thanked him but declined. "We ourselves have the capabilities of laundering five million dollars a day," he said politely. Allowing for weekends and holidays, this would still come to over $1 billion a year for the Sicilians alone—three or four times more than the flow traced in the Pizza case. Just one of the launderers serving Philadelphia, Rosario Dispenza, was found to be handling $1 million a day in Queens, for four seemingly separate Sicilian drug rings along the eastern seaboard.[8]

In the course of nine months, Panessa's targets had informed him that the Sicilian Mafia was a separate entity in the United States; that it had a monopoly on the American heroin market and a sizable chunk of the cocaine market; that it operated out of its own national headquarters in Brooklyn through a network of interlocking rings; that it used American Mafiosi as salesmen only—inferiors, subalterns; that it owned the Dominican Republic, was planning to import liquid morphine from Bulgaria and Yugoslavia, and had a lot going on elsewhere in the world; and that it was making a king-size fortune.

Panessa could hardly have grasped all the ramifications of what he was told at the time. Doubtless he would have been surprised to learn that no other investigator, in either America or Italy, had found out as much in a quarter of a century.

In theory, such remarkable information should have radiated from Philadelphia to law enforcement agencies up and down the country, but nothing of the sort occurred. This was partly an old story of agency rivalry; the DEA was not eager to hand out information that the FBI might grab and run with (and vice versa). Besides, the agency was always chasing drug traffickers somewhere, Sicilians among them. Virtually nobody in authority believed that any two bands of Sicilian traffickers were linked, still less that they all were. "He's just another meatball," Panessa was told when the heroin found on one trafficker in New York proved identical to his own.[9]

Therefore, the New York Task Force drew no benefit from what

Panessa had found out until his mission was nearly over. And even then, it profited only by a fluke.

In the spring of 1983, the DEA, encouraged by Panessa's progress, sent a second undercover named Steve Hopson into Philadelphia. Through Panessa's contacts, Hopson was set up for a half-kilo buy from one Benny Zito, who worked in one of Mannino's Mimmo's Pizza parlors. To relay the order, Zito made a fateful phone call to New York. The man at the other end was Giuseppe Ganci, prominent in what was thought to be the Sicilian faction of the Bonanno Family—by reason of which the FBI was tapping his phone. Once the connection was made, it provided the missing link in the Pizza case.

The FBI had collected monumental evidence of the "Sicilian faction" 's suspicious behavior, but not a grain of powder tying the Sicilians to drugs. The heroin passing from Ganci to Zito to a DEA agent in Philadelphia was all the hard proof the bureau would get until the arrests were made.[10]

Thus, with the missing link in place, New York awoke to the DEA's momentous Philadelphia investigation, and a juridical storm broke. The U.S. attorney in Philadelphia wanted the entire case, as did Brooklyn's Eastern District; Rudolph Giuliani, the new head of Manhattan's Southern District;[11] and even southern New Jersey, where Panessa had also had dealings with La Porta.

After a thunderous sit-down with all four districts, the Department of Justice gave Zito to the Southern District in New York and the rest to Philadelphia. The decision was not uncommon; arguments over venue are normal, and political solutions unavoidable. Nevertheless, a singular opportunity to confront a nationwide menace had been missed.

Once the two court cases were separated, the lines of inquiry pointing to a single organized criminal conspiracy fell apart. The two federal districts ceased to exchange any further information. The hidden world glimpsed briefly by Panessa—the interlocking rings, the corner on the U.S. heroin market, the hold on Brooklyn—remained unexplored.

Eight Sicilian traffickers were tried in Philadelphia, without establishing their links to an immense international consortium. Twenty-two Sicilian traffickers were tried in New York, without establishing their links to those in Philadelphia or thousands of others in America.[12] Paolo La Porta, who had worked with five of the biggest figures in the Pizza case—Gaetano Badalamenti, Cesare Bonventre, Baldo Amato, Filippo Ragusa, Giuseppe Ganci—could not be used as evidence against them. The DEA's own undercover, Frank Panessa, could not testify at the Pizza trial. Prosecutors there could make no courtroom use of what he had learned from Paolo La Porta. His accounts finished up in the archives.

The FBI, knowing nothing of La Porta's indiscretions, could learn next to nothing about the true state of affairs in Brooklyn. Its agents, looking from the outside in, could never figure out the curious status of the Sicilian Mafiosi. Everybody thought they were appendages of Cosa Nostra in America, yet not one of them was known to have been sworn in by an American Family. The latest information suggests one possible exception. Several FBI informants now claim that John Gambino, a made Sicilian Mafioso, has also been sworn in to the Gambino Family. But there is no evidence on the others. "Salvatore Catalano was never identified as made by our informants. Neither were Cesare Bonventre and Baldo Amato. In four years of sophisticated surveillance, we found no evidence that any of them were made here. So we just called them the Sicilian faction of the Bonanno Family," said Assistant U.S. Attorney Louis Freeh, who led the government's team in the Pizza case.

In fact, they were all made in Sicily, as authorities realized in another couple of years. "Sal Catalano was *brought* to New York for heroin," said Tom Sheer, heading the FBI's criminal division in New York. "They were all sent over expressly to take care of the heroin traffic, each for his own Family," wrote a Sicilian judge looking into their money-washing scams.[13]

The first the FBI heard of these transplanted Sicilians was from its star undercover man, Joe Pistone, who had been infiltrating the Bonanno Family since 1975. A Bonanno soldier pointed them out to Pistone at the Toyland Social Club, the Bonanno Family's gathering place in New York's Little Italy. He called them "the zips," Pistone wrote:

He said the zips were Sicilians brought into the country to distribute heroin and carry out hits for Carmine "Lilo" Galante, the boss of the Bonanno Family. . . . This operation, he said, was strictly in the hands of Galante. The zips were effective because, although they were in the family, they were unknown in this country—no police records.

They were set up in pizza parlors, where they received and distributed heroin, laundered money, and waited for other assignments from Galante. . . .

The zips, he said, were clannish and secretive. They hung out mainly by themselves in the area of Knickerbocker Avenue in Brooklyn. They were, he said, the meanest killers in the business. . . .

Two of those he pointed out were Salvatore Catalano and Caesar Bonventre.[14]

That was in 1977, year of the Sicilian heroin pipeline. Sal Catalano, a husky, mean-eyed, taciturn Sicilian in his late thirties, had just taken over Knickerbocker Avenue, after arranging to have its previous street boss shot to death. His inseparable companion, the tall and casually elegant Cesare Bonventre, envied by pudgier colleagues for his Italian look, took care of the matter for Catalano, as he usually did.

Killing a street boss was just the first step in the Sicilian Mafia's remorseless advance. Its people were on their way to controlling the Bonanno Family altogether, and not just the Bonanno Family. While a legion of investigators observed them in Bonanno territory, they were also taking over the Brooklyn turf of New York's mighty Gambino Family.

The Cherry Hill Gambinos, as distinguished from the New York Gambinos, held 18th Avenue in Bensonhurst. They sold quantities of heroin through the New York Gambinos, especially the Family's underboss, Aniello Della Croce, who contributed generously to their financing. ("Don't tell me what it is; just give me back one and a half million for one million," he would say.) But John, Rosario, and Giuseppe Gambino themselves answered to Palermo. John in particular, the eldest brother, was "a different breed," says Mona Ewell—a made Man of Honor from Sicily who towered over his associates in the United States. And he was a much bigger figure in the Sicilian network than any defendant in the Pizza case. Aside from the consignments passing to him through Bonanno territory, he had other copious heroin sources, among them the Alcamo refinery near Trapani, with a capacity of four tons a year.[15] He was "at the vertex," the "converging point [and] final destination in America" for all the heroin sent by Palermo's reigning Families, wrote Italian magistrates in the early 1980s.

But the Italian and American authorities were still not telling each other much in those years. This side of the story was such a forbidding tangle of transatlantic tribal relations that the New York Task Force never went near it. Indeed, John Gambino is still at large.

In both Brooklyn enclaves, the Sicilians were occupying their territory much as a corporate entity occupies leased property. The tenants had the use of the land, and the landlord collected the rent. Naturally, the landlords kept an eye on what went on; and both parties made a careful show of mutual respect. But no Sicilian Men of Honor in Brooklyn were ever called to account by an American Mafia boss: they answered solely to Palermo. Joe Pistone's informant, trying to describe their relations with Carmine Galante, could hardly be expected to know that. Nobody did in those days.

The fearsome Galante, a short, fat, bloody-minded Cosa Nostra boss hated by his soldiers, *looked* like the big man behind the U.S. heroin trade. American Mafiosi were inevitably presumed to be running things in their own country; and next to Vito Genovese, Galante had long been the country's most consecrated and rapacious dope dealer.

Like his fellow American Joe Bonanno, Galante came from Castellammare del Golfo, home port of a flourishing heroin trade since World War II. Bonanno had sent him to organize a drug route through Montreal as early as 1953, and he had met with Lucky Luciano in Italy afterward. Furthermore—this was what really mattered—Galante had attended the October 1957 summit at the Hotel des Palmes in Palermo. As Joe Bonanno's underboss then, he was a party to the Sicilians' heroin franchise deal. Upon replacing Bonanno as the Family's boss, between prison terms in 1974, he had inherited the whole arrangement.

Long after the Sicilian connection grew clear, investigators still didn't know exactly what the Sicilians were paying for their American heroin franchise. "In millions of words under Title 3 surveillance, not a single wise guy ever mentioned a Sicilian heroin payoff to the New York Cosa Nostra Families," says Louis Schiliro of the FBI's Brooklyn-Queens office.

In time, however, U.S. attorneys in the Pizza case concluded that Carmine Galante must have been the American Mafia's rent collector. "He had to be getting the payoffs for the whole Commission," says Richard Martin, chief prosecutor at the Pizza trial. "Whatever the Sicilians were paying, Galante was the guy who got it and spread it around."[16]

The trouble with Galante had always been his ungovernable greed. When he got out of jail again in 1979, he apparently decided to stop spreading the heroin money around. He was shot to death that summer; and Salvatore Catalano, an accredited envoy of the heroin consortium in Palermo, took his place. The takeover had no precedent in Mafia history. A Sicilian Man of Honor now ruled over the American Mafia's entire Bonanno Family, one of the five Families dominating all the others in the United States.

More than two decades had passed since anybody had murdered an American Family boss; wise guys were shocked, and the cops were mystified. Presumably Cosa Nostra's Commission had authorized the hit, a time-honored custom, but the Sicilians had set Galante up.

Cesare Bonventre and Baldo Amato were Galante's Sicilian body-guards and were sitting at his table when three masked gunmen shot him in the courtyard of Joe and Mary's Restaurant on Knickerbocker Avenue. As he fell, Bonventre rose and fired two more bullets into his head. Detective Le Vien, on the scene for the Homicide Squad, saw the evidence of Bonventre's shots, but this part of the story was never published. Joe Pistone himself knew only that Bonventre and Amato had been there, and had walked away. "Supposedly the zips were Galante's chosen people. But two of his prime zips were with him when he got whacked," Pistone wrote.[17]

Later, when the Sicilians had whacked three other ranking Bonanno men, New York's wise guys came to understand them better. "Them fucking zips ain't gonna back up to nobody," said a Bonanno captain to Joe Pistone. "Those guys are looking to take over everything. That's why those three guys were killed—they went against the zips.[18] . . . You give them the fucking power . . . they'll bury you. They don't give a fuck. They don't care who's boss. They got no respect."[19]

Catalano lasted only two years as head of the Bonanno Family. As he conceded when he abdicated in 1981, he could not speak enough English to communicate with his subjects. He held on to his "Sicilian faction," though. In fact, his only notable contribution to the Family's welfare was to renew the Sicilians' lease on Brooklyn.[20]

Nobody in the outside world knew of Catalano's elevation to the late Galante's job at the time. He was just coming under surveillance as one of the Bonanno "zips" when a crucial encounter took place. At one in the afternoon on October 6, 1980, a Cadillac came by for Catalano and the stout, barrel-shaped Giuseppe Ganci at Catalano's bakery in Middle Village, Queens. Proceeding to the Withers Social Club in Brooklyn, they picked up an unknown third man and went on to Martini's Seafood Restaurant in Bay Ridge.[21] Half an hour later, Paul Castellano joined them for lunch. America's Boss of All Bosses, head of the Commission and ruling chief of New York's Gambino Family—the largest and strongest in the American Cosa Nostra—Castellano did not customarily lunch with the Mafia's lower classes. But today he spent two hours with the Sicilians, the first and last time he ever did such a thing.[22]

It took several years to understand that Big Paul Castellano had, in effect, been sitting down with the Great White Father who spoke with forked tongue: Salvatore Catalano and his fellow Sicilian Men of Honor who were colonizing Brooklyn. "They were working out the new terms of payment for the heroin franchise," says Richard Martin of the government's Pizza team. "Carmine Galante was out of the way; now the money would go straight to Castellano himself."[23] This was the informed view of all those close to the Pizza case. "We know that the Sicilians have been paying off the U.S. bosses on the heroin all along," says Louis Freeh. "Paul Castellano got paid, in spite of threatening others with death for dealing."[24]

At the time it happened in 1980, however, the FBI could not imagine why the Boss of All Bosses would confer with an obscure faction of a lesser New York Family. Two young agents newly assigned to the "zips" on Knickerbocker Avenue simply concluded that anybody who could sit down with Big Paul bore watching. So they watched.

The Shock of Recognition

he Pizza Connection was not just a cops and robbers story, though it was a good one. For the two countries hardest hit by the Mafia—Italy and the United States—it marked the passage at last from twenty-five years of mutual frustration and incomprehension to revelation.

There are many misconceptions about the FBI's investigation. It did not trace the Sicilian Mafia's cross-country pizza parlor circuit. (The "Pizza Connection" label was suggested to the press simply because several defendants happened to own pizza parlors in Brooklyn and Queens.) It came nowhere near dismantling the Sicilian Mafia's heroin network in America, which remains in place. It did not find out who was actually carrying the heroin into the country, or how, or who was moving it from coast to coast, along with cocaine; nor did it disrupt the flow through the pipeline for more than a brief interlude.[1]

The investigation also did not break up any of the intersecting Sicilian rings outside of New York. (The DEA broke up the ring in Philadelphia separately.) In particular, it did not affect the Sicilian Mafiosi leasing the Brooklyn property of the American Mafia's Gambino Family. These were John Gambino's Sicilians, the Cherry Hill Gambinos' ring, by all accounts the most important in the United States.

The investigation did dismantle the Sicilian ring operating in the Bonanno Family's Brooklyn enclave. There the traffickers were high-ranking Men of Honor from Sicily, known to have imported at least 150 kilos of heroin a year for five years, perhaps 5 percent of the network's supply in America. (The figure must have been higher, but there was no proof of that.) According to the Justice Department, they were forwarding the drugs to New York City, Newark, Philadelphia, Chicago, and Detroit. The indictment in the Pizza case continued to refer to these traffickers as "the Catalano faction, composed of members and associates of the Bonanno Family." It would take a while before the fact registered that they were made in Sicily and accountable to Palermo.[2]

Sending the traffickers to jail did not mean that the problem was solved, but rather that it had been *recognized* in a court of law, for the first time ever, anywhere. For once, the defendants were not street pushers or couriers. A judge and jury had confirmed the existence of an organized international conspiracy, extending from the raw materials to production to transport, marketing, and money washing.

Finding the proof that would stand up in court took five years, and every step was like walking under water. From two agents watching a couple of "zips," the case progressed to a hundred agents watching a nearly unending procession of them. Men whose faces meant nothing to New York cops moved in and out of a bakery in Queens, a pizzeria near Columbus Circle in Manhattan, a cheese store in Brooklyn, a restaurant in New Jersey, a car cemetery, a garage, a shopping center parking lot. They used roundabout routes, made furtive entrances and exits, carried things in cardboard boxes or paper bags. Some left parcels in car trunks, others removed them. To arrest one or two was to risk driving the others deeper under cover and blowing the whole case. To keep tailing them might have been a lifetime job. Just to match the faces to names took tedious months—years.

The impediments in the case were hard to believe. A couple of dozen shady characters under intensive surveillance were dealing massively in drugs, and *known* to be doing so, and could somehow never be caught at it. The largest concentration of manpower and resources in the history of American law enforcement could barely pierce their defenses until very nearly the end.

The traffickers were not all that clever—some were pretty dim—but they had a big edge. High-level traffickers are never easy to catch in the first place. They operate above the tree line, in a rarified atmosphere where the drug itself is often not even touched; the higher they are, the less likely they are to come anywhere near it.

These particular traffickers were working in a country that was unaware of their criminal past. They spoke in an undecipherable code, changed passports as other men change shirts, melted into a huge, featureless immigrant community. They were practiced in subterfuge and martially disciplined. Above all, they belonged to the world's most subtle and sophisticated criminal brotherhood, by now a huge multinational cartel. The Pizza case was well into its third year before investigators realized this last fact, and its corollary: that the organization could no longer be fought by any one country on its own.

Federal agencies were slow to grasp the point. The FBI, an otherwise admirable police force, was paying for the blindly obstinate rule of its departed chief. After half a century under J. Edgar Hoover, the bureau's agents knew little about the Mafia at home, and embarrassingly little about the one in Sicily or anywhere else abroad. They did not compile a computerized data bank on organized crime until 1980; they did not have a mandate to handle *any* drug cases until 1981.[3]

The DEA had expert agents and a prodigious data bank, but it was apparently not looking for linkage. Between 1969 and 1972, for instance, U.S. narcotics agents had maintained close surveillance on scores of Sicilian Mafiosi gravitating around Buscetta's drug ring in Brooklyn. They had followed the trail to Brazil, and back to Filippo Casamento, whose Eagle Cheese Company had absorbed nearly a ton of heroin in 1972 alone.[4] The arrest that year of this "affable, outgoing, joking, lovable shopkeeper" (to quote his lawyer) was part of the biggest drug bust on record then or since. Yet nobody seemed to grasp the significance of Casamento's past connections when he reemerged as a central figure in the Pizza case.[5]

Therefore, the first two years of the investigation were almost a write-off. By the end of 1982, FBI agents were drowning in paper: printouts, photographs, surveillance reports, bank statements, phone numbers. The case was still so thin that the Justice Department's Eastern District in Brooklyn turned it down, and the Southern District took it on with misgivings. "They certainly had something, but they were reaching," says Richard Martin, whose office would finally haul the Sicilian Mafia into court.

o⊂⊃o

The process of discovery really began in the U.S. attorney's office at One St. Andrews Plaza in Manhattan, just behind the Federal Courthouse in Foley Square. Rudolph Giuliani exerted a magnetic pull on the various agencies in the task force; and he was a great remover of impediments.

Still in his thirties and rising fast, Giuliani hit New York with a bang in 1983. From a big bright room with a stupendous view of the Brooklyn Bridge, he set out to prosecute all five New York Families and the American Mafia's national Commission. When offered what he (and everybody else) thought was the Sicilian faction of the Bonanno Family, he could hardly refuse.

The attorneys preparing the case for prosecution were young and game: Louis Freeh, slight, quiet, and thoughtful; and Richard Martin, jaunty, speculative, watchful.[6] They had a mountain of paper to go on, amounting to little hard evidence on any count but one: there were plentiful records of an enormous cash flow. Sicilians photographed with Sal Catalano and his crowd on Knickerbocker Avenue were bringing $5, $10, and $20 bills to the bank in valises and gym bags: $4.9 million deposited at Merrill Lynch between March and mid-April 1982; $5.2 million at E.F. Hutton from April 27 to July 2; $8.25 million in a different E.F. Hutton account from July 6 to September 27; $1.78 million sent to Switzerland from October 20 to November 21.[7]

Apart from that, nothing. Scores of Title 3 wiretaps authorized in 1983 yielded only cryptic conversations in unintelligible dialect, dwelling largely on shirts and sardines. The transcripts in English were for the most part meaningless, and often comical. (*Porca madonna,* a colloquial phrase used as absentmindedly by Sicilians as some Americans say "mothah," was translated as "pig mother.")

The FBI wanted to drop the case that April, but the Southern District hung in.[8] It did better than that, in fact: breaking virginal ground, Freeh and Martin began searching for historical links. The bureau's agents were looking for anything that might tie one suspect to another; but none had tried to see further into the past than the year they first noticed the Sicilians in Brooklyn. Martin looked back ten years.

Others in key places were beginning to do the same around then, in Italy as well as America. This was the turning point, the moment when a quarter of a century's blurred events began to come into focus. Martin spent the next eighteen months hunting through old DEA files and forgotten court records. Several prime Pizza defendants cropped up again and again: Ganci, Mazzurca, Mazzara, Lamberti, Casamento. "I looked at the Rappa bust in New Jersey in 1971: eighty-six kilos from Badalamenti in Palermo. I looked at Eagle Cheese in 1972. I looked at drug busts in *Italy* that were tied to *America;* that was really something," he told me.

In 1983, it really was something. Though the fact may strain belief, practically nobody on either side of the Atlantic appeared to have done as much up to then. The FBI was running into a wall because people in law enforcement simply didn't think in international terms in those days. Every lead in the Pizza case stopped at the U.S. border, while every suspect was Sicilian-born. Indeed, one good FBI agent sent to Palermo on a fact-finding mission in the early days might have saved many million man-hours later.

In 1981, for instance, the Italian police had issued arrest warrants for three major figures under FBI surveillance in Brooklyn—two of them future Pizza defendants. They were wanted in Sicily on a 1980 drug charge that eventually became the pearl of the American government's case: a beautiful, rounded ball of evidence to bring before the court.[9] The Italians had not only named the three Sicilians but placed them as operating on Knickerbocker Avenue. Upon learning of the warrants, the FBI had simply checked with U.S. Immigration, noting that the three "had immigrated from regions of Italy that are organized crime–oriented."[10] On the other hand, the Italians had not sent a cop after the three in Brooklyn either. Curiously, considering their common need, neither country had more than a hazy idea of what the other was doing.

While Mafia traffickers commuted across the Atlantic with the greatest of ease—first class, with VIP treatment laid on at the airport—a simple exchange of police reports or judicial records between Italy and America could take months or years. (A Sicilian prosecutor working on the same crucial 1980 drug case waited twenty-two months for copies of the DEA's reports.)[11] Different penal codes, disparate extradition procedures, grand jury secrecy in America, and the *segreto d'istruttòrio* in Italy made for paralyzing restraints.[12] Documents went hopelessly astray, through ministerial indifference, ignorance, boredom, or worse. Neither country seemed to sense an urgency to communicate. "Why would those guys know anything?" was their prevailing view of each other.

Yet they were looking at opposite ends of the same enterprise, often at the same people, at exactly the same time. The police in Sicily had found eight large heroin refineries on the island since 1980; Sicilian magistrates had identified thirty-seven Mafia rings producing for the American market; the Cassarà report had shown that a single ruling

directorate controlled them in Palermo; a brilliant cop heading Italy's
Anti–Organized Crime Nucleus, Gianni De Gennaro, was in the process of uncovering its elaborate circuit for shipping and laundering
from Rome, Florence, and Milan to London, Montreal, and Caracas.[13]

In effect, as both countries finally realized, the Americans were
holding half of a torn dollar bill, while the Italians held the other half.

oⒸo

An early tentative exchange—the mere mention of a name in
1981—had shown what could come of comparing notes. Giuseppe
Bono, who had spent a decade helping the Cuntreras mount their operation in Venezuela, had moved on to be the Cupola's new man in New
York in 1980. Caught in a routine snapshot, he was known to FBI
agents only as a middle-aged, professorially bespectacled stranger seen
talking to Sal Catalano and Giuseppe Ganci on a sidewalk in Queens.
But the Italian police knew him as a top-level international trafficker,
an intimate of the Cuntreras, and an engregious Mafia money launderer
whose dummy company in Milan, CITAM, was washing millions of
narcodollars. Indeed, Bono was first on a police list of 162 Mafiosi
dominating the Italian underworld.[14] None of the Italian authorities
had an idea of his whereabouts when he turned up in New York in 1980;
they were thrilled when, a year or so later, the FBI asked if they knew
him.

Identifying Bono was like winning a prize in a lottery. The DEA,
chasing down a Neapolitan associate of Bono's, found out that he had
been married at St. Patrick's Cathedral in November 1980, and had
thrown a grand wedding reception afterward at the Hotel Pierre. Five
hundred guests had all had their pictures taken at Bono's expense. (He
paid the photographer $4,746.)[15] Matching these photos to names be-
came an absorbing game. Eventually—it took three or four years—
agents learned that every man at Bono's party was a Sicilian Mafioso.
All of the FBI's suspects had attended. Dozens of others had flown in
from Sicily, Great Britain, and Canada. Several were dead by the time
they were recognized, killed off in the Great Mafia War.

American and Italian agents took to springing the photographs on
any and every informant. Richard Martin carried a box of two hundred
photos to Italy several times, going over them again and again with the
police in Palermo, Rome, and Milan. He was still at it in 1985, on the
eve of the Pizza trial.[16]

The two-way flow of information grew slowly. Hindsight is intoler-
ant of failure; certainly the failure of both countries to move faster

seems astonishing now. Only at the very last did Italians and Americans find that, between them, they had been sitting on the master key to the Pizza case all along.

The pearl that finally dropped into the hands of Louis Freeh and Richard Martin was a forty-kilo shipment of heroin from Palermo, seized in Milan on its way to New York in March 1980. The seizure was large, but not exceptional. What made it different from any in the history of drug enforcement was that the heroin was traced from start to finish: from producer to shipper to distributor, from Sicily to America.

For Judge Falcone, Sicily's investigating magistrate in the case, the incident became almost magical: as if a thousand multicolored fragments in a kaleidoscope had suddenly formed a brightly lit picture. At first, the seizure in Milan had seemed disconnected, he recalled: "Then I realized that everything started in Palermo. . . . But was it enough to investigate in Palermo, in Sicily, in Italy? If the police confiscate heroin going to the U.S., why not go to the U.S. and study the collateral effects of that operation? Why hadn't others taken that initiative?"[17] Others did in the end, but it took time.

Sal Catalano was still a nonentity for the FBI in Brooklyn when the sequence of events began in February 1980. He was a nonentity for police in Palermo too, but they were familiar with the drug traffickers he met there. Italy's Guardia di Finanza, tapping the phone of one trafficker, learned of their meeting at a bar in Piazza Politeama, the city's busiest square, and sent a photographer. Catalano thus went into local police files as an unidentified white male.[18] The Italian police did not discover who he was until the Americans recognized his photo four years later. But the Italians had known since 1980 that Catalano's companions at the bar—two of them future Pizza defendants—had later inspected a forty-kilo heroin shipment to America.[19]

Both countries might have bottled up the Sicilian Mafia's heroin pipeline at both ends when the forty kilos were seized. The DEA found out who was meant to receive the heroin, and the Italians discovered who had manufactured and sent it. But then the two countries parted ways.

The DEA had gotten on the trail right in the middle of Michele Sindona's fake kidnapping in the summer of 1979. John Gambino had flown over from New York to guide Sindona around Palermo that August. During his month in Sicily, his partners had sent five kilos of heroin to the younger Gambino brothers, Rosario and Giuseppe, in New York, and DEA agents had intercepted it at Kennedy Airport.

In the course of seizing two more consignments in a row at the airport, the DEA acquired an intrepid mole, Frank Rolli, a baggage handler for Alitalia. Like everyone else in the unfolding story, Rolli was Sicilian-born; on and off, he worked for the Cherry Hill Gambinos.[20]

The heroin was arriving in unaccompanied suitcases of "personal effects," packed in "Felce Azzurro" (Blue Fern) talcum powder. Tracking through Alitalia's cargo office, the agents got to Rolli and turned him. He led them to a place in Brooklyn where he had been interrogated under torture by five Sicilians after the first suitcase disappeared. John Gambino's brother Rosario was one of the five interrogators; and Sicily's heroin king, Salvatore Inzerillo, was another. Inzerillo had flown over specially from Palermo for the occasion.[21] "We've lost a million dollars; it can't happen again," he told Rolli.

Rolli must have passed the torture test, since he not only got out alive but was put back to work. The summons came at the start of March 1980 from Emmanuele Adamita, whose name had been cropping up in American police files for the previous fifteen years. One of the Sicilian Mafia's early settlers in Brooklyn—he had set up Buscetta's letter box there in 1965—Adamita had long been the Gambino brothers' chief heroin mover.

Rolli went to meet Adamita, this time with the DEA's blessings and promise of protection, and was taken to the Mille Luci Cafe (Enzo Napoli's on 18th Avenue in Brooklyn) for a meeting with Rosario and Giuseppe Gambino. The brothers wanted to try a new and safer shipping route from Italy. For $30,000, Rolli agreed to set one up with Adamita in Milan.

Two DEA agents tailed their mole and Adamita across the Atlantic; saw the heroin come up from Sicily in a truckload of lemons; and watched Adamita and Rolli ship it off to New York in a zinc container with a hundred LP records of Italian pop music. The DEA then hustled Rolli away to enter the U.S. Witness Protection Program, while the Italian police arrested Adamita and his accomplices in Milan. This was the moment when, incredibly, the Italian and American authorities went their separate ways. The traffickers caught in Italy were tried there; those in America became a separate case (six cases, actually). Nobody was extradited in either direction—not even John Gambino, from the United States to Italy, despite repeated requests from Judge Falcone.[22]

In New York, John, Rosario, and Giuseppe Gambino were arrested on the same day with several of their aides, and bound over to the Eastern District in Brooklyn. In six separate trials, each was acquitted. For the Americans, the Adamita case was closed; FBI agents, just beginning the Pizza investigation, never heard of it. (The DEA, which had a specially targeted team on this trail, apparently did not make the connection.)

In Italy, Adamita and his accomplices were tried with seventy-eight other Sicilian traffickers who kept cropping up as investigators followed the twists and turns of the Sindona kidnapping. The seventy-eight defendants were headed by John Gambino *(in absentia)* and his co-conspirator in Palermo, Rosario Spatola.

Neither country followed the other's case, or saw the other's court records. It was a good four years before the Americans learned that Sal Catalano, along with Ganci and their whole crowd in New York, had owned a big share of Adamita's forty-kilo heroin shipment. The Italians had learned practically everything about the Adamita drug bust long since, except for identifying Sal Catalano's photograph. They had recognized the photo in 1982, but failed to make the connection.

Then a Mafia defector named Salvatore "Totuccio" Contorno came along in Sicily to provide the final, exquisitely incriminating details. Contorno, a burly, gruff, gravelly voiced ex-butcher with heavy black eyebrows and a prizefighter's stance, had been the late Stefano Bontate's faithful Man of Valor since 1975. The atrocities committed by the Corleonesi in the Great Mafia War had made him a *pentito* of inestimable worth. Among his many important revelations to Judge Falcone in Palermo was a particularly significant story about the Adamita heroin consignment. Providentially, if accidentally, he had witnessed the scene firsthand.

The consignment was supposed to have been a trial run for shipments in bulk, a form of supermarket transport serving all of Brooklyn's Sicilian traffickers. The zinc container leaving from Milan contained individual packets for the Cherry Hill Gambinos on 18th Avenue and Catalano's people on Knickerbocker Avenue. Catalano had actually flown over to Palermo to inspect the goods beforehand, with Giuseppe Ganci and three other future Pizza defendants.

Contorno, who had dabbled in all of the Mafia's usual pursuits including drugs, was there by sheer chance. In February 1980, he had just taken a $30,000 flier on a heroin consignment when Catalano and the others got to Sicily for a month's stay. In early March, Contorno gave the fellow who had talked him into the investment, one D'Agostino, a lift to a farmhouse near an iron foundry in Bagheria, on the outskirts of Palermo, where the others were gathered. Their host was the local Mafia boss, Leonardo Greco (no relation to the Ciaculli Grecos). Contorno described what happened:

I didn't understand the procedure, but I saw cellophane packets with a white substance, and something boiling on the stove, and little glass containers, and there was an intense stink of acid. I went out to the car because the air was unbreathable. . . .

Driving back, D'Agostino told me they were American customers for the drug. *He explained that it was merchandise belonging to different people, that would all be shipped at once. To tell the different consignments apart, they made signs on every packet . . . with a pencil or little cut at the end. . . .*

A few days later, I read about forty kilos of heroin getting seized in Milan, and D'Agostino told me it was the shipment I had a piece of.

Contorno identified "the foreigners"—Catalano, Ganci, and three other Pizza defendants—when he was safely in New York, in 1984, and ready to testify at the Pizza trial.[23] Adamita's empty heroin sacks, miraculously preserved in Milan's courthouse, were found to have different colored pencil marks and tiny cuts, exactly as Contorno said.

o⊂⊃o

By the time Contorno talked in 1984, Italian and American authorities were communicating at last. In January of that year, Italy, the United States, and Canada had held a joint conference in Ottawa to talk over the Pizza case and decide whether the American or Sicilian Mafia was in command of the New York drug operation. The decision was unanimous: *all* the operatives in the case were Sicilian.[24]

That October, a high-level Italo-American Working Group on Drug Trafficking met in Rome, to cut red tape and exchange information vital to simultaneous investigations in both countries. Among those present were the U.S. attorney general, the head of the FBI, the head of the DEA, the Italian interior minister, Italy's national chief of police, and the head of the Guardia di Finanza.[25] The Southern District was moving toward the Pizza trial in New York; investigating magistrates in Sicily's anti-Mafia pool were moving toward a mastodonic maxitrial in Palermo. Both made sensational arrests that year; both trials would run concurrently in 1986.

Two-way communication boomed after that meeting. Judge Falcone passed on the Bagheria story to the Southern District. Richard Martin was on the phone to him in Palermo almost daily, and Falcone flew back and forth to New York. FBI agent Carmine Russo went to Rome to consult with Italy's Criminalpol. Falcone's right arm in the Squadra Mobile, Commissario Ninni Cassarà, spent happy days with the FBI in Queens.

Inspector Cassarà told me about these days once, in his cluttered Palermo office. Immersed in preparations for the maxitrial, he was constantly chasing leads to New York. The FBI had made him a temporary U.S. marshal so that he could work in the field. He used to sit with the agents in the bureau's eavesdropping van, translating from Sicilian Mafia jargon. The van was parked down the street from the Al Dente, Catalano's and Ganci's pizzeria on Queens Boulevard; after listening in on their phones all morning, Cassarà and the others would often drop in to pick up a pizza for lunch.

Once the two countries were pooling what they knew, both could finally see the Sicilian Mafia in its full international dimensions. The tons of heroin it was producing and selling were never traced, but the immensity of the Mafia's operations could be measured through the money it took in.

The FBI did a heroic job tracing the money. For upward of two years, its agents had practically nothing to go on beyond a glimpse from the rear of two men lugging a carton into a Manhattan office building. Eventually, pursuing this slender lead, they uncovered a financial cycle in perpetual motion around the globe.

When the Pizza trial opened in 1985, the FBI had turned up thirteen channels used to launder some $60 million. Though considerably less than the $5-million-a-day laundering "capability" that Paolo La Porta had mentioned to DEA agent Panessa in Philadelphia, it was a hearty sum nonetheless. The money had moved out of the United States in multiples of millions, by private plane to the Bahamas, by telex from American to Swiss banks, and by suitcase on turnaround flights to Switzerland. It was then sent straight to Palermo, or directly to pay off Turkish morphine suppliers in Geneva, Sofia, and Istanbul.

Finding the Turkish money link was a tremendous coup. This was the Turkish arms-drugs Mafia, whose secret pact with Sicilian Men of Honor in 1975 had brought their entire chain of heroin refineries into being. The alliance was central—indispensable—to the growth and prosperity of the Cupola's heroin consortium, and still is. As late as 1988, the Turkish Mafia was found to have washed $1 billion through a different international ring, almost twenty times more than the amount traced in the Pizza case. This ring, tracked around the world from Baghdad and Damascus to Istanbul, Sofia, Lugano, Miami, and New York, was spotted when a hundred-kilo morphine shipment for the Sicilian Mafia was intercepted in Switzerland.[26]

The enormous importance of the ten-year-old Turkish-Sicilian Mafia pact was underlined even as the FBI was catching up with Turkish suppliers in Switzerland, in the summer of 1984. Italy's Judge Carlo Palermo had stumbled on the Turkish arms-drugs Mafia in 1980 and pursued it until 1984, precisely the years of the Pizza investigation in America. Stonewalled in Trento, the judge asked for a transfer to Trapani, the Switzerland of Sicily. Fifty days after he arrived in Trapani, on April 2, 1985, the Mafia set out to kill him with a ferocity plainly meant to discourage any possible successors.

The radio-controlled bomb meant for his car "showed high technical competence for maximum impact," wrote the investigating magistrate. It missed Judge Palermo but hit the car ahead, driven by a woman taking her two small twins to school. The woman's car disintegrated. Her face was sucked out, leaving just part of her scalp and left cheek. Viscera spilling out of her body were found a hundred yards away. Nothing remained of the twins but shreds of cloth and shards of bone and teeth; a foot was found in the front yard of a nearby villa.[27]

On April 30, police found the the world's biggest heroin refinery at Alcamo, in Trapani province. Supplied with Turkish morphine base in Bulgarian jute bags, and with high-tech Bulgarian equipment, the refinery was geared to produce four tons of heroin a year: $1 billion worth wholesale.

Not unnaturally, an Italian court concluded that Judge Palermo had gotten too close to the Alcamo refinery and its secrets. Sicily's Mafia bosses would not tolerate interference with their Turkish Mafia lifeline, the court held.[28]

The shock of the hit was barely subsiding in Italy when Louis Freeh and an FBI team reached Switzerland in the summer of 1985 to take depositions from captured Turkish suppliers. Several of importance had been bagged by the Swiss police, though the big one, Yasar Musullulu, got away. He had fled to Bulgaria in 1983, after cheating his Sicilian customers out of nearly $1 million on a ship they thought he was buying for them. He was known to have sold them at least two tons of morphine base over the previous two years, for $55 million.[29]

In his absence, the American team got a fairly full rundown on Musullulu from a fellow countryman and giant-sized scoundrel named Paul Waridel. Also born in Istanbul, Waridel was a high-rolling millionaire who had brokered drug deals in Italy on and off since the Turkish-Sicilian Mafia pact was sealed. Later in the 1970s, he had met some of the best Sicilian bosses in an Italian jail and had been their go-between with Musullulu afterward.[30]

The money changing hands was in the eight-digit range. The biggest Sicilian customer up to 1982, Nunzio·La Mattina, had bought $40 million worth of morphine base on behalf of the Palermo consortium from this one supplier (he had several suppliers). Unfortunately for La Mattina, he failed to pay $13 million on those bills, for which his meticulous superiors in Palermo had him killed.

La Mattina's replacement worked directly for the Sicilian Mafia's treasurer and underground ambassador to Rome—Buscetta's Family boss, Giuseppe "Pippo" Calò.[31] The Mafia's leadership had just passed to Luciano Leggio and the Corleonesi, who saw to paying off all but $1.5 million of the late La Mattina's debt. "Five and a half million dollars was directly deposited in the United States and sent to Musullulu through Bulgaria at a cost of 9 percent," Louis Freeh told the jury in the Pizza case later. The rest was carried from New York to Zurich in six Samsonite suitcases "so heavy that you had to be an athlete to lift them," Waridel said.[32]

Bulgaria's ongoing role in the Turkish-Sicilian arrangement is usually mentioned obliquely if at all, doubtless in the interest of diplomatic peace and quiet. As Louis Freeh pointed out in court, however, its role was significant and direct. "The Bulgarian connection was important for Musullulu because, as Waridel testified, Musullulu told him that he had access to heroin, heroin that was seized by the Bulgarian police and that Musullulu could use to distribute. In fact, Waridel was in jail in Italy for heroin that he said came from Musullulu, which Musullulu said came by way of Bulgaria."

Bulgaria, and Musullulu, are both playing much the same roles to this day, according to the DEA. Reporting from Bern, Switzerland, in January 1989, the DEA's agent there described the global, billion-dollar-a-year money-laundering operations of the Shakarchi Trading Company, exposed a few months previously. The company had been traced after Swiss police seized one hundred kilos of Turkish heroin bound for the Sicilian Mafia in February 1987. The money laundered for these Turkish traffickers was "entering Switzerland from Bulgaria with the active participation of the Bulgarian government officials," said one confidential DEA cable.

The smuggling of the money into Bulgaria for transportation to Switzerland is processed by a Bulgarian import/export firm called Globus, which in reality is an agency of the Bulgarian government operated by the Bulgarian secret police. The Bulgarian government takes a percentage of the value of the goods, whether it be illegal cash, drugs or weapons, and guarantees safe passage of the material through Bulgaria. Globus, formerly known as Kintex, surfaced in the investigation of the attempted assassination of the pope in 1981.

Bulgaria was refining the heroin shipped west from Turkish morphine base, according to another DEA cable. Yasser Musullulu, "one of the largest suppliers of morphine base in the world," had distributed Bulgarian-made heroin as well, and had laundered the Sicilians' payment money through the Shakarchi Company in Switzerland. "Currently a fugitive from Italy and Turkey, Musullulu is believed to be residing in Bulgaria and operating heroin laboratories from that location."[33]

oⒸo

The money discovered in the Pizza Connection case was irrefutable proof that the Sicilian Mafia was operating on a worldwide scale, and could only be dealt with across national boundaries. The FBI could not have followed the trail without substantial help from Italy, Switzerland, Spain, France, Canada, West Germany, and Luxembourg. Italy and Switzerland especially were so closely involved that major Pizza Connection trials were held in both countries for money washers caught on their soil.

And the money made the case against the twenty-two defendants in New York. The millions of dollars changing hands and leaving the country—in cash, in small bills—was crushing evidence to put before a jury. The remaining burden of proof depended largely on saturation surveillance, at which the FBI excelled. A thousand roles of film, fifty-five thousand wiretaps, a million man-hours of surveillance, tipped the balance.

For all the bureau's manpower and resources, however, its agents could not have decoded what they saw and heard in America without knowing what was going on in Sicily.

Sicily was in the midst of a Mafia war, a source of monumental confusion to American agents who had enough trouble as it was. The Corleonesi and their allies had taken over the Cupola and its heroin pipeline in Palermo, impelling the Sicilian Mafiosi in New York to proceed with almost hysterical caution.

The big losers in Palermo were nearly all dead by the end of 1981, leaving survivors like Gaetano Badalamenti in an awkward position. Expelled from the Cupola in 1978, presumably sentenced to be shot on sight, he had nevertheless continued to run drugs out of Sicily until 1982.[34] Then he was apparently obliged to take off and conduct his business elsewhere, confounding everyone on the Pizza case.

Buscetta, testifying at the Pizza trial, swore that Badalamenti was running for his life. If so, he stopped along the way to make a lot of phone calls. Nobody knew where he was calling from; mostly from a public phone booth in Rio de Janeiro, it turned out. The FBI's wizards finally traced the calls to and from tiny towns like Temperance, Michigan (south of Detroit), right off the map in the American Middle West. Apparently, he would trust only his own intermediaries there for his substantial deals with the Sicilians in Brooklyn. To all appearances, the Sicilians shunned Badalamenti even as they bought quantities of heroin and cocaine from him. Supposedly they would have to kill him if they caught him; plainly, they didn't want to catch him.

But if it was true that Badalamenti was running for his life, he could have had no dealings with the Sicilian Mafia's new rulers in Palermo. In reality, he must have been dealing with them, or for them. In fact, he practically gave the secret away, in the single most meaningful conversation among the thousands overheard by the FBI.

Badalamenti was talking to a nephew in Oregon, Illinois, from his favorite phone booth in Brazil, in February 1984. The question was whether to use some foreign supplier who clearly was *not* working with, or for, the Sicilian Mafia, someone who "did not have the license" to bring narcotics into the United States. "It is he who needs us," Badalamenti explained to his nephew. "He does not have an importer's license. *We have the license.* "[35] There, in four words, was the definition of the Sicilian Mafia's heroin franchise. The "we" could only mean that the outcast Badalamenti still enjoyed his trading privileges, if only at a discreet distance.[36]

The Pizza trial was over, and a great deal more was known, before the full import of Badalamenti's phrase sank in. Louis Freeh, going back over this ground with me in 1987, drew the logical conclusion: Badalamenti was referring to the historic decision made by the American and Sicilian Mafias in 1957 at the Hotel des Palmes in Palermo.

This was far beyond anybody's thinking when FBI agents were listening in on Badalamenti's phone calls in 1984. They had heard all about him from the Italians by then, but he was still a hopeless mystery, known merely as "the Uncle" in hundreds of baffling wiretaps. Nobody knew where he was, or whose uncle he was, or *who* he was, until the DEA's Mona Ewell finally matched his disembodied voice on the phone to an answering nephew's in Temperance, Michigan.[37]

Badalamenti was not the only supplier for Catalano's crowd; at least two Mafia Families were shipping directly from Sicily. But he was a storybook Man of Honor, the former crowned head of the Sicilian Mafia, a notorious drug trafficker all his grown life; and in 1984, he was hot.

The phone traffic was frenetic in the early months of that year, from Rio to Oregon, Illinois, to New York and back. Badalamenti was preparing to send twenty kilos of cocaine to the Brooklyn ring via his Midwest nephews: the first clear chance in four years to catch them all in the act. But then the chance came to catch Badalamenti himself, and the Americans went for it. They had the money, the heroin sold to a DEA agent in Philadelphia, the damning reunion in a Bagheria farmhouse, the thousand rolls of film and fifty-five thousand wiretaps—the twenty-two defendants of their choice wrapped up. Badalamenti would be their ultimate reward for all the years of torment.

When the Americans caught up with him in Madrid, in April 1984, the Italian police were there as well. Both countries had come to the end of exhaustive investigations under way since 1980. Both were preparing to put the Sicilian Mafia on trial for a continuing criminal conspiracy dating back to 1975. Both wanted Badalamenti, but they were close enough then to make a swap.

Tommaso Buscetta, arrested in Brazil the previous autumn, was awaiting extradition to either the United States or Italy. Second only to Badalamenti as one of the world's most wanted drug traffickers, he was another prize catch. Both countries wanted him too. By mutual consent, the Americans took Badalamenti and the Italians got Buscetta.

Buscetta's
Fall from Grace

Tommaso Buscetta's last days in the Sicilian Mafia afforded a clear glimpse of the Octopus fully grown. He was known as the Boss of Two Worlds by then: an archetype once, and a victim in the end, of the power reaching from a small Mediterranean island to strategic points around the globe.

Buscetta was captured in Brazil in October 1983, after having just moved to São Paulo from a luxurious apartment in Rio de Janeiro. His lovely young wife, Cristina Almeida de Guimaraes, was with him; an elegant maroon Ford Landau stood waiting. He was unarmed (though a Sicilian bodyguard with a .38 Special hovered nearby).

Eleven others were rounded up with him, in a huge police sweep from São Paulo to Belem to Rio. His wife was arrested. So was her father, Homero Guimaraes, Sr., taken after he shot a police inspector, who shot back. Gaetano Badalamenti's son Leonardo was also arrested, along with a colorful Italian called Zodiaco, who rode around in a Rolls-Royce and owned the longest yacht in Rio's Gloria Marina. It was "the biggest operation against organized crime ever carried out in Brazil," according to the police. "They thought we were just a bunch of

Third World cops. They came here to make Rio de Janeiro the capital of the Mafia, to flood America and Europe with cocaine," said the head of Brazil's Federal Narcotics Squad, Pedro Berwanger.[1]

"They" had been implanted in Brazil since the early 1970s, unnoticed by anybody in authority in or out of the country. "They must have been here at least ten years—*ten years*—and we didn't know a thing about it," the DEA's agent in Rio told me when I got there in 1986. They made up one of the Sicilian Mafia's two chartered branches in South America, as Buscetta revealed later; the other was next door in Venezuela.[2]

By October 1983, the Brazilian branch was expanding rapidly to serve a surging cocaine market in the United States and Europe. The Brazilian police believed that Buscetta had two hundred "cadres" behind him when he was caught (one of the things he preferred not to talk about when he crossed over to the side of the law).

o⊂⊃o

Buscetta had missed the Sicilian Mafia's golden decade, most of which he spent in jail. Extradited from Brazil to Italy in 1972, he had remained behind bars until 1980. Then, with some three more years to go, he got himself out.[3] To say he escaped is to dignify a judicial ruling that caused considerable amusement in Mafia circles. Transferred from the Ucciardone in Palermo to a house of detention near Turin, he was given permission to go out and work by day. Italy often grants this "semiliberty" privilege to model prisoners; Buscetta, a model prisoner up to then, simply went to work one morning and walked away.

The judge who had signed Buscetta's part-time work permit had rejected "negative evaluations" based on his past record. The "spirit of prison reform" provided for a prisoner's "gradual reinsertion into society," and Buscetta had shown high promise in that regard, she wrote:

> The prisoner's conduct has been irreprehensible. He was always respectful to the personnel and sociable with his colleagues, and participated with interest in the process of personal resocialization. . . .
> There is absolutely no sign that the prisoner cultivated or tried to cultivate relations with elements of the Mafia in prison. On the contrary, his personality shows a sincere desire to be resocialized. . . . It is beyond doubt that he is ready to be reinserted into an orderly, civil way of living.[4]

Thus rewarded for behaving exactly as Mafia bosses are supposed to behave in jail, Don Masino Buscetta went home to Palermo. It was June

1980; the heroin pipeline had come on stream three years before; the Sicilian Mafia now owned what an Italian minister of justice has called "the most gigantic commercial enterprise in the world."[5] Every clan in the Sicilian capital was involved in heroin, bar none, and the money was killing them. Discipline, codes of behavior, territorial boundaries and old Family alignments were breaking down. Though a fragile truce still held between the contending armies in formation, Don Masino could hear the distant drums of war.

He was now a mature man of the world in his fifties, traveled, urbane, smooth spoken, well groomed. Prison had in no way diminished him; on the contrary, he had come out after eight years with his legendary aura intact. "I knew Tommaso Buscetta in jail, in Palermo, and I could see that he enjoyed a position of supremacy over the other prisoners. . . . It was notorious that Buscetta and Luciano Leggio had the same importance in the Mafia," testified a fellow convict doing time for drugs.[6] Another described his life-style at the Ucciardone this way:

Buscetta was very meticulous about his person, using only the finest products. He never finished a bottle of toilet water or cake of soap; he gave the rest away as gifts. His casual clothes, his jeans, were always designer-made, perfect. . . .

Only his coffee was prepared in jail; men would take turns to bring it to him piping hot. Otherwise, his breakfast, lunch, and dinner came from the best restaurants in Palermo.

Buscetta was a boss—in fact, The Boss. He never raised his voice, he never asked for anything; but he always knew everything. . . . I never heard him threaten anybody, but I'd hear him say: "That fellow in cell 8 is making too much noise and he'd do well to cut it out." . . .

A prisoner just coming in made sure to pay his respects. A prisoner leaving knew it was his duty to take his leave of Don Masino.[7]

Seemingly friendly to all and an enemy of none, Buscetta was cordially received on returning to Palermo. Throughout the summer and fall of 1980, he lived the life of a visiting high dignitary at some imperial underworld court. Outside, in the other world, he was Italy's most notorious escaped convict, presumably a hunted fugitive. Under the Mafia's wing, he went everywhere and saw everybody (including a parliamentary deputy in Rome, whose name he feels unable to recall).

Seductive propositions came from all sides. The boss of Buscetta's Porta Nuova Family, Pippo Calò, wanted him to take over the Family's affairs in Palermo while Calò himself tended to the Cupola's business in

Rome—reinvestment of narcodollars and morphine deals with Turkish suppliers, mostly. There were billions of lire to be made in the renovation of Palermo's old quarter, Calò said; Don Masino could name his price.

Several top managers in the heroin trade invited him into partnership. Giuseppe Ganci, dropping in from Knickerbocker Avenue that summer, made him an offer, as did the Sicilian Mafia's patriarch in Brazil, Antonio Salamone, just in from São Paulo. Even Salvatore Inzerillo, still the Man in the Cupola's heroin consortium, wanted him for a partner.[8]

Buscetta says he turned them all down. ("I was perhaps the only Man of Honor in Palermo who never took part in the trafficking," he told Judge Falcone later.) The longer he stayed in the Sicilian capital, the less he liked it. Not only could he see the war coming, but he was sure that his natural allies—Stefano Bontate, Salvatore Inzerillo, Gaetano Badalamenti—were going to lose it. Stefano Bontate, the Man of Honor he admired most, had told him all about Leggio's iniquities and the relentless advance of the Corleonesi, and confided that he planned to strike first: he and Inzerillo intended to shoot Leggio's proconsul in the Cupola, Salvatore "Corto" Riina. "You're a lost man," Buscetta warned him sadly.

There was nothing to keep him in Palermo, waiting for the inevitable end. He stayed for Christmas. Bontate, friend and protector of the Salvos, Sicily's millionaire tax collectors, persuaded his friends to put a sumptuous villa at Buscetta's disposal. They also flew down his wife and several offspring from Paris in a private plane. One of the Salvos' hotels sent in a festive Christmas dinner. Then, early in January of the new year, Buscetta drove to Paris and, with yet another false passport, boarded a Concorde for Brazil.

Narcotics agents had lost sight of Brazil since the spectacular demise of Buscetta's Corsican ring in 1972, but all manner of traffickers had soon flocked back. Brazil's geography was an irresistible lure. Apart from thousands of miles of unpatrollable seacoast, empty lands, and jungle, it shared frontiers with the countries producing nine-tenths of the world's cocaine: Colombia, Bolivia, and Peru. Thus, together with Venezuela on its northern border, Brazil made an ideal base for the two-way traffic that would soon escalate to nightmare proportions: cocaine and heroin, the one bartered for the other, moving respectively eastward and westward between the New and Old hemispheres.

Buscetta, arriving in 1981 as Thomas Roberto Felice or Jose Roberto Escobar, could easily be invisible to the official eye. Brazil contained an enormous community of honest and hardworking Italian immigrants. São Paolo in particular was a privileged sanctuary for Sicily's self-made *desaparecidos,* fugitives who had "disappeared themselves" in Italy—abandoning their cars with the doors open, leaving personal effects behind—to simulate forcible kidnapping and a Mafia "white death." This sprawling megalopolis of ten million souls, more than half of them first- or second-generation Italian immigrants, sheltered any number of Sicilian Mafiosi written off as dead by the Italian police. Antonio Salamone, vanishing from guarded exile in the Italian north, was *'u parrinu,* their godfather. A frail, peaceable-looking old man—"a Mafioso with a human face," a Sicilian prosecutor would call him—Salamone was a member of the Cupola on leave when he reached São Paulo in 1974;[9] he remained there eight years before any agent of the law knew he was alive.

Buscetta preferred Rio de Janeiro, also full of faceless Italian immigrants but more frivolous and chic. Upon arriving, he bought a choice high-rise apartment in the Barra da Tijuca quarter on the Copacabana, known as millionaire's row, with magnificent picture windows overlooking the sea. Two floors above him lived another famed Italian fugitive: "a truly singular coincidence," says Buscetta, claiming they never met. He was Don Antonio Bardellino of the Neapolitan Camorra, wanted in Italy for persistent and aggravated cocaine trafficking with South America. The presence of this notorious Camorra boss in the same apartment house in the same city said much for the working relations between Neapolitan and Sicilian traffickers abroad. Bardellino was one of three Camorra chiefs who were also made members of the Sicilian Mafia. The Sicilians had sworn him in to seal their pact with the Neapolitans in 1975.[10]

In Rio, as in Caracas, Los Angeles, Montreal, Paris, and London, the two brotherhoods were inseparably entwined. Time and again over the next two years, police pursuing members of one would come across the other, all over the map; Don Antonio Bardellino himself would be the unwitting cause of Buscetta's downfall.

Those years seemed full of promise when Buscetta settled down in Brazil early in 1981. He was out of jail, still in love, back in his favorite country, and superbly placed to make a mint of money. But the Mafia war broke out in Sicily that very March, and Buscetta's world turned upside down.

The killing in the war was all on one side. This was particularly true of those manning the Sicilian Mafia's overseas outposts. The few Mafiosi murdered here and there abroad, mostly in New York and New

Jersey, were enough to cow the rest. Almost without exception, they surrendered to Leggio overnight—not without anguish and fright. Buscetta, frantic after the murders of Bontate and Inzerillo, found the mighty Salvos no less frantic when he called an in-law of theirs in Palermo:

> IN-LAW: We're going crazy here. . . . I don't see anybody, I haven't seen anybody in a month. . . . There are too many shady things here . . . too much envy, too much betrayal. . . . You don't know who to turn to. . . .
> BUSCETTA: Anyway, if I could talk to Nino [Salvo] . . .
> IN-LAW: But Nino doesn't know anything. . . . He isn't here, he's disappeared. . . .
> BUSCETTA: Then don't look for him, don't look for him. . . .
> IN-LAW: That is, I know where to find him. . . .
> BUSCETTA: No, no. . . . Don't look for him, because I don't want to get in his way. . . . Don't look for him![11]

The Salvos switched sides soon afterward. So did Antonio Salamone in São Paulo, the Cuntreras and Caruanas in Caracas, Montreal, and London, the Sicilian factions in Brooklyn, and nearly all of Buscetta's old associates who survived. Buscetta himself seemed safely above the fray until halfway through the war. Then, in the summer of 1982, Gaetano Badalamenti showed up in Brazil and got him into grievous trouble.

Badalamenti wanted Buscetta to go back and lead a counterattack on the Corleonesi in Sicily. Buscetta refused, but Leggio's men got wind of what looked like a plot to them. That August, Buscetta's Brazilian brother-in-law, Homero Guimaraes, Jr., disappeared. Two weeks after his disappearance, Buscetta's two sons Antonio and Benedetto vanished in Palermo—this with all Italy in shock, just a few days after General Dalla Chiesa was murdered. In late December, Buscetta's son-in-law was shot dead in his Palermo pizzeria. Three days later, Buscetta's older brother Vincenzo was shot dead with his son in their Palermo glass factory.

The December killings followed immediately upon the only direct act of defiance in the Great Mafia War. Reacting to a dozen murders of his own relatives, Badalamenti sent two Men of Valor from Miami to shoot the Corleonesi's most sadistic killer in Palermo, Pino Greco, the holy terror of Ciaculli. But the gunmen missed, and were found dead near Miami six weeks later. What mattered for Buscetta was that one of them had been his trusted gofer in the old days in New York.[12] He was as good as dead himself after that.

Caught up in his own personal tragedies during the autumn of 1982, Buscetta was unaware of doom approaching from another direction. That same autumn, the police of three countries came upon converging trails of the Camorra and Mafia in Paris, leading straight to Venezuela and Brazil.

Don Michele Zaza—Michael the Madman, the not so crazy chief of the New Camorra Family in Naples—had moved long since from contraband tobacco to heroin and cocaine. In the autumn of 1982, with police raiding refineries in Sicily and the Mafia war raging there, he decided to set up his own heroin refinery in France. He had good Corsican friends in Marseilles from the old French Connection days, and all the right Sicilian tie-ins.[13] The Camorristi helping him worked with Giuseppe Bono's people in New York, Antonio Salamone's in São Paulo, and the Cuntreras in Caracas.

Zaza proceeded to buy a cheese factory for $2 million in the northern French city of Rouen; the Camorrista who was planning to run it, a certain Nunzio Guido, was everybody's old friend in the drug business. Garrulous as ever, Don Michele chatted on the phone about all the "mozzarella" they could produce there. "La roba," as he called it—the stuff, the junk—would go to Milan, the United States, and various parts of France. He expected it to net $20,000 or $30,000 a day.[14] But the cheese factory had barely started to produce heroin "samples" for its customers when it was suddenly sold at auction late in 1982, for a fraction of its worth. Don Michele Zaza had just been arrested by the Rome Narcotics Squad.

In the process of tailing him, the Italian police had followed Zaza to a Paris restaurant, where they bumped into the French police and DEA agents tailing his guests. Zaza was having dinner with a dozen characters who had flown in from various parts of the world. One was Giuseppe Bono's brother Alfredo; another was their uncle Antonio Salamone, to whom they deferred as *parrinu*. (godfather). The police concluded that some big heroin shipment had to be going down. And indeed, ninety-three kilos of heroin, worth around $25 million wholesale, arrived at Zaza's mansion in Beverly Hills the following month. DEA agents just missed the heroin—they found its traces in discarded cartons marked "Dinner Plates"—but they had finally picked up the trail of *'u parrinu*.

Antonio Salamone had flown from Paris directly after the meeting to Zaza's California mansion. From there, he had phoned the Cuntreras

in Venezuela, and telexed his nephew in Palermo to pick up Paolo
Cuntrera's son-in-law in Miami and proceed to Caracas. Then Salamone had quietly returned to São Paulo, with DEA agents on his
heels.

Not long afterward, another nephew of his was picked up at the
Palermo airport with a purloined copy of the DEA's report on Salamone. *'U parrinu* left Brazil within twenty-four hours.[15]

o⬯o

By Christmas 1982, the Italian, American, and Brazilian police had
a fairly good fix on the Camorra-Mafia ring in Brazil. Acting on a tip,
Italian investigators flew over in pursuit of Don Antonio Bardellino,
who, as usual, got away a jump ahead of them. When they left, however,
the Brazilian Federal Police (DPF), who took up the search, were told
where to look by an old drug trafficker who had worked with Buscetta
since the 1960s. Arrested yet again that winter, he turned informer and
pointed the cops to the high-rise ocean front residence in Tijuca.[16]

Bardellino had already vacated his apartment on the eighteenth
floor when the cops arrived, and Buscetta was gone as well. Immediately after his gofer was found dead in a car trunk in Florida, Buscetta
had retired to his sixty-five-thousand-acre *fazenda* north of Belem, near
the mouth of the Amazon. There—though he claimed to be a pauper—
he addressed himself to his five hundred horses and herd of cows giving
a thousand liters of milk a day, waiting for the Corleonesi to come and
get him.[17]

But Buscetta's wife, Cristina, was still living on the sixteenth floor in
Rio's Tijuca quarter. She was watched by the Brazilian cops (and the
DEA) from May to October, when she loaded six suitcases into a Chev-
rolet Chevette and drove south to São Paolo to meet her husband, who
had flown down from Belem.

The capture of Buscetta and eleven others in October 1983 made
sensational headlines in Brazil. The police there believed that they had
broken up a colossal intercontinental narcotics ring. The nationwide
hunt had lasted eight months. Two hundred suspects had been identified, working in five interlocking rings from São Paulo to Rio to Belem
in the far north. Dozens of "mules" had been spotted, young women
body carriers of every nationality from Bolivian, Peruvian, Chilean, and
Colombian to Nigerian. Records were found of forty-six trips the
women had made abroad.[18]

According to the federal police superintendent in São Paulo, Romeu
Tuma, Buscetta was at the top of the pyramid. "It is certain that we

have taken the chief of the Latin-American drug connection," he said. To this, the Narcotics Squad's Pedro Berwanger added: "Tommaso Buscetta was the principal coordinator of the cocaine market between Brazil, Bolivia, Peru, Colombia, Europe, and the United States."[19]

Buscetta denied everything. There was no Mafia war in Sicily, he said; his vanished sons had just gotten into a youthful argument with somebody. He knew a few of the other arrestees, but only casually. His father-in-law had shot at the police in the mistaken impression that they were thugs. He himself had done nothing illegal. A reporter asked how Buscetta, after eight years in an Italian jail, could buy a millionaire's apartment in Rio, luxurious cars, and a ranch extending for a hundred square miles. "I brought the money from Italy and invested it in Brazilian savings bonds," he replied.[20]

The Brazilians kept Buscetta in jail for nine months, long after his wife and the others had been bailed out. Buscetta was too big to let go. The Americans still wanted him on the Brazilian ring drug charges going back to 1972, not to mention more current suspicions. The Italians wanted him as an escaped convict and major figure in their entire Mafia investigation. The Brazilians were holding him on a "false document" count—his fake passport as Roberto Escobar—while sifting through crates of incriminating papers seized in the raid. They were finding dummy companies, rigged books, fake shipments abroad, false passports, and long-distance calls and travel vouchers from Rio and São Paulo to Caracas, New York, Montreal, Zurich, Barcelona, Paris, Milan, Rome, and Palermo.

Renowned Sicilian traffickers were drawing money and air fares from a paper corporation called Major Key, which, while it produced nothing, had increased its net assets from $6,000 to $1 million in a year. Buscetta and Gaetano Badalamenti were both getting their bills paid by Major Key. So was Badalamenti's son Leonardo, about to open a Major Key office in Curitiba, Brazil. Badalamenti's nephew Vincenzo Randazzo, a future Pizza defendant, was preparing to set up a branch of Major Key in New York.[21]

After flying down to see what the Brazilians had on Buscetta, the DEA's Mona Ewell and the U.S. Eastern District's Charles Rose reported "documented and circumstantial evidence" to the following effect:

- "Since the spring of 1981, Tommaso Buscetta and several other individuals have conspired to conduct illegal activities, possibly narcotics trafficking."

· The activities "extended beyond Brazil, but the bases of operation appear to be São Paulo, Rio de Janeiro, Betim, and Belem."
· "Several complete passports, driver's licences, etc., were confiscated, revealing aliases for the primary subjects."
· Homero Guimaraes, Jr., had been fitted out with a set of papers as Otto Levy. Cristina Guimaraes' tax records "showed that she had received a great deal of money from Otto Levy."
· Several group members traveled regularly to Caracas, in contact with "case subjects historically associated with Buscetta, suspected of washing money and/or facilitating drug trafficking from South America into the United States."
· Antonio Bardellino, the Camorra boss, was identified with the same group as co-owner of a dummy fish company called CEICO. This company was exporting fish from Rio de Janeiro to Naples, a city that had no need to import fish.

Bardellino's presence in particular gave the game away. As the U.S. report noted, he was "the righthand man of Carlo Zippo"—Buscetta's *"simpatico* Neapolitan friend" and drug-running partner in the early 1970s. The Italians had arrested Zippo again in February 1983, with twenty others, as head of a huge ring smuggling cocaine to Italy from South America.

In conclusion, wrote Ewell and Rose, "The Brazilian Federal Police believe that Buscetta et al. were involved in a cocaine smuggling conspiracy through the use of CEICO via shipments to Italy, and that Major Key was being used to launder the money."[22]

This was their conviction, though they lacked enough hard proof to convict Buscetta in a court of law. Later, Superintendent Tuma suggested that Brazilian police had probably moved too soon. "I think we aborted Buscetta's operation, as he hadn't yet finished setting up the infrastructure," he said.[23]

Waiting it out in a Brazilian jail, Don Masino was a king again, for the last time. "It was a great honor for the other members of the group to be handcuffed together with him," said an aide of Tuma's. "They used to kiss his hands in the morning, and when they were being moved, he always got into the police van first. He kept up the routine of discipline, always giving orders to the others."[24]

Even so, Buscetta was in desperate straits. Cristina made four secret visits to the DEA that winter, begging the Americans to take him, as he was bound to be murdered in prison if Italy got him.[25] But the Americans wanted him sent "wherever the strongest case could be made against him." Together with Italy and Brazil, the U.S. government agreed "to support the country that could obtain the maximum sentence for Buscetta."[26] Italy won.

When he heard the news, Buscetta swallowed strychnine, and barely recovered. He wouldn't have a prayer once he was back in an Italian jail; not long before, an old friend had been stabbed fifty-eight times in the prison yard of the Ucciardone. The sooner he died, he explained afterward, the more chance of survival for what remained of his family. Upon coming out of a coma, however, Buscetta concluded that "dying was not enough." The "terrible Mafioso logic" of those final years had destroyed all the principles of Cosa Nostra as he had known it, he told the press. "Everything changed; only furor, war, blood remained—all for money." He wanted to destroy the Sicilian Mafia.[27]

The Buscetta who turned state's witness has been overtaken by events long since. Others coming after him have been less self-serving and vain, more forthright, closer to the immediate scene. Nevertheless, he was the first, the most prestigious, the most electrifying for having spoken out at all, the most unexpectedly polished and urbane.

Judge Giovanni Falcone, who led the Sicilian team of interrogators, had always maintained that a Mafioso does not defect, by definition. He had never met one who did, and he had met all kinds in two decades on the bench. "There is the Mafioso who barricades himself in his cell," he said, "the one who fakes insanity; the one who is forced by the Mafia to fake insanity; the insolent one who claims he was kidnapped. . . . Then there is the genteel Mafioso, obsequious, with a humble glance, until lightning shoots from his eyes as he pretends to be looking away."[28]

Don Masino did none of these things. He was there to talk, and he talked. Inasmuch as he would not confess to having ever committed a crime, his was not a confession. It was a series of conversations with his Sicilian interlocutors—often informative, frequently reticent, occasionally astonishing—lasting throughout the summer of 1984 and well into the fall.

Much of what he said was no longer new. By the summer of 1984, the anti-Mafia pool in Palermo was already preparing for the biggest Mafia trial in history. Nevertheless, he could piece together a thousand fragments of evidence: he, Don Masino Buscetta, on the witness stand, in a Sicilian courtroom.

The impact could be stupendous, but that was not what mattered most. Buscetta "had been in the eye of the cyclone" for a quarter of a century, as he pointed out himself. He had been in at the birth of the Cupola, the deal for the heroin franchise, the early deployment of Sicilian Men of Honor in the United States, Canada, and South America. He had been intimate with the men who built the Cupola's multinational heroin consortium, and with the men who murdered those men and a thousand of their followers to take it over.

Buscetta might have come nearer to destroying the Sicilian Mafia if he had disclosed everything he knew. As it was, nonetheless, he revealed that the Sicilian Mafia was a separate entity dominating the worldwide heroin market, the cardinal fact that nobody beyond its perimeters had understood in all those years.

Face to Face
in a Court of Law

s judges and jury withdrew to reach a verdict in Palermo's remarkable maxitrial, the head of the Cupola delivered a valedictory message. "Let your conscience guide you," called out Michele Greco, charged with seventy-eight murders, from behind the steel bars of his cage in the bunker-courtroom. "I wish you peace, tranquillity of spirit. . . . *I hope that peace may be with you for the rest of your lives.*"[1]

Submit and live in peace, or you will never know peace again—the Mafia's classic warning to those daring to sit in judgment. The sibylline threat hung over the sealed bomb-proof chamber where the fate of Sicily's big Mafia bosses was being decided. Some might imagine that the Mafia had finally been defeated in a court of law; the judges and jury knew it hadn't.

The killing, suspended during twenty-two months of the maxitrial, began again two hours after sentence was pronounced in December 1987. The first victim had just bought a cake and wine to celebrate his freedom; acquitted by the Palermo court, he was condemned by his own Mafia tribunal. More than two hundred more fell at the Mafia's hand in

Sicily over the following year, the per capita equivalent of ten thousand in the United States.[2] They included two judges, the penultimate mayor of Palermo, a Carabinieri corporal, a Squadra Mobile detective, a dedicated social worker, *picciotti,* Men of Valor, Men of Honor of elevated rank, and wives and children. Sixteen were killed within three days toward the end of 1988. Palermo seemed to have slipped back a decade.

"Everything I was called upon to judge, things that happened in 1981, I find before me again . . . the same dead bodies, the same climate," lamented the co-magistrate in the maxitrial. "I am full of bitterness . . . 1981 is almost history now, but today, in 1988, nothing has changed."[3] Yet Palermo's court of assizes had sentenced 19 *mammasantissima* to life imprisonment, and 323 other Mafiosi to some twenty-six centuries in jail. Was it possible for even the Mafia to come out as strong as ever—stronger?

In reality, something did change. The Sicilian Mafia, passing for over a hundred years as a mere "frame of mind," emerged at last as an organized international crime syndicate. The evidence showed it to be "a state within a state, an antistate, with its own government, army, territory, rituals, moral code, and juridical order," said the prosecutor in his summation.[4] Therefore the Mafia could be investigated and prosecuted as a corporate entity. Mafia bosses could be found collectively guilty of its crimes, meaning literally that they could no longer get away with murder. They might never be caught with a smoking gun, but they could be held accountable for telling a subaltern to do the shooting (as was customary). Indeed, they were punishable for any of the Mafia's illegal acts, if they took part in making its decisions. Eight members of the Cupola were sent up for life on those grounds in the maxitrial.

The Mafia's seeming indifference to this momentous verdict did not signify that the trial was a flop. On the contrary, it was a monumental victory for justice in the highest legal sense. As always in Sicily, however, the court could go only so far. The rest was largely a matter of obscure menace, recondite maneuvers, rigorous juridical niceties, and politics.

Getting the trial under way was peculiarly difficult. It was improbably oversized, with 464 defendants, a juridical monstrosity, according to some. This couldn't be helped, the judges held. The Mafia had proved to be a single organization, with "a single criminal strategy," requiring a single judicial response. Its "oneness"—*unicità* is the untranslatable Italian word—meant that everything was interlocked. For instance, the same Kalashnikov was used to kill a Carabinieri colonel near Corleone in 1977, Stefano Bontate and Salvatore Inzerillo in Palermo in 1981, a close ally of theirs in Catania in 1982, General Dalla Chiesa, and Salvatore Contorno (though he beat the shooters to the draw). How could that be handled piecemeal?

Size was not the only problem. The trial was also unwelcome to the Italian establishment: a direct, dramatic confrontation with the Mafia that the state could not afford to lose—and, for unspoken but compelling political reasons, could hardly afford to win either.

There had never been such a trial anywhere. The bunker-courtroom built onto a wall of the Ucciardone prison held thirty steel cages for the 464 defendants. Two hundred lawyers defended them. Fifty more lawyers represented friends of the court: relatives of the dead, the city of Palermo, the Sicilian Region. Two full sets of judges and jurors sat on the dais by special governmental decree, so that death, natural or otherwise, could not interrupt the proceedings. Seven magistrates declined the post of presiding judge before an eighth, Alfonso Giordano, accepted "the Sicilian risk."

The indictment, drafted by five investigating magistrates in Sicily's anti-Mafia pool, ran to 8,607 pages, with over a quarter of a million pages of documentation. Some 400 pages were taken up just to list the names of the defendants and the charges against them. Apart from multiple murder, they were accused of mounting a worldwide heroin network under the Mafia's auspices. The charges covered the period from 1975 to 1985. That was the fatal decade, the judges wrote—the time when the Sicilian Mafia became an international crime cartel and a primary purveyor of narcotics. The ease with which it did so, the incredible laxity of an entire governing class during those years, made for a devastating indictment within the indictment.

Throughout the 1970s, continued the judges, a parliamentary commission had gathered thirty-five volumes of explosive information about the Mafia. Gradually, however, "a veil of sovereign institutional unconcern" was drawn over these findings:

Ten years of almost total disattention to the Mafia phenomenon allowed Cosa Nostra Families, disunited by internal warfare and the pressure of a parliamentary commission, to reorganize and take over the channels of production and distribution of drugs.

There were no police investigations for six months after Boris Giuliano was killed [Palermo's Squadra Mobile chief, in 1979]. On the judicial level, his findings met with disconcerting delays and dubious acquittals. . . .

The forces of order were lacking; a strategy of battle was lacking; the judiciary lacked adequate knowledge of the new Mafia reality. . . .

A vacuum, made up of indifference and skepticism, surrounded the individual magistrates and police officers who, in spite of themselves, became solitary
paladins of legality, involuntary heroes.[5]

The solitude surrounding this small band of investigators was ac-
centuated as the trial drew near. They lived as if under siege, cut off
from their families, camping in heavily guarded wings of Palermo's
courthouse or at Squadra Mobile headquarters, venturing out only
when strictly necessary, in caravans of bullet-proof Alfa Romeos with
sirens screaming. They were "militarizing the city," complained the
local press. They were guilty of "protagonism" as well, of "drawing
morbid attention to Sicily," of mounting an "inquisition," added a
chorus of critics.[6]

The Mafia had rarely been so mortally dangerous as in those last
months before the maxitrial. Even with hundreds of its members in jail
and the law on its back, the organization continued to kill until the last
of its formidable adversaries in Sicily's corps of police was wiped out.

Commissario Ninni Cassarà was murdered in August 1985, after
leaving his cramped quarters at the Squadra Mobile for an unannounced visit to his family. Some mole in the office, or in the little park
facing it, must have signaled his departure. By the time he reached his
door fifteen minutes later, ten hit men with Kalashnikovs were waiting
for him.

The saddest memory I have of those tense times was flying down to
Palermo for Cassarà's funeral. Few had done more to break the Mafia's
oppressive grip on Sicily. Apart from his grieving family and colleagues,
however, scarcely a hundred mourners were at the church for his me-
morial mass. *Palermo-bene,* the Palermo that mattered, was not there.

oᴐo

Many will doubtless remember the trial as theater, at times comic
opera. The great pale-green octagonal hall, the semicircle of human
cages, the mass of black-robed lawyers, the witness chair set in a booth
of clear bullet-proof glass, made an extravagant stage set. The cast—
possibly the largest assortment of scoundrels ever assembled in a courtroom—was worthy of it.

The clowns acted their part. One defendant entered with his lips
stapled together; another had swallowed six-inch nails; yet another did
a striptease in his cage and threw a shoe at his lawyer. Avuncular elders
with comfortable paunches, angel-faced boys, and villainous-looking

hoods shouted greetings over an acre of green-carpeted space to relatives in the visitors' gallery.

Ranged among the bit actors, however, were the *mammasantissima* who had terrorized Sicily for decades; who had ordered the murders of General Dalla Chiesa, Judge Terranova, Judge Costa, Judge Ciaccio Montalto, Judge Chinnici, Boris Giuliano, and Ninni Cassarà; who had carried heroin around the world and made the Mafia "one of the worst plagues of our century," according to Judge Falcone. Always beyond the reach of the law, they were matching all their wits and immense power against it now.

Over a hundred defendants were still missing when the trial opened in February 1986, but many celebrities were present: Michele Greco, "the Pope"; Leonardo Greco, boss of Bagheria; Antonio Salamone of São Paulo; Giuseppe Bono of Caracas, New York, Paris, and Milan, with his brother Alfredo; Pippo Calò, the Mafia's ambassador to Rome; Giuseppe Fidanzati, the Mafia's ambassador to the Neapolitan Camorra; and Gerlando Alberti, the "tireless fabrics salesman" in charge of Palermo's proliferating heroin refineries.

Luciano Leggio had a cage of his own. Brought down for the occasion from his maximum security prison in Sardinia, he sat heavy and hunched, decked out with casual insolence in a track suit and Adidas tennis shoes, reading a newspaper, lighting up a black Tuscan cigar as he took a lazy look around the courtroom. He was plumper after twelve years in jail, but still indefinably chilling. Respect, obeisance, and near reverence radiated from adjoining cages toward "the unchallenged chief, the summit of the Mafia organization, the strategic intelligence of Cosa Nostra," in the prosecutor's words.

Most defendants had been in and out of the courts before, but never to be so humiliated, outraged, galled. The *pentiti,* parading to the witness stand to testify against their fellow Mafiosi, were an unthinkable affront.

Italy knew of "penitents" from previous experience with defectors from the Red Brigades, who did much to deliver the country from raging terrorist warfare in the early 1980s. Though their contribution was invaluable—decisive, in fact—many Italians thought of them as turncoats, traitors, and rats all the same. The Mafia's defectors could expect still less public favor, and certainly fewer rewards. Terrorist collaborators could have their sentences cut in half and even walk free under a special parliamentary law; Mafia *pentiti* had no such chances, no leniency to speak of from the court, no assured government protection for themselves and their families. Only Tommaso Buscetta and Salvatore Contorno were free, subsidized and safe in America, for bearing witness at the Pizza Connection trial. (Contorno, like Buscetta, was in the Federal Witness Protection Program.) A score or more in Palermo lived in constant fear, with nothing to gain but revenge and (for some) a weight off their chests.

Yet their help was not just valuable, but indispensable. In the process of questioning them all, Judge Falcone had come upon a structured subterranean society of unimagined complexity, impenetrable to any but its own members. "The Mafia is more than a simple criminal association. . . . It is a world apart," he said. "At the center is Cosa Nostra. Then, around it, is everything extraneous to it. Only those who live inside it can really know how things are. Only he who takes the oath is a Mafioso."[7]

So, for the first time since its birth around 1865, the Mafia was split open to public view. One by one, the *pentiti* stripped it of all romance and demolished the most useful of its myths, starting with the evergreen fiction that it did not exist.

The Mafia they described in close detail was "global, unitary, rigidly regimented, and vertically structured, governed from the top down by a Cupola with absolute powers over policy, money, life, and death. . . . It is only now that we can see this globality, but it was always there," says Judge Giusto Sciacchitano of Sicily's anti-Mafia pool.[8] The line of command rose geometrically, in a pyramid whose base covered practically every village in Sicily. (Its extension to every corner of the Italian mainland was not discovered until 1988.)[9] At the base were the *capi-Famiglia* (Family bosses). Every three contiguous Families answered to a *capo-mandamento,* who represented them on provincial commissions, dominated in turn by the Commission or Cupola in Palermo, the supreme governing body. An ultrasecret *Inter-Provinciale* coordinated its decisions island-wide.

This whole chain of command became known as Buscetta's Theorem. Others confirmed it amply, but his version was definitive, especially in regard to killing procedures. "No representative [*capo-Famiglia*] would take it on himself to kill a person without asking his *capo-mandamento,* who refers it to the Commission. . . . The Commission knows about every murder, especially of important people," he declared.[10] Those few lines of testimony sent a number of his enemies to jail for many years.

Buscetta, in Palermo solely for these proceedings, shone at the trial. Entering a taut courtroom under armed escort, seated in the bullet-proof glass booth with his back to the men who had wrecked his life, he was calm, dignified, implacable. Leggio, from his cage, called him a worm; Pippo Calò implied that his Brazilian wife was a tart. Buscetta quelled them both with a few glacial words, in his velvety baritone. He was not a *pentito,* he said, "because I have done nothing to repent of. What I was, I remain." It was Cosa Nostra that had changed. Since the 1970s, it had "subverted the ideals that are frowned upon by those who live within the law, but are beautiful for us, who live inside this association."

Here Buscetta managed to sell the public a second, more pernicious theorem—the Good and Bad Mafias, the before and after of Luciano Leggio's rise to power, virtue and vice respectively—a view that gained surprisingly wide acceptance. In fact, the two were not opposites; one was simply, inarguably, worse than the other.

The ideals in question—respect, courage, honor, tradition—were strictly in-house rules for members, in no way inhibiting their cold violence and piratical greed in the outside world. The rules did not exclude collection of *'u pizzu* by bombing, arson, or a bullet in the head. Building the heroin consortium had not bothered Buscetta when he worked with friends like Badalamenti and Inzerillo, sticking more or less to their code. Murder was not just condoned but required.

Nevertheless, the Mafia of bygone days had imposed respect, maintained internal law and order, and refrained from killing women and children, distant relatives, even cops and judges (with occasional lapses). That was possible so long as profits remained within bounds, by a Man of Honor's standards. When the profits from heroin ran wild, so did the Mafia.

Though Buscetta did not put it quite that way, he was plainly sickened by what the Sicilian Mafia had become. Few doubted that he really wanted to destroy it.

He talked for a week, reviewing the Mafia scene since the 1950s, tracing its moves into heroin, naming major traffickers from the mid-1970s on and Leggio's prime killers in the Great Mafia War. The first witness to be called, Buscetta laid out the three tremendous counts on which the Mafia would stand convicted: its organized "oneness"; its capture of the worldwide heroin market; and its secret heroin network in the United States. "All the drug activity I know of in America is done by Men of Honor sent there by the Sicilian Cosa Nostra," he testified, advancing worldwide understanding of the problem by some twenty or thirty years.[11]

That said, however, Buscetta chose to say no more. He did not begin

to explain how these Sicilian Men of Honor had deployed an occupation army on American Mafia territory, or who ran it, apart from those
already identified in the Pizza case. He claimed to know nothing about
the Cherry Hill Gambinos—indeed, to have met them only once, by
chance, in a New York bar. He even assured an incredulous audience
that Gaetano Badalamenti "could not have participated in the drug
traffic, because he always told me that he was extraneous to it."[12]

Most of his friends in Sicily were spared as well; those he did tag for
drugs were nearly all dead. Above all, he refused blandly to identify the
politicians covering for the Mafia down the years. The single person he
selected as a sacrificial offering was former mayor Vito Ciancimino—
Leggio's man. "When we're on the Other Side, and I'll be there first
because they're going to kill me, I will tell you who the politicians are,
and even then you'll be surprised," he told his Italian biographer later.[13]

In the end, Buscetta's awesome authority counted less for the jury
than the candor of *pentiti* from the lower orders. He would not confess
to murder, drugs, or any of his own guilty acts; they did. It was not
the elegant Don Masino but the hapless Vincenzo Sinagra, recount-
ing his days among the torturers and stranglers in the death chamber at
Piazza Sant'Erasmo, whose testimony doomed some of the Mafia's
most vicious killers. (He was sentenced to twenty-one years in jail all
the same.)

The hero of the trial was the late Stefano Bontate's Man of Valor,
Salvatore "Totuccio" Contorno, also on loan from America. An unvar-
nished and unashamed ruffian, crook, extortionist, kidnapper, and drug
trafficker, he testified in a rapid, often incomprehensible Mafia jargon
that had to be translated for the official record. ("Would Your Excellency ask the witness to speak Italian?" an exasperated defense attorney
demanded of the judge. "I wouldn't trust myself," responded Contorno.) Even so, he held the courtroom enthralled with his passion, and
his open contempt for the brotherhood he had once believed in. Cosa
Nostra was "just a gang of bullies and murderers," he said.

Contorno had been on his way to kill Pippo Calò in Rome when he
was arrested in 1982. "Too bad I didn't succeed," he observed. (Calò
had betrayed Bontate to the Corleonesi, he believed.) After two at-
tempts on his own life following Bontate's death, he had acquired a pair
of bullet-proof cars and an electronic device to start them up from a
distance.

Contorno had a personal war going with the winning clans who had
killed twelve of his relatives, and didn't try to hide it. "They wanted to

kill me and they couldn't and now I'm a *pentito*. Here I am, Mr. President," he told the presiding judge. "They" were the Corleonesi. "The winning and losing clans don't exist, because the losers don't exist; they killed them all," he said.

He named upward of 150 made Mafiosi, rising in his glass booth and wheeling around to face the vilest, picking them out of a lineup one by one. The judge ran down the alphabet calling out names, and Contorno answered bluntly, amid dead silence:

"Is Giuseppe Abate a Man of Honor?"
"Yes."
"Filippo Argano?"
"Yes."
"Pietro Alfano?"
"Yes."
"Francesco Adelfio, Mario Adelfio, Salvatore Adelfio, Giovanni Adelfio known as 'Giannuzzo'?"
"Yes."
"Did Franco Adelfio traffic in drugs?"
"All his life."[14]

Contorno's evidence on the drug traffic was crushing, and not just because of his spectacular contribution to the Pizza case. His accidental glimpse of Sal Catalano and Giuseppe Ganci in a Bagheria farmhouse in 1980—when he saw them "testing this drug to see if it was any good, or nothing doing"—was just one of many episodes.

Contorno had not operated at Buscetta's altitude, but at ground level, from the year he was sworn in—1975, around the time of the crucial deals with the Camorra and the Turkish Mafia. He knew all about the morphine base coming from Turkey and Bulgaria, and had sat in on meetings with the Camorristi in Naples. "They were Mafiosi like us, the Bardellinos, Zazas, Nuvolettas, all Men of Honor, not Camorra, they say Camorra but it doesn't exist. They were Men of Honor in Palermo," he stated flatly.

Contorno had seen several of the island's refineries personally, including one on Don Michele Greco's five-hundred-acre estate in Ciaculli, La Favarella. But La Favarella, where the Cupola usually met and Mafia fugitives hid out, was too exposed. "There was too much confusion, too many cops around, so they moved the lab," he said.

Everybody in Sicily's Cosa Nostra was involved in heroin except Bontate, Contorno declared, loyal to the memory of his revered boss:[15]

It wasn't as if Stefano Bonta' said they mustn't so they didn't, he couldn't control it in our Family. . . . Because they told him, "I have to do drugs, my family has to eat." . . .

They were all in it, because there was a great wad of money in it, it was better than building houses, better than anything. If you invested a hundred million lire, right away you'd get three hundred back, so everybody jumped into it . . . they dropped everything else, they only did drugs. . . .

If I wanted to do drugs by myself I could do it alone. If we were in three or four in the Family we could do it, no problem. . . .

There was a general agreement, because the morphine came in a big load at a time. . . . If I was the one interested in the ship coming in, I would take care of getting the morphine turned into heroin, and vice versa for everybody else.

Everybody had his part to do. . . . If I wanted a hundred kilos, they'd give me a hundred kilos. . . . They refined it in Palermo and everybody took what he wanted and sent it out however he wanted to.[16]

Then the dollars would come back from America in suitcases or plain wrapped parcels. Changing the money into lire was easy. "We had the bankers, there were bankers inside the banks who were 'friends.' . . . No problem."

The Sicilian Mafia controlled the entire drug trade, continued Contorno. "I'm saying Sicilians, not Milanese or Turinese, or French— Sicilians. We Palermitani of Cosa Nostra, that is, I don't mean the public. . . . Cosa Nostra had the whole drug trade in hand, everything had to be in Palermo, everything went back to Palermo."[17] And the Sicilians were answerable to no one else, including Cosa Nostra in America. When asked if the Americans had requested an explanation for the murder of Franco Mafara, the Cupola's heroin marketing manager in Italy, Contorno seemed surprised: "No, no . . . if they had to kill Franco Mafara, it was of no interest to the Americans. . . . So many things happen in Palermo! And why should they go to the Americans? They weren't authorized to give explanations. They had to kill Mafara? So they killed him, end of the story."

Luciano Leggio, following Buscetta and Contorno to the witness stand, was respectful, obsequious, and aggrieved. Impeccably dressed for this appearance in a dark suit, silk pocket handkerchief, and striped tie, Leggio professed himself amazed by a hair-raising list of charges against him. He had no idea what the Mafia was and did not even know what drugs were, he declared. "I have never done anything in my life to reprove myself for. I've never been an enemy to anyone. I've always been a tranquil man. . . . They can slander me, but nobody can say a word against me."

He reminded the court of all the times he had been tried and acquitted—he was in prison now only for a single murder committed a quarter of a century earlier—noting with the faintest whiff of irony that nobody still alive had ever testified against him up to then. True, a boss named Di Cristina had said shocking things about him to the Carabinieri before being murdered (on Leggio's orders, allegedly). "But if this fellow is dead, it's only in dreams now that he can go around saying certain things," Leggio concluded neatly.

To all these charges, I have one answer: I was in jail. I'm still in jail. Excuse me, but how could I be running around the country, walk the streets, return to my cell, unless all this was done with permission?

If so, I must have been helped by various prison guards, prison directors, sergeants who check the mail and the telephones. But I'm here in a cage, and I don't see any sergeants or prison guards or prison directors in a cage. If such people helped me, why haven't they been charged?[18]

They hadn't been charged because not a soul in the Italian prison system was imbecile enough to go up against Leggio. He had been stopping courts with that argument since his sentence to life imprisonment in 1974, and would do so again. Nobody could use the law to paralyze the law more triumphantly than Luciano Leggio.

o◯o

Some 1,337 witnesses were summoned to testify after the stars appeared. Many lied, retracted previous statements, or broke down, visibly half-dead with fright. But the charges did not stand or fall with them. Independently of the *pentiti* or any backsliding witnesses, the body of evidence was more than enough to make the case stick.

The evidence showed a Mafia in disquieting expansion. From the "epicenter" in Palermo, its lines had spread across Sicily to the Straits of Messina, and jumped the water to Calabria, Naples, Rome, and the far Italian north.

A colossal Mafia-Camorra installation for extortion, kidnapping, drug running, and money laundering had been uncovered in Milan, in which 159 stalwarts of the international drug trade were involved: the Bono brothers, the Fidanzati brothers, the Salamone brothers, the Cuntrera brothers, the Nuvoletta brothers, the Zaza brothers, and Buscetta, among others. They had been on the verge of buying Milan's San Siro racetrack and Hilton Hotel for around $100 million when they were found out.[19] Tapping their phones in Milan had pointed Italian investigators to the Cuntrera-Caruana Families in Venezuela, Canada, and Great Britain, and the Pizza Connection had filled in part of the New York picture. International movements of narcodollars had been traced through Caribbean, Swiss, Milanese, and Sicilian banks. The facts were in on the Turkish Mafia's supply lines from Istanbul and Sofia, and on a hitherto unknown direct line from Palermo to the Golden Triangle in the Far East.

This newly opened channel belonged almost exclusively to Leggio's closest allies in Palermo and Catania, headed by "the exquisitely Mafioso clan" of one Nitto Santapaola. They had begun to tap this bottomless source of morphine base and heroin around 1979, developing rapidly once police began to close down the refineries in Sicily. It was cheaper, easier, and safer to buy refined heroin in Thailand and move it straight to the Western market.

By 1983, Thailand swarmed with Sicilian traffickers, whose Chinese suppliers were selling to the Mafia by the ton. A single supplier, a native of Singapore called Koh Bak Kin, had consigned 3,750 kilos of morphine base in his first delivery to Palermo from Bangkok via Copenhagen—enough to produce nearly four tons of heroin, two-thirds of the annual supply for America's half-million addicts.[20] Koh Bak Kin had delivered at least 280 kilos of refined heroin in 1982; in 1983, he had taken an order for half a ton more and shipped another 233 kilos, which were seized in the Suez Canal.[21] The carrier vessel, the *Alexander G.,* had been loaded by armed men on the tiny island of Ko-Fra-Kong, fifteen miles off Thailand's coast. Arrested in Bangkok and brought to testify in Palermo, Koh Bak Kin said not a word more than he knew that the court knew already. No more was needed, really.

The verdict, reached in December 1987 after nearly two years of hearings, confirmed the cardinal points in the indictment: the "oneness" of the Mafia, the heroin net built under its auspices, the murders done to order, the collective guilt of its governing body. All the members of the Cupola were convicted, along with 323 others. Over 100 lesser figures got off for lack of evidence, but no Mafia boss of stature was acquitted, save Leggio. His glint of malicious amusement on the witness stand had been justified; everybody knew, but nobody could prove, that he ran the Mafia from his prison cell.

The maxitrial was never more than a sporadic feature story in the foreign press. Few realized what a titanic battle had been fought in a distant Palermo courtroom. Nor did they realize that there was scarcely a country in East and West Europe, North and South America, Africa, the Middle East, and Asia that the Sicilian Mafia did not work in, or corrupt in passing. Switzerland, West Germany, Spain, Greece, Great Britain, and Canada were among its staging areas and banking centers. France was once again a center of heroin production, this time under the Sicilian Mafia's management. Bulgaria and Yugoslavia were part of its lifeline. Lebanon, Syria, Iran, Pakistan, and Turkey were among its providers. Sri Lanka's Tamils were financing their insurgency by dealing heroin through the Mafia. Kenya was one of its meeting places. Guinea-Bissau was buying weapons and Mirage jets through a front company it ran on the northern Italian coast (in partnership with right-wing terrorists). Vianatu, Aruba, the Seychelles, Malta, the Dominican Republic, and Venezuela were its privileged sanctuaries. Even Katmandu, near the top of the Himalayas behind a range of inaccessible mountains, was found to have a ring of bent army officers and politicians in Palermo's pay.[22]

No country had lifted a finger against the Sicilian Mafia for a quarter of a century. The United States, its earliest and choicest victim, had managed after all that time to lop off only a single limb: a certifiable band of drug runners, important but expendable. The trial in Palermo was the first serious assault ever made on the entire, infinitely complex Mafia phenomenon.

The courage of the judges, the jurors, and the policemen behind them could probably not be found anywhere but in Palermo—could scarcely be imagined elsewhere. Each was putting his life on the line; and the chances of surviving the trial, whatever the verdict, were not good. Doubtless there were many reasons for their courage, but the overriding one was that they were all Sicilians. They had an intimate, lifelong knowledge of the Mafia, and they had had enough. "I feel like a Garibaldino coming to liberate Sicily," said a member of the jury.

Being Sicilian, the judges and jurors sensed that they were going to be left alone in this fight, and they were. The trial was viewed by outsiders with curious detachment. Many abroad still thought of Italy as a land of guitar-playing Neapolitans and Mack Sennett comedy cops. Not many had the smallest idea of the heroic detective work that had brought the Mafia to book.

None of the countries concerned was more than a spectator nor, by and large, was the Italian establishment. A handful of Sicilians onstage, and a growing number of ordinary citizens applauding them, were left to get on with it. "First they said, 'Go to war, we're all with you.' Now they say, 'Go to war, but don't bother us,' " said Judge Falcone on the eve of the trial.[23]

The bravery of those who fought it out was all the more admirable for their knowing that they could not win on their own. In fact, it was worse than they thought. Their achievements in the maxitrial began to come undone as soon as it was over. Within barely another year, nearly everything they won was lost.

The Octopus
at Large Again

The frailty of a free society's defenses against the Mafia grew painfully clear by 1989. As the law took its course in Italy, judges and jurors were overruled, truth gave way to juridical nit-picking, and a host of Mafiosi duly tried and convicted were turned loose. In a grotesque parody of justice, the vanquished became the victors.

At the start of the new year, only 60 of the 342 defendants convicted in Palermo's maxitrial were still in custody. The others had either gotten out provisionally and vanished, or gotten out, period. Michele Greco, sentenced to life imprisonment, stood to be released in two or three years. Gaetano Fidanzati, sentenced to twenty-two years, was out already. Giuseppe Bono and his brother Alfredo, sentenced to twenty-three and eighteen years respectively, were out in style; Giuseppe was relieved of having to pay bail, set originally at a quarter of a million dollars, on the grounds that he was a pauper.[1] (The Bonos kept their money in Switzerland.) Antonio Salamone, sentenced to twenty-two years, had been sent home by the Supreme Court on the grounds of his "advanced age" and "grave state of health," whereupon he had

promptly left the country. (He is said to be back in Brazil.)[2] Even
Luciano Leggio, thought to be inside for good, was expecting his freedom soon.

Hundreds of other unregenerate Mafiosi were back in circulation.
Don Michele Zaza, sentenced to nine and a half years on heavy drug
charges in 1984, was driving around the Continent in a new Mercedes.[3]
All the defendants convicted by an Italian court for their money laundering in the U.S. Pizza case were out, as were two of the three Mafia
bosses convicted of murdering Carabinieri captain Basile—the third
was murdered by fellow Mafiosi in prison—and the boss indicted for
killing Judge Ciaccio Montalto.[4] So were 100 of the 120 convicted in
Turin, where the "Catanese clan" operating there had received twenty-
six life sentences and over seven centuries of imprisonment. Also free
were the two men convicted of murdering Judge Chinnici: this after six
trials and retrials. Michele Greco, thrice convicted in other courtrooms
of ordering Chinnici's murder in 1983, was finally acquitted along with
these two.

It seemed like old times, but a crucial decade had passed. The
Mafia's cover had been blown in Italy and America. Betrayed and debunked by its own members, raked over in the press, decapitated by
round after round of arrests, damned in millions of pages of courtroom
testimony, Cosa Nostra had been condemned in a dozen landmark
cases; its members could be prosecuted now in ways unthinkable just a
few years earlier.

In a highly civilized democracy, however, a Man of Honor could be
arrested, tried, and convicted and still walk free. Concern for the rights
of every citizen was necessarily paramount. Where the law was not
explicitly permissive, it had loopholes enough to be pounced on by
smart lawyers, designing politicians, and inflexibly exacting jurists.
Thus, the Mafia could beat the law without even bending it.

Italy had in fact approved enlightened legislation for its prison and
penal codes at the very time the judiciary started to bear down on the
Mafia. No sooner were its members captured than the new laws worked
(inescapably, if unintentionally) toward their release.

In 1984, Parliament had set strict time limits for prisoners awaiting
trial: two years from the day of arrest to a sentence in the lower court,
another year and a half for the appellate court, a further year for the
Supreme Court. The deadline was automatic, however complex the
proceedings. A defendant could leave in the middle of his trial, if the
time was up; he could also leave if sentence was passed but not yet filed
in chancery, which alone could take months.

This provision was workable for normal crime, but a Mafia case could tie a court in knots. Men of Honor generated monumental paperwork. Locked into a worldwide circuit—traveling back and forth to America, shopping for morphine in Sofia or Bangkok, paying a Turkish supplier in Zurich, laundering money in London—they required foreign police and banking reports, interrogations abroad, authorized translations. Even the U.S. government, committing massive resources, needed three years to convict twenty-odd defendants in the Pizza case.

Another parliamentary act, in 1986, offered discounts to Italy's model prisoners. (Men of Honor are always model prisoners.) Those who behaved well got six weeks of furlough each year, and three months off their sentences for every year in jail. After ten years of good behavior, they were entitled to "semiliberty," spending their days outside and only their nights in a cell.[5]

In the last half of 1988, 2,992 convicted prisoners out on furlough or daytime permits disappeared. Thousands of others reported back, but it was "the quality, not the quantity, that mattered," as Italy's Minister of the Interior Antonio Gava observed. Half the fugitives were ranking Mafiosi convicted for murder, theft, kidnapping, and drug-trafficking. Most were from Palermo, Catania, and Naples; one was a member of the Cupola.

Nearly all the Cupola's members still in custody had found the next best solution. They were certified invalids, comfortably installed for an indefinite stay in a wing of Palermo's Civico Hospital. (Among the ailments diagnosed by physicians with a straight face were a stiff neck, hernia, "excessive sweating," fainting spells, and a physiological need for sea air.)[6]

The scandal flared with the news that Luciano Leggio might be out next. It had taken a quarter of a century to put him behind bars, and now the prisons seemingly couldn't hold him. He was already claiming his right to semiliberty. Totting up his assorted discount points, he could look forward to being a free man altogether by 1991. This prospect jarred the government into thoughts of tightening the law, for Mafia convicts at any rate. Nobody was going to make honest citizens of them, and letting them out on trust was tantamount to legalizing their escape.

Where an act of Parliament could be reversed, however, a crippling assault from within the judiciary could not. Even as 464 alleged Mafiosi came before a court of assizes in Palermo, a superior court was establishing the ground rules that would get them off the hook. Starting in 1986, Italy's Supreme Court (Court of Cassation) threw out nearly every important lower court verdict against the Mafia.

Most of the rulings came from an eminent jurist, Corrado Carnevale, known as "the sentence basher." Many rulings were based on
hairsplitting "defects of motivation," "defects of notification," "errors
of form," and "errors of procedure." Others simply rejected a jury's
view of the evidence. Annulling a lower court's convictions in Italy's
Pizza case, for instance, Judge Carnevale found:

- The "cryptic conversations" overheard in America by the FBI
  were too cryptic to be taken for a reference to drugs.
- The defendant Antonio Salamone, though "adhering to Mafioso
  methods," could not be considered a member of the organization
  at least partly because "he lived on another continent."
- A major money launderer in the Pizza case could reasonably
  claim to have been unaware of handling drug money; this although he admitted that the dollars he laundered came in "small
  bills, tattered and filthy, in enormous quantity," passed to him by
  "Sicilians in the strongest odor of the Mafia."[7]

Judge Carnevale's integrity could not be impugned, nor could his
rulings be appealed; his was the court of last resort. The lower courts
were helpless as the nation's highest tribunal proceeded to undo virtually everything that Sicily's anti-Mafia pool had done, and finally to
undo the pool itself.

In the autumn of 1988, the Supreme Court discarded the only premise on which the judiciary could ever catch up with the Sicilian Mafia—
its *unicità,* or "oneness." The Mafia did not "correspond to a unitary
and vertical structure," the ruling said. Rather, it was "composed of
single Families, operating in diverse territories, without any hierarchical ties to the Cupola of Cosa Nostra."[8]

Investigators who had labored for a decade to prove the opposite
were staggered. They had been losing ground steadily since the maxitrial began. Now, scarcely a year after the verdict, its main pillar was
cut away, and the foundations of the anti-Mafia pool collapsed. It was
not just the Supreme Court that undercut Judge Falcone's team. The
judiciary's own governing body let it fall. Though defended by a passionate minority in the Magistrates' Higher Council, the team was
abandoned by a rhetorically virtuous majority. No member of the Italian cabinet lifted a finger to save it.

The atmosphere had grown heavier month by month, as if the
judges working against the Mafia, not the Mafia itself, were the enemy.

Silky voices of reason questioned their wisdom and motives. They were accused of careerism, of "handcuffs for headlines," of inflicting their screaming sirens on Palermitani to enhance their macho image, of bucking for rank and glory. Backbiting and sly innuendo spread turbulence through Palermo's courthouse, which came to be called "Poison Palace."

A fastidious chorus deplored the use of *pentiti,* whose testimony had revealed the dark side of the Mafia planet. The *pentiti*'s urgent pleas for more safeguards were ignored. "If they don't protect me now, now that I've served the state, you can imagine what will happen afterward. What will happen? They'll kill me, that's what will happen," said one.[9] Nevertheless, no party introduced a Witness Protection Bill in Parliament. The state could not protect the defectors and their families anyway, conceded the Socialist minister of justice.[10]

The fate of one Antonino Calderone, Sicily's latest and most important *pentito,* who talked in 1988, was a clear portent. A lifelong Man of Honor from Catania, Calderone had moved in the highest Mafia echelons until 1982, when his brother was murdered by the Corleonesi. The brother, Giuseppe, had controlled eastern Sicily and headed the Cupola's *Inter-Provinciale.* Admitting to seven murders of his own, Calderone laid out the Mafia's links to citizens above reproach, its hold on the world of finance in Sicily and Milan, its intimate relations with politicians of high degree—everything Buscetta never talked about. "He spilled it all out, without sparing his friends or even himself, without reservations, without asking for anything except protection for his family," said the head of Italy's Anti-Crime Squad, who was keeping watch over Calderone in a special prison wing.[11]

Where Buscetta had been welcomed as a marvel in 1984, however, Calderone was relegated to something bordering on outer darkness in 1988. Having admitted to multiple murder, Calderone himself was doomed to spend much of his remaining life in prison. Yet his tremendous revelations hardly left a mark on others. The investigation deriving from his confession was broken up and divided among ten different judicial districts. Politicians and financiers "contiguous" to the Mafia were filtered out of the case. Of the 160 arrested after Calderone talked, all but 11 were released.[12]

By the end of 1988, "the slow agony of the anti-Mafia investigation" was over, as a Sicilian magistrate put it. The life had gone out of the whole gallant enterprise.

Judges, cops, and *pentiti* who had laid their heads on the line were disavowed. Palermo's anti-Mafia pool, invaluable for its accumulated knowledge and broad overview, was disbanded (in fact if not in form),[13] and the police team working with it was dispersed. (Those police still alive were sent elsewhere, one to mind the post office in Reggio Calabria.) Major cases were divided into disconnected parts and assigned to routine magistrates scattered across the island. In May 1989, an appellate court ruling in Rome actually maintained that the Mafia had never existed; as if we were still back in 1963, when the cardinal primate of Sicily declared that the Mafia was a communist invention.[14]

"The state has surrendered," a front-line judge had said halfway through 1988. "The anti-Mafia pool is in ruins. The past has been cut off. The police don't know what's going on in Cosa Nostra any more; not a single police formation here can turn in a report on the Mafia worthy of the name. . . . We are risking the creation of a dangerous vacuum. . . . We're going backward, to the way we were ten or twenty years ago."[15]

The hopes rising among Sicilian Mafiosi were conveyed in a brief exchange between two of them in Brooklyn, recorded by the FBI around that time:

"Has Falcone resigned yet?"
"No, he changed his mind."
"Shit."

Tremors of alarm were spreading among U.S. law enforcers. "Without the Italian pool, the Mafia will win," warned Louis Freeh, head of the Eastern District's Organized Crime Unit. "Dismantling the Italian group would create insoluble problems for us here. . . . The Mafia has been destabilized in both countries, but it isn't finished. This is the critical moment for both of us. Without the Italian pool, we would be paralyzed too."[16]

When the Italian anti-Mafia pool fell apart after all, the United States did not feel the impact at once. Italian and American judges and cops continued to work closely together, and even made dramatic drug arrests.[17] As Freeh observed, however, "The people [in charge] have changed, but the system hasn't."[18] The New York–Palermo drug axis was still working, he said, despite the legal battering it was taking at both ends.

Traffickers caught in America were always expendable, so long as the organization flourished. In Italy, their international headquarters, the Mafia was surging back with frightening virulence. Everybody conceded that it was winning; many thought it had won already. "Dear

Cossiga, The Mafia has won," wrote the president of Parliment's Anti-Mafia Commission to the president of the Italian Republic in the summer of 1989.[19]

◦⟨⟩◦

What was it that prevented a sophisticated democratic society from mobilizing against the Mafia as it had mobilized against terrorism? Not just permissive laws, or a jurist of exceptional punctilio, but myriad elements adding up to a lack of political will.

Not many Italians, other than its victims, saw the Mafia as a far deadlier menace to their freedom than the Red Brigades ever were. The Red Brigades had also enjoyed a curiously uninterrupted interlude of growth in Italy. Intellectuals shielded them as misguided comrades. Politicians could use them to show off as custodians of law and order. The Italian establishment did not perceive them as a threat to its own existence. The police and courts, understanding little of their true intent—to destroy the democratic state—arrested them only to turn them loose again and again. By 1980, Italy was second only to Turkey as a victim of raging terrorist warfare.

Then also, a handful of brave Italian magistrates risked death to expose the nature of the conspiracy. Several judges were killed, but the Palazzo finally recognized that the threat was intolerable. Once this was plain, the entire nation closed ranks and the Red Brigades' "long march through the institutions" was over.

But nothing of the sort ever happened to the Mafia. Perhaps it was too familiar, too closely woven into the social and economic fabric, too well protected and camouflaged. Whatever the reasons, it appeared to have anesthetized Italy's governing class. While the whole country deplored Cosa Nostra verbally, people did not make a point of voting against it. No trade union opposed it with genuine vigor. No mainland politician ran on an anti-Mafia ticket. No political party made the Mafia a major plank in its national election platform. Those who were not corrupted or intimidated seemed overcome by lassitude or resignation.

Yet the Mafia could blackmail and dictate terms to the country as no political terrorists could. It could remove an inquisitive cop merely with an anonymous death threat on the phone—Palermo's chief of homicide got shipped out that way in 1989—and murder the highest representatives of the state with impunity. It could fleece the state of many billion dollars a year, regularly, flagrantly, and defy the law to come and get it.

The Mafia had "capillary control over every quarter of Palermo,"

said a magistrate in the anti-Mafia pool in 1988. It had "total possession
of entire areas of the national territory," added Italy's High Commissioner to Combat the Mafia, Domenico Sica, referring to Sicily, Calabria, and the Campania region around Naples. Cosa Nostra had made
justice "impossible" in Sicily, and rendered the wealthy city of Catania
"ungovernable," according to the Anti-Mafia Commission of the Magistrates' Superior Council. It was "contaminating the entire national
economic mechanism" by "investing dirty capital in a healthy economy," said the governor of Italy's central bank. It was "financing the
state's debt" by "rinsing its narcodollars in Treasury bonds," said the
minister of the interior. It was "buying the Italian state piece by piece,"
declared the mayor of Palermo, Leoluca Orlando.[20]

Mayor Orlando, a Christian Democratic reformer, spoke for a
growing number of Sicilians and mainland Italians who had begun to
fight back politically around 1985. The effort had transformed him
from a hopeful young believer to a weary, harrowed, and sadly battle-
scarred figure in just four years. He was the first reformer in a century to
last that long in office; the few others who had tried were out within
weeks or months. A recent predecessor had been murdered to boot.[21]

The murdered ex-mayor had left behind a political testament, con-
veying something of the atmosphere at City Hall. "How long do you
want to be mayor? A month? Five years? If it's five years, you'll have to
deal with me," he had been told in 1984 by former Christian Democratic mayor Vito Ciancimino, who ran Palermo for three decades on
behalf of the Mafia and himself. (Ciancimino was pocketing a quarter of
a million dollars a month when he was arrested later in 1984.)[22]

To dislodge the Mafia—just to try—was to touch the most delicate
nerves in Italy's body politic. The Mafia was every party's guilty secret,
though guiltier for some than others. Even the communists had their
peccadilloes, though their record was cleanest.[23] Sicily was the poorest
region in Italy, and left to fester in its poverty; "Born and Died Unem-
ployed" might be the epitaph for much of its postwar generation. But
the island was an immense reservoir of hidden wealth, surreptitious
power, and votes, largely at the Mafia's disposal.

Sicilian barons of finance, secretly connected, made generous contributions to nearly all Italian parties. Most parties had strong Sicilian
contingents in Parliament as well, and needed them. The Sicilian electorate is almost a tenth of the nation's—a crucial margin in a country
where no party has had an absolute majority for forty years. Several
parties cohabiting in precarious government coalitions could not do
without the Sicilian vote.

All but the communists and neofascists, barred from the feast, had votes thrown their way in Sicily, to candidates meeting with Mafia approval. The other kind of candidates could be knocked out of the race in similar fashion (where they weren't wiped out physically). Not everybody got elected that way, to be sure, nor were their parties necessarily consulted. The Mafia made the decisions, calculated to its best advantage. National party leaders might hate the thought, but they lived with it.

By court estimate, the Mafia had upward of half a million captive votes to spread around: 150 Families times 50 to 150 members apiece times 50-odd relatives and friends in each member's pocket.[24] Half a million votes meant one in every five or so in Sicily, one in every two polled by the Christian Democrats, more than the total polled by any other party. Regularly, at election time, the top brass decided how to hand them out, as an authoritative *pentito* from Catania has explained:

The Families vote for all the parties except the communists and the [neofascist] MSI. . . . Before the elections, we'd get the signal for certain names and parties, and the provincial [Mafia] commissions would take charge. Every Family's members, relatives, and friends could amount to thousands and thousands of votes—two hundred thousand for the province of Catania alone.[25]

The swing vote could have a paralyzing effect on minor parties, the small but exceptionally decent Republican party, for one. The Republicans' national leader, Giorgio Lamalfa, was an admirable and honest man, among the most respected in Italy, but he had a problem; the Republicans' leader in Sicily had been on extremely questionable terms with Mafia bosses for a long time. Lamalfa might yearn to get rid of him, but he delivered more votes for the Republicans in Sicily than they polled anywhere else save in northern Lombardy; and he controlled a quarter of the party's enrolled membership besides.[26]

The problem was much more acute for the Christian Democrats, whose power-sharing deals with the Mafia dated back to World War II. Sicily was their fortress. They always dominated its local and regional governments. Every cabinet they headed in Rome included a couple of Grand Sicilian Electors. Christian Democrats gathered a million votes there, three times more than the nearest runner-up. Italy's most powerful politician at present, Giulio Andreotti, had controlled a quarter of their Sicilian vote for a good twenty years. Without his Sicilian base, he would lose a critical part of his strength.

Such was the Christian Democrats' dilemma that none of their na-

tional leaders ever denounced Andreotti's official party spokesman in
Palermo, former mayor Salvo Lima. Although he was described by a
later Christian Democratic mayor as "the most disquieting and corrupting element" in the Sicilian capital,[27] Lima is still defended vigor-
ously by Italy's distinguished prime minister. "If anybody has something to charge Lima with, let him produce it," Minister Andreotti has
said, rounding on his critics. Indeed, Lima has never been convicted of a
crime. Nevertheless, he was cited 163 times in a ten-year study by
Italy's Parliamentary Anti-Mafia Commission.[28]

Politicians everywhere are familiar with the principle involved,
blandly referred to as realpolitik. The Mafia, a master of the art, has
been setting honeyed traps for Americans as well since the days of the
Unione Siciliana. Some might dodge them where others could not. But
few candidates for high office in the United States could be unaware of
Cosa Nostra's formidable electoral machines in a dozen strategic states.
As one example in many, John F. Kennedy would have lost the 1960
presidential election if not for the two hundred thousand or so votes
thrown to him by Chicago's Mafia boss, Sam Giancana. Unfortunately
for Kennedy, he did not repay his debt. He and his brother Robert went
after the Mafia instead. Many authorities believe they got themselves
killed for that.[29]

Perhaps the proud Kennedys did not understand that the Mafia
always collects. A child of ten in Sicily would know as much, however.
The Mafia there was repaid in a thousand ways, with rigged public
contracts, giveaway state credits, pork-barrel jobs, plummy government posts, and golden gifts of silence. Incriminating evidence against
the *mammasantissima* disappeared. Dossiers on compliant politicians
were sealed away. Unwelcome prefects and police chiefs were transferred, and judges ran into invisible barriers.

In effect, the Italian establishment did not try to stop the Mafia until
the early 1980s, when it began to make so much money in drugs that
there appeared to be no stopping it.

When the narcodollars swelled to billions, the Mafia moved north
and hooked into the nation's financial heart. The north, which made
Italy the world's fifth richest industrial nation, had looked to the south
mostly for cheap labor in the past. Then, around 1981, the Mafia set up
an elaborate investment branch in Milan with the Bono brothers, the
Cuntrera brothers, the Salamone brothers, the Zaza brothers, and Buscetta, among others. Within a short while, the branch was a major

source of big, tax-free capital.[30] Mafia money invaded the stock exchange, bought into legitimate industry, enriched the banks. The organization became an enormous untraceable supplier of foreign exchange for importers, investors, and currency speculators: dollars abroad for lire at home.

The Mafia also found channels to bypass the local system of rigging public contracts in Sicily. Respectable northern companies, secretly taken over by Mafia frontmen, were already replacing disreputable Mafia firms on the island. "Firms somehow connected to Cosa Nostra in Palermo will no longer have to bid at auction; the bids will be made by corporations seemingly above suspicion," reported the Carabinieri in 1988. Some $16 billion worth of public works contracts were scheduled for auction in Sicily at the time.[31]

Boring further into the money market, Catania's clans launched their own underground bond issues. Go-go investors in the north (or anywhere) could lend the Mafia half a million dollars or more, at 20 percent a month, to finance its wholesale heroin purchases. Rolled over, $500,000 could bring in $1.2 million a year.[32] Meanwhile, as Interior Minister Gava disclosed, Mafia drug money was conditioning the value of the lira, and underwriting Italy's national debt. Working through foreign banks—especially in Spain, bridgehead for Sicilian-Colombian joint operations in Europe—billions of narcodollars were flowing into Italy for investment in anonymous government bearer bonds.[33] The force of such enormous, corrupting wealth would appear to explain the intangible obstacles eternally blocking anti-Mafia forces in Sicily. But the Mafia's inexorable advance could also have the reverse effect; it could shock the Italian establishment into fighting back.

A country with Italy's vitality, resilience, and intuitive common sense does not give up its freedom so easily. Italian politicians may not be saints, but neither are they all incurably venal. Much of the problem all along was their continuing failure to comprehend the Mafia's magnitude.

The Mafia could have its way with many people because they saw it as a peculiarly Sicilian phenomenon; it was dangerous, violent, grasping, arrogant, but sophisticated political leaders thought they could handle it. Once it became a national incubus—the source of a nationwide narcotics epidemic, an arbiter of the nation's finance, a direct menace to the nation's governing class—they were no longer so sure.

On the eve of the 1990s, there were perceptible breaches in establishment ranks. The signals from the Palazzo still called for an end to the "culture of emergency" and for "normalized" relations with the Mafia:

a return to peaceful coexistence, in a word. Nevertheless, influential men in government were trying to turn this around.

Popular resistance was becoming a fact of political life, in Sicily first of all. Students, intellectuals, housewives, and young political activists were driving a wedge into local parties. The Catholic clergy was speaking out against the Mafia from the pulpit, backed by the island's increasingly forthright cardinal primate. (The figures in Cardinal Pappalardo's crèche for Christmas 1988 were women weeping over graves, *carabinieri* struggling to keep order, and a giant Polyphemus, violence incarnate.)[34] Several powerful Christian Democrats had been determined to change their party's posture in Sicily since the mid-1980s. The then prime minister, Ciriaco De Mita, sent a party commissar to Palermo to shake out corrupt political hacks. Mayor Orlando was his idea, and his protégé, and the mayor's policy was paying off. By the spring of 1989, De Mita's forces had gained enough popular votes in Sicily to alarm the traditional Christian Democratic establishment. Even ex-mayor Salvo Lima was demanding "maximum solidarity for the war on the Mafia."

By that time, the five parties in the government coalition had appointed a tough and vigorous magistrate, Domenico Sica, as the Interior Ministry's High Commissioner to Combat the Mafia, and granted him the special powers withheld from General Dalla Chiesa six years earlier. In fact, they gave him more than Dalla Chiesa ever asked for: the run of the country's prisons to interrogate Mafia suspects, a special force to coordinate intelligence from all sources, access to the secrets gathered by investigating magistrates.

Yet a year after Sica's appointment, the Mafia had attained new heights. Deftly, unerringly, it was pitting Italy's anti-Mafia forces against one another, sending insidious anonymous letters, planting inflammatory rumors, casting unthinkable suspicions over Sicily's frontline magistrates, even as it tried to murder their standard bearer— Giovanni Falcone, saved by a near-miracle from a fifty-kilo bomb planted near his seaside villa. (Brought in by sea-borne commandos, the bomb in its Adidas gym bag was spotted by a bodyguard at the last moment.)

The air was growing unbreathable in Palermo's Palace of Justice. Judges were investigating fellow judges; Sica and Falcone were no longer on speaking terms; the whole judiciary appeared to be in shambles. In the midst of this wreckage, the Mafia's heroin-cocaine business flourished—over half a ton of refined heroin was seized in Italy in 1988, a worldwide record—and killerism was rampant once again. In just the first six months of 1989, 428 men and women were murdered by the Mafia in Sicily and its partners in the Neapolitan Camorra and Calabrian 'Ndrangheta: too many, said incoming Prime Minister Andreotti, promising a new war on organized crime.[35]

Though every incoming prime minister since World War II has made the promise, the war has yet to be fought to the end. Some day, Italy might gather its full strength and put finish to the nightmare. Not yet.

Standoff

Italy and the United States had what some thought was a last piece of unfinished business regarding the Sicilian Mafia in America; and shortly before Christmas 1988, they finished it. They broke the Cherry Hill Gambinos' heroin ring.

The teamwork was magnificent. American and Italian agents synchronized their movements for months, and a dozen specially trained Italian cops went over to New York to give the FBI a hand. On the night of December 1, 1988, 133 traffickers were arrested in various regions of Italy, and another 75 in New Jersey, Pennsylvania, California, Illinois, Florida, and Brooklyn. The choicest arrests were made in Brooklyn, on 18th Avenue, in the Gambino brothers' grandly renovated hangout, the Cafe Giardino (their old Cafe Valentino). A Sicilian tenor was enjoying a round of hearty applause at 2:00 A.M. when an FBI agent took the mike and invited the assembled guests to put their hands up. "This is your last dance, folks," he said.

Operation Iron Tower, as it was named, had the makings of a considerably more important drug bust than the one that had caught a hundred-odd Sicilian traffickers in America and Italy the previous

April. The FBI had believed at the time that it had "dismantled the Sicilian drug connection," but the connection had grown to dimensions almost beyond discerning by December.

The star arrestee in the spring bust, Emmanuele Adamita, had been moving heroin for the Cherry Hill Gambinos since the 1960s. By April 1988, when agents caught up with him, he was engaged in an enormous two-way traffic directed from Palermo, moving heroin to America and cocaine to Europe. His arrest did not make the smallest dent in the traffic.[1] Iron Tower at the year's end did not dismantle the Sicilian connection either, but it exposed much more of the whole subterranean enterprise. As always, the magnitude of the Sicilians' operation was a continuing surprise.

The Cafe Giardino, bugged in spite of its denizens' elaborate precautions, yielded evidence enough to bag just one of the Gambino brothers, Giuseppe, by no means the brightest of the lot. The youngest, Rosario, had already been sent up for forty-five years on a heroin rap. John, the big prize, slipped through the net again; the FBI still couldn't gather enough evidence to jail him. (Though John Gambino faced a six-and-a-half-year jail sentence in Italy—a sentence *in absentia* confirmed by Italy's Supreme Court in 1985—the United States has never agreed to Italian requests for his extradition.)

Gambino's old Palermitano partner in crime got away too. Rosario Spatola—billionaire drug trafficker, second-in-command under the late Salvatore Inzerillo, cosponsor of Michele Sindona's fake kidnapping—had vanished from Sicily in 1986. (Convicted in Palermo three years earlier, he had walked away when the case failed to get through an appellate court in time.) Though Spatola was photographed with the same crowd in Brooklyn, the FBI missed him somehow. (Spatola was finally arrested five months later.)

Even so, the haul proved amazing. This was not just the Cherry Hill Gambinos' ring. It included all the Families who had once run the old Mafia in Palermo, presumed to be extinct. Half a dozen Inzerillos, an assortment of other Gambinos, a Di Maggio, a Badalamenti, and several Manninos—uncles, nephews, and cousins of the Palermo Gambinos, and owners of the Mimmo's Pizza chain in Philadelphia—were picked up in the raid.[2] These Families, making up the Gambino-Inzerillo-Spatola–Di Maggio superclan, supposedly killed off years ago by the Corleonesi, had continued to ship heroin from Sicily right through the Great Mafia War. Not only had the Families survived, but they were busier and richer than ever, though their status had changed. Once the overlords, they were plainly Luciano Leggio's vassals now. "You don't move a leaf if they don't know about it in Corleone," said Giuseppe Gambino at the Cafe Giardino to a visitor just in from Palermo. "They're running the show; everything comes from Corleone," the visitor agreed.[3] (The Man in Corleone during Leggio's absence was "Corto," they said, meaning Salvatore "Corto" Riina, Leggio's chief proconsul and designated heir, a fugitive from the law since 1969.)

Although the Corleonesi had known of their activities all along, the old superclan had escaped detection in the outside world throughout a decade of discovery and revelation. Its people had managed to keep their own shipping lanes open and their own refineries going, through all the arrests and trials on both sides of the Atlantic. They had always had a direct line to the U.S. market, even before the 1957 heroin franchise deal. Consignments of theirs had been seized as far back as 1947. The nearby Alcamo refinery on the Sicilian coast, the largest heroin lab ever discovered anywhere, was theirs. Sicilian magistrates believe that they must have sent tons and tons of heroin to America down the years.[4]

Despite the misfortune befalling some Family members, their multitudinous relatives and associates are still shipping and reportedly still refining heroin; police are hunting for their labs in western Sicily, as this is written.[5]

The prodigious staying power of these clans said something that few American investigators seemed able to hear, even by the end of 1988. There was no sign of historical memory in their announcement of the raid on the Cherry Hill Gambinos' ring. At best, some of the biggest traffickers creating and feeding America's dope habit for decades on end appeared in the U.S. media as merely picturesque. Incredibly, U.S. authorities still seemed to think of them as the "zips" working for the Brooklyn Mob, menials in the service of New York's Cosa Nostra Families. They were indicted as "the Brooklyn-based Sicilian faction" of the American Gambino Family. Where had everybody been since Big Paul Castellano, America's Boss of All Bosses, had sat down to lunch in 1980 with Sal Catalano, the Great White Father from across the waters?

For all the mass of evidence, investigators accustomed to dealing with the American Mafia apparently had yet to grasp the fact that the head of the Octopus was in Palermo, not New York. "The head is here, here, *here,*" fumed an exasperated chief of detectives at Palermo's Squadra Mobile headquarters, when the press kept getting it wrong.[6]

The home base for the superclan's ring was the outwardly unpretentious hamlet of Torretta, on a hilltop lying off the Palermo-Trapani highway. This was the domain of the late Mafia patriarch Rosario Di Maggio, the Man of Honor who dropped dead in fright when he thought the police coming for him were Mafia killers in disguise.

Torretta was the village where Italian police had found gold faucets in the bathrooms of humble peasant cottages early in 1986, the fruits of a humming cottage industry. They had come upon the place after catching a mother of eight trying to get through Palermo's Punta Ráisi airport with two kilos of heroin in her girdle—gusts of Trussardi's perfume, drenching her bosom to disguise the drug's scent, had given her away.

She was one of Torretta's many mules, housewives of all ages carrying three or four kilos at a time to New York, four or five times a year, for ten million lire and a free week at the Sheraton Hotel. Upon raiding the village, police had found the special girdles, with hand-sewn cotton sacks stitched in rows to fit around the waist without bulging unduly. Special cotton leggings to fit under men's trousers were found as well. "The whole village was in on it," said Gianni De Gennaro, who guided the investigation.[7]

It took nearly three years to follow the leads from Torretta to the United States, and not just to the United States. When several different Italian and American investigations hooked together to focus on Torretta, the evidence became a mirror of the Sicilian Mafia's wide-ranging interests. The ring uncovered by investigators included not just Sicilian Mafiosi but traffickers from the Neapolitan Camorra and Calabrian 'Ndrangheta. By now, the three brotherhoods were so entwined as to be scarcely distinguishable one from the other. Their members were all inveterate world travelers.

Several members of the ring met with FBI undercovers in Amsterdam and London. A member in Los Angeles was bringing in Chinese heroin across the Pacific from the Far East. Another was picking up heroin shipped from Asia to San Francisco, by men working for the son of the high commissioner of Mauritius in the United Kingdom.[8] Yet another in Miami was negotiating to bring heroin straight from Pakistan "for John" (Gambino), and had stored a ton of pure cocaine in a warehouse, brought in uncut from Colombia, for export to Europe. (He was Salvatore Rina, a crony of Enzo Napoli's and Buscetta's and an intimate part of their Brooklyn circle in the 1960s.) An Inzerillo in the Dominican Republic was overseeing "the wine matter," a major international project involving Bulgaria and Yugoslavia. The "wine matter" was the plan described to DEA undercover Frank Panessa by his friendly mark in Philadelphia, Paolo La Porta, in 1983. Liquid heroin procured in Sofia was going to be bottled as wine in Sicily and shipped to Santo Domingo for reshipment to the United States via Mexico. "We own the Dominican Republic," La Porta had said at the time, though not many in authority appeared to be listening.

All this was happening in 1988, nearly half a decade after the momentous discovery that the Sicilian Mafia was an independent entity dominating the American heroin market. Some of the traffickers who had kept crossing the FBI's line of vision since 1980—and the DEA's since 1970—were still operating on the same Brooklyn turf. The same men who had come over from Palermo to set things up a quarter of a century earlier were still at it. Judging by the evidence, furthermore, they had the same deal with the American Mafia that had made the setup possible in the first place.

Authorities in 1988 didn't know who had taken over collection of the heroin payoffs on the American Mafia's behalf, after Paul Castellano was murdered in New York in December 1985. Barely more than a year later, however, the FBI picked up some highly suggestive information in that regard.

Since early in 1987, John Gambino has been seen visiting John Gotti, the biggest man on the American Mafia scene, reigning chief of New York's Gambino Family, once a week. These contacts go back to March 7, 1987, when an eyewitness informed the bureau that "five different *capos* from five different La Cosa Nostra Families met with John Gambino in the back room of the Cafe Giardino." The *capos* "went back one at a time and discussed business with Gambino."[9] Just a few weeks later, on April 27, John Gotti paid a personal visit to the Cafe Giardino. Drawing up in a limousine with three bodyguards, he was closeted privately with Giuseppe Gambino for an hour.[10]

The boss of America's mightiest Cosa Nostra Family does not pay state visits to underlings. Gotti in particular would certainly not have so honored the leaders of the "zips" without compelling reason. He detested them, as they did him. (He was not of Sicilian birth, a source of deep distrust for both.) His opinion of Sicilian Mafiosi in general emerged in a piquant exchange with a couple of his soldiers, recorded by the FBI:

> 1ST SOLDIER: They're opening up all over the fuckin' place, these zips, ain't they? There's three of them right on this avenue here, they all make money. . . .

2ND SOLDIER: Johnny's been here fifteen years, you know. . . . If they run a game, you know, Johnny will go along with another game. . . .

GOTTI: They're not gonna play nothin'. . . . I got four thousand guys I'll send from every neighborhood, I'll put in there. . . . Let 'em come ahead, let's see what they'll do.

SOLDIER: Whaddya expect them to do? Who brought the fuckers here?

GOTTI: I'm dying for someone to come forward. . . . He better go to Russia and get a guy, he can't get it away from the five crews we know. . . .

SOLDIER: They make like they don't understand, the motherfuck-ers. . . .

GOTTI: They don't understand what they don't wanna understand. . . . They go around with hundreds of thousands in their pockets, and you're going around with your hat in your hand."

Operation Iron Tower was hailed by some FBI enthusiasts not only as the swan song of the "zips" in America, but as a sign of the entire American Mafia's dying fall. "The New York Families are on their knees. The Mafia is falling apart. It's collapsing under our blows," asserted one of the bureau's special agents covering organized crime.[12]

American authorities had indeed inflicted tremendous blows in the course of the 1980s. Some 2,500 American Mafiosi and their associates had gone to prison. Leaders of every Cosa Nostra Family in the United States had been indicted, and most had been tried and convicted. Their entire national Commission had been convicted, its members drawing sentences of up to a hundred years. A lot of money was taken away from them, and they lost access to much more, especially in the labor unions. Their leadership passed to younger men, inexperienced, brash, several generations removed from the old Mafia culture, and lacking their own historical memory. Not only did these new leaders upset delicate, long-standing business arrangements, they took to killing each other off to move up the ladder, something Mafiosi hadn't done since Lucky Luciano had imposed his new order in the 1930s. Many qualified crime analysts thought the organization was really on its last legs.

Nevertheless, the United States too had perceived the frailties of the law where the Mafia was concerned. John Gotti, whose ascendancy in Cosa Nostra after Castellano's death has not been equaled since World War II, was acquitted by a Brooklyn court in 1987. (The aide who betrayed him to the FBI was murdered the following year.)[13] Gotti's brother Gene was also acquitted then; and in 1988, after being charged with multimillion-dollar heroin deals, he was freed in two mistrials.[14] He was finally convicted on the third try, in May 1989.

In New Jersey, also in 1988, twenty ranking bosses of the Lucchese Family—its entire leadership—were acquitted of running a criminal enterprise together with the Genovese Family. The trial lasted twenty-one months, a third of a year longer than the Pizza case, and produced a mountain of wiretaps and ninety witnesses. But the evidence failed to persuade the jurors, several of whom even hugged the freed defendants and wished them luck.[15]

Grave in themselves, these defeats in the courts were indications of an underlying strength too readily dismissed. America's Cosa Nostra was weathering not just assaults by the law, but more competition than it had ever faced. The area of organized crime had been invaded by innumerable ethnic and indigenous groups: Colombians, Bolivians, Mexicans, Cubans, Puerto Ricans, West Indians, Vietnamese, Koreans, Chinese, Japanese, Israelis, Russians, ghetto blacks, and scores of motorcycle gangs led by Hell's Angels, the Outlaws, the Pagans, and the Bandidos.

Several criminal groups had international connections. The Chinese Triads, two centuries older than the Mafia, operated in many parts of the world. So did the Japanese Yakuza, five times bigger than the Mafia in size. Even Hell's Angels, with thirty-five chapters in the United States, formed as many again abroad, from Canada, Britain, and Denmark to West Germany, France, Japan, New Zealand, and Brazil.[16]

But not many had the stuff to stand up to Cosa Nostra, which was actually hiring some of these gangs for piecework in the United States and making pacts with others. Hell's Angels were "working partners with Cosa Nostra Families in several illegal activities," said a high FBI official. Cubans were paying a tax to New York's Families for the numbers games in Harlem. Chicago's Family employed Mexicans, Puerto Ricans, and Colombians. The Caribbean Westies carried out contract killings for the New York Families, and even provided their bodyguards. Boston's Patriarca Family supplied loan sharks to gambling joints run by by Chinese Triads, who were buying guns from New York's Families. The Yakuza had "forged a specific operational link with elements of La Cosa Nostra in New York City," with whom the Colombians also maintained "a kind of co-existence agreement."[17]

The American Mafia was not like the other ethnic groups. It was more versatile, its ethnic community was more thoroughly integrated into the national society, its network of protection and political cover was incomparably more secure; and it had the Sicilian connection for drugs, the product of consuming interest to the others. The more various groups flocked to feed in America's narcotics fields, the more some form of orderly government was needed for the underworld. Cosa Nostra was the nearest thing to such a government. "Instead of being threatened and limited by so many criminal organizations, Cosa Nostra has hegemonized and utilized them," declared the FBI's assistant director for criminal investigation, Floyd Clark, in the spring of 1989. "It is still the most important criminal organization in the United States."[18]

The notion that this organization had lost its indispensable secret partner—that the Sicilian Mafia was finished in America after the FBI's spectacular raid in December 1988—was the stuff of an evening news broadcast, no more. No criminal band could boast anything comparable to the Sicilian traffickers' alternative life-support system in the United States, reinforced by so many privileged sanctuaries, from Venezuela, Brazil, and the Dominican Republic to Bulgaria and the Seychelles, sustained by such imperial power at home.

Sicilian traffickers might need an interval to regroup after the Cherry Hill Gambinos were hit, as they did after the Pizza ring was hit. But they had recovered "quickly and well" before, as Louis Freeh observed, and were already doing so again. Indeed, said Freeh, the Sicilian and American Mafias together continued to be "the superpowers in the world of drugs."[19]

There is plenty of room in the international drug trade, valued at several hundred billion dollars yearly. Traffickers have been turning up from everywhere to move dope anywhere, but not many could be called world-class. Only three formations are capable of handling narcotics on a wholesale, intercontinental scale: the Chinese Triads for heroin, the Colombian cartels for cocaine, and the Sicilian Mafia for both. And there lies the advantage assuring the Sicilian Mafia's supremacy; it is the only one of the three that handles both drugs of preference in the worldwide marketplace. Apart from selling its own product, furthermore, it acts as broker for the other two groups.

The three don't fight. Just as America's Cosa Nostra does not push the Sicilian Mafia around, neither do the Chinese or Colombian traffickers, who would readily kill almost anybody else in sight. Palermo's Men of Honor can move safely through the treacherous jungles of the drug trade because their point-to-point distribution system abroad is necessary to all, reaching where others cannot.

The Mafia has been buying or brokering the Colombians' cocaine for upward of thirty years, heavily since 1978 and massively since 1983.

Today the quantity is appalling. Sal Rina's ton of Colombian cocaine in a Miami warehouse could be lost without pain (except to Rina), when he was pulled in with John Gambino's other helpers. He was just one in an army of Sicilian Mafiosi engaged in the great transatlantic heroin-cocaine swap.

In February 1989, for instance, the French police in collaboration with Italian police and the DEA seized half a ton of cocaine on its way to Italy, the second-largest cocaine seizure ever made in Europe. (Spain had made a record two-ton haul in 1988.) The cocaine had been shipped from Colombia through the French Antilles to Le Havre on the coast of France, where it was loaded on a thirteen-foot sloop for overland transport by TIR truck. Traffickers of several nationalities were involved, but the cocaine was the Sicilian Mafia's.[20]

Some months before, London's Metropolitan Police had uncovered a plan to immerse Britain with a hundred kilos of cocaine weekly—over five tons a year. The cocaine was going to be welded into tractors and mechanical diggers and flown to Heathrow Airport, where detecting it was "almost impossible," according to the prosecutor in the London court. The cocaine was produced in Cochabamba, Bolivia. The "Sicilian faction" of the Mafia in Detroit, Michigan, was moving it on from there.[21]

Such are their talents for dissembling that Palermo's Men of Honor are just now beginning to be mentioned as purveyors of cocaine. They might still be escaping notice, if not for an increasingly obsessive concern with the spread of cocaine across the world. Oddly, popular worries about cocaine have tended to eclipse worries about heroin, an infinitely deadlier scourge. Heroin kills much faster, costs much more, and generates by far more street crime. And contrary to certain perplexing comments of late, its use is not in decline. If the class of users may be changing in America, the addict population is not dropping there, and is growing to epidemic proportions elsewhere: all over Europe, for instance.

The Italian port of Naples, with a population of 3 million, has 20,-000 heroin addicts by now—1 in every 150 inhabitants, compared with 1 in 500 for the United States. Over a quarter of a million used syringes were gathered by the city's street cleaners during the first nine months of 1988. The pushers came from Ghana, Nigeria, Senegal, and Tunisia, but their suppliers were the Mafia's primary allies, the Neapolitan Camorra.[22]

The Sicilians' own heroin syndicate has changed in understandable ways. After police discovered fifteen-odd refineries inside Italy, they moved production facilities abroad. In 1986, in France, police came across a startling resurrection of the old French Connection under new management. Corsican gangsters, and the chemists they had once utilized—still the world's finest—were back in production in Marseilles. As always, the morphine base was coming from Turkey, and the finished product was going mostly to New York. As a French court found in December 1988, however, the Sicilian Mafia was putting up the money this time, and was unmistakably in charge. Indeed, the evidence revealed "the Sicilian Mafia's firm hand on everything affecting heroin in the Mediterranean Basin," according to the court.[23]

Meanwhile, Sicilian traffickers were tending more and more to buy heroin ready-made in the Near and Far East and ship it wherever they pleased, bypassing Sicily entirely. Bangkok was thronged with traffickers as the 1990s neared, which alone suggested the need to look beyond appearances.[24]

"China White," bursting into the Western marketplace from Southeast Asia, was thought to be moving almost wholly through Chinese channels by 1989. The Triads were certainly picking up a larger share of the market; they were actually caught with a whopping cargo of four hundred kilos in the United States. Whether as the Triads' broker or on their own, however, Sicilian traffickers working in the shadows continued to be an incalculable force.

Istanbul also swarmed with buyers from Palermo and Catania. Three hundred TIR trucks were crossing daily into Turkey from Iran, gateway to the world's largest opium-producing area in southwest Asia. Turks, Syrians, Lebanese, and Palestinians saw to the refining, and the TIR trucks moved on to Italian staging areas.

In January 1989, a single TIR truck detained and searched in Milan yielded 115 kilos of "brown sugar" heroin in four Samsonite suitcases. Men from the Turkish Mafia were riding in the truck; Sicilian traffickers waiting to pick up the load slipped away. DEA agents, working in tandem with Italian police, knew it was a Mafia cargo. More important, they knew this was just one of the shipments planned for regular delivery every two weeks—two and a half tons of refined heroin a year through this single source, half for the United States and half for Western Europe. Two other rings under investigation in Sicily were believed to be picking up 50 kilos a month each from their Turkish suppliers.[25] The Sicilian-Turkish Mafia axis was as strong as ever.

"The Sicilian Mafia is still the biggest," said the FBI's Floyd Clark in the spring of 1989. "They still have routes that we've never found and know nothing about. We're still naive about the major drug structure.

We still haven't found the linkage between the drugs and the money laundering. We'll never get a handle on all this until we see the international connections."[26]

So matters stood on the threshold of the 1990s. The Mafia, revealed at last for the startlingly dangerous enemy of society that it was, nevertheless seemed impervious to exposure so long as the evidence coming to light was ignored, belittled, or papered over. There was an odd perversity, almost like a death wish, in the unwillingness or inability of countries and continents under siege to credit what they saw and heard. The evidence had shown that the Mafia was an abnormal criminal phenomenon, impossible to resist where it was imperfectly understood.

The police could not deal with Cosa Nostra as they would a gang of hoods. Judges could not perceive it that way either, without endangering their own sacrosanct institutions. Politicians could not leave it solely to the police and the courts. The law alone could not destroy it—and, as Mussolini proved for all time, profaning the law to smash it would be not only dangerous but useless.

No single country could contain the Mafia, nor could it be hacked away piece by piece. The head and limbs would all have to be chopped at once. This would take an act of iron will such as the international community has rarely displayed. It could happen, but there isn't much time. In the spring of 1989, the Guardia di Finanza issued a Red Alert regarding "new dimensions" opening up for the Sicilian Mafia in the international financial market. The new dimension was the Common Market itself. In 1992, Europe's Common Market countries will abolish their internal boundaries. Virtually the entire western side of the Continent will be freed of customs barriers, passport controls, police roadblocks.

Like everyone else in the European community. Men of Honor and their associates will then be able to move undisturbed from the Mediterranean to the Baltic, and from the Danube to the Atlantic coast of Ireland. Not even they might have expected as much of an obliging world: a Mafia without frontiers.

Epilogue

This book should end, as it began, with Detective Douglas Le Vien because he held the key to the Sicilian Mafia's secret invasion of the United States. Nobody in American or Italian law enforcement, to my knowledge, had crossed so many bureaucratic boundaries with such pigheaded determination, to fill so many unread pages of remarkable information. Not until I returned to Italy from New York in 1986, with thirty-five tapes of Le Vien's private diary covering events from 1976 to 1978, did I see the outlines of the Mafia's grand design.

I was filled with admiration for this stubborn and irreverent young cop, his passionate commitment to a lost cause, his flair for following a scent, his impatience with plodding hacks and contempt for the "empty suits" behind imposing desks. He would not learn to keep his head down, and was perpetually baffled by so many others who did. Were they blind, buffaloed, bent, or what? "They just don't *want* this case. They'll be happy to get Enzo off the street and close this case, and we don't find out *nothing*. It fucking appalls me! I swear to Christ I don't understand it!" he raged into his tape recorder.

What Le Vien had turned up, as a dogged, street-smart detective, would not begin to come out of federal computers for another decade. The names of Sicilian operatives manning several of Palermo's strategic heroin outposts—Emmanuele Adamita, Salvatore Rina, the Cherry Hill Gambino brothers, and Salvatore Catalano in Brooklyn, Nick Rizzuto in Canada, the Cuntreras in Venezuela—figured prominently in Le Vien's reports to all government agencies.

In spite of everything known about them, the Napoli brothers themselves, made in Villabate, Sicily, are still in federal files as members of the American Gambino Family. In fact, all three are John Gambino's people, exalted in rank and still at large.

Gaetano Napoli, the youngest and seemingly least important, actually played host to John and Giuseppe Gambino for a weekend at New Jersey's Playboy Hotel in 1975. He was photographed sitting at the head of their table, and he picked up their weekend tab.[1] That was about as high as a Sicilian Man of Honor could get.

Antonino Napoli has been part of John Gambino's innermost circle in New York since the 1960s. The two went on to Caracas around the same time in the early 1970s and became business partners of the Cuntrera Family in its proliferating enterprises there.

Enzo Napoli was checking in almost daily with John Gambino in 1976 and 1977, the years of Operation Earn. Le Vien, dining with Enzo at the Ritz or the "21," would often tail him to John Gambino's home in Bensonhurst afterward. He saw them together dozens of times at the Mille Luci, Enzo's own café on 18th Avenue—the terminal for Luigi Ronsisvalle's massive heroin deliveries from Knickerbocker Avenue.

Enzo was still checking in with John and Giuseppe Gambino in December 1988, when the FBI raided the Cafe Giardino. He was always dropping by there during the bureau's investigation, and was picked up on tape in a couple of interesting conversations. In the summer of 1988, for instance, he was overheard complaining to Giuseppe Gambino and one Francesco Inzerillo (a nephew of the late Salvatore Inzerillo). Somebody had owed him $150,000 for too long, it appeared. "Vincenzo, you *like* him," remarked Inzerillo reprovingly. "Some people would have done better to make certain other people cry, instead of crying themselves. . . . You have a good heart. . . . So we'll call him. My heart isn't like yours. I'm bad. I'll tell him what he has to be told."[2]

Enzo's kind heart might have brought Le Vien face to face with the Gambino brothers and their crowd in 1976, circumstances permitting. Increasingly fond of his bent millionaire friend "Tommy Russo," he invited Le Vien to meet some of "his people" on 18th Avenue. For a detective whose face was familiar to half the wise guys in Brooklyn, this was a freezing prospect.

"I nearly got myself whacked trying to get out of it," Doug noted in his tape diary. "He wants me to meet some people. I say, 'Why not just us two?' He gives me a look. I'm telling ya', this guy has a frightening face. Only he made a mistake; he never asked me who my mother was and who my grandmother was." Le Vien managed to elude Enzo's invitation in the one way likely to impress his target. As Enzo was leaving an East Side restaurant, he saw Tommy Russo shove a terrified black man to the sidewalk, raise a .22 with a silencer, fire (a blank), and bundle a limp body (an agent's) into the trunk of his Mercedes. Enzo never spoke of it, but his faith was renewed.

Wary of meeting Napoli's people in the flesh, Le Vien took to drawing labyrinthine charts of their interlocking names, relationships, and known habits, which amounted to a family album of the Gambino brothers' transatlantic superclan. Had Le Vien been allowed to pursue his leads to Europe, he might have brought the clan into better focus. But he never got that far.

Operation Earn was barely half a year old when the DEA arrested Enzo Napoli for importing a single kilo of heroin from Thailand. DEA agents had worked the case for months, tapping phones, tailing accomplices, and infiltrating an undercover agent as Enzo's courier. By March 1977, they knew that his man in Bangkok, Sicilian-born Freddy Porcello, "was capable of importing ten kilos of pure Asian heroin into the U.S. every fifteen days."[3]

Surveillance had shown that the single kilo was only a sample—that Napoli was going to be receiving and passing on a quarter of a ton of heroin a year. "Listen, it's only once a month," he was overheard telling his man from Milan. He might have led narcotics agents to those who would be moving the heroin on from there in America, but he was arrested instead.[4] Out on bail for another year, Napoli gave Le Vien a chance to look further, across the Atlantic. Credit card charges and toll calls showed that Enzo had made at least six trips to Europe previous to his drug arrest; and he was often on the phone to two of Europe's biggest heroin dealers.[5]

The number he called in Munich belonged to Agostino Flenda, "the Prince." The DEA had been investigating Flenda since 1975, and considered him "a major Sicilian underworld figure in Munich." Its Bonn agent maintained that Flenda was "the Cosa Nostra representative in Munich, with direct contact to Cosa Nostra headquarters in New York." Actually, Flenda was the *Sicilian* Cosa Nostra's representative in Munich; and he was working in tandem with a well-known Turkish Mafia trafficker there, Ertem Tegmen.[6]

DEA agents, apparently unaware of the connection, were still investigating Flenda when they arrested Enzo Napoli in May 1977. As it happened, Napoli was also telephoning frequently at the time to the people in Sicily who gave people like Flenda their orders.

His calls had been traced to one Salvatore Montalto, a native of Villabate residing in Palermo. Upon receiving Enzo's calls from New York, Montalto would call Enzo's brother Antonino in Caracas, who would call a cutout in Miami, who would call Enzo in New York.[7]

The Italian police did not carry the matter further because they didn't know who Salvatore Montalto was in 1977. They thought he was a respectable merchant in heating fuels. He turned out later to be the boss of Villabate, a member of the Mafia's Cupola, a major drug trafficker, and the late Salvatore Inzerillo's chief lieutenant. (He was sentenced to life imprisonment in Palermo's maxitrial.)

These were Enzo Napoli's people at home.

oⵔo

Operation Earn ended on April 12, 1978, when the Strike Force decided to pull Enzo in as he sold Le Vien another gun. He was still out on bail for the single-kilo drug charge. Now, in lieu of half a million dollars' bail, he was taken off the street.

Most of the Strike Force turned out to watch "Tommy Russo" make his final buy from the target, in the parking lot of an airport hotel near Kennedy Airport, whereupon both of them were arrested. The *New York Daily News* gave the story a brief flutter. Napoli was described as "an international broker for New York's five Families," whose arrest "would be a major break in cracking an international smuggling ring for fake money, stolen art, drugs and weapons."

But there were no major breaks, no rings cracked, no other charges brought, no further investigation of Napoli's singular connections and criminal career. He pleaded guilty, avoiding all the pitfalls of a courtroom hearing. Sentenced to thirteen years for the guns and kilo of heroin both, he was paroled and back on the street in four.

For all their fifty-five taped conversations—the coded signals exchanged from public phone booths, the talk of money in eight digits, the drinks at the Plaza and dinners at the Palace, the cruise up the Hudson and plans for a yachting expedition down the coast to Miami and Caracas—Le Vien never did buy anything but guns from Enzo. The sixth and last brought the sum of his purchases to $6,500. His cover was still intact when he walked into a small gray room at the Brooklyn head-quarters of the Strike Force, for an awkward meeting with Enzo. "Mr. Napoli, I am not who you think I am. I am Detective Douglas Le Vien of the New York Police Department," he said. Enzo, ashen, responded after a long silence, "You done a good job."

Le Vien's instructions were to turn Enzo if he could, but he was sure he couldn't, and he didn't. Enzo put out a contract on him just a few weeks later, or so an informant said. The tip was hard to believe because the American Mafia does not kill cops as a rule. "I have never heard of an alleged organized crime figure killing a cop. It's unprecedented," declared Edward McDonald, chief of the Organized Crime Strike Force in Brooklyn, when one of his undercover agents was shot some years later. "This is a mistake the mob doesn't tolerate. The killers who got away will be found all right—dead," predicted an aide.[8]

The last thing the American Mafia wanted was a head-on collision with the law. Where courtship and corruption were not enough to keep the peace, some kind of live-and-let-live balance could still be struck: an understanding tacitly accepted by both sides.

"He made the mistake; shame on *him,"* was how Le Vien saw the situation at the time. How a made Mafioso from Sicily might see it was something else. The Sicilian Mafia did kill cops, part of a truculent posture that seemed to hold even the American Mafia transfixed. "They're shit-scared of the 'siggies,' " said Le Vien when he was older and wiser.

It was more than likely that Enzo did put out a contract on Le Vien; the "Tommy Russo" he had trusted was now walking around with mortally dangerous knowledge of Enzo's people. At the time, however, the New York police had no idea of that. They simply reacted to the fact that Enzo Napoli had turned out to be a "siggy"—a "zip," a "geep," therefore unpredictable if not uncontrollable.

Over Le Vien's strenuous protests, he became the only cop ever taken into the Federal Witness Protection Program. Agents armed with machine guns blocked off the street and helicopters circled overhead as Le Vien, his wife, and two young sons were hustled out of their Brooklyn home and sent into hiding for the next six months. Then one day Le Vien's commanding officer, Lieutenant Joseph Harding, went to the Great Western Beef Restaurant for a sit-down with Big Paul Castellano. Flanked by his attorney, the most powerful Mafia boss in America would not talk, but he listened. Lieutenant Harding told him that the

New York Police Department would not stand for a hit. They would pick up every gambling game, move into the social clubs, grab the shylocks—in short, make life hell for the Mob.

Castellano would not answer directly. He simply turned to his attorney and said: "I know Enzo and his brother Nino. I have nothing but ill respect for both." He would never have said that if the Napoli brothers had been his. In the Mafia, respect is all.

Not long afterward, Le Vien received a letter from the Manhattan Correctional Center, where Enzo was lodged. It hung framed on Le Vien's wall in Washington, D.C., when he went to work years later for the President's Commission on Organized Crime. Enzo wanted to make it clear that he had no hard feelings. He admired people who did their job diligently, as Le Vien did, "and manipulated me to your advantage." In the few years of their relationship, he wrote, he himself had kept his word. He concluded (the italics are his): *"I as a man, I tell you, I carry no grudge. . . . If I was in your predicament, I would have done the same."*

Chronology

1904:   Cascio Ferro becomes first *capo di tutti capi*

1927–29: Mussolini's war against the Sicilian Mafia

1931:   Lucky Luciano modernizes the Mafia in America

1946:   Lucky Luciano deported to Italy

1951:   Kefauver hearings

1957:   Palermo summit, heroin franchise decided upon, Sicilian Commission (Cupola) formed, Greco first president

Apalachin (New York) meeting ratifies heroin franchise

1962:   Lucky Luciano dies

1963:   Greco, Leggio, and Buscetta engage in shooting war with the La Barberas

Ciaculli bomb, Cupola disbanded, Sicilian Mafia fans out into the world, Judge Terranova begins investigation

McClellan hearings

1964:   Leggio arrested for the first time

1967:   Trial of 114 and other big Mafia trial

1968:   Casamento opens Eagle Cheese in U.S.

1972:   Corsican drug ring busted in Brazil, Buscetta arrested and deported to Italy

1974:   Leggio sent to jail

       Sicilian Mafia forms pact with the Camorra

1975:   Sicilian Mafia forms pact with Turks

1976:   Operation Earn (Le Vien and Enzo Napoli) begins

1977:   Pete Licata shot, Catalano takes over Knickerbocker Avenue

       Sicilian Mafia inaugurates heroin pipeline to U.S.

1979:   Ronsisvalle turns himself in

       Sindona kidnapped

       Galante shot, Catalano takes over Bonanno Family

1980:   Pizza investigation begins

       Judge Palermo begins arms-drug investigation in Trento

       Adamita 40-kilo heroin case

1981:   Bontate killed

1981–83: Great Mafia War

1982:   Dalla Chiesa killed

       Cassarà submits seminal report, "Greco + 161"

       Spatola trial in Palermo, 79 Mafiosi accused

1983:   Buscetta arrested in Brazil

1984:   Buscetta extradited to Italy, talks

1985:   Pizza trial begins in New York

1986:   Maxitrial begins in Palermo

       Italy's Supreme Court begins to overturn Mafia convictions

1988:   Operation Iron Tower (Cherry Hill Gambinos)

       Maxitrial sentence

       Italy's anti-Mafia pool finished

The Dead
(a partial list)

DISTINGUISHED CADAVERS

ANTIOCHIA, ROBERTO: detective, Squadra Mobile, Palermo, August 6, 1985

BASILE, EMMANUELE: Carabinieri captain, Monreale, May 5, 1980

CACCIA, BRUNO: state prosecutor, Torino, June 27, 1983

CASSARÀ, ANTONINO: assistant chief, Squadra Mobile, Palermo, August 6, 1985

CHINNICI, ROCCO: judge, Palermo, July 29, 1983

CIACCIO MONTALTO, GIANGIACOMO: judge, Trapani, January 25, 1983

COSTA, GAETANO: state prosecutor, Palermo, August 6, 1980

DALLA CHIESA, CARLO ALBERTO: prefect, Palermo, September 3, 1982

FAVA, GIUSEPPE: journalist, Catania, January 5, 1984

GIALLOMBARDI, CARMELO: agent, Carabinieri, Altavilla, December 12, 1988

GIULIANO, BORIS: chief, Squadra Mobile, Palermo, July 29, 1979

IEVOLELLA, VITO: inspector, Carabinieri, Palermo, September 10, 1981

INSALACO, GIUSEPPE: former mayor, Palermo, January 12, 1988

LA TORRE, PIO: Communist party leader, Sicily, April 30, 1982

MANCUSO, LENIN: agent, Squadra Mobile, Palermo, September 25, 1979

MATTARELLA, PIERSANTO: president, Sicilian Region, January 6, 1980

MONDO, NATALE: detective, Squadra Mobile, Palermo, January 14, 1988
MONTANA, GIUSEPPE: inspector, Squadra Mobile, Palermo, July 28, 1985
REINA, MICHELE: secretary, Christian Democrats, Palermo, March 9, 1979
ROSTAGNO, MAURO: journalist, Trapani, August 1, 1988
RUSSO, GIUSEPPE: Carabinieri colonel, Ficuzza, August 20, 1977
SAETTA, ANTONINO: judge, Caltanissetta, August 1, 1988
TERRANOVA, CESARE: judge, Palermo, September 25, 1979
ZUCCHETTO, CALOGERO: detective, Squadra Mobile, Palermo, November 14, 1982

MAFIA LOSERS

ALONGI, SEBASTIANO: boss of Prizzi, white death (no body found), September 9, 1983
BADALAMENTI, ANTONINO: shot, *lupara* (shotgun), August 19, 1981
BONTATE, STEFANO: shot, Kalashnikov, April 23, 1981
BOSIO, SEBASTIANO: shot, *lupara*, November 6, 1981
BUCCELLATO, ANTONINO: shot, *lupara,* Castellammare del Golfo, September 30, 1981
BUSCEMI, RODOLFO: strangled, dumped in harbor, 1982
BUSCETTA, ANTONIO: white death, September 11, 1982
BUSCETTA, BENEDETTO: white death, September 11, 1982
CARUANA, LEONARDO: shot, Palermo, September 2, 1981
CHIAZZESE, FILIPPO: white death, June 8, 1981
D'AGOSTINO, EMMANUELE: white death, May 28, 1981
D'AGOSTINO, IGNAZIO: *lupara*, January 11, 1982
DI CRISTINA, GIUSEPPE: boss of Riesi, shot, May 30, 1978
DI FRANCO, CARLO: white death, May 26, 1981
DI GREGORIO, SALVATORE: white death, January 4, 1982
DI MAGGIO, CALOGERO: white death, May 25, 1981
FALLUCCA, GIOVANNI: strangled, dissolved in acid, 1982
FEDERICO, ANGELO: white death, May 26, 1981
FEDERICO, SALVATORE: white death, May 26, 1981
FERLITO, ALFIO: shot, Kalashnikov, Catania, June 16, 1982
GALLINA, STEFANO: shot, *lupara,* Palermo, October 1, 1981
GNOFFO, IGNAZIO: boss of Palermo-Centro, white death, June 15, 1981
GRADO, ANTONINO: white death, October 14, 1981
GRADO, ANTONINO: shot, *lupara*, January 11, 1982
GRAVIANO, GIUSEPPE: shot, dumped in harbor, 1982
IMPASTATO, GIACOMO: shot, *lupara,* January 15, 1982
IMPASTATO, LUIGI: shot, *lupara,* Palermo, September 22, 1981
INZERILLO, GIUSEPPE: white death, July 31, 1981
INZERILLO, PIETRO: shot, in U.S., January 15, 1982

INZERILLO, SALVATORE: shot, Kalashnikov, May 11, 1981

INZERILLO, SANTO: white death, May 25, 1981

LO JACONO, CARMELO: strangled, dissolved in acid, 1982

LO PRESTI, IGNAZIO: white death, August 1982

LO VERSO, MAURIZIO: strangled, dissolved in acid, 1982

MAFARA, FRANCESCO: white death, October 14, 1981

MAFARA, GIOVANNI: shot, *lupara,* Palermo, October 14, 1981

MAMOLA, EMMANUELE: shot, *lupara,* Palermo, October 5, 1981

MANDALA, FRANCO: shot, *lupara,* April 5, 1982

MANDALA, PIETRO: shot, *lupara,* Palermo, October 3, 1981

MARCHESE, PIETRO: stabbed, in prison, February 25, 1982

MARSALA, MARIANO: boss of Vicari, white death, February 1983

MIGLIORE, ANTONIO: strangled, dumped in harbor, 1982

MISURACA, CALOGERO: shot, *lupara,* Palermo, October 9, 1981

PANNO, GIUSEPPE: boss of Casteldaccia, white death, March 11, 1981

PECORELLA, STEFANO: white death, July 31, 1981

PIOMBINO, NICOLO: shot, *lupara,* January 26, 1982

RICCOBONO, ROSARIO: boss of Partanna, white death, November 1982

RICCOBONO, VITO: beheaded, left in parked car, 1982

RIMI, VINCENZO: shot, *lupara,* Alcamo, 1981

RIZZUTO, MICHELE: strangled, dumped in harbor, 1982

ROMANO, GIUSEPPE: shot, dumped in car trunk, U.S., February 8, 1983

RUGNETTA, ANTONIO: strangled, dumped in harbor, 1982

SETTECASE, GIUSEPPE: shot, *lupara,* Agrigento, March 23, 1981

SEVERINO, SALVATORE: white death, Palermo, May 29, 1981

SEVERINO, VINCENZO: white death, Palermo, May 29, 1981

SPICA, ANTONIO: shot, in Milan, February 2, 1982

SOLLENA, MATTEO: shot, dumped in car trunk, U.S., November 19, 1983

SOLLENA, SALVATORE: shot, dumped in car trunk, U.S., November 10, 1983

SORCI, NINO: boss of Villagrazia, shot, *lupara,* April 12, 1983

TERESI, "MIMMO": shot, fed to pigs, 1982

TRAMONTANA, GIUSEPPE: shot, dumped in car trunk, U.S., February 8, 1983

VITALE, LEONARDO: shot, *lupara,* Palermo, December 2, 1984

Notes

PROLOGUE

1. Excerpts from the taped dinner conversation at the Palace Restaurant, January 13, 1977.
2. The fact that Vincenzo Napoli was made by the Villabate *cosca* was confirmed to Doug Le Vien by Luigi Ronsisvalle. See chapter 10.
3. These were the destinations Napoli charged on his own American Express credit card. Where he may have gone on other people's credit cards is not known.
4. Taped phone conversation, April 1974, Public Morals Division, New York Police Department.
5. The Eastern District represents the U.S. Department of Justice in Brooklyn, Queens, Staten Island, and Long Island.
6. Memo to Eastern District Strike Force from Commanding Officer, Central Gambling Unit, NYPD, November 4, 1976.
7. Secret Service case cited in Department of Justice file on Vincenzo Napoli, January 25, 1975, on sale of Treasury notes. Justice Department printout, January 25, 1977. INS (Immigration and Naturalization Service): alien-smuggling reports cited in New York State Police Report, August 18, 1970. Customs: Report by Steve Rogers, February 10, 1977. BNDD (Narcotics Bureau) on Enzo Napoli, October 30, 1970. Miami Police file: Enzo Napoli was arrested, but not arraigned, for passing stolen checks in August 1976; Luigi Ronsisvalle was arrested with him and jailed briefly. FBI: all three Napoli brothers were suspected of "handling the smuggling of illegal aliens into New York"; informant cited in FBI Report, November 5, 1973. Assorted police

reports cited in Report of NYPD, Special Forces, September 8, 1975: Vincenzo Napoli was believed to be involved in "loansharking, fraud, sale of handguns, sale of stolen merchandise, robberies." Association of all three Napoli brothers with Paul Castellano and Gambino Family *consigliere* Joe N. Gallo cited in NYPD Report, December 4, 1976. New York Police Intelligence Report, August 5, 1976.

8. The Rubens and Terborch were recovered in the Abscam case.

9. *New York Times,* April 12, 1977; *Time,* April 18, 1977.

10. U.S. Attorney Tom Puccio, incoming head of the Eastern District, had one good reason to stall. An FBI agent was under investigation at the time for selling information to the Mafia. The first bureau agent ever found to be bent, he pleaded guilty and was sentenced to a year and a day in prison. The FBI's report on the rifle was inconclusive.

11. Napoli's accomplices in Miami were Luigi Ronsisvalle and Giuseppe Mirabile, both *picciotti* in the Sicilian Mafia.

12. *New York Times,* January 16, 1977; *New York Daily News,* January 26, 1977.

13. The First National City Bank in Staten Island was swindled out of the money in April 1976 by Enzo Napoli and another Italian named Frank Resto. After testifying before a grand jury, Resto was found hanging on a doornail in his New York apartment. As Le Vien discovered a year later, customs had followed the trail to St. George, Grenada, where Resto and Napoli had laundered most of the Staten Island loot through their own phony bank, the First National City Bank and Trust Company, at 11 Halifax Street. "Frank Resto and Riccardo LNU [last name unknown] own this bank," customs agent Steve Rogers reported. " 'Riccardo' is Vincent Napoli, a mover in stolen Treasury notes." Report by Steve Rogers, February 10, 1977.

14. *New York Daily News,* October 5, 1977. Following Enzo Napoli's arrest on heroin charges in 1978, he was interrogated by the FBI and U.S. Secret Service on counterfeiting, bank fraud, embezzlement, and interstate dealings in stolen checks. But he was not charged on any of these counts.

15. The diamonds were stolen by Luigi Ronsisvalle and Giuseppe Mirabile, on Enzo Napoli's instructions, as Ronsisvalle later confirmed (see chapter 10). They were taken from Henry Grosbard's, on West 47th Street.

16. DEA Reports, March 9 and April 18, 1977.

1. THE VIEW FROM PALERMO

1. The expert was Washington agent Frank Storey, quoted in *U.S. News and World Report,* April 11, 1988. The spokesman was William Carter, quoted in the *Corriere della Sera* (Milan), April 1, 1988. See chapter 20.

2. The $12 billion estimate for retail U.S. heroin sales is based on an average $20 per fix, an average three fixes daily for confirmed addicts, and an official figure of 500,000 confirmed addicts. U.S. Attorney Rudolph Giuliani of New York's Southern District gave me the $20 billion estimate in 1986. The overall narcotics trade figure comes from the President's Commission on Organized Crime, "America's Habit: Drug Abuse, Drug Trafficking, and Organized Crime," and from the UN Conference on Narcotics, as reported by RAI (Italian TV), May 19, 1989. The Italian figure was issued by Italy's Higher Magistrates' Council on January 31, 1989. The estimate of $110 billion generated by narcotics in the United States was given to me by the DEA's New York office in March 1986. Previous estimates cited by Francis Mullen, head of the DEA, to the Senate Judiciary Committee, February 23, 1983, put the figure at $79 billion.

These and practically all similar figures on narcotics consumption and profits are approximate at best. Few narcotics experts believe, for instance, that statistics are accurate on the American heroin addict population and the total amount of heroin entering the country annually. Educated guesses tend to double the official estimates.

3. Statement by the FBI's then director, Judge William Webster, to the U.N.'s Seventh World Congress on Crime, August 27, 1987. Profit figures in the dossier *Illecito* by the Italian governmental research institute Censis, April 4, 1985, put the estimated return on investment at 1,667 percent.

4. Interview with Frank Panessa, DEA, Rome, August 1988. Interview with Floyd Clark, deputy director of the FBI's Criminal Investigation Division in Washington, and Anthony Daniels, inspector–deputy assistant director of the same division, March 14, 1989.

5. Unofficial memorandum given to me by the State Department's Bureau of International Narcotic Matters, March 1989.

6. Estimate by Italian Ministry of the Interior Central Anti-Narcotics Service, August 10, 1988. Reported in *Corriere della Sera* (Milan) of that date. Italy's 1988 OD figures from General Sotgiu, head of the Interior Ministry's Anti-Narcotics Service.

7. *Time,* August 1, 1988.

8. British figures from my interview with Colin Hewett, Scotland Yard's National Drugs Intelligence coordinator, February 1987. French figure from International Committee for the Struggle Against Drug Abuse, reported in State Department cable from U.S. embassy, Paris, March 1988.

9. The worldwide heroin addict population was set at 2.5 million and rising in 1987 by the DEA (interview with Tom Angioletti, then head of DEA's Rome bureau). Figures for European addiction from the U.S. State Department's Bureau of International Narcotics Matters, April 24, 1988. European heroin seizures for 1984 and 1985 are given in the National Narcotics Intelligence Consumers' Committee Report for 1985–86. Heroin seizure figures for 1987 from Interpol Bulletin *Quest,* second and third trimesters 1987. Heroin seizure figures in United States for 1987 from DEA Rome office. The DEA estimates that a kilo of 95 percent pure heroin makes 45,000 fixes at 5 percent.

10. DEA Director Francis Mullen's statement to a U.S. Senate committee, *New York Times,* July 4, 1983: "Officials now believe that organized crime Families in New York are importing 85% of the heroin entering the United States." In 1983, no public authority was yet aware of the fact that the direct heroin importers were not New York's Mafia Families, but the Sicilian Mafia, given the franchise by its American counterparts. William Sessions' Report to the Committee on Governmental Affairs, Permanent Subcommittee on Investigations, U.S. Senate, April 11, 1988.

11. Sessions' Report to the Committee on Governmental Affairs, Permanent Subcommittee on Investigations, U.S. Senate, April 11, 1988. According to the then attorney general William French Smith, the Sicilian Mafia had supplied "perhaps 80% of all the heroin entering the northeastern United States." See "The Impact: Organized Crime Today," President's Commission on Organized Crime, p. 57. "Ordinanza di Rinvio a Giudizio" (Indictment), maxitrial of 464 alleged Sicilian Mafiosi, cited in Violante, La Mafia dell' eroina.

12. Interview with Frank Storey, the FBI's top expert on organized crime, April 28, 1988.

13. Interview with Mike Spataro, the DEA's New York expert in this field, April 25, 1988. "The Chinese don't like to deal with blacks; they get ripped off. They prefer dealing with the Sicilians," he said. This was confirmed in my interview with Jules Buonavolonta, the FBI's Organized Crime supervisor in New York, April 19, 1988. Confirmed to me also by Louis Freeh, assistant U.S. attorney in New York's Southern District, who led the investigation in the 1985 Pizza Connection case. I was told essentially the same thing by the FBI's Frank Storey in Washington.

14. Interview with DEA Rome director Frank Panessa, January 30, 1989.

15. National Narcotics Intelligence Consumers' Committee Report, 1985–86. The tripling rate in Europe cited in *Time,* August 1, 1988.

16. Interview with Mona Ewell, DEA intelligence analyst. See chapter 7.

17. Interview with the DEA's agent in Caracas, October 1987. His estimate is based on seizures of eight tons of cocaine emanating from Venezuela that year. The standard calculation—admittedly rough—is that seizures represent 10 percent of the traffic.

18. The DISIP study, made in 1982, was never published, and some of the most interesting material it contained seemed to have disappeared. The contents were revealed in Parliament in 1984 by Deputies Carlos Tablante and Vladimir Gessen, of the Anti-Mafia Commission, who had consigned the key documents to DISIP. See *El Diario de Caracas,* December 12, 1984.

The *El Diario* article on the Mafia's cocaine role, dated October 13, 1985, was part of a well-researched series by Rodolfo Schmidt on the Sicilian Mafia in Venezuela. Vladimir Gessen, then head of the Parliamentary Anti-Narcotics Commission, confirmed the essential facts in an interview with me in Caracas, October 1987. The figure cited for the Sicilian's share of the traffic was 60 percent.

19. Interview, in New York, April 12, 1988.

20. Estimate in the Stewart-Clark Report to an Investigating Committee of the European Parliament, 1986, cited in Violante, *La Mafia dell'eroina,* p. 19.

21. Arlacchi, *La Mafia imprenditrice;* Hess, *Mafia.*

22. Gambino, *Blood of My Blood.*

23. Peterson, *The Mob,* p. 444.

24. *New York Times,* December 18, 1985.

25. Ianni and Reuss-Ianni, *The Crime Society,* p. 99.

26. Cressey, *Theft of the Nation,* pp. 19, 181–82.

27. Ianni and Reuss-Ianni, *The Crime Society,* includes contributions by several well-known commentators, including Daniel Bell.

28. Peterson, *The Mob,* p. 440.

29. Interview with the FBI's Floyd Clark, March 14, 1989.

30. *The Economist* (London), quoted in *Giornale di Sicilia* (Palermo), April 2, 1988. The $30 billion figure was given by the Guardia di Finanza to the Parliamentary Anti-Mafia Commission, May 4, 1989.

31. The Sicilian Mafia income estimate was made by the Guardia di Finanza, reported in the *Corriere della Sera* (Milan), October 1, 1983. Pino Arlacchi, noted Italian crime analyst, gave me the comparative estimate for the Sicilian regional government budget.

32. U.S. Mafia size from "The Impact: Organized Crime Today," p. 36. Sicilian Mafia membership figure by Emanuele De Francesco, former head of the Italian Ministry of the Interior's Anti-Mafia Commission.

33. Anastasia's membership racket was reported by Joe Valachi; see Maas, *The Valachi Papers,* p. 256. The membership figures are reported respectively by the President's Commission on Organized Crime ("The Impact: Organized Crime Today") and the Italian Ministry of the Interior's Anti-Mafia Commission.

34. Stajano, *Mafia: L'atto d'accusa,* pp. 40, 72.

35. Falzone, *Storia della Mafia,* pp. 76–115.

36. This derivation is suggested by Giuseppe Guido Loschiavo, a highly esteemed Sicilian magistrate and author, in his book *Cento anni di Mafia.* It is cited by many other authors, including Gaetano Falzone, Rosario Poma, and Enzo Perrone. In *Blood of My Blood,* Richard Gambino refers to the "squadre della Mafia" on p. 296.

37. Falzone, *Storia della Mafia,* p. 126; Servadio, *Mafioso,* p. 19; Hess, *Mafia,* pp. 5–6.

38. Poma and Perrone, *La Mafia,* p. 6; Hess, *Mafia,* p. 5; Servadio, *Mafioso,* p. 23.

39. Petacco, *Joe Petrosino,* p. 119.

40. Giuseppe Guido Loschiavo, noted historian, cited in Poma and Perrone, *La Mafia,* p. 50.

41. Giuseppe Pitrè, *Usi e costumi, credenze e preguidizi del popolo siciliano* (Palermo: Clausen, 1889).

42. The former curator is Gaetano Falzone, an esteemed Sicilian historian. His book *Storia della Mafia* is full of valuable information.

43. Hess, *Mafia,* pp. 70–71; Servadio, *Mafioso,* pp. 55–59.

44. Americans had been hearing of the Black Hand since 1890, when a hysterical mob lynched eleven Sicilians in New Orleans. The victims had just been acquitted on charges of murdering the city's police chief, Dave Hennesey. The facts were obscure— Hennesey was not a saint's shin, as Italians say—but the city's large Sicilian colony was certainly infested with Mafiosi from the Old Country.

45. Petacco, *Joe Petrosino,* p. 135.

46. For a fuller account of Cascio Ferro's career in New York, see Petacco, *Joe Petrosino.* This reference is on p. 75.

47. Ibid., pp. 218–25; Pantaleone, *Mafia e dròga,* p. 24. Petrosino was murdered on March 12, 1909.

48. Servadio, *Mafioso,* p. 74.

49. Duggan, *La Mafia durante il Fascismo.*

50. Smith, *Storia della Sicilia medievale e moderna,* p. 701; Duggan, *La Mafia durante il Fascismo.*

51. Pantaleone, *Mafia e politica,* p. 58.

52. Barzini, *The Italians,* pp. 345–46.

53. Gosch and Hammer, *The Last Testament of Lucky Luciano,* p. 98.

54. Ibid., p. 101.

55. The bloody conflict between Joe Masseria of Trapani and Salvatore Maranzano of Castellammare del Golfo became known as New York's "Castellammarese War." For Lansky quote, see Gosch and Hammer, *The Last Testament of Lucky Luciano,* pp. 115, 146; *The Autobiography of Joseph Bonanno,* p. 150.

56. The books remained closed from 1931 until 1954: McClellan Committee Report, March 4, 1965, p. 13.

2. Don Luciano Leggio, the Winner

1. The name "Leggio" is often and mistakenly spelled "Liggio" in the press.

2. Told to me by Judge Falcone of Palermo. He estimates that some six hundred were killed in Palermo and its outlying province alone, and another four hundred in Mafia-infested areas such as Trapani, Agrigento, and Catania.

3. "During World War II there was a lot of hocus-pocus about allegedly valuable services that Luciano, then a convict, was supposed to have furnished the military authorities in connection with plans for the invasion of his native Sicily. We dug into this and obtained a number of conflicting stories," Senator Kefauver wrote.

4. Probably the most authoritative account of the Allied landing in Sicily may be found in a recent voluminous and heavily documented history of Sicily by the noted Sicilian historian Francesco Renda. His complete work is entitled *Storia della Sicilia dal 1860 al 1970.* Volume 3 covers the Allied landing, under the title *Dall'occupazione militare alleata al centro sinistra.*

Describing the Allied military operation in general, Professor Renda shows clearly that its conception and outcome depended on many more complex factors than a simple under-the-table deal with Mafia bosses. Among other things, he writes: "The Anglo-American victory was not as complete as had been hoped, nor was it carried out without difficulty. . . . The invasion was anything but a pushover . . . Italian and German resistance was stronger than expected" (pp. 19–20).

"What determined the behavior of Italian troops and the civilian population was [primarily] the balance of strategic-political forces. It was impossible, in those circumstances, that the Allies would not win, and people still in possession of their faculties to think and decide with their own heads drew the necessary conclusions" (p. 25). "People wanted peace, and the only way of getting it was the arrival of the Allies."

Referring specifically to the tale of Lucky Luciano's yellow silk kerchief, Professor Renda notes: "The mechanism of Mafioso pollution of the island administration and the Allied Military Government was self-propelling in an altogether spontaneous way, also because it met no obstacles on the part of various Civil Affairs officers. There is no proof, and no motive to suppose a kind of pre-determined and intentional plot, involving occupation authorities at high and low levels, to consign Sicily into the hands of the Mafia."

For other references, see Servadio, *Mafioso:* "The alleged role of some Cosa Nostra criminals and Sicilian *cosche* in the war effort is and will always be controversial. There are several versions, many of which come from the same sources (like Moses Polakoff, Lucky Luciano's lawyer, who told conflicting stories). The truth is probably somewhere in the middle. . . .

"While I strongly doubt that there were ever big deals between American officials and gangsters, it is more than possible that promises and exchanges of favours happened somewhere in the middle ranks" (pp. 82–83).

As for Lucky Luciano's own role, Servadio writes: "Lucky Luciano had been too long in prison by then to be able to control the New York 'families,' and everybody was out of touch with Sicily because of the Fascist regime. Calogero Vizzini had no overall power, since Mori's operation had actually succeeded in disconnecting the Sicilian underworld network. . . . He became a prominent figure only after becoming Mayor of Villalba."

5. Renda, *Storia della Sicilia dal 1860 al 1970,* vol. 3.

6. Luciano Leggio's testimony in Palermo's maxitrial; *Giornale di Sicilia* (Palermo), May 25, 1986.

7. Pantaleone, *Mafia e politica;* Nese, *Nel segno della Mafia,* p. 16.

8. Nese, *Nel segno della Mafia,* p. 16.

9. Ibid., p. 21.

10. This in-between verdict, known as the Scotch Verdict, was abolished under a new Italian judicial code in 1988.

11. Nese, *Nel segno della Mafia,* p. 22. Nese's excellent book on Leggio relies for much of its documentation on reports of Italy's Parliamentary Anti-Mafia Commission.

12. Report of Carabinieri general Amedeo Branca, brigade commander in Sicily, October 9, 1946.

13. Fava, *Processo alla Sicilia,* p. 194.

14. Ibid.

15. Nese, *Nel segno della Mafia,* p. 66; Pantaleone, *Mafia e politica,* pp. 127–28.

16. Pantaleone, *Mafia e politica,* p. 120; Sterling, "Portrait of a Mafia Killer"; Nese, *Nel segno della Mafia,* pp. 34–42; Poma and Perrone, *La Mafia.*

17. Sterling, "Portrait of a Mafia Killer"; Nese, *Nel segno della Mafia,* p. 34; Poma and Perrone, *La Mafia,* p. 216.

18. "Relazione sull'Indagine Riguardante Casi di Singoli Mafiosi," Italian Parliamentary Anti-Mafia Commission.

19. Ibid.

20. Leggio's appearance before the Cupola is reported in the texts of Tommaso Buscetta's interrogation by Judge Giovanni Falcone of Palermo, September 1984.

21. Nese, *Nel segno della Mafia,* p. 79.

22. The Land Reform Bill limited maximum holdings to two hundred hectares, or five hundred acres.

23. *La Repubblica* (Rome), April 17, 1987.

24. Hess, *Mafia,* p. 212.

25. Mori, *Con la Mafia,* pp. 128–29, cited in Duggan, *La Mafia durante il Fascismo,* p. 20. Trapani had 700 homicides a year by 1924, Palermo 278.

26. Poma and Perrone, *La Mafia,* p. 61. There were two thousand known homicides and disappearances in Sicily's four western provinces between 1944 and 1962.

27. The visitor was the journalist and editor Indro Montanelli, who told this to me.

28. The judge was Cesare Terranova, assassinated in 1979. See chapter 8.

29. Report by Carabinieri officer Mario Malausa, cited in "Relazione sull'Indagine Riguardante Casi di Singoli Mafiosi," Parliamentary Anti-Mafia Commission, quoted in Sterling, "Portrait of a Mafia Killer."

30. Fava, *Processo alla Mafia,* p. 196.

31. Ibid., pp. 196–97.

32. *Giornale di Sicilia* (Palermo), August 3, 1986.

33. Pantaleone, *Anti-Mafia, occasione mancata,* p. 113.

34. Fava, *Processo alla Mafia,* p. 194.

35. Ibid., p. 196.

36. Ibid., p. 25. The permits were issued between 1959 and 1963.

37. Pantaleone, *Anti-Mafia, occasione mancata,* p. 19. Anti-Mafia Commission Report to Parliament, July 8, 1965. The commission had begun its investigation in 1963.

3. Don Tommaso Buscetta, the Last of the Big Losers

1. Interview with Judge Falcone, February 1985.

2. Enzo Biagi's book *Il Boss è solo* was awarded Italy's prestigious Premio Bancarella in 1987.

3. McClellan Committee hearings, p. 184.

4. Maas, *The Valachi Papers,* p. 35.

5. Ibid., p. 44.

6. McClellan Committee hearings, September 25–October 9, 1963, p. 120.

7. DEA debriefing of Buscetta by Anthony Petrucci, April 22, 1985.

8. Pistone, *Donnie Brasco,* p. 330.

9. Arlacchi, *La Mafia imprenditrice,* p. 153.

10. The same oath has been described by a score of *pentiti* over the past decade.

11. DEA debriefing of Buscetta, May 1, 1985.

12. Biagi, *Il Boss è solo,* p. 181.

13. The murdered men were Giulio Pisciotta and Natale Carollo. Buscetta was sentenced by the court of assizes in Catanzaro on December 22, 1968. Together with Angelo La Barbera and Salvatore Greco, he was found guilty of "the unlawful continuing detention of the so-wronged persons, Giulio Pisciotta and Natale Carollo," who were never seen alive again.

The conviction was reversed by a court of appeals "on a technicality," according to Buscetta's lawyer. See "Sentenza di Rinvio a Giudizio," Judge Cesare Terranova; "Sentenza della Corte d'Assise di Catanzaro"; Anti-Mafia Commission Report 1976, excerpt from *I Boss della Mafia.* "Acqua in bocca" literally translated is "water in your mouth."

14. "Sentenza di Rinvio a Giudizio" by Judge Terranova, and "Sentenza della Corte d'Assise di Catanzaro." The builder's name was Giuseppe Annaloro. Despite Annaloro's testimony, Buscetta was acquitted on this charge "for lack of sufficient evidence."

15. Report of Italy's Parliamentary Anti-Mafia Commission, 1976. The quantity seized was 3,815 kilos: 3.8 tons.

16. Pantaleone, *Mafia e dròga,* pp. 64–70.

17. "Sentenza di Rinvio a Giudizio," Judge Cesare Terranova, p. 95; Pantaleone, *Mafia e dròga,* pp. 92–93.

18. *I Boss della Mafia,* pp. 295–315.

19. Gosch and Hammer, *The Last Testament of Lucky Luciano,* pp. 292–93.

20. Testimony of John J. Shanley, McClellan Committee hearings, September 25–October 9, 1963, p. 251.

21. Gosch and Hammer, *The Last Testament of Lucky Luciano,* pp. 301–2.

22. Pantaleone, *Mafia e politica,* pp. 213–14.

23. Pantaleone, *Mafia e dròga,* p. 98.

24. Ibid. Others named by Pantaleone were Rosario Mancino, Calcedonio Di Pisa, Antonino Sorce, and Pietro Davì, notorious heroin smugglers. Luciano went into business with Antonino Sorce and Rosario Mancino in 1951 to finance construction activities in Palermo. Their firm was called ISEP (Istituto Sovvenzioni e Prestiti). After Luciano's death, a document found in his safe deposit box showed that the three together had bought fifty acres of priceless parkland in the heart of Palermo from Princess Anna of France.

25. Buscetta's account of his relations with Lucky Luciano is given at length in Biagi, *Il Boss è solo,* pp. 147–53.

26. Claire Sterling, "The Boys Who Made Bad," *The Reporter,* October 17, 1957.

27. Short, *Crime, Inc.,* p. 160; Gosch and Hammer, *The Last Testament of Lucky Luciano,* p. 362. The heroin was diverted by corrupt officials of the Schiaparelli Company in Milan, three of whom were arrested. The American Mafioso involved was Joe Biondo, presented to one of these officials by Luciano.

28. See chapters 4 and 8.

29. Buscetta disclosed the fact of the 1951 rupture, though not its motivation, in his interrogation by Judge Falcone. See "Interrogazione di Buscetta," October 1984, and Buscetta's testimony in New York's Pizza Connection trial, October 1985.

30. Petacco, *Joe Petrosino,* p. 121.

31. Debriefing of Tommaso Buscetta, DEA (Huber and Petrucci), March 20, 1985.

32. Gosch and Hammer, *The Last Testament of Lucky Luciano,* p. 146.

33. Cressey, *Theft of the Nation,* p. 46. Joe Bonanno imported soldiers from Castellammare in the 1960s, when he was fighting to keep control of his Family.

4. THE DEAL

1. The American delegation included Carmine Galante, John Bonventre, Frank Garofalo, John Di Bella, John Priziola, Santo Sorge, Nick Gentile, Gaspare and Giuseppe Maggadino, and Vito Vitale. The Sicilian contingent included Genco Russo, Vincenzo Rimi of Alcamo, Salvatore and Angelo La Barbera, Salvatore Greco, Diego Plaja, Don Mimi La Fata, and Calcedonio Di Pisa.

2. The Judge, Aldo Vigneri, issued arrest warrants for Carmine Galante, John Bonventre, John Priziola, Frank Garofalo, Santo Sorge, Vito Vitale, Genco Russo, Calcedonio Di Pisa, Angelo and Salvatore La Barbera, and Joe Bonanno. Poma and Perrone, *La Mafia,* p. 92; Falzone, *Storia della Mafia,* p. 286.

3. McClellan Committee hearings, October 10–16, 1963, p. 777. This was the first mention of the summit in the United States.

4. See Pantaleone, *Mafia e Dròga* and *Mafia e Politica;* Poma and Perrone, *La Mafia;* Servadio, *Mafioso.*

5. Bonanno, *Man of Honor,* pp. 198–200.

6. "Interrogazione di Buscetta," July 21, 1984, p. 303.

7. DEA debriefings of Buscetta, March 20 and July 14, 1985.

8. Biagi, *Il Boss è solo,* pp. 147, 154.

9. DEA debriefing of Buscetta (Huber and Petrucci), March 20, 1985.

10. Testimony of John Shanley, head of New York City Police Department's Central Investigation Bureau, McClellan Committee hearings, September 25–October 9, 1963.

11. Estimate of U.S. Bureau of Narcotics, McClellan Committee hearings, March 4, 1965. p. 56.

12. Bonanno, *Man of Honor,* p. 270.

13. Gosch and Hammer, *The Last Testament of Lucky Luciano,* p. 314.

14. Testimony of Henry L. Giordano, commissioner of Bureau of Narcotics, McClellan Committee hearings, March 4, 1965, p. 70.

15. They were "Big John" Ormento and Natale Evola.

16. Servadio, *Mafioso,* p. 187.

17. Short, *Crime, Inc.*

18. Gosch and Hammer, *The Last Testament of Lucky Luciano,* p. 348.

19. Ibid., p. 372.

20. Pizza Connection proceedings, p. 37566.

21. Text of recorded conversation made by Royal Canadian Mounted Police in 1974 and transmitted to the Italian police that same year. The text was submitted as evidence a decade later, in Palermo's maxitrial. Paul Violi was murdered by Sicilian Mafiosi in 1978.

22. Poma and Perrone, *La Mafia,* p. 86; Pantaleone, *Mafia e dròga,* p. 38.

23. Barrese, *I Complici,* p. 85. The police report, among documents submitted to Judge Aldo Vigneri in 1964, stated that the Palermo meeting and the one at Apalachin a month later "were interdependent: their aim was to settle certain open questions within Cosa Nostra, reorganizing its top leadership. The elimination of Albert Anastasia . . . was part of this program."

24. Pennsylvania Crime Commission Report, "A Decade of Organized Crime," 1980.

25. Among those attending were the heads of all five New York Families, Carlos Marcello of New Orleans, Louis Trafficante, Jr., of Florida, Angelo Bruno of Philadelphia, Joe Zerilli of Detroit, Sam Giancana of Chicago, Steve Maggadino of Buffalo, Sam De Cavalcante of New Jersey, John Scalise of Cleveland, Frankie Zito of downstate Illinois, and James Coletti of Colorado, as well as John Ormento and Natale Evola of the Lucchese Family, especially notorious drug traffickers.

26. Those attending both the Palermo and Apalachin conferences were John Bonventre, Carmine Galante, John Priziola, John Di Bella, Santo Sorge, the Maggadinos, Frank Garofalo, and Joe Bonanno himself. The visits to Luciano are described by Gosch and Hammer, *The Last Testament of Lucky Luciano.*

27. Servadio, *Mafioso,* p. 192.

28. Gosch and Hammer, *The Last Testament of Lucky Luciano,* p. 400.

29. Short, *Crime, Inc.,* pp. 33–36.

30. Ibid.

31. Cressey, *Theft of the Nation,* p. 58.

32. McClellan Committee hearings, October 11–16, 1963, p. 777.

33. See note 23.

34. Mangano disappeared in 1951. Insider accounts have always named Anastasia as his killer.

35. DEA debriefing of Buscetta, July 14, 1985.

36. McClellan Committee hearings, September 25–October 9, 1963, pp. 319–23.

37. Maas, *The Valachi Papers,* p. 32.

38. Gosch and Hammer, *The Last Testament of Lucky Luciano,* pp. 402–4. The meeting between Luciano and Carlo Gambino was in Santa Marinella.

39. Interview with Ralph Salerno, New York, May 1986. Salerno, now retired, had long headed the New York Police Department's Central Intelligence Unit.

40. Buscetta's interview with *Corriere della Sera* (Milan) correspondent Paolo Graldi, October 28, 1984.

41. "Interrogazione di Buscetta," pp. 253–54.

42. Pizza Connection proceedings, p. 37562.

43. Ibid., p. 37552. See chapters 15 and 16.

44. Transcript of Badalamenti's calls in February 1984, Chronology of Events for Pizza Connection proceedings, p. 233.

45. Interview with Louis Freeh, May 1987; interview with Judge Giusto Sciacchitano, Palermo, August 1987.

5. EXODUS FROM PALERMO

1. Judge Cesare Terranova, "Sentenza di Rinvio a Giudizio," for the Trial of 114 in Catanzaro, May 31, 1965, p. 125.

2. Buscetta's interrogation by the DEA in New York, March 18, 1985. See also DEA debriefing of July 14, 1985.

3. McClellan Committee hearings, October 10–16, 1963; McClellan Committee Report, March 4, 1965, p. 121.

4. This was another Salvatore Greco, a cousin of Cichiteddu's known as "L'Ingegnere," the Engineer, or "Salvatore Il Lungo," because he was taller than Cichiteddu. He was also as big, or bigger, in the heroin business.

5. This was Pietro Davì, an internationally notorious heroin trafficker throughout the postwar years. Pantaleone, *Mafia e dròga,* p. 92.

6. Profile of Buscetta in Parliamentary Anti-Mafia Commission Report, 1965, published in *I Boss della Mafia.*

7. This was the figure for 1985 in a University of California study, among the few serious studies available.

8. Luciano told Gosch and Hammer that he decided to go into narcotics in 1961. See *The Last Testament of Lucky Luciano,* pp. 422–23.

9. Ibid., pp. 432–33.

10. Galluzzo, *Tommaso Buscetta,* p. 30.

11. Pantaleone, *Mafia e dròga,* p. 82. The wax oranges were discovered by Italy's Guardia di Finanza in 1959.

12. Ibid., p. 108.

13. Under interrogation in 1984, Tommaso Buscetta revealed that Di Pisa had actually been killed by Michele Cavatoio, a leader of the Greco faction in the Cupola. Accordingly, Cavatoio and five others with him had been mowed down by machine-gun fire in 1969, in what became known as the Viale Lazio massacre.

14. Poma and Perrone, *La Mafia.* See also *Il Giornale* (Milan), March 14, 1981.

15. Poma and Perrone, *La Mafia,* p. 65; Pantaleone, *Mafia e dròga,* p. 116.

16. Pantaleone, *Mafia e dròga,* pp. 119–21; Fava, *Mafia,* pp. 66–67.

17. "Sentenza di Rinvio a Giudizio," Cesare Terranova.

18. Barrese, *I Complici,* p. 60. In 1984, during his interrogation by Judge Giovanni Falcone, Buscetta confirmed the dissolution of the Cupola.

6. STARTING UP: NORTH AMERICA

1. Biagi, *Il Boss è solo,* pp. 170–72.
2. Ibid.
3. McClellan Committee hearings, September 25–October 9, 1963, p. 294.
4. Buscetta told his DEA baby-sitters about the card games with Paolo Gambino. According to James Kallstrom, who investigated the Gambino brothers for the FBI in 1970, Paolo headed the Sicilians' alien-smuggling ring in New York. See New York FBI memo, November 5, 1973.
5. "The Sicilian Mafia and Its Impact on the United States."
6. The fact that John, Rosario, and Giuseppe Gambino were made in Palermo was confirmed to me in October 1987 by Dr. Pansa, a close aide to Gianni De Gennaro, who headed Rome's Anti–Organized Crime Nucleus. Both men are among the most knowledgeable investigators of the Mafia in Italy. The fact was corroborated later by Mona Ewell, one of the DEA's most brilliant intelligence analysts.
7. The books were closed by Lucky Luciano in 1931 and not reopened until 1954. See Maas, *The Valachi Papers,* p. 256. They were closed again at the Livingston, New Jersey, Mafia summit in October 1957, until 1974. See "A Decade of Organized Crime." The books were closed again until 1977, when each Family was allowed to swear in a maximum of ten new members.
8. A local police officer in Delran, New Jersey, Art Saul, still has his notes on meetings in the early 1970s, naming John, Rosario, and Giuseppe Gambino, Filippo Casamento, Emmanuele Adamita, Salvatore Inzerillo and his uncle Antonio, and Tommaso Buscetta and his son Antonio.
9. Rosario Gambino was seen hustling Melchiorra and Felicia Buscetta out of the house, in an attempt to avoid the police directly after Buscetta's first arrest in August 1970. See Charbonneau, *The Canadian Connection,* p. 295.
10. INS report, September 11, 1969. Adamita asked his uncle Domenico to let Buscetta use his address as a letter drop.
11. Report of Italy's Parliamentary Anti-Mafia Commission, cited in Galluzzo, *Tommaso Buscetta,* p. 43.
12. Letter from Italy's Guardia di Finanza to the BNDD, July 19, 1966. Exchange of confidential correspondence between the BNDD and Italy's Carabinieri, Guardia di Finanza, Nucleo Polizia Giudiziario: "Re: Conspiracy involving Calcedonio Di Pisa, Joe Profaci, Jr., Antonino Napoli, and Tommaso Buscetta," February 28, 1966.
13. Buscetta's son Antonio told this to New York State Police officer Mike Minto, after Buscetta's arrest in 1970. Minto Report, August 18, 1970; FBI Report, July 22, 1975. There is no evidence that Buscetta's wife and daughter were involved in the heroin trade; Lisa Wigs also did a legitimate business in wigs.
14. Italian Parliamentary Anti-Mafia Commission Report, cited in Galluzzo, *Tommaso Buscetta,* p. 48.
15. DEA debriefing of Buscetta, March 18, 1985. Buscetta told the DEA that his partnership with Napoli in Pizza City "existed in fact but was not reflected in ownership records." See also New York State Police Report, August 18, 1970. New York City Police Report, September 8, 1975, speaks of Buscetta's employment at the Dolce Vita.
16. Le Vien's police reports on the Murray Hill Town House and Pizza City pizzeria; New York FBI memo on Falcone and Antonino Napoli's gambling club, November 5, 1973. See "A Decade of Organized Crime" and "Organized Crime's Infiltration of the Pizza and Cheese Industry." The latter report, p. 23, speaks of the Alburg creamery as having been "destroyed by fire of suspicious origin. Subsequent suits and other legal actions eventually led to the conviction of Joseph Falcone and his office manager." The FBI informant's version was just one of several of why the factory burned down.

17. The closest associates were Salvatore Inzerillo, Giuseppe Tramontana, Salvatore Rina, Emmanuele Adamita, Bruno Pennisi, Filippo Casamento, Antonio Settimo, and Pietro Davì. New York State Police Report, August 18, 1970; FBI Report by Charles Rooney, September 24, 1981; FBI Report, December 14, 1982 (Genus Cattails); Report of U.S. Attorney's Office, Southern District of New York, to Joint Strike Force, August 26, 1970; Report by Jack Ricciardi, INS, on Brooklyn Strike Force, July 27, 1970; New York State Police Report, January 14, 1970, on surveillance of Giuseppe Tramontana. See also testimony of Buscetta's son Benedetto, debriefed by New York detective Frank Alessandrino, January 31, 1973; and his debriefing by the BNDD, December 11, 1972.

18. FBI NADDIS printout (Narcotics and Dangerous Drugs Information Systems) from EPIC (El Paso Intelligence Center), cited by agent Charles Rooney, September 4, 1981. Among those listed as Filippo Casamento's close associates were all three Napoli brothers, Salvatore Inzerillo, and "Carlo Zippo's narcotics organization." An FBI report by Carmine Russo, December 14, 1982, cites the fact that Buscetta and Carlo Zippo were frequently seen visiting Eagle Cheese. An FBI Brooklyn-Queens report, October 4, 1982, states that "Buscetta was employed by Frank Casamento at Eagle Cheese, in the early 1970s."

Buscetta now denies that he ever knew Casamento, and has even refused to identify his photograph. Nevertheless, Casamento's lawyer at the Pizza Connection trial spoke of their friendship in Palermo. A DEA NADDIS printout refers to Buscetta as one of Casamento's close associates, and to his employment at Eagle Cheese. See FBI Brooklyn-Queens Report, September 21, 1981.

19. Report of Italy's Parliamentary Anti-Mafia Commission, cited in Galluzzo, *Tommaso Buscetta,* p. 47.

20. They met in Montreal with Guido Orsini and Frank Cotroni, both notorious drug traffickers, according to Catania's later confession. See Charbonneau, *The Canadian Connection,* pp. 451–53.

21. Ibid.

22. Giuseppe Catania's confession, supported by Jorge Asaf y Bala's. See note 49 below.

23. Biagi, *Il Boss è solo,* pp. 125–27.

24. See chapter 1.

25. Buscetta sent this message to Gaetano Badalamenti and Stefano Bontate in Palermo. See note 26.

26. DEA debriefing of Buscetta, July 14, 1985. Buscetta is quoted as saying: "In approximately June 1970, I met with Stefano Bontate, Gaetano Badalamenti, and Salvatore Greco in Rome. At that meeting, I suggested to Bontate, Badalamenti, and Greco that they attempt to reestablish the Sicilian Cosa Nostra Commission, which they did, together with Salvatore Riina." Bontate is often referred to by the press as "Bontade."

27. Prosecutor Ayala's summation, maxitrial. See *La Repubblica* (Rome), April 15, 1987.

28. The other Cupola member was Giuseppe Calderone of Catania. The drug trafficker was Gerlando Alberti, presently serving a life sentence for drugs in Italy.

29. The episode is described at length in a report by Jack Ricciardi of the U.S. Immigration and Naturalization Service, July 27, 1970. Buscetta denies categorically that he was the Adalberto Barbieri in the car. "I was in the U.S., so it wasn't me," he told Judge Falcone. Nevertheless, the Canadians had his passport application as Barbieri, with his photograph. He had gotten the passport on February 10, 1970, and used it at once to visit Spain and Mexico. He was demonstrably in Italy that June; and the Carabinieri placed him in Zurich, a day's drive from the northern Italian border, just around the date in question.

30. The report was discussed in the 1973 court of appeals hearings for the Trial of the 114, and included the identification of Buscetta's photograph by the hotel porter in Zurich. Buscetta says the identification was made in 1972, too late to have any meaning. See *Il Giornale* (Milan), January 31, 1982.

31. Interview with Minto, Ft. Lauderdale, Florida, October 1986.

32. BNDD Report, August 19 and October 30, 1970. The shipment never arrived, presumably because police surveillance was noticed.

33. BNDD Report, October 30, 1970.

34. Interpol Rome had sent a telex to the BNDD and other U.S. authorities the day after Buscetta's arrest, reporting only an old arrest warrant for Buscetta on double murder and conspiracy charges, going back to 1963. As far as I know, not even these charges were raised in court. Interpol telex, August 26, 1970. Actually, Buscetta was convicted of the double murder and conspiracy after the famous Trial of the 114 in Catanzaro, in 1968.

35. Catania's initial confession to BNDD agent Ronald Provencher, cited in Charbonneau, *The Canadian Connection,* p. 453.

36. National Institute on Drug Abuse, Report on Black Tar Heroin Field Investigation, June 1986. This report discusses an "epidemic" from 1967 to 1972, without going into more detailed statistics. Heroin seizures nevertheless indicate that the huge increase in supply happened between 1969 and 1972.

37. FBI Report from Brazilia, "Mafia Suspects in Brazil," November 17, 1972.

38. Told to me by two of Buscetta's DEA baby-sitters in New York, March 1985.

39. The shipments were planned by the head of the Corsican Union for all South America, Lucien Sarti, who spoke of them to Pino Catania and Carlo Zippo.

40. From 1963, when Senator McClellan's committee made the estimate of fewer than 50,000 American addicts, no official figures were gathered in the United States until 1979. The estimate of 720,000 for 1971 was given to me in March 1989 by a spokesman for the U.S. State Department's Bureau of International Narcotics Matters. A DEA estimate put the figure at 750,000 by 1977: the number of addicts had plummeted after the breakup of the Brazilian ring, and climbed back after the Sicilian Mafia opened its own pipeline to the United States via Montreal in 1977.

41. National Narcotics Intelligence Consumers' Committee Report, 1987.

42. The President's Commission on Organized Crime, at its Miami hearings, put the number of Pakistani heroin addicts at 300,000 on February 20–21, 1985. The testimony was given by a Pakistani narcotics official. By 1988, the figure had risen to 600,000 in the U.S. State Department's International Narcotics Control Strategy Report, March 1988. The same State Department Report in March 1989 raised the estimate to a million.

43. *The Muslim* (Islamabad), March 19, 1984.

44. Michel Nicoli referred to this meeting in his lengthy debriefing by the DEA, September 9, 1974. The meeting took place in May 1971, he said. June seems the more likely date, judging from several other accounts.

45. A British TV network, Central Television, made the charge in a lengthy documentary in November 1988. It also named Christian David, another member of the gang, as Sarti's accomplice in the Kennedy shooting. David was notorious as the enforcer for the Corsicans' South American ring. Under torture in Brazil, he confessed to having assassinated the Moroccan opposition leader, Mehdi Ben Barka, in Paris in 1965. See *Newsday* team, *The Heroin Trail,* pp. 154–55.

46. Newsday team, *The Heroin Trail,* pp. 152–56.

47. Michel Nicoli, a leader of the Corsican ring, testified that a Portuguese TAP pilot had brought 440 kilos into New York for Eagle Cheese within a one-and-a-half-month period, in September–October 1971. The heroin was supplied by Nicoli's boss in the ring, Lucien Sarti. The TAP pilot, who later confessed, was Luis Felipe Estores Da

Costa Pires. The same pilot told drug courier Claude Pastou that "Carlo Zippo told me that Eagle Cheese was the recipient of all the loads he had done in New York."

48. U.S. Southern District case file on Filippo Casamento, backgrounding charges in the Pizza Connection trial. Claude Pastou, an important courier for the Corsicans' ring in Rio, affidavit for New York Southern District, January 4, 1973: "Carlo Zippo told me that the recipients at Eagle Cheese were also the recipients of all the other loads he had done in New York." Pastou named one recipient as Filippo Casamento.

49. Charbonneau, *The Canadian Connection,* p. 450.

50. Benedetto Buscetta's debriefing by BNDD, December 11, 1972.

51. Sentence, Salerno Court of Appeals, July 5, 1978, confirming the lower court's sentence, July 12, 1977. The sentence was upheld by the Italian Supreme Court on February 19, 1979. Italian and American authorities have been reluctant to discuss Buscetta's record on drugs since his defection. Many insist now that his guilt has never been established. Nevertheless, in his summation for the Pizza Connection trial, Assistant U.S. Attorney Richard Martin said: "Buscetta himself was involved in narcotics trafficking in the 1970s. He got involved because he had contacts in the U.S. and could move between the U.S., Canada, Italy and Brazil easily" (trial proceedings, p. 37567). Rudolph Giuliani, then head of the Southern District, also conceded Buscetta's past guilt.

52. DEA debriefing of Michel Nicoli, September 9, 1974.

53. The confessions having to do with all the transactions listed here are Michel Nicoli, BNDD debriefing, January 20, 1973; Michel Nicoli, DEA re-interview, September 9, 1974; Michel Nicoli, Affidavit in the Matter of the Extradition of Tommaso Buscetta, January 1984; Jorge Asaf y Bala, DEA debriefing, July 19, 1974; Alfredo Asaf y Bala, DEA debriefing, February 7, 1974; Benedetto Buscetta, New York Police debriefing, January 31, 1973; Claude Pastou (courier), statement to New York Southern District, January 4, 1973; Giuseppe Catania, BNDD debriefing, October 3, 1973; Giuseppe Catania, testimony before Eastern District grand jury, October 16, 1973; Giuseppe Catania, Affidavit for U.S. Eastern District Regarding Buscetta's Extradition, February 27, 1974; excerpts of various confessions cited, Sentence of the Court of Appeals, Salerno, July 5, 1978; Eastern District grand jury charges, October 16, 1973; Luis Felipe Da Costa Pires, Affidavit, New York Southern District, December 27, 1973. Corroborative police reports on Carlo Zippo: BNDD, August 19, 1970; BNDD, October 30, 1970; BNDD, April 10, 1970.

54. Though Helene Ferreira is often described as a "ballet dancer," she is listed in Brazilian police reports as a prostitute.

55. Newsday team, *The Heroin Trail,* p. 155.

56. Pino Catania was rearrested by Mexican police for dealing cocaine in February 1989.

57. Newsday team, *The Heroin Trail,* p. 155.

58. FBI Report, "Mafia Suspects in Brazil," November 17, 1972.

59. Statement by U.S. Circuit Judge M. I. Gurfein, July 7, 1975; letter from Filippo Casamento, December 14, 1974; letter from Brooklyn pastor, Our Lady of Grace Church, December 7, 1974; letter from Palermo priest, Cathedral of Carini, December 16, 1974.

60. The court of assizes in Catanzaro issued the fourteen-year sentence on December 22, 1968. This was reduced to three years on appeal in 1974. The court of assizes in Salerno convicted Buscetta on the drug charges on July 12, 1977. Salerno's court of appeals upheld the sentence on July 5, 1978, but reduced the penalty to eight years. The Court of Cassation (Supreme Court) upheld the appeals court verdict on February 19, 1978. The Eastern District in New York had requested Buscetta's extradition for these charges on September 16, 1973.

7. STARTING UP: SOUTH AMERICA

1. From a series of well-researched reports by Venezuelan investigative journalist Rodolfo Schmidt, in *El Diario de Caracas,* December 5, 1984. DISIP stands for Dirección de los Servicios de Inteligencia y Prevención.
2. Buscetta told his DEA baby-sitters in New York that the Sicilian Mafia had chartered branches in Brazil and Venezuela. Interview with the baby-sitters, May 1986.
3. Cited in two-volume report of Italy's Criminalpol in Milan and Rome, "Bono + 159," p. 220.
4. See chapter 1, note 9.
5. Rodolfo Schmidt, in *El Diario de Caracas,* November 22, 1984. The Commissioner of DISIP who conducted the investigation and arrived at this estimate was Camilo Cussati.
6. Puccio's description of Antonino Napoli was given to Detective Douglas Le Vien in December 1976. His statement was also relayed to a meeting of the Eastern District Strike Force by Attorney-in-Charge Charles Weintraub, December 14, 1976. New York Police Report, memo from Detective Joseph Conway to Eastern District Strike Force meeting, December 14, 1976.
7. She married Nino Mongiovi, said by the DEA to be one of the biggest narcotics brokers in Miami.
8. Italian arrest warrants were first issued for Pasquale and Paolo Cuntrera in 1984, following a lengthy investigation of the Sicilian Mafia's activities abroad by the Criminalpol in Milan and Rome. Formal requests for their extradition from Venezuela followed, and were ignored. Warrants for Alfonso and Pasquale Caruana, then in Montreal, were issued in 1985. Their brother Gerlando was already imprisoned in Canada on heavy drug charges by then.
9. *International Herald Tribune,* March 30, 1988. The minister denied any wrongdoing, the paper added.
10. Interview with Judge Fulvio Salamone, Agrigento, October 1987.
11. The Guardia di Finanza informed the Questura of Agrigento that the Cuntreras had gone to Brazil in 1963 and spent a year there. Rome and Milan Criminalpol Report, "Bono + 159," p.256.
12. Interview with Judge Salamone, Agrigento, October 1987.
13. Royal Canadian Mounted Police transcript of tapes recorded April 22, 1974.
14. "Sentenza di Rinvio a Giudizio," Agrigento.
15. Interview with Judge Salamone, Agrigento, October 1987.
16. *Corriere della Sera* (Milan), November 8, 1986.
17. DEA Report, December 6, 1982. The delegation included Galante and Frank Petrula of the Montreal Mafia.
18. Stajano, *Mafia: L'atto d'accusa,* p. 208.
19. DEA Report, December 6, 1982. Nino Mongiovi's role in Miami was confirmed to me by DEA intelligence analysts in Washington in October 1987.
20. *El Diario de Caracas,* October 23, 1985; *The Gazette* (Montreal), April 8, 1988 (part of an excellent series by William Marsden).
21. Interview with Vladimir Gessen, former head of Venezuela's Parliamentary Anti-Narcotics Commission, October 1987.
22. *El Diario de Caracas,* November 19, 1984.
23. DEA Report, December 11, 1982; *El Diario de Caracas,* November 17, 1984; *The Gazette* (Montreal), April 8, 1988; interview with Gianni De Gennaro, Anti–Organized Crime Nucleus, Rome.
24. Documents submitted by Carlo Tablant of Venezuela's special Parliamentary Anti-Mafia Commission, cited in *El Diario de Caracas,* December 12, 1984.

25. Interview with Gianni De Gennaro.

26. Cited in William Marsden's series of articles in *The Gazette* (Montreal), April 7, 1988.

27. Testimony in Pizza Connection trial by Luigi Ronsisvalle. See chapter 10 for the heroin pipeline.

28. Italian police recorded several phone conversations from the Italian end. See "Bono + 159."

29. Interview with Colin Hewett, Scotland Yard's National Drugs Intelligence co-ordinator, March 1987. The last-semester figure for 1987 is from Interpol's *Quest,* 2nd and 3rd Trimester 1987.

30. These included Dr. Pansa of Rome's Anti–Organized Crime Nucleus and the brilliant Ninni Cassarà, assistant director of Palermo's Squadra Mobile until he was killed by the Mafia in August 1985.

31. Interview with Colin Hewett, March 1987. The chief lieutenant was Francesco Di Carlo, sentenced by a London judge to twenty-five years' imprisonment on March 11, 1987. He was caught transshipping sixty kilos of heroin to Gerlando Caruana in Montreal.

32. *Daily Express,* March 13, 1987.

33. "Ordinanza di Rinvio a Giudizio, Michelangelo Aiello + 32," pp. 71–72. This Italian indictment names Kingsland specifically and traces the whole operation. Inter-viewed on Grenada TV's "World in Action," Kingsland denied any wrongdoing and was never charged. Money laundering at the time was not a crime under British law.

34. *Corriere della Sera* (Milan), September 14, 1988.

35. *The Gazette* (Montreal), April 8, 1988.

36. *Giornale di Sicilia* (Palermo), March 12, 1987. Di Carlo and his accomplices were sentenced to twenty-five years apiece by a London court on March 11, 1987.

37. State Department cable from U.S. embassy, London, citing U.K. Annual Nar-cotics Report for 1986–87.

38. London *Evening Standard,* March 12, 1987.

39. Ibid. See also London *Times,* March 13, 1987.

8. THE SCARLET PIMPERNEL OF CORLEONE

1. Nese, *Nel segno della Mafia,* pp. 115–16. Apart from being shot in 1973, Man-gano was also subjected to a virulent and ultimately ruinous campaign of defamation.

2. Nese, *Nel segno della Mafia.*

3. Poma and Perrone, *La Mafia,* p. 291.

4. Pantaleone, *Mafia e dròga,* p. 121.

5. Barrese, *I Complici,* p. 88.

6. Stajano, *Mafia: L'atto d'accusa,* p.14.

7. The judge was Aldo Vigneri of Palermo. The United States refused to extradite the American defendants he named because it had no law against "organized delin-quency," the Italian law used to charge them.

8. Judge Vigneri prepared the indictment in 1965. Among those who had died since the 1957 summit at the Hotel des Palmes were Lucky Luciano, John Di Bella, Gaspare Maggadino, and Frank Garofalo. Poma and Perrone, *La Mafia,* pp. 94–95.

9. "Sentenza di Rinvio a Giudizio," Judge Cesare Terranova, pp. 59, 71–72.

10. Nese, *Nel segno della Mafia,* pp. 120–22.

11. See chapter 6.

12. A few who got light sentences in the Catanzaro trial were rescued by a general amnesty, a not infrequent occurrence in Italy.

13. *La Repubblica* (Rome), November 9, 1982, citing Judge Terranova's interview in *Giornale di Sicilia* (Palermo), in 1978.

14. The reporter was Marco Nese.
15. Nese, *Nel segno della Mafia,* p. 124.
16. Ibid.
17. Poma and Perrone, *La Mafia,* p. 294.
18. Ibid.
19. Leggio's interview with Guido Guidi of *La Stampa* (Turin), cited in Nese, *Nel segno della Mafia.*
20. Nese, *Nel segno della Mafia,* p. 155.
21. Barrese, *I Complici,* pp. 195–99.
22. Poma and Perrone, *La Mafia,* pp. 296–97.
23. Attorney General Pietro Scaglione was killed near his Palermo home in May 1971. Buscetta has testified that Leggio in person fired from a passing car. The Mafia boss of Riesi, Giuseppe Di Cristina, said more or less the same thing in his long statement to the Carabinieri before being killed by Leggio's men. Both stated that Scaglione was about to get a favorable verdict on Vincenzo Rimi, boss of Trapani, an enemy of Leggio's at the time. Another *pentito,* Salvatore Contorno, has confirmed Leggio's guilt. The courts have twice acquitted Leggio on this count, however.

Another explanation for Scaglione's murder is that Leggio simply did not want him to leave Sicily with his incriminating secrets. Writing in the weekly *Panorama,* Romano Cantore observed: "Everybody in the Palermo courthouse—ushers, chancellors, lawyers, and judges, knew that denunciations and anonymous letters, memorandums with names and undertakings of the Mafia, were shoved into a drawer by Scaglione, who would say, 'What a bore' "; cited in Nese, *Nel segno della Mafia,* p. 169.
24. Nese, *Nel segno della Mafia,* p. 169.
25. The reporter was Marco Nese.

9. ISTANBUL, SOFIA, NAPLES, AND THE GOLDEN CRESCENT

1. Prominent among the Sicilian Mafiosi moving in on Naples were Gerlando Alberti, Giuseppe Di Cristina, and Rosario Riccobono. Violante, *La Mafia dell'eroina,* p. 81.
2. I am especially grateful to Judith Harris for her careful reconstruction of these events in an as yet unpublished manuscript.
3. Southeast Asian heroin "constituted less than 20 percent of the total supply in the United States as in Western Europe," reported the National Narcotics Intelligence Consumers' Committee in June 1987. The export figures for Burma are cited in the U.S. State Department's International Narcotics Control Strategy Report, March 1988.
4. Bartels is quoted in *Oui,* December 1976.
5. The Italian detective who tracked down the Sami Duruoz story was Cristoforo La Corte, attached to the Criminalpol in Trieste at the Yugoslav border. Later, La Corte helped in Judge Carlo Palermo's investigations and accompanied him to Sofia. La Corte gave details of the Duruoz story to American journalist Judith Harris. The Turkish envoy who replaced Duruoz was Cevdet Cil, brother of the big Istanbul boss and drug trafficker Huseyn Cil.
6. Statement of John Lawn, head of the DEA, to U.S. House of Representatives Foreign Affairs Committee, Task Force on International Narcotics Control, June 7, 1984.
7. Statement of R. M. Palmer, deputy assistant secretary of state for European and Canadian affairs, to the same House committee.
8. Ibid.
9. Sterling, *The Time of the Assassins,* pp. 79–80, 96, 125. The fact that Ugurlu carried a Bulgarian passport was told to me by former Turkish minister of the interior Hasan Fehmy Gunes.

10. Testimony given to Judge Palermo by Hakim Nasser, who worked with Ugurlu's liaison man in Milan, Salah Al Din Wakkas. Stajano, *Mafia: L'atto d'accusa,* p. 53.

11. Cunningham Report to the DEA, February 14, 1981.

12. Sterling, *The Time of the Assassins,* p. 220. The source of this information was Interpol in Turkey.

13. Agca was in Sofia from July 3 or 4 to August 31, 1980, as established by Italian court records. See the explanation of sentence for the Papal Shooting trial; also Sterling, *The Time of the Assassins,* p. 103.

14. Sterling, *The Time of the Assassins,* pp. 220–24; Stajano, *Mafia: L'atto d'accusa,* pp.62–63; Struffi and Sardi, *Fermate quel giudice,* p. 85. Celenk was also tracked by Swiss and Dutch police to a drug pickup in Amsterdam, according to a DEA report.

15. Testimony of R. M. Palmer to House committee.

16. Struffi and Sardi, *Fermate quel giudice,* p. 49.

17. This description comes from my *Time of the Assassins.* The features are listed in the Vitosha's brochure.

18. Nathan Adams, "Drugs for Arms," *Reader's Digest,* November 1983. The Sicilian delegation was led by Francesco Mafara, the traffic manager in Italy for the Cupola's heroin consortium from the late 1970s until he was murdered in 1982.

19. *Newsday* team, *The Heroin Trail.*

20. By international convention, TIR trucks can cross all frontiers in Europe without customs inspection until reaching the country of destination.

21. Stajano, *Mafia: L'atto d'accusa,* pp. 8–9.

22. The Turkish Mafia's Rome office in Via Barberini, WAPA, was near the Iraqi Airways office. See Judge Carlo Palermo's "Rinvio a Giudizio" in Trento, 1984. See also Struffi and Sardi, *Fermate quel giudice,* p. 52.

23. Stajano, *Mafia: L'atto d'accusa,* pp. 8–10.

24. Testifying before the same House Foreign Affairs Committee in 1984, the DEA's Acting Director John Lawn said: "Since 1970, and continuing to date, the DEA has received statements from several different sources delineating Bulgaria's involvement in illicit trafficking activities. Information about the involvement of government officials, government agencies, and the descriptions of selected arms and narcotics traffickers has remained consistent over the years."
In 1973, the DEA's Special Agent Tom Angioletti submitted a special report summing up knowledge gained in a series of 1972 interviews with Henri Arsan, the arms-drugs titan working out of Milan. Syrian-born, Arsan had spent a decade in Istanbul and another in Sofia before setting up operations in Italy. An informant for the DEA and the Italian intelligence service for a few years, Arsan was then dumped—and allowed to get on with his business. The Americans and Italians both considered him to be a double agent, working for the Bulgarians and above all for the Syrians. See Stajano, *Mafia: L'atto d'accusa.* Included in this volume is also a secret U.S. memorandum on Kintex, submitted to the Italian authorities in 1973.

25. "Interrogatorio di Michele Zaza," Judge Aurelio Galasso.

26. This was the old Camorra, revived by 1975 and in fierce competition with Raffaello Cutolo's NCO (Organized New Camorra).

27. Stajano, *Mafia: L'atto d'accusa,* pp. 94–95.

28. Ibid., pp. 91–94.

29. *Corriere della Sera* (Milan), April 1, 1988.

30. Wakkas first met Ugurlu together with a brother of Huseyn Cil's in Bucharest in 1969. The three men arranged with a Rumanian minister to smuggle cigarettes down the Danube to the Black Sea and across to Turkey. From then on, Ugurlu was the man to whom Wakkas was ultimately responsible. See his testimony to Judge Carlo Palermo, in Stajano, *Mafia: L'atto d'accusa.* For the statement that he "answered to

Ugurlu," see DEA Report by Cunningham, December 30, 1980, cited by Italian Crimi-nalpol, February 14, 1981, in Judge Palermo's indictment.

31. Report by LABPS (Laboratorio per le Politiche Sociali) attached to Italy's Ministry of the Interior, December 11–12, 1986.

32. Ibid.

33. Stajano, *Mafia: L'atto d'accusa,* pp. 48–49.

34. The Sicilian Mafia's main northern branch officers for this purpose were the Grado brothers, cousins of Salvatore Contorno. See ibid., pp. 90–95, notable mainly for the statements made by Buscetta and Salvatore Contorno.

10. THE HEROIN PIPELINE

1. FBI Report, "Luigi Ronsisvalle, Information Concerning Murder," Queens, New York, April 30, 1979.

2. These and all ensuing statements of Ronsisvalle's are textual excerpts from his testimony before the President's Commission on Organized Crime, February 20–21, 1985, Miami.

3. Interview with James Kallstrom, May 1986.

4. Interview with Louis Schiliro, FBI, Brooklyn-Queens headquarters, May 1986.

5. The carrier was Frank Rappa.

6. The hit man's name was Sebastiano Pisciotta. A victim of the Great Mafia War, his body was found just outside Palermo in 1982. Pisciotta's was one of the two names that turned up most often on the toll records of Enzo Napoli's phone calls to Palermo.

7. Interview with James Kallstrom, FBI, New York; Pennsylvania Crime Com-mission report, 1980 ("A Decade of Organized Crime") and 1985; Sean McWeenie's case study "The Sicilian Mafia and Its Impact on the United States"; Metropolitan Police Department, Washington, D.C., Investigative Service Division Report, Decem-ber 21, 1984.

8. The other two on Bonanno's hit list were Gaetano Lucchese and Stefano Maggadino. Demaris, *The Last Mafioso,* p. 179.

9. The agent was Frank Panessa, now head of the DEA's Rome office. He cited the figure in testimony before the President's Commission on Organized Crime, Miami hearings, February 20–21, 1985.

10. New York State Police Intelligence Summary, Tramontana-Settimo Investiga-tion, August 18, 1970. FBI Report by Sean McWeenie, "The Sicilian Mafia and Its Impact on the United States."

11. Ronsisvalle told this to Detective Le Vien, at variance with FBI and press reports.

12. See chapter 12.

13. Sindona was convicted by a Milan court on March 18, 1986, of sending a contract killer named William Arico to assassinate Ambrosoli. He died in his prison cell of strychnine poisoning two days after his conviction (see chapter 12). The contract killer died of a fall from a high-rise window, while trying to escape from the Manhattan Correctional Center. The assistant U.S. attorney he wanted Ronsisvalle to murder was John Kinney.

14. See chapter 15.

15. Frank Panessa, now the DEA's Rome director, was an undercover narcotics agent in New York and Philadelphia during those years. He has described several such scenes to me.

16. "America's Habit," President's Commission on Organized Crime, pp. 25–26, figure 5. The addict population was put at 750,000 for 1977. According to a University of California study, it was 625,000 by 1985.

17. *New York Times,* January 31, 1986.

18. Ronsisvalle was paroled in April 1985 on the recommendation of U.S. Attorney Rudolph Giuliani, head of the Southern District, and went straight into the Witness Protection Program with his wife and three daughters. After a triumphant performance as a star witness at the Pizza trial, he recanted, only to recant his recantation soon afterward. He claimed to have been terrorized into taking back his testimony incriminating Salvatore Catalano.

11. FROM THE PIPELINE TO THE PIZZA PARLOR

1. The President's Commission on Organized Crime estimated in October 1984, in "The Cash Connection," that U.S. heroin sales were generating $2.5 billion a year for the American Mafia, of which about $1 billion went back to Sicily. At the time, however, U.S. intelligence estimates were based on the assumption that the "Sicilian faction" was part of the American Mafia. It is now recognized that the Sicilian Mafia controlled the trade in American Mafia territory. The estimated revenue concerns wholesale trading. At street levels, the value would be ten times higher.

The estimate does not include profits from cocaine, which the Sicilian Mafia was also selling in large quantities through the same network. No estimates of how much are available.

2. The Telran computer check was made by U.S. Customs on July 28, 1977.

3. "Pennsylvania Crime Commission 1985 Report," p. 17.

4. Ibid., p. 18.

5. Metropolitan Police Investigation Service, Washington, D.C., December 21, 1984.

6. The pizzeria's owner was Pietro Alfano, Gaetano Badalamenti's nephew.

7. "Pennsylvania Crime Commission 1985 Report," p. 18. The report says that 8,862 illegal Sicilian aliens were deported between 1978 and 1983.

8. Others included Salvatore Rina, Giuseppe Tramontana, and Bruno Pennisi.

9. Interview with James Kallstrom, May 1986.

10. New Jersey State Police Confidential Intelligence Report, February 22, 1973. In "The Sicilian Mafia and Its Impact on the United States," Sean McWeenie of the FBI wrote in 1985: "The Federal Bureau of Investigation, Drug Enforcement Administration and Immigration and Naturalization Service, along with their Italian counterparts, have confirmed that between the mid-1960s and early 1970s, the U.S., Canada and parts of South America were flooded with Sicilians departing Italy. . . . Most illegally entering the U.S. were fugitives from Italy on charges ranging from murder to narcotics trafficking."

11. New Jersey State Police Report, February 22, 1973.

12. Ibid., pp. 4–5, 20–21.

13. Ibid., pp. 18–19.

14. Ibid., pp. 16–20.

15. Short, *Crime, Inc.,* pp. 318–19.

16. "A Decade of Organized Crime," Pennsylvania Crime Commission Report.

17. *Washington Post,* June 30, 1985.

18. Pennsylvania Crime Commission Reports, "A Decade of Organized Crime" and "Organized Crime's Infiltration of the Pizza and Cheese Industry."

19. Adamita owned the franchise for the Pizza Palace in Wrightsville, New Jersey, and Levittown, Pennsylvania. Matteo Sollena had the franchise in Perth Amboy and Bedford, New Jersey. See Pennsylvania Crime Commission's "Organized Crime's Infiltration of the Pizza and Cheese Industry," p. 34; New Jersey State Police Report, February 22, 1973.

20. These and preceding facts on Piancone brothers in the Pennsylvania Crime Commission's "Organized Crime's Infiltration of the Pizza and Cheese Industry," pp. 27–34.

21. Blumenthal, *Last Days of the Sicilians.*

22. Cable News Network, April 12, 1988.

23. *Washington Post,* June 30, 1985.

12. MICHELE SINDONA AND
THE BILLION-DOLLAR BLACKMAIL SCAM

1. Di Fonzo, *St. Peter's Banker,* p. 25.

2. Ibid., p. 75.

3. Ibid., p. 79.

4. Ibid., chapter 9.

5. Ibid. See also *Sindona: Gli atti d'accusa,* p. xvii.

6. The senator was Graziano Verzotto, who signed kickback checks for the boss of Riesi, Giuseppe Di Cristina, a close ally of Buscetta, Salvatore Inzerillo, and Stefano Bontate. See Di Fonzo, *St. Peter's Banker,* p. 7.

7. "The Cash Connection," Interim Report to the President's Commission on Organized Crime.

8. Di Fonzo, *St. Peter's Banker,* pp. 213–14.

9. Ibid.

10. Sindona's later statement to the FBI, in an interrogation dated May 20, 1980. This statement was accepted as valid by Italy's investigating magistrates. According to Sindona, Gambino helped out with the passport "because he also was a Sicilian patriot and wished to fight communism."

11. "Requisitoria, Rosario Spatola + 84," by Sicilian prosecutor Giusto Sciacchitano, December 20, 1981.

12. "Requisitoria, Sindona + 11," by Judge Guido Viola, p. 102. See also Prosecutor Giusto Sciacchitano's "Requisitoria, Rosario Spatola + 84," p. 205.

13. Di Fonzo, *St. Peter's Banker,* p. 225.

14. *Sindona: Gli atti d'accusa,* p. 26.

15. Bontate's brother-in-law was named Giacomo Vitale. His "preeminent role" is described in the "Requisitoria, Rosario Spatola + 84" of Prosecutor Giusto Sciacchitano.

16. Statement by Boris Giuliano's brother Emmanuele to the *Corriere della Sera* (Milan), June 27, 1985.

17. Sindona was convicted of ordering Ambrosoli's murder by a court in Milan on March 18, 1986.

18. *Sindona: Gli atti d'accusa,* p. 205.

19. Report of Tina Anselmi's parliamentary commission investigating the P-2, summary in special edition of *L'Espresso* (Rome), May 20, 1984, p. 47. The Squadra Mobile chief was Giuseppe Impallomeni, the *questore* was Giuseppe Nicolicchia.

20. Ibid. See also "Ordinanza di Rinvio a Giudizio" for the Palermo maxitrial trial, 1987.

21. Confession of Antonino Calderone, *La Stampa* (Turin), October 2, 1988.

22. FBI interrogation, June 17 and July 1, 1980.

23. "Interrogazione di Buscetta," Italian text, p. 129.

24. "Requisitoria, Sindona + 11," pp. 110.

25. *Sindona: Gli atti d'accusa,* pp. 188–89.

26. Ibid., p. 192.

27. Sindona had even threatened to kill Ambrosoli in the prime minister's name,

flaunting his hold over the nation's most powerful politician. Ambrosoli recorded the chilling phone call from Sindona's hired killer, published in the *Corriere della Sera* (Milan), May 20, 1984:

> KILLER: They're pointing the finger at you, I'm in Rome and they're pointing the finger, as if you don't want to collaborate. . . .
> AMBROSOLI: But who are "they"?
> KILLER: The Big Boss. . . .
> AMBROSOLI: Who's the Big Boss?
> KILLER: You understand me. The Big Boss and the little boss, everyone is blaming you. . . . You're a nice guy, I'd be sorry . . . The Big One, you understand? Yes or no?
> AMBROSOLI: I imagine the Big One is Sindona.
> KILLER: No. It's Andreotti.
> AMBROSOLI: Who? Andreotti!
> KILLER: Right. He called and said he had everything taken care of, but it's all your fault. . . . So watch it. . . .

For Andreotti's support of Sindona's "rescue operation," see Larry Gurwin, *The Calvi Affair*, p. 24.

28. The minister was Attilio Ruffini, longtime minister of defense, and brother of the then cardinal primate of Sicily. Quotation cited in the "Requisitoria, Spatola + 84." See also *La Repubblica* (Rome), January 25, 1984.

29. Hess, *La Mafia*, p. 272.

30. "Requisitoria, Spatola + 84," by Giusto Sciacchitano, December 20, 1981.

31. Arlacchi, *La Mafia imprenditrice*, p. 130. The figure given in lire is one thousand billion. The holdings in Palermo passed mostly through Inzerillo Sanitari (Building Supplies) and Valentino Construction.

32. *Nuova Polizia* (Palermo), June 1981.

13. PALERMO'S GREAT MAFIA WAR

1. For profit estimate, see chapter 1, note 3. Participation in the heroin pool by all Mafia clans is described in a report to the Sicilian judiciary by Commissario Antonino Cassarà, "Greco + 161," dated July 13, 1982. This report was a landmark in the judicial assault on the Mafia, summing up confidential information from a range of astonishing sources. Among these were Salvatore Contorno, Bontate's most trusted Man of Valor (killer), and Ignazio Lo Presti, a made member of Inzerillo's Passo di Rigano Family and in-law of the powerful financier Nino Salvo, also a made member under Bontate's protection.

2. Testimony by Tommaso Buscetta, Salvatore Contorno, and others in Palermo's maxitrial. Stajano, *Mafia: L'atto d'accusa*, pp. 208–9.

3. Interview with Gianni De Gennaro, Anti–Organized Crime Nucleus, Rome, February 1987; verdict of Court of Assizes, Palermo, February 26, 1988.

4. Statement of William Sessions, Director of the FBI, to U.S. Senate Permanent Subcommittee on Investigations, April 11, 1988.

5. Interview with Tom Angioletti, then head of the DEA's Rome bureau, March 1985.

6. "Ordinanza di Rinvio a Giudizio," maxitrial, cited in Galluzzo et al., *Rapporto sulla Mafia degli anni '80*, p. 319. This was the lab in Via Messina Marina.

7. Galluzzo et al., *Rapporto sulla Mafia degli anni '80*, p. 307. This lab was run by

the Grado brothers, closely associated with the Fidanzatis in the Mafia's Milan operations.

8. "Ordinanza di Rinvio a Giudizio, Calabrò, Gioacchino + 19," by Judge Claudio Lo Curto. The Alcamo refinery was found on April 30, 1985.

9. Panessa's testimony before the President's Commission on Organized Crime, Miami hearings, February 20–21, 1985. The trafficker was his target in Philadelphia, Paolo La Porta.

10. This and the sequence of events that follows are detailed in Commissario Cassarà's report "Greco + 161."

11. Mafara was arrested in 1982 and confessed. He was murdered by the Corleonesi later that year.

12. "Ordinanza di Rinvio a Giudizio, Calabrò, Gioacchino + 19," p. 397.

13. Cassarà Report, "Greco + 161."

14. Gambling was legalized in Atlantic City in 1977. The Sicilian Mafia's Atlantic City project was reported in Commissario Cassarà's report "Greco + 161." See also testimony of FBI agent Richard Ross to President's Commission on Organized Crime, Miami hearings, February 20–21, 1985. Ross was in charge of organized crime investigations in Atlantic City.

The special relationship between the Cherry Hill Gambinos of southern New Jersey and the Bruno Family in Philadelphia was described to me by Frank Panessa, head of the DEA in Rome, who worked as an undercover narcotics agent in that city.

15. Cassarà Report, "Greco + 161." During this period, the Gambino brothers' cousin Emmanuele tried to buy a hotel in Atlantic City under a false name "for the simple reason that if I introduced myself as a Gambino, the guy wouldn't have dealt with me." See Pennsylvania Crime Commission Report, "A Decade of Organized Crime," p. 72.

16. Cassarà Report, "Greco + 161."

17. The fifty-kilo story is told not only in Cassarà's report but also by Buscetta. He specifies that Inzerillo did not pay for the fifty kilos, adding that Inzerillo thought Leggio wouldn't dare kill him until he paid up.

18. Cassarà's report "Greco + 161" notes that Giuseppe Di Cristina was the last important boss to be murdered from 1978 to 1981. The boss of Catania then was Giuseppe Calderone, one of the five in the Alfa Romeo with Buscetta when a police patrol stopped the car near the northern Italian border in 1970. Calderone was killed by the Corleonesi's Catanese allies. In 1988, his brother Antonino became perhaps the single most important Mafia defector in Italy.

19. The victim was Luigi Corleo, father-in-law of financier Nino Salvo.

20. According to Buscetta, Badalamenti was expelled from Cosa Nostra in 1978. Nevertheless, he remained in Palermo until 1982, when he fled to the north and eventually to Brazil.

21. This information was given to me by Cassarà. He was told by Francesco Mafara, the Cupola's marketing manger, who got the information in 1979 from two Belgian chemists working in the Sicilian refineries named Albert Gillet and Eric Charlier.

22. Cassarà Report, "Greco + 161."

23. The trusted lieutenant who betrayed Inzerillo was Salvatore Montalto, Enzo Napoli's Mafia boss. The Corleonesi rewarded him by making him boss of Villabate and giving him a seat on the Cupola, for which he was later sentenced to life imprisonment.

24. This was Pietro Marchese, the "good" brother of Filippo Marchese, a psychopathic killer heading Palermo's Corso Dei Mille clan.

25. They were Giuseppe Calderone and, later, Alfio Ferlito. Ferlito was ambushed while four Carabinieri agents were escorting him from one Sicilian prison to another.

26. Sinagra's testimony at Palermo's maxitrial, June 15–19, 1986.

27. Excerpts from Sinagra's testimony to Judge Falcone, published in *La Repubblica* (Rome), January 24, 1984.

28. The detective was Beppe Montana, murdered by the Mafia in July 1985.

29. High Commissioner Boccia's report to the Italian minister of the interior, published textually in *Cronache Parlamentari Siciliane,* December 1986, p. 34.

30. *Corriere della Sera* (Milan), May 24, 1986, quoting Leggio's testimony at Palermo's maxitrial.

31. Leggio was formally accused of using Antonino Faro as his prison killer, in Palermo's maxitrial.

32. Cassarà Report, "Greco + 161." See also Giuseppe Di Cristina's secret confession to the Carabinieri before his murder. Stajano, *Mafia: L'atto d'accusa,* p. 21.

33. Explanation of sentence, maxitrial October 1, 1988.

14. DISTINGUISHED CADAVERS

1. "Ordinanza di Rinvio a Giudizio," maxitrial, p. 1888. The joint investigation with the DEA was called Operation Caesar, and got under way in 1978.

2. The money in the suitcase had been sent to the Cupola's marketing manager, Francesco Mafara, by Gaetano Badalamenti's nephew in New Jersey, Salvatore Sollena, in payment for a shipment from Palermo by Badalamenti himself. See "Greco + 161."

3. From the secret dossier M. Fo. Biali, seized by police in the Rome office of a murdered editor-blackmailer, Mino Pecorelli, cited by Sandra Bonsanti in *La Repubblica* (Rome), September 12, 1982.

4. The president of the Sicilian Region was Piersanto Mattarella, killed January 6, 1980. The Carabinieri captain was Emmanuele Basile, killed May 3, 1980. The state prosecutor was Gaetano Costa, killed August 6, 1980. The Communist party secretary was Pio La Torre, shot April 30, 1982. General Dalla Chiesa was killed September 3, 1982.

5. Galluzzo et al., *Rapporto sulla Mafia degli anni '80,* p. 32.

6. Contorno is quoted at length as "Prime Luce" in Cassarà's report. His identity was revealed in 1984. See *Il Giornale* (Milan), November 16, 1984, and *La Repubblica* (Rome), April 12, 1986.

7. Stajano, *Mafia: L'atto d'accusa,* pp. 318–19.

8. The Mafia's roots in Catania have now been established in voluminous testimony by Mafia defectors. Its foundations there going back to 1925 were cited in the confession of Antonino Calderone, whose brother Giuseppe had been head of the regional Mafia commission in Catania and the entire Mafia's *Inter-Provinciale* until he was murdered by Leggio's Catanesi allies. *Giornale di Sicilia* (Palermo), March 11, 1988.

9. Giorgio Bocca's series on Catania, *La Repubblica* (Rome), March 24, 1988.

10. The deputy was Nino Drago. *Corriere della Sera* (Milan), January 9, 1984.

11. See Report of the First Parliamentary Anti-Mafia Commission, a ten-year study filed in 1974.

12. Dalla Chiesa had denounced several others as well, including a former Christian Democratic cabinet minister, Giovanni Gioia, now dead, and the Republican party's leader in Sicily, Aristide Gunnella.

13. Dalla Chiesa, *Delitto imperfetto,* p. 34. Nando Dalla Chiesa, a sociology professor in Milan, was a rebel of the 1968 generation and a member of the Communist party. Though certainly not in agreement with his father politically, his evident love and respect were such that it is difficult to imagine him distorting the circumstances that surrounded Dalla Chiesa's mission to Sicily.

14. The prime minister was Giovanni Spadolini, then head of the small and moderate Republican party.

15. Dalla Chiesa, *Delitto imperfètto,* pp. 48–49.

16. Explanation of sentence, by Judges Alfonso Giordano and Pietro Grasso, cited in *La Repubblica* (Rome), October 2, 1988.

17. One employee he found in the Prefettura was the brother of Joseph Miceli Crimi, who had played a major part in the fake kidnapping of Michele Sindona. He has never been formally charged with wrongdoing.

18. Dalla Chiesa, *Delitto imperfètto,* p. 64.

19. Ibid., p. 53.

20. "Today the Mafia is strong in Catania also. With the consent of the Palermo Mafia, the four biggest Catania construction companies are operating in Palermo today. Do you think they could do that if there weren't a new map of Mafia power behind them?" Dalla Chiesa, interview with Giorgio Bocca.

21. The visit to Ralph Jones is described in an admirable series by the *Wall Street Journal*'s Roger Cohen, February 12, 1985.

22. Stajano, *Mafia: L'atto d'accusa,* p. 226.

23. Report by Carabinieri Captain Ganzer, "Sentenza di Rinvio a Giudizio," maxitrial; Stajano, *Mafia: L'atto d'accusa,* p. 293.

24. The official was De Francesco, the prefect of Palermo who replaced Dalla Chiesa after the latter's death, and the first anti-Mafia high commissioner.

25. Forty percent of Sicily's bank deposits, in six regional banks, twenty-eight provincial banks, and hundreds of savings banks, are in Trapani.

26. Trapani province includes Alcamo, Castellammare del Golfo, Partanna, Castelvetrano, Marsala, Mazara del Vallo, and Salemi.

27. The shipments had come from Salvatore Zizzo, one of the big Mafia bosses of all time, to his brother Nitto in Canada. *La Repubblica* (Rome), January 26, 1983.

28. *La Repubblica* (Rome), May 13, 1987.

15. THE OCTOPUS EMERGES

1. The figure of twenty made Sicilians is given by Sean McWeenie in his special FBI report "The Sicilian Mafia and Its Impact on the United States." The figure of a thousand was given to me by U.S. Attorney Louis Freeh in 1987.

2. On October 31, 1988, I had a long transatlantic telephone conversation with Mona Ewell; I was in Rome, she in Washington.

3. See "Bono + 159," two-volume report by Toni De Luca of the Milan Criminalpol and Gianni De Gennaro, head of the Anti–Organized Crime Nucleus in Rome, February 7, 1983.

4. He paid the Philadelphia ring $880,000 in all. The price of heroin was around $220,000 a kilo, but Panessa did not pay for his last consignment. When his superiors decided to pull in his target, they no longer saw a need to make payment. Later, with the target in prison, Panessa offered to make the payment good, but was told sadly, "It's too late." The Sicilians had already put out a contract on him.

5. Panessa's testimony before the President's Commission on Organized Crime, Miami hearings, February 21–22, 1985.

6. Ibid., February 20–21.

7. La Porta's group did set up a refinery in the Dominican Republic, raided by police before it could begin operations, in September 1983.

8. Interview with Panessa, Rome, October 31, 1988.

9. The heroin signatures were identical on the heroin Panessa was buying in Philadelphia and five kilos found on Ambrogio Farina, captured in New York in the summer

of 1983. Farina and his son Salvatore were later extradited from the United States to Italy and eventually convicted for the murder of Judge Ciaccio Montalto.

10. Zito sold Hopson two and a half kilos in all. During the roundup of Pizza defendants in April 1984, a few ounces of cocaine were found in possession of Sam Evola, Gaetano Badalamenti's nephew by marriage. By the time of the Pizza trial in New York, four defendants were also tied to a forty-kilo heroin case in Italy going back to 1980. See chapter 16.

11. Giuliani had left the Department of Justice in Washington to head New York's Southern District in July 1983.

12. Paolo La Porta was sentenced to thirty-five years, his brother Giovanni to twenty years, and their closest aide, Alberto Ficalora, to thirty years.

13. "Ordinanza di Rinvio a Giudizio, Aiello + 32," p. 42.

14. Pistone, *Donnie Brasco.*

15. See Judge Claudio Lo Curto's indictment ("Ordinanza di Rinvio a Giudizio") for the murder of Judge Ciaccio Montalto.

16. Interview with Richard Martin in Rome, October 31, 1988. There have been reports that Galante was getting $5,000 for every kilo of heroin the Sicilians brought in. Other reports say that Pasquale Conte, a Sicilian regarded by New York cops as a captain in the American Gambino Family, was collecting this fee. According to Martin, however, these reports were based on statements by an unreliable informant, unconfirmed by any others. The figure would seem absurdly small for Carmine Galante and the entire American Mafia Commission, anyway—$5 million a ton, perhaps $15 to $20 million a year, hardly something the American Mafia would get excited about.

17. Pistone, *Donnie Brasco,* pp. 204–5.

18. The three Bonanno men killed were Domenick Trinchera, Alphonse "Sonny Red" Indelicato, and Philip Giaccone, murdered in 1981.

19. Pistone, *Donnie Brasco,* pp. 356–57.

20. The story of Salvatore Catalano's abdication as head of the Bonanno Family was told to me by the FBI's Carmine Russo, who happened to be doing surveillance at the Cafe Roma on Knickerbocker Avenue on that night in 1981. Agent Russo said that Catalano had reached this agreement with the Bonanno Family bosses during a sit-down at the Fern Cliff Caterers near Kennedy Airport, and had then gone on to explain it to the Sicilians first at the Cafe Roma, later at "a big round table" in the Cafe Viale.

21. The third man was Pasquale "Patsy" Conte, who owned several Key Food supermarkets in the New York area and was on the board of directors of the Key Food chain. According to Buscetta, he paid $100,000 to be sworn in to the Gambino Family. Judging from the company he kept, however, he is more likely to have been made in Sicily. Enzo and Gaetano worked in his meat market when they first came to New York. Luigi Ronsisvalle saw him frequently with Catalano, Bonventre, and Amato on Knickerbocker Avenue, and once attended a sit-down at which Conte presided.

22. "Chronology of Events," Pizza trial, p. 13.

23. Interview with Richard Martin, Rome, October 31, 1988.

24. Interview with Freeh, April 12, 1988.

16. THE SHOCK OF RECOGNITION

1. For detailed accounts of the investigation, see Blumenthal, *Last Days of the Sicilians,* and Alexander, *The Pizza Connection.*

2. From figures in the drug ledger found when the defendant Salvatore Mazzurco was arrested, the Southern District calculated that the ring was planning to bring in a ton and a half "between part of 1982 and 1983." The five-year estimate of 330 pounds (150 kilos) a year actually imported was given to the press by Attorney General William French Smith at the time of the Pizza arrests on April 9, 1984.

3. It was through Rudolph Giuliani's efforts that the Justice Department authorized the FBI to work with the DEA on drug cases in 1982. See Attorney General William French Smith's statement to press conference, April 9, 1984.

4. See BNDD Reports, 1970–72, on Carlo Zippo ring, Antonio Settimo investigation: April 8, 1970, Surveillance Report on Settimo identifies Antonino and Vincenzo Napoli of Lisa Wigs; October 4, 1970, Surveillance Report on Settimo identifies Michael Piancone, Emmanuele Adamita, Antonio Minore, Carlo Zippo, Tommaso Buscetta, and Giuseppe Tramontana; September 18, 1970, Report is on surveillance of Settimo and Zippo. The BNDD's Ross Riley, summarizing 1970 investigation on October 30, 1970, profiles sixteen Sicilians figuring in the investigation, including Settimo, Adamita, Nick Rizzuto (of Montreal and Caracas), Giuseppe Catania (of Mexico City, New York, and Montreal), Giovanni Caruana (in Montreal), and Liborio Cuntrera (in Montreal, phoning Sicily, Brazil, and Venezuela). The entire investigation turned out to revolve around Casamento and his heroin receivers at Eagle Cheese.

In the 1972 Eagle Cheese case, the Eastern District estimated that Eagle Cheese had taken consignments of nine hundred kilos of heroin in that year. See chapter 9.

5. Casamento's connections to Ganci and Castronovo were used as "probable cause" to get the first Title 2 wiretaps in the Pizza case. But this did not happen until early 1983.

6. New Jersey's older and relentlessly methodical U.S. attorney, Robert Stewart, worked closely with them.

7. "The Cash Connection," President's Commission on Organized Crime, pp. 33–35.

8. Interview with Richard Martin, Rome, October 31, 1988.

9. This was the Adamita drug case, merged into the Spatola case. The three major figures were Frank Castronovo, Filippo Ragusa, and Onofrio Catalano, Salvatore's brother.

10. Charles Rooney's Report to the FBI (Genus Cattails), May 15, 1981.

11. The prosecutor was Giusto Sciacchitano, preparing the Spatola case. He blamed the delay largely on foot-dragging in his own ministry. See his "Requisitoria, Spatola + 84," 1981.

12. The *segreto d'istruttorio* precludes disclosures of any information gathered by an Italian investigating magistrate until his case goes through the courts. The system is due to be changed in 1989.

13. "Bono + 159," two-volume report by Gianni De Gennaro to the Rome Questura. For figures on heroin refineries seized in Sicily and Mafia rings broken up there, see the *Washington Post,* October 3, 1984; see also *Giornale di Sicilia* (Palermo), January 14, 1988.

14. "Bono + 159."

15. The DEA found the date of Bono's wedding to be November 16, 1980. The bill, discounted, was $63,120. Bono was in the DEA files as a member of the Bonanno Family. See ibid., pp. 155–56.

16. Among those present at the wedding from Brooklyn were Giuseppe Ganci, Sal Catalano, Cesare Bonventre, Baldo Amato, the Cherry Hill Gambino brothers, Filippo Casamento and his brother Franco, and Enzo Napoli's brother Gaetano. (Enzo was in prison then.) Buscetta, shown 138 selected faces, picked out 18. He denied recognizing Filippo Casamento, but did identify Sal Catalano, Gaetano Napoli, Nunzio Guido of the Camorra in Canada and Brazil, and Antonio Inzerillo, an uncle of the late Salvatore Inzerillo.

In 1985, Luigi Ronsisvalle identified Pasquale Conte as the unknown third man who went to lunch with Big Paul Castellano in October 1980.

17. Galluzzo et al., *Rapporto sulla Mafia degli anni '80,* pp. 28–29.

18. The trafficker whose phone was tapped was Giorgio Muratore. The others were Frank Castronovo and Filippo Ragusa. Onofrio Catalano, Salvatore's brother,

was not present but had hired the black Mercedes that picked the others up at the bar.

19. "Requisitoria, Spatola + 84."

20. The shipments amounted to thirty-eight kilos in all.

21. "Requisitoria, Spatola + 84."

22. The United States never answered Italian requests for John Gambino's extradition, a fact that continues to baffle Sicilian magistrates.

23. Stajano, *Mafia: L'atto d'accusa,* pp. 212–13. Apart from Catalano and Ganci, Contorno named Salvatore Greco (brother of the Bagheria boss), Gaetano Mazzara, and Frank Castronovo, known as Ciccio L'Americano. A major figure in handling drugs and laundering money, Castronovo was co-owner of Roma Restaurant in Menlo Park, New Jersey, where many drug transactions went down. His partner was Michael Piancone, one of the famous Piancone brothers who were sugar daddies for the Sicilian Mafia's string of pizzerias in America. See "A Decade of Organized Crime," "Pennsylvania Crime Commission, 1985 Report," and "Organized Crime's Infiltration of the Pizza and Cheese Industry." See also New Jersey State Police Confidential Intelligence Report, February 22, 1973. While in Palermo with Catalano and the others in February 1980, Castronovo completed a million-dollar real estate deal for John Gambino and Salvatore Inzerillo. In 1982, he was indicted by Judge Falcone in the Spatola case.

24. Interview with Judge Giusto Sciacchitano, Palermo, August 4, 1987.

25. See *Giornale di Sicilia* (Palermo), October 3, 1984. The U.S. attorney general was William French Smith, the FBI head was Judge William Webster, and the DEA head was Francis Mullen.

26. *La Repubblica* (Rome) and *Corriere della Sera* (Milan), November 6, 1988; *Corriere della Sera,* February 2, 1989. The breaking story generated a sensational scandal in Switzerland, whose minister of justice, Elizabeth Kopp, was forced to resign because of her husband's reported involvement in the laundering operation. She was said to have warned him improperly of an imminent investigation.

27. Indictment by Judge Claudio Lo Curto, "Ordinanza di Rinvio a Giudizio, Calabro, Gioacchino + 19."

28. Three Mafiosi from Trapani were sentenced to life imprisonment for the attempted assassination of Judge Palermo by the Caltanissetta Court of Assizes, on November 19, 1988.

29. Stajano, *Mafia: L'atto d'accusa,* pp. 200–1, 204.

30. Waridel was in jail from 1978 to 1979, where he met Giuseppe Ferrera, a high Mafia boss allied with the Catania clans, and Leggio, who played a major role in their morphine procurement.

31. The replacement was Antonino Rotolo, arrested with Pippo Calò in 1985. Calò was the boss of Buscetta's Porta Nuova clan, to which Rotolo and La Mattino both belonged.

32. Summation by Louis Freeh at Pizza Connection trial, pp. 37791–92.

33. For press reports, see *Forbes,* April 1989; *Newsday,* April 1, 1989; *Washington Times,* April 2, 1989. Source material from confidential DEA cables and a lengthy report dated January 3, 1989.

34. See statements by Salvatore Contorno and Gennaro Totta in Cassarà Report, "Greco + 161."

35. "Chronology of Events" prepared for Pizza trial jury, p. 233.

36. The Corleonesi were not above using other expelled members as well, if there was money in it. Francesco Di Carlo, working with the Cuntreras and Caruanas in London, was also expelled from the Mafia on the insistence of the Corleonesi, for whatever reasons of expediency. Nevertheless, they put his brother in as boss of his Altofonte Family, and used Di Carlo as their own man in London anyway.

37. The nephew by marriage was Sam Evola.

17. Buscetta's Fall from Grace

1. *Corriere della Sera* (Milan), October 12, 1984 (article by Giangiacomo Fo, on rearrest of Homero Guimaraes, Sr.).

2. Interview with Buscetta's DEA baby-sitter, Tony Petrucci.

3. Buscetta was sentenced to fourteen years for criminal association and ten for drug trafficking by two courts of assizes. The sentences were reduced on appeal to three and eight years respectively. See Buscetta's testimony in maxitrial, textually reported in *Giornale di Sicilia* (Palermo), April 4, 1986.

4. Statement of Judge Lina Monge, Turin, January 28, 1980, cited in Galluzzo, *Tommaso Buscetta,* pp. 104–5.

5. Justice Minister Nino Martinazzoli, *Il Giorno* (Milan), March 12, 1984.

6. Testimony of Francesco Gasparini to Judge Falcone, in Stajano, *Mafia: L'atto d'accusa,* p. 115.

7. Galluzzo, *Tommaso Buscetta,* pp. 90–91.

8. State's summation, Pizza trial, pp. 33579–81.

9. The prosecutor was Giuseppe Ayala, in the maxitrial.

10. Buscetta himself disclosed this to Judge Falcone in 1984, naming Antonio Bardellino, Antonio Nuvoletta, and Michele Zaza as the three Camorra chiefs.

11. Stajano, *Mafia: L'atto d'accusa,* pp. 319–20. The in-law was Ignazio Lo Presti, Nino Salvo's brother-in-law by marriage, who disappeared in August 1982, a presumed "white death."

12. The gunmen were Giuseppe Tramontana and Giorgio Romano. Tramontana had been Buscetta's trusted courier for most of the drug deals transacted while he lived in New York, and best man at Buscetta's bigamous marriage to Vera Girotti in New York.

13. The Corsicans working with Zaza were Paul Graziani and Bernard Quilichini.

14. For a full account, see "Bono + 159," pp. 319–338.14.

15. Ibid., pp. 115–25. Buscetta has testified that Antonio Salamone left Brazil to avoid having to kill Buscetta himself on the Corleonesi's orders. But it is hard to get around the dates of Salamone's departure. His nephew Francesco Di Matteo, one of those attending the Paris dinner, was arrested at Punta Ráisi Airport with the DEA report on Salamone on October 24, 1982. Zaza, on a tapped phone, said that Salamone left Brazil on October 25.

16. The informer was Paolo Lelio Gigante, who had carried heroin and cocaine for the Corsican ring all through the 1960s and early 1970s. He was arrested and indicted with Buscetta and the Corsicans when their ring was broken up in 1972. See *Giornale di Sicilia* (Palermo), October 26, 1983. The tip from Gigante contradicts the usually accepted story that Buscetta's apartment was found accidentally; the resident manager had reportedly identified Buscetta's picture among many while being shown a picture of Bardellino. This became the official version, perhaps to protect the informant. Nevertheless, in an interview with me in Rio de Janeiro in October 1986, the DEA's agent in charge said "it was no accident" that Buscetta's apartment was discovered.

17. The bodies of Giuseppe Tramontana and Giorgio Romano were found in Florida on February 1983. Buscetta left Rio a few days later. Some reports say there were no horses or cattle on Buscetta's ranch when he was captured. Buscetta himself described his herds in this way to his biographer: Biagi, *Il Boss è solo,* p. 224.

18. *Veja* (Brazilian weekly), November 2, 1983; DEA Report, December 15, 1983.

19. Romeu Tuma was quoted in the popular Brazilian weekly *Veja* on November 2, 1983. São Paulo police chief Pedro Berwanger and anti-narcotics chief Ugo Pavoa spoke to a press conference on October 24, 1983. See Galluzzo, *Tommaso Buscetta,* p. 157.

20. Press interview with Buscetta in São Paulo jail, *Giornale di Sicilia* (Palermo), October 27, 1983.

21. The other defendant was Salvatore Mazzurco.

22. Report to DEA by Mona Ewell, Charles Rose, and John Huber, December 15, 1983.

23. Shawcross and Young, *Men of Honor.*

24. Ibid., p. 183.

25. Interview with DEA agent in charge, Rio de Janeiro, October 1986.

26. Mona Ewell's report to DEA, U.S. government memorandum, December 15, 1983.

27. Interview with Paolo Graldi of the *Corriere della Sera* (Milan), October 28, 1984.

28. Galluzzo et al., *Rapporto sulla Mafia degli anni '80,* pp. 35–36.

18. Face to Face in a Court of Law

1. All Italian newspapers, November 12, 1987.

2. The death figure given by Prime Minister De Mita was 135 for the months from June to November 1988. A previous figure for the year was 180, but the number was rising toward the last months. By the year's end, the commonly accepted figure was a rounded 200. These figures did not include "white deaths."

3. Judge Pietro Grasso, comagistrate known as *giudice in latere* under Italian law, in *La Repubblica* (Rome), October 1, 1988.

4. Summation by Prosecutors Ayala and Signorino, April 17, 1987. The indictment itself defined Cosa Nostra as "an organization with a rigidly vertical structure, with its epicenter in Palermo, with a substantial *'unicità'* [oneness] notwithstanding periodic crises. Cosa Nostra, thanks to the victorious ascent of the Corleonesi, has become ever more rigid: a concept such as spontaneous germination of the Mafia phenomenon does not apply." *Corriere della Sera* (Milan), November 9, 1985.

5. "Ordinanza di Rinvio a Giudizio" for maxitrial, February 4, 1986.

6. Giampaolo Pansa, in *La Repubblica* (Rome), February 6, 1986, quoting the dean of Palermo University's Law Faculty, among others.

7. Galluzzo et al., *Rapporto sulla Mafia degli anni '80,* pp. 33–38.

8. Interview with Giusto Sciacchitano, August 4, 1987.

9. A *pentito* from Catania, Giuseppe Calderone, made this and other startling revelations in 1988.

10. Buscetta's testimony at maxitrial, textually reported in *Giornale di Sicilia* (Palermo), April 4, 1986.

11. Ibid.

12. Stajano, *Mafia: L'atto d'accusa,* p. 97.

13. Biagi, *Il Boss è solo,* p. 21.

14. Contorno's testimony, reported textually in *Giornale di Sicilia* (Palermo), April 17, 1986.

15. Though Inspector Cassarà had incriminating evidence on Bontate's interest in the drug trade, Contorno may actually not have known about that. He claimed to have known nothing about Bontate's plan to kill Salvatore Riina in 1981, perhaps because Bontate did not confide such things to him. Bontate did tell Buscetta about those plans, however.

Questioned on Bontate's role in the drug traffic, Buscetta said: "Stefano Bontate maintained that he was extraneous but, for love of the truth, I wouldn't know if what he said corresponded to the truth, because in this field everyone kept what he was doing to himself." See Stajano, *Mafia: L'atto d'accusa,* p. 97.

16. Contorno's testimony, reported textually in *Giornale di Sicilia* (Palermo), April 23, 1986.

17. Ibid., April 24, 1986.

18. Leggio's testimony, reported textually in *Giornale di Sicilia* (Palermo), May 24, 25, 26, 1986.

19. "Bono + 159." The Mafia's plan to infiltrate Milan's financial structure was also described by the defector Antonino Calderone, who has testified that his late brother Giuseppe had actually fathered the plan in late 1979.

20. Stajano, *Mafia: L'atto d'accusa,* pp. 112–35.

21. The five-hundred-kilo order was made by Nitto Santapaola, who talked the deal over with Koh Bak Kin directly. Ibid., p. 112.

22. Ninety-five Tamils were arrested in Italy on March 18, 1985, for heroin trafficking in complicity with the Sicilian Mafia in Naples, Palermo, and Catania. They were Tigers of Elam, financing their insurgency in Sri Lanka. Eventually, they were released because no court interpreter could be found who spoke their language. *La Repubblica* (Rome), March 19, 1985; *L'Espresso* (Rome), December 1, 1985.

In 1987, British customs agents traced the Sicilian Mafia trafficker Francesco Di Carlo to a hotel he had stayed at in Mombasa, Kenya. The register showed that he had met with other Sicilian Mafia bosses there, and that several other hotels and casinos in Mombasa were being used for Mafia money laundering. BBC, March 11, 1987.

The arms deals with Guinea-Bissau were made through a company called Euro-Gros in Massa Carrara. Details emerged in an arrest order on January 30, 1989, for thirty-seven Italians, including twelve Mafiosi in the Corleone and Trapani clans. The Mafiosi had been working with (or under) the Mafia's treasurer, Pippo Calò, until his arrest in 1985. Their partners had been right-wing terrorists in NAR and Ordine Nuovo. See *La Repubblica,* January 31, 1989.

Aruba, off the Venezuelan coast, has been used for temporary or lengthy shelter by many Sicilian traffickers. At the height of Italy's investigation into the Cuntrera-Caruana operations abroad, in 1985, the entire Cuntrera family moved out of Caracas altogether and lived in Aruba for a while. Interview with Dr. Pansa, Rome's Anti–Organized Crime Nucleus.

In the summer of 1987, Nepalese authorities arrested a group of army officers found to be working for the Sicilian Mafia.

The Katmandu source is the BBC, July 12, 1987.

23. Interview in *La Repubblica* (Rome), April 13, 1985.

19. THE OCTOPUS AT LARGE AGAIN

1. Ruling by the Supreme Court (Court of Cassation), *Corriere della Sera* (Milan), September 29, 1988.

2. *La Repubblica* (Rome), February 11, 1989.

3. Zaza was picked up again in France for smuggling cigarettes, in March 1989.

4. The boss indicted for murdering Judge Ciaccio Montalto was Calogero Minore of Trapani, a close ally of the Corleonesi. His release was ordered by Italy's Supreme Court (Court of Cassation) on November 23, 1988.

5. *Corriere della Sera* (Milan), November 4, 1986.

6. *La Repubblica* (Rome), March 12 and 14, 1989; *Corriere della Sera* (Milan), March 12, 13, and 17, 1989.

7. "Sentenza della Corte" by Judge Carnevale, Supreme Court (Court of Cassation), pp. 85–86, 121, 128.

8. *Corriere della Sera* (Milan), December 30, 1988.

9. Vincenzo De Caro, *Giornale di Sicilia* (Palermo), March 23, 1988.

10. Justice Minister Giulio Vassalli, a Socialist, quoted in *La Repubblica* (Rome), February 4, 1988.

11. *Corriere della Sera* (Milan), March 13, 1988.

12. Ibid., December 30, 1988. In Agrigento, where magistrates had labored for years for the evidence that convicted thirty Mafia notables, only one remained in custody by the end of the same year.

13. Falcone's lengthy statement in *L'Espresso* (Rome), September 18, 1988. Over the next months, one judge left the pool voluntarily; two were withdrawn and assigned to non-Mafia cases; all were given routine cases adding to their already enormous professional burden. Officially, the pool was still supposed to be the repository for all material pertaining to the Mafia in Palermo itself, though nowhere else. In reality, even this had unworkable limitations. For instance, a case based on major arrests in Termini Imerese—a summer hangout just twelve miles from Palermo, frequented by Palermo's biggest bosses—was withdrawn from the anti-Mafia pool's jurisdiction by Supreme Court judge Carnavale, and assigned to the local court in Termini Imerese.

14. Ruling of appellate court in Rome on the Christmas train bombing of 1984, reversing the convictions of Pippo Calò and his codefendants, who, the court declared, did not belong to any Mafia association. The cardinal primate's statement is from the *Corriere della Sera,* April 16, 1989, citing a letter written by Ernesto Ruffini to the papal secretary of state two months after the Ciaculli bomb.

15. Judge Paolo Borsellino, formerly in Palermo's anti-Mafia pool, later chief prosecutor in Marsala. *La Repubblica* (Rome), July 20, 1988.

16. Freeh interview in *La Repubblica* (Rome), August 14, 1988.

17. For example, the big drug bust in December 1988, described by an FBI expert as "the biggest in the history of mankind." Several members of John Gambino's Cherry Hill ring were rounded up at the time, starting with his favorite heroin courier, Emmanuele Adamita. See chapter 20.

18. *La Stampa* (Turin), October 7, 1988.

19 *La Repubblica* (Rome), July 28, 1989.

20. Interior Minister Antonio Gava in *La Repubblica* (Rome), July 6, 1989. The capillary control of Palermo statement made by Judge Giuseppe di Lello of the anti-Mafia pool, *Giornale di Sicilia* (Palermo), July 28, 1988. Sica's statement on control of the Italian south, *Corriere della Sera* (Milan), November 16, 1988. His statement on control of institutions and terrorists, to the Parliamentary Anti-Mafia Commission, March 1, 1989. Governor of the central bank, Ciampi, *La Repubblica*, March 29, 1985. Mayor Orlando's statement, *Corriere della Sera,* August 6, 1988. The Superior Magistrates' Council Report by Judge Carlo Smuraglia, *La Repubblica,* February 4, 1988.

21. Former Mayor Giuseppe Insalaco was killed by the Mafia on January 11, 1988. He had been the mayor of Palermo for three months in 1984.

22. *Corriere della Sera* (Milan), January 29, 1988.

23. The Italian Communist party's large cooperative movement had some dealings with Mafia-dominated produce companies in Sicily, and individual party leaders have occasionally been brushed by similar contacts. See *Corriere della Sera* (Milan), March 14, 1989. Nevertheless, they do not ordinarily receive Mafia favors. The fact that they do miserably at the polls in Sicily may be because of or in spite of that. See Galasso, *La Mafia non esiste.*

24. Estimate in maxitrial indictment.

25. Antonino Calderone, interrogation by judges in Palermo, *Corriere della Sera* (Milan), March 15, 1988.

26. The Republicans' leader in Sicily was Aristide Gunnella. See Miriam Mafai in *La Repubblica* (Rome), July 11, 1987.

27. Former mayor of Palermo Elda Pucci, testimony before Parliamentary Anti-Mafia Commission, *La Repubblica* (Rome), October 4, 1984.

28. In *Anti-Mafia occasione mancata,* Michele Pantaleone wrote: "Lima's political career is a continuous crescendo in a single direction: the conquest of power, all power in the party, always more power in any case, and by every means. In his rapid and fortunate career, for the open-mindedness of his methods, Lima has been the most talked about political figure. Mayor of Palermo in 1958, reconfirmed in 1960 until 1962, reelected again in 1964, provincial secretary of the DC, Lima manages to block all internal opposition in the party and the city council. . . . In April 1964, the second working group of the Parliamentary Anti-Mafia Commission specifically studying Palermo noted that Salvatore Lima should be suspended from his job as extraordinary commissioner on the Board of Agrarian Reform for Sicily (ERAS). The Anti-Mafia Commission, among other things, had received from the general command of the Guardia di Finanza the file on Angelo La Barbera, which showed that La Barbera and his brother Salvatore had carried out political activities in 1958 for the election of Lima as mayor and 'for the protection of Lima's person' " (pp. 40–45).

For Andreotti's defense of Lima, see Andreotti's interview with *Il Messagero* (Rome), cited in *Panorama,* December 10, 1984, and *Corriere della Sera* (Milan), November 13, 1986. See also "Un amico a Strasburgo," assorted extracts of documents gathered by the Anti-Mafia Commission on Salvo Lima, during his term as a deputy in the European Parliament at Strasbourg, prepared by the Centro Siciliano di Documentazione Giuseppe Impastato.

29. Davis, *The Kennedys,* pp. 304–6. John Kennedy won the presidency by a nationwide margin of only 118,550 popular votes: 49.7 percent to Richard Nixon's 49.6 percent. The Illinois Republicans did an unofficial check of 699 paper-ballot precincts in Cook County after the election, turning up a net gain of 4,539 votes for Nixon— enough to have thrown Illinois and the entire national election to Nixon. But Mayor Daley's political machine was able to block an official recount. According to author John Davis (a cousin of Jacqueline Kennedy), Giancana himself boasted later that he had "elected" Kennedy. See Blakey and Billings, *The Plot to Kill the President;* Hurt, *Reasonable Doubt;* Summers, *Conspiracy;* Scheim, *Contract on America.*

30. This was the operation investigated by the Criminalpol's Gianni De Gennaro and Toni De Luca, in the report "Bono + 159," February 7, 1983. Antonino Calderone, whose confessions in 1988 far outweighed Buscetta's, has described how the Milan operation was set up, directed in part by Calderone's brother Giuseppe, head of eastern Sicily's regional Mafia commission and the island-wide *Inter-Provinciale.*

31. Public works amounting to 21 trillion lire, roughly $16 billion, have been scheduled for Sicily covering the years 1989–94: *La Repubblica* (Rome), January 18, 1989. The warning about "respectable" companies fronting for the Mafia was repeated by High Commissioner Sica and Judge Di Pisa, a specialized investigating magistrate in Palermo: *La Repubblica,* January 17, 1989.

32. Catania-based news report, gleaned from the Guardia di Finanza, *La Repubblica* (Rome), January 21, 1989.

33. *La Repubblica* (Rome), July 6, 1989.

34. *La Repubblica* (Rome), December 22, 1988.

35. The heroin seizures are reported in *La Repubblica* (Rome), July 6, 1989; Andreotti's figures on the killings, *Corriere della Sera* (Milan), August 10, 1989.

20. STANDOFF

1. Gaetano Fidanzati was named as Adamita's main partner in that enterprise but is still a fugitive. Sentenced to twenty-two years in the maxitrial in Palermo, he was released pending appeal under Italy's time-limits law.

2. The Sicilian Mafioso considered to be the head of the Torretta group in New

York was Francesco "Cheech" Gambino, whose mother was Rosa Mannino. This was told to me by Di Gennaro and Pansa of Rome's Anti–Organized Crime Nucleus.

3. U.S. Southern District Complaint, November 30, 1988.

4. Interview with Judge Claudio Lo Curto of Caltanissetta, who has since been transferred to Florence. The late Judge Ciaccio Montalto is thought to have been murdered in Trapani primarily because he was getting too close to this operation.

5. Interview with Frank Panessa, head of the DEA in Rome.

6. He was Ignazio D'Antone, on an RAI (Italian TV) program.

7. Interview with De Gennaro, Rome, April 1986.

8. His name was Nigel Sevan Soobiah, indicted in this case but still a fugitive, believed to be living in Amsterdam. See U.S. Southern District Complaint, November 30, 1988.

9. Ibid., p. 35.

10. Ibid. Also *New York Times,* December 2, 1988.

11. As reported in the *Corriere della Sera* (Milan) from New York, December 3, 1988.

12. *La Repubblica* (Rome), December 13, 1988.

13. The informant was Willie Boy Johnson, murdered on August 31, 1988.

14. *New York Times,* July 28, 1988.

15. *New York Times,* August 28, 1988; *La Repubblica* (Rome), August 28, 1988.

16. Speech to the International Association of Chiefs of Police, Houston, Texas, October 13, 1985, by Oliver Revell, the FBI's executive assistant director for investigations.

17. President's Committee on Organized Crime, hearings, October 23–25, 1984. See also testimony by Floyd Clark, assistant director of criminal investigation for the FBI, before the Senate Subcommittee on Investigations, April 1988; and Oliver Revell's speech in Texas.

18. Interview with Floyd Clark, March 14, 1989.

19. Freeh's interview with Ennio Caretto, *La Stampa* (Turin), October 2, 1988.

20. Frank Panessa, DEA, Rome.

21. London *Times,* October 12, 1988. The *Times* refers only to "the Mafia in Detroit" as responsible, but DEA sources add that the traffickers were "the Sicilian faction" of the Detroit Mafia.

22. A meticulous study on the Naples drug scene was completed in 1988 by the Osservatòrio sulla Camorra, whose findings shocked the nation. See *Corriere della Sera* (Milan), November 19, 1988, and *La Stampa* (Turin), same date.

23. The French "Pizza Connection" trial, beginning in September 1988, reported in *Le Figaro,* December 12, 1988.

24. DEA, Rome.

25. Interview with Frank Panessa, DEA, Rome, April 1989.

26. Interview, March 14, 1989.

EPILOGUE

1. New Jersey State Police Intelligence Report, February 22, 1973.

2. Judicial report by Italy's Anti–Organized Crime Nucleus, regarding Francesco Inzerillo and sixty-nine other Sicilian Mafiosi in the United States, November 11, 1988.

3. DEA Report, March 9 and April 18, 1977.

4. Enzo Napoli's gofer caught in this heroin transaction was Victor Amuso, who later became boss of New York's Lucchese Family.

5. Napoli's American Express credit card reports registered the following flights to Europe, among others: to Milan, February 1975; Paris, May 1975; Milan, October

1975; Lugano-Rome, January 1976; Munich, Rome, Lugano, and Zurich, February 1976.

6. DEA Reports on Flenda, June 13, 1977; Bonn agent's telex, February 13, 1977. The DEA's ongoing investigation lasted at least through the summer of 1977. A decade later, when the relevant facts came to light, the DEA's Rome office confirmed that Flenda had been working for the Sicilian Mafia.

7. Information on Napoli's toll calls to Germany and Italy was reported by Detective Le Vien's superior, Lieutenant Joseph Harding, in a "Summary of Highlights—Operation Earn," on July 7, 1977. The information had arrived during the month of May—the month of Enzo's arrest on the drug charge. It "showed a connection to international organized crime figures," Harding said.

8. *New York Post,* January 23, 1986.

Bibliography

BOOKS AND ARTICLES

Albini, Joseph. *The American Mafia: Genesis of a Legend.* New York: Appleton-Century-Crofts, 1971.

Alexander, Shana. *The Pizza Connection.* New York: Weidenfeld and Nicolson, 1988.

Anderson, Annelise Graebner. *The Business of Organized Crime.* Stanford, Calif.: Hoover Institution Press, 1979.

Anonimo. *Uomo di rispetto.* Milan: Arnaldo Mondadori, June 1988.

Arlacchi, Pino. *La Mafia imprenditrice.* Bologna: Societa Editrice il Mulino, 1983.

Arlacchi, Pino, and Nando Dalla Chiesa. *La palude e la città.* Milan: Arnaldo Mondadori, 1987.

Armi e dròga: L'atto d'accusa del giudice Carlo Palermo. Rome: Editori Riuniti, January 1988.

Barrese, Orazio. *I complici.* Milan: Feltrinelli, November 1983.

Barzini, Luigi. *The Italians.* New York: Atheneum, 1977.

Benson, George C. S. *Political Corruption in America.* Lexington, Mass.: Lexington Books, D.C. Heath, 1978.

Biagi, Enzo. *Il Boss è solo: Buscetta, la vera storia d'un vero padrino.* Milan: Arnaldo Mondadori, October 1986.

Blakey, G. Robert, and Richard N. Billings. *The Plot to Kill the President: Organized Crime Assassinated J.F.K.* New York: Times Books, 1981.

Blok, Anton. *The Mafia of a Sicilian Village.* New York: Harper and Row, 1975.

Blumenthal, Ralph. *Last Days of the Sicilians.* New York: Times Books, 1988.

Bonanno, Joseph, with Sergio Lalli. *A Man of Honor: The Autobiography of Joseph Bonanno.* New York: Simon and Schuster, 1983.

Bresler, Fenton. *The Chinese Mafia.* Briarcliff Manor, N.Y.: Stein and Day, 1981.

Brill, Steven. *The Teamsters.* New York: Simon and Schuster, 1978.

Calvi, Fabrizio. *La vie quotidienne de la Mafia.* Paris: Hachette, 1986.

Charbonneau, Jean-Luc. *The Canadian Connection.* Ottawa: Optimum, 1976.

Cressey, Donald R. *Theft of the Nation.* New York: Harper and Row, 1969.

Dalla Chiesa, Nando. *Delitto imperfètto.* Milan: Arnaldo Mondadori, 1984.

Davis, John H. *The Kennedys.* New York: McGraw-Hill, 1984.

Demaris, Ovid. *The Last Mafioso.* New York: Times Books, 1981.

De Sanctis, Riccardo. *Delitto al potere.* Rome: Las Nuova Sinistra–Edizioni Samona' e Savelli, 1972.

Diapoulous, Peter, and Steven Linakis. *The Sixth Family.* New York: Dutton, April 1976.

Di Fonzo, Luigi. *St. Peter's Banker: Michele Sindona.* New York, London, Toronto, Sydney: Franklin Watts, 1983.

Dolci, Danilo. *Fare prèsto (e bene) perchè si muore.* Turin: Francesco De Silva, 1954.

———. *Banditi a partinico.* Bari: Editori Laterza, 1956.

Duggan, Christopher. *La Mafia durante il Fascismo.* Cosenza: Rubbetino Editore–Soveri Mannelli, 1987.

Falcone, Nino, and Bruno Caruso. *Almanaccu sicilianu.* Messina: Pungitopo Editrice, 1986.

Falzone, Gaetano. *Storia della Mafia.* Palermo: S.F. Flaccovio, 1973.

Fava, Giuseppe. *Mafia: Da Giuliano a Dalla Chiesa.* Rome: Editori Riuniti, 1986.

———. *Processo alla Sicilia.* Palermo: Editrice Ites, 1971.

Gage, Nicholas. *The Mafia Is Not an Equal Opportunity Employer.* New York: Dell, 1970.

Gage, Nicholas, ed. *Mafia, U.S.A.* New York: Playboy Press, 1972.

Galasso, Alfredo. *La Mafia non esiste.* Naples: Tullio Pironti, 1988.

Galli, Giorgio. *Storia del partito armato.* Milan: Rizzoli, 1986.

Galluzzo, Lucio. *Tommaso Buscetta: L'uomo che tradì se stesso.* Aosta: Musumeci, 1984.

———. *Meglio morto: Storia di Salvatore Giuliano.* Palermo: S.F. Flaccovio, 1985.

Galluzzo, Lucio, Francesco La Licata, and Saverio Lodato, eds. *Rapporto sulla Mafia degli anni '80.* Palermo: S.F. Flaccovio, 1986.

Gambino, Richard. *Blood of My blood.* Garden City, N.Y.: Anchor Press/Doubleday, 1974.

Giancana, Antoinette, and Thomas C. Renner. *Mafia Princess.* New York: Avon, 1984.

Gosch, Martin A., and Richard Hammer. *The Last Testament of Lucky Luciano.* Boston, Toronto: Little, Brown, 1974.

Gurwin, Larry. *The Calvi Affair.* London: Macmillan Ltd., 1983.

Hess, Henner. *Mafia.* Rome, Bari: Laterza and Figli Spa, April 1984.

Hoffa, James R., as told to Oscar Fraley. *Hoffa: The Real Story.* New York: Stein and Day, 1975.

Hurt, Henry. *Reasonable Doubt.* New York: Holt, Rinehart and Winston, 1985.

Ianni, Francis A. J., and Elizabeth Reusss-Ianni, eds. *The Crime Society.* New York: New American Library, 1976.

I Boss della Mafia. Preface by Girolamo Li Causi. Rome: Editori Riuniti, August 1971.

Jannuzzi, Lino. *Così parlò Buscetta.* Milan: Sugarco Edizioni, 1986.

Kaplan, David E., and Alec Dubro. *Yakuza.* Reading, Mass.: Addison-Wesley, April 1986.

Kennedy, Robert F. *The Enemy Within.* New York: Harper and Row, 1960.

Kwitny, Jonathan. *Vicious Circles.* New York: Norton, 1979.

Lampedusa, Giuseppe Tomasi di. *Il gattopardo.* Milan: Feltrinelli, 1960.
Lane, Mark. *Rush to Judgment.* New York: Holt, Rinehart and Winston, 1966.
Lernoux, Penny. *In Banks We Trust.* New York: Anchor Press/Doubleday, 1984.
Lewis, Norman. *The Honored Society.* New York: Putnam, 1964.
Maas, Peter. *The Valachi Papers.* New York: Putnam, 1968.
Marrazzo, Giuseppe. *Il Camorrista.* Naples: Tullio Pironti, 1984.
Mills, James. *The Underground Empire.* Garden City, N.Y.: Doubleday, 1986.
Moldea, Dan. *The Hoffa Wars.* New York, London: Paddington Press, 1978.
Moore, Robin. *The French Connection.* London: Hodder and Stoughton, 1969.
Mustain, Gene, and Jerry Capeci. *Mob Star: The Story of John Gotti.* New York, Toronto: Franklin Watts, 1988.
Nese, Marco. *Nel segno della Mafia.* Milan: Rizzoli, 1976.
Newsday staff and editors. *The Heroin Trail.* New York: New American Library, 1973.
Nicolosi, Pietro. *Palermo fin de siècle.* Milan: U. Mursia Editore, 1979.
Pantaleone, Michele. *Mafia e dròga.* Turin: Einaudi, 1966.
———. *Mafia e politica.* Turin: Einaudi, 1962.
———. *L'industria del potere.* Bologna: Cappelli, 1984.
———. *Anti-Mafia occasione mancata.* Turin: Einaudi, 1969.
Petacco, Arrigo. *Il prefetto di Ferro.* Milan: Arnaldo Mondadori, 1975.
———. *Joe Petrosino.* Milan: Arnaldo Mondadori, 1972.
Peterson, Virgil. *The Mob.* Ottawa, Ill.: Greenhill Press, 1983.
Pileggi, Nicholas. *Wiseguy.* New York: Simon and Schuster, 1985.
Pistone, Joseph D., with Richard Woodley. *Donnie Brasco: My Undercover Life in the Mafia.* New York: New American Library, 1987.
Poma, Rosario, and Enzo Perrone. *La Mafia: Nonni e nipoti.* Florence: Vallecchi, 1971.
Puzo, Mario. *The Godfather.* New York: Putnam, 1969.
Renda, Francesco. *Storia della Sicilia dall 1860 al 1970.* Vol. 3. Palermo, 1986.
Saladino, Giuliana. *De Mauro: Una cronaca palermitana.* Milan: Feltrinelli, 1972.
Scheim, David. *Contract on America: The Mafia Murders of John and Robert Kennedy.* Silver Spring, Md.: Argyle Press, 1983.
Schiraldi, Vittorio. *Siciliani si nasce.* Milan: Rusconi Libri, 1983.
Sciascia, Leonardo. *The Day of the Owl.* Boston: David R. Godine, 1984.
Scott, Peter Sale, Paul L. Hoch, and Russell Stetler, eds. *The Assassinations: Dallas and Beyond.* New York: Vintage Books/Random House, 1976.
Servadio, Gaia. *Mafioso.* New York: Stein and Day, 1976.
Shawcross, Tim, and Martin Young. *Men of Honor: The Confessions of Tommaso Buscetta.* London: Collins, 1987.
Short, Martin. *Crime, Inc.* London: Thames Methuen, 1984.
Sindona: Gli atti d'accusa dei giudici di Milan. Rome: Editori Riuniti, May 1986.
Smith, Denis Mack. *Storia della Sicilia medievale e moderna.* Milan: Editori Laterza, 1983.
Stajano, Corrado, ed. *Mafia: L'atto d'accusa dei giudici di Palermo.* Rome: Editori Riuniti, January 1986.
Stendal, Russell. *Rescue the Captors.* Burnsville, Minn.: Ransom Press International, 1984.
Sterling, Claire. "Portrait of a Mafia Killer." *Reader's Digest,* June 1973.
———. *The Time of the Assassins.* New York: Holt, 1984.
Struffi, Maurizio, and Luigi Sardi. *Fermate quel giudice.* Trento: Luigi Reverdito, 1986.
Summers, Anthony. *Goddess: The Secret Lives of Marilyn Monroe.* New York: Macmillan, 1985.
———. *Conspiracy.* New York: McGraw-Hill, 1981.
Talese, Gay. *Honor Thy Father.* New York: Dell, 1986.

Teresa, Vincent, with Thomas C. Renner. *My Life in the Mafia.* Garden City, N.Y.: Doubleday, 1973.
Violante, Luciano. *La Mafia dell'eroina.* Rome: Editori Riuniti, April 1987.
Waller, Leslie. *The Swiss Bank Connection.* New York: Signet Books, 1972.
Welch, Neil J., and David W. Marston. *Inside Hoover's FBI.* Garden City, N.Y.: Doubleday, 1984.

DOCUMENTS: ITALIAN

"Annullamento di Sentenza." By the Court of Cassation, reversing the Caltanissetta Appeals Court confirmation of the above convictions for the murder of Judge Rocco Chinnici. Judge Corrado Carnevale. Rome, June 3, 1986.
["Bono + 159."] "Rapporto Giudiziario di Denuncia a Carico di Bono, Giuseppe + 159, Ritenuti Responsabili d'Associazione per Delinquere di Tipo Mafioso e Finalizzata al Traffico delle Sostanze Stupefacènti." Report by the Questura of Rome, Squadra Narcotici (headed by Gianni De Gennaro). Prepared by the Centro Interprovinciale Criminalpol of Lombardia, Lazio-Umbria, and Sicily-Palermo. Two volumes. Rome, February 7, 1983.
Complete File of Testimony in Palermo's Maxitrial (Maxi-Processo). As reported textually in *Giornale di Sicilia* (Palermo). February 10, 1986, to April 1, 1987.
["Greco + 161," Antonino Cassarà Report.] "Rapporto Giudiziario di Denuncia a Carico di Greco, Michele più Altri 161 Persone." Submitted to the Palermo judiciary by the Questura of Palermo, Centro Interprovinciale di Coordinamento delle Operazioni di Polizia Criminale, Sicilia Occidentale. July 13, 1982.
"Interrogatorio d'Angelo Epaminonda." By Prosecutor Francesco di Maggio of the Milan Tribunal (in various sessions filling 230 pages). November 19, 1984, to February 4, 1985.
"Interrogatorio di Michele Zaza." By Judge Aurelio Galasso, at trial of Salvagore Amendolito + Altri. Rome, April 23, 1985.
"Interrogatorio di Pietro Luigi De Riz." By Judge Giovanni Falcone and Public Prosecutor Giuseppe Ayala. Rome, October 20, 1988.
"Interrogazione di Buscetta, Tommaso." By Judge Falcone in Palermo. Series of *verbali* (written accounts of questions and answers). July 16, 1984, to September 12, 1984.
"Mandato di Cattura Contro Abbate, Giovanni + 351." Palermo, September 29, 1984. First arrest orders and charges for Palermo's maxitrial, signed by Judges Antonino Caponnetto, Giovanni Falcone, Paolo Borsellino, Leonardo Guarnotta, and Giuseppe Di Lello Finuoli. Motivation (explanation) of arrest orders by Judge Falcone.
"Ordinanza di Rinvio a Giudizio." Indictment by Judge Claudio Lo Curto, for the murder of Judge Ciaccio Montalto. Caltanissetta, January 25, 1988.
"Ordinanza di Rinvio a Giudizio, Baddar Hakam Hussein + 21." Indictment by Judge Vittorio De Cesare of 22 Palestinians and Italians on drug-smuggling charges. Rome, October 12, 1985.
"Ordinanza di Rinvio a Giudizio Contro Calabrò, Gioacchino + 19." Indictment by Judge Claudio Lo Curto, Tribunal of Caltanissetta, for trial of 20 defendants accused of attempting to murder Judge Carlo Palermo. June 26, 1986. Motivation of the order.
"Ordinanza di Rinvio a Giudizio, Michelangelo Aiello + 32." Indictment by Judge Aurelio Galasso on money-laundering charges connected with drug trafficking in the Pizza Connection case and otherwise. Rome, October 6, 1986.
"Ordinanza di Rinvio a Giudizio, Salvatore Amendolito + 35" (including Michele Zaza). By Judge Aurelio Galasso. Rome, October 6, 1986.

"Ordinanza-Sentenza Contro Abbate, Giovanni + 706." Order for the trial known as the Maxi-Processo (maxitrial). Forty volumes. Palermo, November 8, 1985.

"Relazione sui Lavori Svolti e Sullo Stato del Fenomeno Mafioso al Termine della V Legislatura." Document XXIII, no. 2.

"Relazione sui Mercati all'Ingrosso." Report by the Parliamentary Anti-Mafia Commission. May 1971. Document XXIII, section *(ter)* 2.

"Relazione sulle Risultanze Acquisite sul Comune di Palermo." Report by the Parliamentary Anti-Mafia Commission. May 1971.

"Relazione sull'Indagine Riguardante Casi di Singoli Mafiosi." Report by the Parliamentary Anti-Mafia Commission, communicated to the Italian Senate July 1971. Document XXIII.

"Relazione sull'Indagine Svolta in Merito alle Vicende Connesse all'Irreperibilità di Luciano Liggio." Published by the Commissione Parlamentare d'Inchiesta sul Fenomeno della Mafia in Sicilia, communicated to the Italian Parliament February 26, 1970. Document XXIII, no. 2.

"Requisitoria Contro Calò, Giuseppe + 14." Recommendation for indictment and trial for drug trafficking and bombing of Christmas train near Bologna. Office of the Procura. Rome, June 18, 1987.

"Requisitoria, Michele Sindona + 11." Recommendation for indictment of Sindona and other defendants, including John Gambino. By Public Prosecutor Guido Viola. Milan, June 6, 1984.

"Requisitoria nei Confronti di Calò, Giuseppe, Carboni, Flavio + 25." By Public Prosecutor Domenico Sica. Rome, April 6, 1985.

"Requisitoria, Rosario Spatola + 84." Recommendation for indictment by Prosecutor Giusto Sciacchitano. Palermo, December 7, 1981.

"Sentenza della Corte d'Assise d'Appèllo di Caltanissetta Contro Rabito, Vincenzo + 5" (verdict). Confirmation of lower court conviction of Rabito and five others including Michele Greco for the murder of Judge Rocco Chinnici. By Judge Antonino Saetta. Caltanissetta, June 14, 1985.

"Sentenza della Corte d'Assise di Catanzaro." December 22, 1968.

"Sentenza della Corte Suprema di Cassazione." On appeal in Judge Carlo Palermo's arms-drugs case. August 7, 1985.

"Sentenza della Corte Suprema di Cassazione." Partial annulment of lower court verdict on Turkish-Italian drug traffickers indicted by Judge Carlo Palermo. Rome, August 7, 1985.

"Sentenza della Corte Suprema di Cassazione sul Ricorso Proposto d'Amendolito + 26." Reversal of convictions in Italy's Pizza Connection trial. By Judge Corrado Carnevale. Rome, November 5, 1988.

"Sentenza di Rinvio a Giudizio." By Judge Cesare Terranova. Palermo, May 31, 1965.

"Sentenza di Rinvio a Giudizio." For maxitrial. Palermo, November 8, 1985.

"Sentenza di Rinvio a Giudizio." Indictment of entire Mafia membership in Agrigento, 56 in all. By Judge Fabio Salamone. Agrigento, April 2, 1986.

"Sentenza di Rinvio a Giudizio." Excerpts of arms-drugs indictment. By Judge Carlo Palermo. Trento Tribunal, November 15, 1984.

DOCUMENTS: AMERICAN AND CANADIAN

"America's Habit: Drug Abuse, Drug Trafficking, and Organized Crime." Report to the President and Attorney General of the United States by the President's Commission on Organized Crime. Washington, D.C., 1986.

"The Cash Connection." Interim Report on Organized Crime, Financial Institutions, and Money Laundering, President's Commission on Organized Crime. Washington, D.C., October 1984.

"Chronology of Events." Prepared by U.S. Southern District, Manhattan, for jury in Pizza Connection trial. 1985.

"Colombian Narcotics-Trafficking Organizations." Criminal Investigative Division, Federal Bureau of Investigation. Washington, D.C., June 1986.

"Complaint by U.S. Southern District against Giuseppe Gambino and 26 Others." By Assistant U.S. Attorney Andrew C. McCarthy. New York, November 30, 1988.

"A Decade of Organized Crime." Pennsylvania Crime Commission. Commonwealth of Pennsylvania, St. Davids, Pennsylvania, 1980.

Full Testimony at Pizza Connection Trial of Salvatore Contorno, Tommaso Buscetta, Luigi Ronsisvalle, Gaetano Badalamenti, FBI agent Charles Rooney, FBI agent Carmine Russo, FBI agent Joe Pistone.

"The Impact: Organized Crime Today." President's Commission on Organized Crime. Washington, D.C., April 1986.

Indictment by Federal Grand Jury, Manhattan, of Gaetano Badalamenti and 34 others for Pizza Connection drug charges. Complaint by U.S. Attorney Rudolph Giuliani. New York, April 19, 1984.

Indictment of Anthony Salerno, Paul Castellano, and 7 others accused of belonging to the American Cosa Nostra's ruling national council. By Federal Grand Jury. Manhattan, February 26, 1985.

"International Narcotics Control Strategy Report, March 1988." U.S. State Department, Bureau of International Narcotics Matters. March 1, 1988.

"International Narcotics Control Strategy Report, March 1989." U.S. State Department, Bureau of International Narcotics Matters. March 1, 1989.

"La Cosa Nostra in Canada." Criminal Investigative Division, Federal Bureau of Investigation. Washington, D.C., March 1985.

[McClellan Committee hearings.] "Organized Crime and Illicit Traffic in Narcotics." Senate Hearings, Permanent Subcommittee on Investigations of the Committee on Government Operations, 85th Cong., 1st Sess. September 25–27, October 1, 2, 8, 9, 10–16, 29, 1963; July 28–30, 1964. Final Report of the McClellan Subcommittee, March 4, 1965.

"Narcotics Intelligence Estimate, 1983." National Narcotics Intelligence Consumers Committee (NNICC). Washington, D.C.

"National Drug Strategy." Federal Bureau of Investigation. Washington, D.C., 1986.

"The NNICC Report, 1985–6." NNICC. Washington, D.C., June 1987.

"The NNICC Report, 1987." NNICC. Washington, D.C., April 1988.

"Organized Crime and Cocaine Trafficking." Hearings of the President's Commission on Organized Crime. Washington, D.C., November 27–29, 1984.

"Organized Crime and Heroin Trafficking." Hearings of the President's Commission on Organized Crime. Miami, February 20–21, 1985.

"Organized Crime of Asian Origin." Hearings of the President's Commission on Organized Crime. New York, October 23–25, 1984.

"Pennsylvania Crime Commission, 1985 Report." Commonwealth of Pennsylvania, Conshohocken, Pennsylvania, 1985.

"A Report of the Study of Organized Crime's Infiltration of the Pizza and Cheese Industry." Pennsylvania Crime Commission. March 1980.

"The Sicilian Mafia and Its Impact on the United States." Sean M. McWeenie. Federal Bureau of Investigation, Criminal Investigative Division. Washington, D.C., 1986.

Superseding indictment February 20, 1985. Sealed complaint by Assistant U.S. Attorneys Louis J. Freeh and Richard A. Martin. April 3, 1984.

Transcript of tapes made by Royal Canadian Mounted Police, recording conversation between Paul Violi and visitors from Sicily. Montreal, April 22, 1974.

Index

Calò, Giuseppe (Pippo), 147, 149 261,
    267–68, 284
    at maxitrial, 281, 283
CAMEA lodge, 194
Camorra brotherhood, 75, 138, 144, 206,
    207, 271–72, 303, 307, 312
    Sicilian Mafia and, 156, 157, 163, 164–65,
    269, 285
    tobacco of, 163–65
Canada, 258, 262
    Bonanno Family in, 89, 134
    heroin pipeline from, 175–76, 206
    heroin trafficking in, 134–35, 141
    Sicilian Mafia in, 34, 89, 110, 133–35, 137,
    206, 288, 289
capi-Famiglia (Family bosses), 282
Capo-Mafia, 47, 72, 89, 171, 213
capo-mandamento, 282
Capone, Al, 53, 237
Carabinieri (Italian paramilitary police), 40,
    58, 64, 112–13, 144, 145, 216, 217, 220
    on Camorra-Mafia pact, 164–65
    Ciaculli bombing and, 102, 103, 150
Caracas, Sicilian Mafia in, 112, 130–32, 135
Caribbean Management Corporation, 188
Carnevale, Corrado, 294
Caruana, Alfonso, 137, 140
Caruana, Giovanni, 133
Caruana, Leonardo, 134
Caruana, Pasquale, 140
Caruana Family, 132, 134, 206, 239, 288
Casamento, Filippo (Tizio), 109, 127, 128, 187
    Pizza Connection and, 140, 251
Casamento, Franco, 114, 128
Cascio Ferro, Vito, 48–51, 62–63, 80
Cassarà, Antonio (Ninni), 209, 217–19, 230,
    258–59, 280
Castellammare del Golfo, 76, 83, 205
Castellano, Paul, 96, 178, 187, 247–48, 306,
    308
    Harding and, 319–20
Catalano, Salvatore, 106–7, 110, 140, 206, 244,
    285, 306, 316
    Bonanno Family taken over by, 246–47
    Knickerbocker Avenue taken over by, 170,
    174, 177, 245
    Pizza Connection and, 140, 254, 255, 257
    Ronsisvalle's testimony on, 176–77
    trial of, 149, 150, 174, 177
"Catanese clan," 292
Catania, 206, 219, 232
Catania, Giuseppe (Pino), 110, 114, 125–26,
    127

Catanzaro, Mafia trial in, 150
"Catarina la Licatisa nomata ancor Maffia,"
    46
Catholic Church, Roman, 47, 48, 191, 302
cattle trade, in Venezuela, 136
Cavalieri di Lavoro (Knights of Labor), 219,
    232
Cavatoio, Michele, 111–12
CEICO, 274
Celenk, Bekir, 160
Central Intelligence Agency, 116, 160, 196
cheese makers, priority status of, 184
Cherry Hill Gambinos, 109, 135, 170, 182,
    188, 199, 207, 241, 245, 284, 316
    breaking of, 304–9
    description of, 107
    Pizza Connection and, 250, 256, 257
    Sindona and, 193–95
China, People's Republic of, 116, 163
"China White," 158, 204, 313
Chinese Triads, 38, 310, 311, 313
Chinnici, Rocco, 219, 230, 235, 242, 292
Christian Democratic party, Italian, 63,
    65–66, 74, 146, 197, 199, 216, 219,
    299–300
    advocates for change in, 302
    Dalla Chiesa and, 220, 229, 232
    Sindona and, 191, 192
CIA (Central Intelligence Agency), 160, 196
Ciaccio Montalto, GianGiacomo, 234–35,
    292
Ciaculli, 212
    bombing of, 102–3, 111, 131, 133, 145,
    150
Ciancimino, Vito, 66, 229, 284, 298
cigarettes, black market, 75, 164
Cil, Huseyn, 165
CITAM, 254
Clark, Floyd, 311, 313–14
Clement, Harry, 139
cocaine, 11, 36, 100, 141, 239, 249, 264, 307,
    311–12
    cattle trade and, 136
    cost of, 38, 39
    growth in use of, 38–39
    as payment for heroin, 38, 39
    seizures of, 138, 312
Coccia, Ciccio, 51
Colombia:
    cocaine trafficking in, 39, 131, 311–12
    Sicilian Mafia in, 39, 211–12
Colombo, Joe, Jr., 186
Colombo, Joe, Sr., 186